SAGE ELECTORAL STUDIES YEARBOOK

VOLUME 4

Political Parties:
Development and Decay

edited by
LOUIS MAISEL
and
JOSEPH COOPER

SAGE Publications   Beverly Hills / London

For information address:

SAGE PUBLICATIONS, INC.
275 South Beverly Drive
Beverly Hills, California 90212

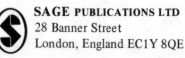

SAGE PUBLICATIONS LTD
28 Banner Street
London, England EC1Y 8QE

Printed in the United States of America

Library of Congress Cataloging in Publication Data
Main entry under title:
Political Parties: Development and decay

   (Sage electoral studies yearbook; v. 4)
   1. Political parties—Addresses, essays, lectures. I. Maisel, Louis.
II. Cooper, Joseph, 1933-
JF2011.D45   329'.02   76-46782
ISBN 0-8039-0738-9
ISBN 0-8039-0739-7 pbk.

FIRST PRINTING

POLITICAL PARTIES

SAGE ELECTORAL STUDIES YEARBOOK

Series Editors

Louis Maisel, *Colby College*
Joseph Cooper, *Rice University*

Editorial Advisory Board

Other volumes in this series:

1. The Future of Political Parties
   LOUIS MAISEL and PAUL M. SACKS, editors

2. Changing Campaign Techniques:
   Elections and Values in Contemporary Democracies
   LOUIS MAISEL, editor

3. The Impact of the Electoral Process
   LOUIS MAISEL and JOSEPH COOPER, editors

CONTENTS

Chapter 1

PROBLEMS AND TRENDS IN PARTY RESEARCH: AN OVERVIEW

JOSEPH COOPER
LOUIS MAISEL

I

The organizing theme of this, the fourth volume of the *Sage Electoral Studies Yearbook,* is party development and party decay. The study of political parties has been one of the primary concerns of political scientists since the formal beginnings of the discipline. Nor is it surprising that from the first party politics has stood at the vanguard of research in political science. Both the theoretical importance of parties and electorates in the functioning of democratic politics and the dominant positions parties actually occupied in American and British politics in the early decades of this century gave them an appeal and prominence for scholars which they have never relinquished. Nonetheless, in this traditional area of concern even more than in many others, World War II marks a watershed in the breadth, depth, and sophistication of research.

Three prime factors have combined to change the character of research on political parties drastically during the past quarter century.

AUTHORS' NOTE: We would like to thank Colby College for generously supporting our research.

The first is one whose influence has been general or pervasive over the whole discipline since 1945—the emergence and rise to dominance of a stricter set of beliefs and norms regarding the scientific character of research. Commonly called "behaviorism," this orientation or movement differed from the past primarily in terms of emphasis and aspiration. As is clear from the work of Lowell, Ostrogoroski, Holcombe, Schattschneider, Gosnell, and others, regard for data, theory, laws, and verification was not new (Ranney, 1954; Somit and Tanenhaus, 1967). What was new was the degree of insistence on relating data and theory, the degree of attention paid to research methods and techniques, and the degree of faith in the possibility of establishing more general laws or explanations regarding political phenomena. Moreover, despite some initial rigidity and excessive evangelical zeal, there was, as became apparent with time, ample room within the new movement for a large variety of approaches, themes, and methods. The net result, in the area of political parties as elsewhere, has been substantial growth in the degree of sophistication with which research is conducted. Beginning with the publication of Maurice Duverger's (1954) pathbreaking work on political parties, in which he pointed out the need for and sought to begin the construction of a general theory of political parties, significant progress has been made both in developing and applying sets of explanatory concepts and in refining techniques for gathering and treating data.

The second factor for purposes of brevity may be termed the "internationalization" of the study of politics. Its impact has been far less pervasive than that of behaviorism, but in the area of parties it has been highly influential. Prior to World War II, the study of political parties was culture-bound. The lion's share of attention was devoted to the United States and to the Western European nations. Such work as was done on other nations was not only limited but also not easily relatable to the work done on parties in Western democracies. After 1945, however, the decline of colonialism, the emergence of a host of new nations, and the expansion of one-party states broadened the vistas of students of party politics. In the context of stricter scientific perspectives and aspirations, these events became both meaningful and directive. Suddenly, all the many forms of party experience began to be seen as highly relevant and important. As a result, both the range of parties and party systems brought under scrutiny and the richness of data and theory greatly expanded. The whole world, in short, became a laboratory for students of party politics, and comparative analysis, for the first time, became a real possibility rather than an ideology or slogan.

The third factor is even more directly tied to events and restricted in impact to the area of party politics. In the 1960s, students of parties in the most developed and successful democracies began to notice serious gaps and anomalies in their understanding of parties and electorates. To be sure, many of the factors and trends that came to the forefront had been previously identified or suspected—the decline of party organization, the decline in the strength of party identification, the increasing salience of issues, the growing isolation and personalization of candidates and campaigns, the declining hold of party on legislatures and bureaucracies, and so forth. Yet, these factors and trends began to combine in ways that were unanticipated and to produce both concrete events and scholarly findings that shattered key articles of the conventional wisdom and left professional observers doubtful as to how to interpret the present or forecast the future. This was especially true in the United States. Perhaps, the prime scholarly catalyst has been Walter Dean Burnham, who in various works (1965, 1970, 1975) has pointed out the overall trend toward party disaggregation and speculated on its causes and outcomes. However, a number of other insightful students of American parties, such as Frank Sorauf (1976), Austin Ranney (1974), and James Wilson (1966), have also been involved in identifying major aspects of the decline of party in America and their combined efforts have raised the specter not simply of significant change, but of gradual decay. These themes were explored in the first volume of this series (Maisel and Sacks, 1975).

The realization that the stable, moderate, and pragmatic American party system, captured and enshrined in all the textbooks, was not necessarily a basic and enduring aspect of reality, but perhaps only a historic stage, has had a profound impact on students of American politics. It has encouraged such students to adopt research strategies and perspectives similar to those employed by students of parties in new nations—that is, to approach party developmentally. In doing so, it has also encouraged them to seek to place American party politics in broader and more comparative perspective. The net result has been to add a new dimension to the research enterprise of perhaps the largest single group of professional students of party politics and to call into question their previous reliance on static rather than dynamic premises and models for pursuing research.

Yet, if it is true that in the past few decades the study of political parties has attained a level of sophistication and a richness in results that exceeds most, if not all, other fields of political science, it is also true that the sum of our knowledge remains far less than the parts. Here, as elsewhere, there are substantial elements of confusion and contradiction both in approaches and findings. Indeed, the very richness and sophistication of research in this area only serve to highlight the problems and difficulties that continue to plague it. These relate to basic organizing concepts and categories as well as to substantive results and will briefly be reviewed here as background for the articles that follow.

II

The progress that has been made in the study of political parties has been attained despite continued inability to resolve a number of key conceptual problems. Most prominent among these are: how to define party; how to classify or categorize parties and party systems; how to conceptualize the environment or context within which party functions; how to conceptualize the operations and impact of party; and how to conceptualize the interaction between party and environment.

It would seem that commonly agreed upon and standardized definitions of basic terms constitute a necessary foundation for success in any rigorous or scientific study of parties. Such definitions provide essential building blocks for conceptual frameworks, but they should not be confused with them. Their purpose is simply to provide a basis for identifying and distinguishing the objects of analysis.

Ironically, however, this is an objective that has frustrated students of parties for decades. A variety of definitions of party, often associated with lists of discrete characteristics that purport to distinguish it from other political groups, exist. Many of the definitions stress the tie between parties and elections and the lists of distinguishing characteristics typically focus on party as an agent of linkage between the mass public and the government. Nonetheless, despite the similarities, significant differences of inclusion and emphasis exist in terms of the treatment of such factors as ideology or principle, structure or organization, and function or activity (Sorauf, 1976; Sartori, 1976). Equally important, the distinctions ultimately established between parties and other political groups— e.g., factions and interest groups—are highly relative with the result that the universe of political groups remains exceedingly kaleidoscopic in character.

A number of deleterious consequences for the construction of viable conceptual frameworks and subsequent analysis ensue. Confusion over basic terms prevails. For example, as has been true since Madison, the differences between party and faction remain unclear. Similarly, it becomes difficult to construct subsidiary or secondary definitions or terms that are needed for analysis. For example, confusion over party and faction has impeded the construction of standardized terms for party components or subunits.

Nor is confusion the only source of difficulty. Those aspects of party which are common to or shared by most definitions are so elastic as to permit students of parties to apply a wide variety of approaches and delineate a multitude of objects of analysis. As a result, the very coherence of the field as a field is threatened, ranging as it does from psychological studies of voting to spatial or dimensional studies of cleavage to organizational studies of party units and activists to historical and functional studies of the role of parties in the development and maintenance of political systems. Conversely, this same elasticity also sparks controversy over appropriate objects of analysis and leads to substantial conceptual anomalies. For example, should entities as different as the Soviet Communist Party and the Republican Party in the United States be included under the same rubric? How justified is it to treat the Democratic Party and the Prohibition Party under the same heading and the AFL-CIO under a different one, given the similarities between the Democratic Party and the AFL-CIO and their shared differences from an entity such as the Prohibition Party?

Another critical ingredient in a conceptual framework is classification or categorization. Since the examination of variation provides the key to explanation and knowledge, it is essential to categorize forms of the phenomenon under investigation in ways that will facilitate the examination of relationships and dependencies. Here too, however, the area of party politics suffers from lack of consensus (Sartori, 1976).

Most students employ one or various combinations of the following approaches. The most traditional and perhaps still the most prevalent approach is to classify simply on the basis of number. Thus, party systems are classified as one-party, two-party, and multiparty. A related approach is to use number as as an indicator of the manner in which power is distributed or shared. Thus, party systems are classified as unipolar, including different types of one-party states, bipolar, including different types of two-party states, and multipolar, including different types of multiparty states. A third approach is to apply substantive criteria, such as ideological intensity, organizational character, or functional significance. A final approach is to use the type of polity as a criterion, classifying party systems into competitive or noncompetitive or pertaining to a mature or developing nation.

The combinations and permutations of these approaches that can be found in the literature are substantial. Such diversity in classification both impairs the ability to cumulate knowledge and breeds confusion. For example, students of American parties have distinguished one-party states from two-party states, though these types of one-party situations are quite different from one-party situations at national levels. To add to the confusion, what is basically involved here is a form of factional politics, though definitionally party and faction are supposed to be distinct.

Equally important, the variety of classificatory schemes that exist serves to mask a variety of complex and unresolved issues. What aspects of party and environment should be identified as basic variables and what is the character of their internal relationships? If more than a single continuum has to be employed, what are the sets of basic variables that define these continua? Do they differ significantly in relation to whether party is treated as an independent or dependent variable or in terms of the aspect or level of party under consideration? How should the classification of parties within party systems be pursued and related to the classification of party systems per se?

Thus far, conceptual problems regarding the definition of terms and the delineation of categories or classes have been discussed. Conceptual frameworks, however, require more than basic terms and categories. They require standardized conceptions of basic variables and the broad nature of the relationships among them. As has been suggested, such conceptualization is also involved in establishing standardized classificatory schemes. Inability to resolve this lesser problem thus signifies the presence of substantial conceptual gaps and deficiencies.

This is not to say that the rudiments of a standardized conceptual framework do not exist. Rather, most students of party politics conceive parties to exist in environments with which they interact both in terms of impacting them and being impacted by them (Chambers, 1975; Sorauf, 1975). This commonly shared notion, however, provides only highly general guidance as an operative theoretical framework and serves largely as a basis for dividing labor. The great majority of scholars choose, explicitly or implicitly, to treat party either as a dependent or independent variable. Moreover, in so doing they differ widely on the level at which they operate, the aspects of party or environment they choose to emphasize, and the approach or orientation they employ.

A number of partial and differing ways of conceptualizing the environment as a variable or set of variables thus exist. Facets of the electoral system or electoral politics, political institutions or arrangements, systemic characteristics or needs, policy outcomes, and broad social or cultural factors have all served as bases for defining the environment as a variable. However, emphasis tends to differ depending on whether environment is treated as an independent or dependent variable. For example, those who treat environment as an independent variable tend to conceptualize it in terms of factors rooted outside the political system, changes in the political system tied to such factors, or basic structural or institutional features of the political system. In contrast, those who treat it as a dependent variable tend to conceptualize it in terms of abstract characteristics or needs of political systems per se.

Similarly, there are a variety of partial and differing ways of conceptualizing party as a variable or set of variables. Concrete roles and activities, abstract functions, facets of structure, electoral groupings, policy positions, and broad aspects of electoral or party politics have all served as bases for defining party as a variable. The number of options is further compounded because several of the most popular bases of conceptualization, i.e., functions, roles, and/or activities, can be interpreted in different senses and elaborated in different ways even when interpreted in the same sense. Here too, however, emphasis tends to differ depending on whether party is treated as an independent or dependent variable. Conceptualization, for example, tends to focus on structure alone or structure and concrete activities in the latter case and on function, in the systems sense, in the former.

This division of labor and the profusion of separate treatments testify to the existence of a maturing but nonetheless troubled state of conceptual development.

Students of the impact of environment on party carry on a long tradition in the field and can well argue that party should be approached more as effect than cause. Nonetheless, partial and differing conceptualization of environmental factors breeds confusion, impairs the build-up of knowledge and leads to flawed results. Such conceptualization does little to resolve such basic questions as what factors should be included in the political environment, the internal relation and status of factors in this environment, and the manner in which the broader societal environment should be related to the political environment and treated. Nor can it firmly establish the independence of the environmental variables applied or their general applicability. Current conceptualization of environmental variables thus tends to result in the delineation of factors whose range and significance across polities and even within them remain clouded.

Students of the impact of party on environment have developed a variety of findings on the role or impacts of party on political systems. This is true both statically and dynamically. Yet, once again, partial and differing conceptions of the independent variable breed confusion, impair the build-up of knowledge, and lead to flawed results. As noted above, the prevailing tendency is to conceptualize party as an independent variable in terms of abstract functions. Analysts, however, not only employ varying catalogs of functions, but also usually fail to treat the ties or relations between function in any of its senses and structure. Rather, as previously suggested, those who attempt to deal with party as structure or organization typically treat it as a dependent variable or without explicit regard for its environmental impacts. Moreover, due both to the state of conceptual development with regard to the environment and the problems of functional analysis, conceptualization of party impacts tends to self-confirming results. Systems are presumed to have certain needs, and parties are accorded functions that satisfy them. As Frank Sorauf (1975) has argued, this imputes a primacy to parties they may not deserve. Here too, then, current conceptualization of party as a variable tends to result in treatments that do not firmly establish its range, significance, or independence.

Finally, given the difficulties of dynamic analysis in social science generally and the problems that remain unresolved in conceptualizing party and environment in the area of party politics, it is hardly surprising that ability to treat these variables in an interactive fashion is severely limited. As a result, analysts usually proceed either by treating one or the other exclusively as the independent variable or by alternating such treatment in a separate and isolated fashion (Chambers, 1975; Sorauf, 1975; Weiner and LaPalombara, 1966). The dynamic or developmental aspects of analysis thus derive simply from the fact that it is carried out over time. In a few cases, however, analysts have defined models that qualify as inter- active ones. Walter Dean Burnham (1970), for example, posits that critical realignments proceed from shocks or tensions in the socio- economic environment and impact institutions, policy, elite roles, and so on. Nonetheless, such models are few in number and limited in scope. Moreover, key variables and relationships in them often lack the specificity or concreteness needed for operationalization and testing. In sum, then, the point remains that, though the rela- tionship between party and environment is highly interactive, the conceptual apparatus available for treating them rigorously and comprehensively in this fashion is inadequate. It is as if the problem were to analyze how persons climbed stairs and the conceptual frameworks available did not include or provide for coordinated use of the feet.

III

This catalog of conceptual gaps and deficiencies in party research should not be misconstrued. The profusion of treatments and lack of consensus testifies not simply to the existence of problems, but also to the rich and extensive body of data, concepts, categories, and approaches that has emerged in recent decades. Indeed, the same type of critique could be made of fields in the "harder" sciences that have undergone rapid development in terms of data gathering and theory construction in the past few decades, e.g., cancer research.

The substantive findings produced by party research since World War II accordingly reflect both its strengths as a rapidly maturing area of research, perhaps the most so in the discipline, and its weaknesses as an area of research in which a variety of basic conceptual issues remain unresolved. Hence, as is invariably true in fields of knowledge that are rapidly progressing, two somewhat contradictory statements apply. Our knowledge has substantially improved; yet puzzling questions of great importance still exist.

Our purpose in this section of this paper is to complement our brief discussion of the conceptual problems in party research with a brief discussion of major substantive problems or questions. Given the varying levels of analysis, objects of attention, and orientations or approaches present in party research, there are a multitude of ways in which such a discussion could be organized. However, since the theme of this volume is party development and party decay, the following three categories seem logical and appropriate: the origins or emergence of party systems; change or development in party systems; and decline or decay in party systems.

Students of party development agree that the entities now commonly identified as parties are radically different from the cliques, factions, or groups of notables that were referred to as parties in earlier times. It is also commonly argued that contemporary party systems are a product of modernization, that they emerge as a result of rapid social change along a variety of interrelated dimensions (Huntington, 1968; LaPalombara and Weiner, 1966). Such change is perceived as increasing the need for governors to secure the support of larger publics because of its impact in heightening societal complexity and interdependence and altering political beliefs, attitudes and expectations. In addition, the current literature on party origins deals with such topics as why particular types of party systems emerge, the developmental process through which party systems emerge, why in a number of cases the process aborts, and the impact that the manner in which a party system emerges has on its subsequent functioning and development. In all these respects, however, significant questions remain open. Not only does conceptualization or definition of the key components of modernization vary in the case of different authors; in addition, there is a pronounced tendency to treat key variables in an ambiguous manner. For example, political participation is often treated both as an essential element of modernization and as a critical consequence of it. In addition, vague and abstract strands or elements of the theory are employed to cover the origins of parties in highly diverse circumstances over periods of several centuries, e.g., to deal with both 18th century America and 20th century Ghana.

As might be expected, substantial explanatory gaps and anomalies result. To cite perhaps the most basic: if party systems are a product of modernization, why do not all contemporary states have them? In general, the answer given by students of party development is that modernization is a necessary but not sufficient condition for the existence of party systems, and thus that the process by which party systems emerge can abort. Yet, if the relationship between modernization and party systems is as direct and significant as postulated, it is difficult to understand how and why this occurs. Typically, such results are explained in terms of the excessive loads that crises of nation-building, industrialization, mass mobilization, and so on impose on new nations. However, while theorizing of this sort may be the start of explanation, it cannot be accepted as more than that. Rather, the theory of modernization itself requires further elaboration and refinement. If this theory is to explain the basic dynamics of the emergence of party systems, the strength and relationship of the intervening variables between forms of social change and the emergence of party systems need to be explored and clarified in a more rigorous fashion. Moreover, as part and parcel of doing so, the components of modernization and the character of system loads need to be pinned down so that the status or standing of nations can be more definitively assessed and compared.

Significant explanatory gaps and anomalies also exist with respect to the origins of particular types of party systems and the process or stages by which party systems emerge. Though the conception of system crises and loads provide some unifying themes and modes of analysis, answers to the question of why particular types of party systems emerge tend to vary in relation to the concerns and perspectives of the analysts. Thus, those who focus on developing nations often differ in approach, emphasis, and findings from those who focus on developed ones. Similarly, though aspects of development theory have also been frequently used to trace the stages by which party systems emerge, such analyses tend to focus on individual nations and to be highly historical in character.

As a consequence, while much is known about the details of the emergence of particular party systems, ability to generalize concerning the reasons different types of party systems emerge or the process or stages by which they do so remains weak. Explanations that can encompass a large variety of cases in different contexts are limited in number, especially as regards crossing broad regional areas or levels of system development. Some noteworthy attempts, however, have been made. Seymour Lipset and Stein Rokkan (1967) have applied Parsonian theory to the analysis of cleavages in order to explain the emergence of a large number of European party systems and Lipset (1970) has also speculated on applications to party systems in developing nations. Samuel Huntington (1968) has put forward a theory that both explains the basic stages or processes by which party systems emerge and the reasons why different types of party systems result.

Finally, as might be expected, analysis of the impacts that the origins of a party system have on subsequent functioning is a topic that has been pursued largely in terms of development theory. Emphasis has been placed on the order in which system crises occur and important insights have resulted. Nonetheless, this concern has often been secondary or tangential to other concerns and knowledge remains either highly general and speculative or tied to quite concrete historical circumstances.

The literature that deals with development or change in party systems is extremely diverse. Studies involve a number of cross-cutting dimensions. There are one-nation, regional, and cross-regional analyses. There are analyses of new or developing nations and regions, and analyses of developed or mature nations and regions. As noted earlier, the manner in which party and environment are conceptualized as variables can and does vary widely. Similarly, there is variation in terms of whether party is treated as an independent variable, dependent variable, or in some mixed and/or interactive fashion.

Given the highly variegated character of research, it is difficult to summarize concrete findings. Contexts, variables, and treatments differ so that it is hard to find solid ground on which to generalize. Indeed, even such traditional questions as the impact of proportional representation on types of party systems remain in dispute (Santori, 1976). Nonetheless, two common or pervasive aspects of substantive research on party development or change exist which can be coherently and profitably discussed, even within the confines of a brief essay. One relates to several basic or underlying problems or dilemmas that students of party development or change confront and the other to the broad theories or frameworks that are currently available for organizing and directing research.

In the latter regard, five such theories or frameworks deserve mention. As in the case of the origins of party systems, modernization or development theory serves as a frequently relied upon framework. Once again three aspects of the approach are particularly widely applied: the notion of systemic crises, such as nation-building, industrialization, mass mobilization, and so on; the notion of broad systemic needs or functions, such as integration, legitimization, conflict management, and so forth; and the notion of system loads, i.e., the burdens imposed by the order in which system crises occur.

Nonetheless, some important differences also exist among those who rely on development theory to analyze party development or change. As already noted, conceptions of development or modernization vary. This is true both with respect to the level of specificity adopted and the degree of emphasis placed on development as a process as opposed to development as a state of being. For example, Chambers (1975) insists on a highly explicit and normative definition of development in terms of system characteristics and capabilities, e.g., adaptive capacity, structural differentiation, maintenance of integration, and so on. Weiner and LaPalombara (1966) deliberately refrain from positing or adopting any specific definition of development and rather approach it in terms of solving system crises and meeting system needs. Huntington (1968) defines development or modernization in terms of system characteristics, such as the rationalization of authority, differentiated structures, and mass participation, but argues that, empirically, only the concept of modernization as participation or mobilization is generally applicable to the "developing" world.

Here again, these differences seem to be tied to and perhaps dependent on the concerns of the analyst. Thus, Chambers's object of attention is the United States and he provides a careful and historically detailed analysis of stages in the growth of the American party system. Huntington and Weiner and LaPalombara are engaged in cross-regional analysis with emphasis on new or developing nations.

Cleavage theory provides another common or popular framework. Once again the approach permits substantial differences in definition or conceptualization. Thus, cleavage can be and has been defined in terms of a variety of categories: economic, religious, regional, urban-rural, ethnic or tribal, conceptions of legitimate authority, and so on. In addition, analysts can and do emphasize various combinations of these categories (Lipset and Rokkan, 1967; Allardt and Rokkan, 1970).

Aspects of cleavage theory can be and have been combined with development theory. But its thrust is nonetheless quite different. Since cleavages are typically defined in terms of broad societal or cultural factors, those who rely on cleavage as an approach tend to treat party as a dependent variable. The opposite tends to be true in the case of development analysts. For similar reasons, students of cleavage frequently treat party as an electoral entity or group and do statistical analyses of voting. In contrast, students of development tend to treat party in terms of function or activity and can operationalize their primary hypotheses only infrequently. Finally, students of cleavage have tended to focus on mature or developed systems where the processes of nation-building have been completed. Again, quite understandably, the opposite is true of development analysts.

A third theory or framework that has focused and directed the work of many students of party development or change is realignment theory. This approach is limited in ways that development and cleavage theory are not. In its present form, at least, it is applicable primarily to stable two-party systems and has been applied in depth only to the United States and Britain. Moreover, in pure or pristine form, its basic view of changes is cyclical, not developmental, though it can be integrated with a developmental perspective and used to assist in analyzing the historical stages of a party system.

Yet, if realignment theory is more circumscribed in scope or range than development or cleavage theory, it too is broad enough in terms of conception or definition to permit considerable variation in application. What realignments are, how they should be classified and measured, when they occur, what their causes and impacts are, what processes or stages they involve—all have been treated differently by different authors. Overall, however, two basic orientations can be identified. One is to treat realignments as electoral phenomena that involve widespread and durable changes in party grouping and allegiances and, in a derivative manner, important changes in governmental policy (Sundquist, 1973). The other is to treat realignments as far broader types of phenomena, which encompass such factors as changes in the levels of political participation, in the intensity and divisiveness of partisan feeling, in the distribution of political and economic power among elites, and in the character of key political institutions (Burnham, 1970).

Two remaining theories or frameworks deserve mention: spatial theory and party reach or permeation theory. In neither case has the approach been as widely applied as development, cleavage, or realignment theory. Yet, in each case, the explanatory potential is significant. Spatial theory might be viewed as a specialized form of cleavage theory. However, it differs by focusing more directly on issue divisions and approaching them in terms of economic assumptions and techniques of analysis (Sartori, 1976). Party reach or permeation theory might be viewed as an aspect of development theory. However, it is concerned with the degree to which party elites in fact permeate the institutional structures of a political system and the results that follow from varying degrees of success (Daalder, 1966). Use of this approach thus allows analysts to treat the role and impact of party as problematic, rather than being led by assumptions concerning abstract functions and system needs to treat them as givens.

So much, then, for theories or frameworks. Whatever approach or combination of approaches students of party development or change apply, certain basic and pervasive problems exist in carrying on such research that are very difficult to resolve.

The first is whether the primary object of attention and analysis should be development or change. Our discussion thus far has deliberately obscured this issue. This is because these terms are often treated uncritically in the literature and used as if they were interchangeable. But, in fact, they are not. Development is a particular type of change and involves the assumption that change is somehow linear in a positive fashion. Change, on the other hand, is a much more comprehensive concept and can be approached in terms of cyclical assumptions as well as negative linear ones. Analysts who adopt a developmental view, either implicitly or explicitly, thus make a choice, even though they may not be fully aware of the restrictive implications of their choice. Yet, not to adopt a developmental view also presents serious problems. The number of broad theories or frameworks available for organizing and directing the analysis of change as it relates to parties is limited. Moreover, the frameworks that are nondevelopmental in character involve their own distinctive types of restrictive assumptions. Still, to seek to explain change without the aid of a broad theory or framework is to risk isolating one's research and focusing on minutiae. Difficult issues in terms of the proper approach or orientation toward change thus confront each and every analyst. Nor can they be avoided by failing to face them. To do so simply allows decision by default.

A second underlying problem is the degree to which a theory of the political system must be defined before the investigation and explanation of development or change can proceed. The need for such theory is particularly apparent when party is treated as an independent variable so that attention focuses on its functions or impacts, when the primary analytic concern is to explain the transition from one type of party system to another, and when parties in one-party systems become the topics or objects of analysis. Nonetheless, the problem has general relevance or applicability. In investigating party systems all analysts make assumptions, implicitly and/or explicitly, about the political system or systems in which the party or parties under examination operate. The question that thus always exists, whether directly confronted or not, is the degree to which it makes sense to seek to explain aspects of party politics without explicit and developed conceptions of systemic variables. If this issue is not deliberately and carefully thought through, the worth of an analyst's work can easily be undermined. Yet, when so confronted, the analyst usually must deal with a variety of problems and questions he cannot easily resolve. Extant theories of the political system are at least as ambiguous and conflicting as extant theories of party. Here too, then, difficult issues confront the student of party development or change, issues he must nonetheless seek to meet and accommodate in order to guard the validity and significance of his work.

A third and final problem is related to the second. It concerns the degree to which it is advisable at this point in time to rely on comprehensive or general theories that presume to span highly different contexts. Though development or modernization theorists, in particular, believe this to be desirable, the question remains as to whether current frameworks are powerful enough for analysts to apply them with profit to stable as well as unstable systems, to new as well as mature systems, to one-party as well as competitive party situations. The issue here is not whether theories or frameworks are needed. Obviously, they are. Nor is it whether general theory is desirable. Obviously, it is. The issue is rather whether the concepts and findings now available provide a viable platform for general theory or whether they are so limited and ambiguous as to lead to deceptive and superficial results when organized and applied in a comprehensive fashion.

Analysis of party decline or decay has focused on three primary aspects of the topic: the repression of parties, the breakdown of competitive party systems, and the erosion of party power and functions within the confines of an ongoing party system. As is the case generally, substantial differences of approach and view exist.

Students of developing nations interested in the problem of decline have devoted some attention to party erosion or decay, particularly with reference to the loss of party power and function in one-party systems as party leaders become ranking state officials (Wallerstein, 1966). However, such students have devoted most of their attention to forms of party decline that involve regime change, that is, instances in which party systems are repressed or transformed into one-party systems through coups or revolutions.

Two continuing problems may be noted in the analysis of these forms of decline. Students of party politics generally have not resolved the question of whether the transition from a competitive party system to a one-party system is a form of change or a form of decline. Thus, among students of developing nations argument continues on this matter not only in terms of normative considerations, but also in terms of the impact on development per se. In addition, development theory has an implicit bias that militates against its ability to analyze decline. It is true, of course, that development theorists do not posit any inevitable connection between the presence of modernizing conditions and the emergence and success of party systems. Still, treatment of party as a critical agent of development leads to treatment of decline in a derivative and negative manner. Nonparty states, in which party has been repressed, are accordingly regarded as states in which there are serious barriers to development and stability (LaPalombara and Weiner, 1966; Huntington, 1968). This may well be true empirically, but for those who rely on development theory it becomes true almost by definition.

Students of party decline or decay in developed or mature nations also have been long concerned over the breakdown of competitive party systems. And this tradition continues in contemporary research (Sartori, 1976). Nonetheless, the focus is as much, if not more, on the atomization of existing party systems (nonregime change) as on the transition to one-party systems (regime change). Equally if not more important, since the 1960s a new theme—the erosion or decay of party systems—has emerged among students of party decline in modern industrialized nations and become quite prevalent, if not dominant. In short, what is only a secondary concern to students of developing nations has become a primary concern to students of developed nations.

Analysis of the erosion or decay of party systems has been largely a product of the work of American political scientists and most of this work has been focused on the United States. Yet, here as elsewhere, significant disagreements exist. Both the extent of decline and its implications for the American political system are disputed.

Some find the evidence of decline impressive and believe it signifies basic and decisive change. For example, students of American party politics, such as Frank Sorauf (1976) and Gerald

Pomper (1977), have emphasized the declining role and power of party as an organization. They see party as becoming just one of a number of contestants for power in the system, rather than the preeminent link between the electorate and the government, and they believe that this involves critical and permanent change both in the character of the political process and the operations of American democracy. Others take an even bleaker view. Walter Dean Burnham (1970, 1975), for example, has gathered together a large amount of data on the onward march of party decomposition or disaggregation as an electoral group or alliance. On the basis of these data, he argues that the United States may well have entered a new postindustrial era in which politics will grow more issue-oriented and polarized and parties will continue to dissolve into increasingly discrete and transitory electoral coalitions. If so, Burnham believes that the result will not only be a drastic alteration in the character of American politics, but ultimately a change in the nature of the political system itself.

In contrast, other students of American party politics take a far less pessimistic view. James Sundquist (1973), for example, argues that many of the aspects of decomposition, which analysts such as Burnham have found, are typical features of a prerealignment period. He therefore believes that the march toward decomposition could well be checked, at least in the short run, and the New Deal realignment reinvigorated. Similarly, Warren Miller and Teresa Levitin (1976) discount negative interpretations of evidence bearing on party strength. They argue that the party system remains largely intact and that the degree of alienation has been exaggerated. They therefore believe that the future is open, not closed, and that it will be determined by the degree of skill political leaders possess and can successfully bring to bear.

This dispute is of great significance. Theoretically, what is at issue is whether party development is subject to a final and conclusive stage, whether the party cycle resembles the life cycle, even for healthy party systems. Practically, and more importantly, the argument is also an argument over the viability of democratic government in the modern world. What is basically at issue is whether the most stable and successful democratic regimes this planet has ever known can continue to survive, whether democracy can, in fact, cope with complexity.

IV

The articles in this volume could have been organized in any number of ways. In earlier volumes of this series, for example, we have organized the articles according to the geographic subject area covered in each article. In this volume, we could have chosen to organize the chapters according to the conceptual problems in party research which the authors address or according to the orientation or approach of the authors. We have decided, however, to follow the outline presented in the section of this chapter just concluded, dealing first with the emergence of party systems, then with change in existing party systems, and finally with decline or decay in party systems.

Two of the articles in this volume deal with the origins of new political parties. Charles Hauss and David Rayside look at the large number of recent examples in which new parties have emerged in ongoing party systems. Hauss and Rayside present a first approach toward developing a theory of how and why such parties appear and whether or not they will be successful. Party emergence is the dependent variable in this theory, a variable to be explained in terms of factors they call "political facilitators," such as the organization and behavior of these parties and the existing ones, rather than in terms of the social and legal factors stressed often in the literature.

Ralph M. Goldman's chapter on the emerging transnational party system points to many of the problems in research on party origins. Goldman maintains that transnational parties do exist and are very active in many spheres but that Americans do not take them seriously because of perceptual difficulties, the tradition of anti-partyism, our unwillingness to compare our experience to others, and like reasons. This chapter, which puts transnational parties into an analytical framework similar to that commonly used for national party systems, speculates on the implication of a transnational party system for the current American party system.

Marsha Hurst's chapter is the first which looks at development or change in an ongoing party system. She examines the political development of one particular segment of American society for one brief period of time. Her analysis of the blacks in the Republican Party in New York City in the early decades of this century parallels the themes developed by others in this volume. Specifically, Hurst demonstrates that black party development was dependent on power struggles within the political system, particularly the structure of inequality between blacks and whites. Hurst generalizes from her analysis not only about what politics based on race has and will mean to party development, but also on the implications of political participation based on race or ethnicity for the continuation of barriers between groups in society generally.

In her chapter, Kay Lawson presents 10 hypotheses explaining how existing party systems, once created, are likely to change over time. She uses France, Nigeria, and the United States to test her theories of party change. Briefly summarized, Lawson's theory relates party action to whether or not the party is in power and second to the nature of policymaking in the regime in which the party exists. Lawson suggests a new interpretation for why parties might be declining—a mini-theory of self-destruction—but she also presents reasons why this tendency is not irreversible, that is, why parties can continue to develop in a positive direction.

In their chapter, Raymond Wolfinger and Robert Arseneau discuss changes in the party system in the South. Many observers have noted changes in the voting coalitions in the South, as that region has moved from a solid Democratic vote. Wolfinger and Arseneau discuss the nature of the Southern political system as it has evolved.

In the first of the articles that focus on party decline, Martin Shefter looks at the history and the structure of both political parties and public bureaucracies and the relationship between the two in the United States. Shefter argues that social change, which has been used to explain "critical realignments" in the American party system, is a contributing but not a sufficient cause for the changes he sees in parties and bureaucracy and the relationship between the two. Rather, Shefter maintains that the variables he examines have been used as tools in ongoing party struggles in the United States. He maintains that American parties are on the decline today in part at least because the major struggles for power are taking place outside of the party system. Party in this case is a dependent variable which can be explained in terms of the strategies of those struggling for power. Party is on the decline today because it is irrelevant to that more significant power struggle.

Walter Dean Burnham's chapter on the British party system questions whether the British parties, with which we have become familiar since World War II, are currently dying off because the collectivist consensus so long accepted is now in doubt. Burhnam's work relates to a number of the themes we have discussed. It deals with the decline of an existing party system, it is specifically comparative in its approach, going beyond the work on American parties for which Burnham is so well known, and it explicitly deals with the relationship between environment and party system, positing that the nature of the party system is a dependent variable, changes in which can be explained by changes in the independent variable, the state of the political economy. This chapter presents a new aspect of Burnham's work. In our view, it is an important contribution toward clarifying some of the ambiguities in the field of party development.

The final chapter, T.J. Pempel's essay on the experience of parties in Japan, is similar in' many ways to Burnham's. Pempel sees the Japanese parties in decline and explains this decline in terms of two environmental factors, the degree to which parties can control policymaking and changes in the significance of social groupings in Japan. Pempel maintains that contemporary Japanese parties are following a pattern set up by their prewar predecessors; they are becoming irrelevant because they are not important to those currently making major policy decisions and they depend for their support on socioeconomic sectors which were once dominant but which today are less so. While the environmental factors Pempel emphasizes are different from that studied by Burnham, Pempel agrees with Burnham that party should be viewed as a dependent variable to be explained in terms of other factors in the political, social, and economic life of a country. Pempel even more explicitly than Burnham discusses the relevance of his theoretical findings beyond the context of the single case he examines.

As we stated earlier, despite its long and rich history, party research still suffers from conceptual problems, from definitional problems, and from problems of deciding just what it is relevant to study. It would have been impossible to collect a series of articles which solved problems that have confronted generations of political scientists. We feel that we have collected a series of exceptional articles in this volume. They do not solve the problems of the discipline, but they do deal with some of the major questions of party research in a way which also contributes to our understanding of the conceptual problems still inherent in that research.

REFERENCES

ALLARDT, E., and ROKKAN, S. (eds., 1970). Mass politics: Studies in political sociology. New York: Free Press.

BURNHAM, W.D. (1965). "The changing shape of the American political universe." American Political Science Review, 59(March):7-28.

——— (1970). Critical elections and the mainsprings of American politics. New York: W. W. Norton.

——— (1975). "Party systems and the political process" and "American politics in the 1970's: Beyond party." In W.N. Chambers and W.D. Burnham (eds.), The American party systems: Stages of political development (2nd ed.). New York: Oxford University Press.

CHAMBERS, W.N. (1975). "Party development and the American mainstream." In W.N. Chambers and W.D. Burnham (eds.), The American party systems: Stages of political development (2nd ed.). New York: Oxford University Press.

DAALDER, H. (1966). "Parties, elites, and political development in Western Europe." In J. LaPalombara and M. Weiner (eds.), Political parties and political development. Princeton, N.J.: Princeton University Press.

DUVERGER, M. (1954). Political parties. New York: John Wiley.

HUNTINGTON, S.P. (1968). Political order in changing societies. New Haven, Conn.: Yale University Press.

LaPALOMBARA, J., and WEINER, M. (1966). "Origin and development of political parties." In J. LaPalombara and M. Weiner (eds.), Political parties and political development. Princeton, N.J.: Princeton University Press.

LIPSET, S.M. (1970). "Political cleavages in 'developed' and 'emerging' politics." In E. Allardt and S. Rokkan (eds.), Mass politics: Studies in political sociology. New York: Free Press.

LIPSET, S.M., and ROKKAN, S. (1967). "Cleavage structures, party systems, and voter alignments: An introduction." In S.M. Lipset and S. Rokkan (eds.), Party systems and voter alignments: Cross-national perspectives. New York: Free Press.

MAISEL, L. and SACKS, P.M. (eds.) (1975). The Future of Political Parties. Beverly Hills, Calif.: Sage.

MILLER, W.E., and LEVITIN, T.E. (1976). Leadership and change: The new politics and the American electorate. Cambridge: Winthrop.

POMPER, G.M. (1977). "The decline of partisan politics." In L. Maisel and J. Cooper (eds.), The impact of the electoral process. Beverly Hills, Calif.: Sage.

RANNEY, A. (1954). The doctrine of responsible party government. Urbana: University of Illinois Press.

——— (1974). Curing the mischiefs of faction. Berkeley: University of California Press.

SARTORI, G. (1976). Parties and party systems: A framework for analysis. Cambridge: Cambridge University Press.

SOMIT, A., and TANENHAUS, J. (1967). Development of American political science from Burgess to behaviorism. New York: Irvington.

SORAUF, F.J. (1975). "Political parties and political analysis." In W.N. Chambers and W.D. Burnham (eds.), The American party systems: Stages of political development (2nd ed.). New York: Oxford University Press.

————— (1976). Party politics in America (3rd ed.). Boston: Little, Brown.

SUNDQUIST, J.L. (1973). Dynamics of the party system. Washington, D.C.: Brookings.

WALLERSTEIN, I. (1966). "The decline of the party in single party African states." In J. LaPalombara and M. Weiner (eds.), Political parties and political development. Princeton, N.J.: Princeton University Press.

WEINER, M., and LaPALOMBARA, J. (1966). "The impact of parties on political development." In J. LaPalombara and M. Weiner (eds.), Political parties and political development. Princeton, N.J.: Princeton University Press.

WILSON, J.Q. (1966). The amateur democrat. Chicago: University of Chicago Press.

Chapter 2

THE DEVELOPMENT OF NEW PARTIES IN WESTERN DEMOCRACIES SINCE 1945

CHARLES HAUSS
DAVID RAYSIDE

In the study of industrialized democracies, the words "party" and "development" have been most commonly linked in sweeping historical works like those of Lipset and Rokkan (1967), Chambers and Burnham (1967), or Daalder (1966). These authors have dealt perceptively with the impact of large-scale structural transformations of the 16th through the early 20th centuries on the development of today's parties.

While we agree that the impact of the upheavals of the last five centuries can still be seen in Western Europe and North America, their party systems have also changed markedly in our lifetimes. There has been a spate of new parties since World War II, not to mention the 1920s—the time at which Lipset and Rokkan argue European party systems were fixed. For example, only one party—the Communists—that contested the 1973 French legislative elections remained from those that ran in 1946. Not even countries like the United States, known for the stability of their party systems, have escaped the intrusion of new parties.

These parties have taken several forms. There are "new left" parties like the French PSU; new parties of the "radical right," most notably the German neo-Nazi NPD; and ethnically or linguistically based parties like the Scottish Nationalists (SNP) or the *Parti Québécois* (PQ). Unfortunately, we do not have a very clear under-

AUTHOR'S NOTE: We would like to thank Colby College for generously supporting our research.

standing of how or why these parties have developed. Many have been extensively and insightfully studied, but they have largely escaped comparative analysis, and, consequently, we know little about their development in general terms.

Improving that understanding is the task we have set for ourselves in this paper. We have consciously set our sights broadly to include perhaps too many parties and too many countries. We have had to rely on secondary sources and have not been able to generate an adequate body of directly comparable evidence. We are certainly guilty of being "airport comparativists" who are not sensitive enough to the peculiarities of the countries and parties we touch on. Nonetheless, we feel our efforts have paid off. We have developed a general argument for the development of new parties in industrialized democracies which downplays factors most commonly stressed in the literature—cleavages, strains, and electoral laws—and emphasizes instead what we call "political facilitators," including the behavior of existing parties, the nature of mass commitments, and the activities and organizational bases of the new parties themselves.

THE PARTIES

The analysis that follows is based on the experience of new parties in Canada, Italy, Norway, France, West Germany, the United States, the United Kingdom, and Sweden. In these countries, one finds a wide variety of parties and party systems. Some (France or Canada) have had to cope with several new parties, while others (the United States) have had few or even none at all (Sweden).

In all, we have examined 23 "cases." A case, however, is not necessarily a party. We have included a number of cases, like the American new left, in which no party emerged even though one might well have. We feel that an examination of the nondevelopment of new parties is just as important and worthy of explanation as the retrospective study of the growth of existing parties. In fact, it is because this is a prospective analysis that we have been able to show that cleavages and electoral laws are not as important in the development of political parties as the political facilitators.

The parties can be divided into four types. Ten are left wing, including parties of "orthodox socialist revival," formed in reaction agains the rightward swing of established socialist parties, and "new left" parties, inspired by the protest movements of the late 1960s and early 1970s. We consider the Canadian New Democrats (NPD), the Italian Socialist Party of Proletarian Unity (PSIUP), and, at least at first, the French Unified Socialists (PSU) to be parties of orthodox revival. New left parties include the Italian Il Manifesto and German Extra-Parliamentary Opposition (APO) as well as still-born radical parties in the United States, United Kingdom, Belgium, and Sweden.

Four parties—George Wallace's American Independent Party (AIP), the French *Poujadistes,* the neo-Nazi German National Party (NPD), and the Canadian Social Credit Party—are populistic and right wing. Ethnic and/or linguistic parties form our third group. They include some of the most successful and most publicized of the new parties—the Scottish Nationalists, *Parti Québécois,* and three Belgian parties representing the interests of the Flemings (*Volksunie*), Walloons (Walloon Rally—RW), and the *Bruxellois* (Democratic Front of Francophones—FDF). Not all ethnically based parties have been so successful, however, as we will see by considering the failures of American blacks and French Bretons to form their own parties.[1] Finally, the French Gaullists (UDR)[2] do not fit in any of these three basic groups of parties, but, because of their success at the polls, must be considered.

In the pages that follow, we will be explaining the development of these parties. In particular, we will try to show why some have done rather well while others have failed miserably. Eight of the parties within our horizon never got anywhere. New left parties of any significance have not developed in the United States, the United Kingdom, or Sweden, even though each country experienced major protest movements in the 1960s and 1970s.

In the United States, radicals have run for President and have occasionally done well in local elections, especially in university communities (Mazmanian, 1974). The organizers of groups like the People's Party, who have tried to build a national new left party, have, however, met nothing but failure. In Britain, the new left sects that have contested elections have done poorly even in depressed areas and when they have run luminaries, such as Vanessa Redgrave, as candidates. No new left party has developed in Sweden, although the old Communist Party took up some of the radicals' issues and demands after it transformed itself into the Communist-Left (Tarschys, 1977; Hancock, 1972:128-130; Cyllenstein, 1972).

New left parties have fared only marginally better in West Germany and Italy. The German APO polled only 0.3% of the vote in 1969, and the new Communist Party (DKP) did not do much better in either 1972 or 1976 (Shell, 1970; Merritt, 1969; Laux, 1973). Despite high hopes, the Italian Il Manifesto won less than 1% of the vote and no seats in 1969 and ran no candidates in subsequent national elections until 1976.

Our last two examples of parties that have done poorly or even failed to materialize are ethnically based. These parties have not always developed where they might have. In the United States, the civil rights movements spurred black involvement in politics, but blacks have not sought to form their own political party except in the South and then only in local elections (Carmichael and Hamilton, 1967, Chaps. 1 and 2; Walton, 1969, 1972). Nationalist movements have enjoyed growing popularity in Brittany and elsewhere in France since 1970. Yet, the Bretons have been reluctant to go beyond replacing the "F" on the backs of their cars with the Breton "Bzh" and vote for the FLB (Breton Liberation Front) (Gourevitch, 1977; *Critique Socialiste,* 1973).

Another four of our parties represent ephemeral "flash parties" which suddenly emerge, do rather well in an election or two, and then, equally suddenly, disappear (Converse and Dupeux, 1962). The *Poujadistes* won 11% of the vote in 1956, but by 1958 had been all but swallowed up by the new Gaullist party (Hoffmann, 1956). The NPD won between 6% and 8% of the vote in *Land* elections between 1966 and 1969, leading observers in Germany and a-broad to fear the rise of a new Nazism (Nagle, 1970; Warnecke, 1970; Dittmer, 1969). But, the NPD failed to top 5% in the 1969 federal elections and declined rapidly thereafter, winning only 0.6% of the vote in 1972.[3] George Wallace won 8.5% of the presidential vote in 1968, but, after he returned to the Democrats, the rump AIP could not even muster 1% in 1972 (Mazmanian, 1974). The PSIUP split off from the larger Socialist Party and did well in the mid-1960s, but it saw its vote wither away in the 1970s until most of its leaders decided to merge with the Communists.

Nationally, the Canadian Social Credit movement is neither a new nor a flash party. Under the leadership of William Aberhardt, they scored their first successes in the prairie provinces during the 1930s where they have continued to win between 10% and 20% of the vote (Pinard, 1971, Macpherson, 1962). In Quebec, however, the *Créditistes* all but disappeared after the war, then reemerged in the 1960s, only to be supplanted by the PQ. Our concern, then, is with Social Credit's postwar reincarnation as a flash party in Quebec.

One party, the PSU, seems to have a weak but stable following (Criddle, 1971; Hauss, 1978). It has won between 2% and 4% of the vote in the five national elections it has contested. And, despite the loss of its most popular leaders and the success of the Communist-Socialist alliance, most polls show the party winning its now normal share of the vote in elections which must be held by March 1978.

Eight parties have enjoyed more success than either the PSU or the flash parties. Both the Norwegian SEV and the NDP have won over 10% of the national vote. The SEV profitted from its opposition to Norwegian entry into the Common Market and from the growing dissatisfaction with the Labour Party among its left wingers (Means, 1977; Tarschys, 1977; Hibbs, 1976). The NDP has strong bases of support in the Western provinces and the urban areas of Ontario, although Canada's plurality electoral system has kept its parliamentary representation far below the 20% of the vote it normally wins (Irving, 1959; Lipset, 1968; Young, 1969; Zakuta, 1964).

Five of the ethnic parties—the SNP, PQ, FDF, *Volksunie,* and *Rassemblement Wallon*—have also done relatively well. Each has become one of the two strongest parties in its region and except for the PQ, which probably will not contest national elections, they hover around 10% of the national vote. The case of the SNP is typical. After doing poorly through the mid-1960s, the SNP grew rapidly, beginning with by-elections held in 1967 (W. Miller et al., 1977; Bochel and Denver, 1972; Kellas, 1975; Jaensch, 1975; Mansbach, 1973). By the October 1974 elections, the SNP was able to win 30% of the Scottish vote and was second only to Labour in Scotland.

There is some indication that parties like the SNP which have done rather well only in recent years have "soft" support that may not last (Bochel and Denver, 1972). They could, then, turn into flash parties. Still, they have done better longer than the flash parties we are considering, and they have what appears to be a larger more or less permanent base of support than the PSU.

Finally, only the French Gaullists have become a governing party (Charlot, 1971; Wright, 1975; Hofferbert and Cameron, 1973; Cameron, 1977). From 1958 until 1974, the UDR dominated the right wing coalition that ruled France. Since then, the UDR has remained a pivotal though declining force in the coalition supporting President Valéry Giscard d'Estaing.

These, then, are the parties who successes and failures we are about to examine.

A FRAMEWORK FOR THE STUDY OF
NEW POLITICAL PARTIES

There is no theory of the development of new parties we could have tested in this paper. There are, however, a number of variables that other researchers have found to be related to their growth. These variables form a loose framework which has guided our research.

Most observers agree that new parties form when "something is wrong." "Something wrong" may, first of all, be a deep division or cleavage caused by a major social or political transformation. Lipset and Rokkan (1967) have shown that European parties have their roots in reactions to the "great revolutions" of the last five centuries. Presumably, they would also argue that new cleavages would produce new parties. "Something wrong" need not entail anything as sweeping as divisions resulting from the industrial revolution or the Reformation. More fleeting issues or "strains" have been show to lie behind the development of some new parties (Pinard, 1971; Nagle, 1970).

We believe, however, that one has to go far beyond cleavages and strains in order to understand the success or failure of new parties. Their mere existence is not enough. The development of a new party is eased if its potential supporters are concentrated in one region. More importantly, dissatisfaction engendered by cleavages or strains must be politicized, a process which does not always occur and does not always manifest itself in new political parties. To understand when and how strains and cleavages are turned into new

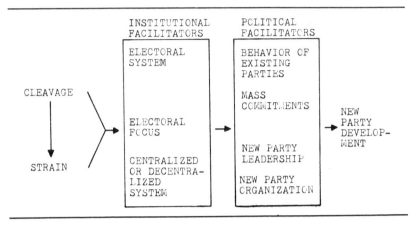

Figure 1

parties, two sets of facilitating factors, through which the strains and cleavages are filtered, must be explored. (These factors are summarized in Figure 1.)

The first of these are institutional and have received considerable attention from other scholars. The most commonly cited of these involves a country's electoral system and the proposition that proportional representation allows for the proliferation of parties while single member districts and simple plurality systems encourage the growth of a two-party system and discourage the development of new parties (Rae, 1971; Hermens, 1941; Duverger, 1954).

A country's electoral focus may also make a difference. When the key electoral unit is the parliamentary seat, there seems to be little discouragement of new parties. If, on the other hand, attention is focused on the single office of the presidency, its zero-sum nature encourages the bipolarization of the party system and makes it hard for weak parties (which most new parties, at least initially, are) to compete effectively (Cameron, 1977; Wright, 1975; Mazmanian, 1974). Finally, regional parties supposedly develop most readily in decentralized federal systems.

The other set of facilitators includes more clearly political variables which have received far too little attention from other scholars. First, what the elites, who could lead a new party, decide to do has a bearing on a new party's development. Leaders of the aggrieved group simply may not be interested in forming a political party. For example, from the 1840s until the present, most French Canadian leaders have preferred to work through established national parties instead of forming distinctively Francophone organizations, at least insofar as federal politics is concerned, Also, few leaders of the protest movements in the United States during the 1960s showed any interest in forming a new party; most, in fact, rejected all participation in electoral activities (Sale, 1973).

Once a party does emerge, what its elite does and the problems— e.g., factionalism—it faces can have a considerable impact on the party's evolution (Nagle, 1970; Hauss, 1978, Chaps. 6 and 7). Highly popular or charismatic leaders, like George Wallace or General de Gaulle, can be extremely effective in attracting new support for a party. Similarly, the existence of a strong organizational base, either within the new party or affiliated to it, can provide considerable help for its leadership. The absence of such a base can be a major hindrance to a party's success. For example, the NDP (Lipset, 1968; Young, 1969) and the Gaullists (Charlot, 1971) benefitted from already existing organizational support, while attempts to build a new party in the United States were stymied by the radicals' weak national coordination and their failure to establish ties with labor and other interest groups.

The other political facilitators represent conditions largely beyond the control of the potential new party. First, what other parties do or do not do is of critical importance. If voters believe that the existing parties have failed to provide a solution for the aggrieved group problems (W. Miller et al., 1977; Macpherson, 1962; Morton, 1960; Pinard, 1971), the chances of a new party's developing are rather good. If, however, the existing parties respond to a new issue or strain and the voters accept that response, the development of a new party is hindered, if not altogether destroyed.

Finally, we have to consider the attitudes of the voters toward both the possibility of creating a new party and the party system as a whole. In some countries, most people's strong identification with a party means that there is no pool of available voters in which a new party can build a base of support (see, in particular, Converse and Dupeux, 1962; Burnham, 1972). Similarly, American voters seem to believe in their two-party system and reject most new parties because of the challenge they pose to it.

So far, we have done little more than present a shopping list of explanatory factors drawn largely from existing literature. Yet, it is our hope that our efforts have proven to be more than a simple summary of what other people have found. In the pages that follow, we examine these factors comparatively and prospectively, reaching what we believe are rather novel conclusions.

CLEAVAGES AND STRAINS: NECESSARY BUT NOT SUFFICIENT PRECONDITIONS

One of our major arguments is that cleavages and strains are not as important in the development of new parties as some scholars have led us to believe. True, when new parties emerge, deep divisions can be found. But such divisions can exist without spawning new parties. Cleavages and strains, then, are necessary but not sufficient preconditions for the development of new parties.

Most European and North American party systems have long reflected class differences, pittings an often socialist, anti-clerical, and working class-based left against a more middle-class and business-oriented right. Since 1945, however, the nature of class conflict and the party systems have changed markedly. All of our countries experienced considerable economic growth through the mid-1960s and, in some cases, beyond. The benefits of this growth trickled down to the working class. Workers were far more affluent than they ever were before, and many were able to join the middle class or at least enjoy a more middle-class life-style. With this improvement in workers' lives as well as the development of the welfare state, workers and their parties began to tone down their demands in the 1950s and early 1960s (Lipset, 1963; Kircheimer, 1966).

After the mid-1960s, these societies began to come unglued. The changes of the postindustrializing world, like those of the great transformations of earlier generations, weighed heavily on the new social groups they created and on the old ones whose standing was most threatened. With the Vietnam War and the problems of the young often serving as catalysts, these groups began to form a new left and a new right, including, in some cases, new political parties

(Mallet, 1963; Marcuse, 1968; Touraine, 1969; Inglehart, 1971, 1976).

They formed, first, parties of "orthodox socialist revival" during the early 1960s. While the moderation of social democratic parties had electoral payoffs, particularly in Great Britain and West Germany, some leftists rejected this "end of ideology." In France, Italy, and Norway, dissident socialists formed their own parties which continued to support orthodox marxist goals.

Later attempts were made to form radical new left parties, in order to support the protests of the 1960s and to capture the votes of the radicalizing students and young workers (Inglehart, 1971, 1976; Burnham, 1970). Finally, some of the groups most threatened by postindustrializing society have turned more conservative. New right wing parties, like the AIP, NPD, Social Credit, and the *Poujadistes*, have appealed to the losers in this new world—the rural middle class, farmers, small-scale merchants, elements of the working class displaced by automation, and, in the United States, working and lower-middle-class whites.

There clearly is a relationship between these changes in cleavage structure and the development of new parties. In statistical terms, it is "one way" and by no means perfect, however. New cleavages or changes in old ones do not automatically yield new parties. Not all of the countries which are postindustrializing most rapidly have had new left or new right parties. No serious radical parties have developed, for example, in Sweden, the United States, or Canada. Moreover, the existence of a new cleavage tells us little about how or when a new party develops. The cleavage must be politicized if it is to be the basis for a party. The Canadian, Swedish, and American cases attest to the fact that this process does not always occur. Furthermore, even if the cleavage is politicized, the new parties that develop are not necessarily successful. In fact, of the new left wing parties, only the SEV, NPD, and PSU have achieved any kind of permanent success, and the PSU has reached only a tiny fraction of the radicalizing groups in postindustrializing France.

One can make the same basic argument for the second cleavage, which separates national centers from their peripheral regions and ethnic or linguistic minorities. This cleavage has produced many new parties since the end of World War II. In Great Britain, Belgium, and Canada, postwar politics has been marked by the spectacular entry of parties whose electoral appeals have been directed at one ethnic group (Rayside, 1976, Chap. 1; Kellas, 1975). On the other hand, American blacks and French Bretons (along with other non-French ethnic groups), while becoming more nationalistic, have not turned to their own political parties.

In other words, center-periphery cleavages are not always politicized into political parties. Peripheral parties have only developed where their potential supporters are geographically concentrated. The willingness of the residents of the South Tyrol and Val d'Aosta in Italy to vote for regionalist parties indicates that the limited size of a minority group is not necessarily an impediment to party development (Wildgen,1973). What does seem to be critical is the concentration of the group as the majority in its own region. This is the one thing that the Flemings, Walloons, Quebecers, Scots, and Welsh have in common but do not share with American blacks. Blacks constitute the majority of the electorate only in a few dispersed cities and in a few countries of the rural South. That dispersion makes it hard for a party appealing only to blacks—not all of whom would respond to such appeals—to win elections even at the local level. In contrast, a party has a much greater chance of success if its target population is heavily concentrated, as in the province of Quebec which is more than 80% French speaking. While, as we will see, other factors have hampered the development of a black party, the dispersion of the black population throughout the United States has certainly inhibited black leaders from thinking about forming a party (Carmichael and Hamilton, 1967, Chaps. 1 and 2).

The link between the existence of highly concentrated ethnic minorities and the development of new parties in thus clear and close.[4] Below the surface, however, lurk inconsistencies which again show cleavages to be necessary but not sufficient causes of the development of new parties. Not all regionally concentrated minorities have produced parties. The Bretons, for example, are highly concentrated, but have never developed much support for nationalism or regionalism, let alone a party of their own. One might argue that there simply are not enough Bretons to make a regional party viable. Yet, as we have already seen, far smaller groups have formed and supported regional parties in Italy. Also, Breton nationalism is still tainted by earlier nationalists' collaboration with the Nazis. And, nonnationalist elites control local politics and retain the electoral loyalties of most Bretons. Still, if cleavages and concentration of supporters necessarily produced political parties, we should find a Breton party, but we do not.

More important, the link between this cleavage and new parties tells us little about how and when the parties actually develop. The fact is particularly important for the ethnically and linguistically based parties, because the center-periphery cleavages are by no means new. In fact, the cleavages and tensions associated with them have existed for centuries, but have only been expressed through regional political parties in the last generation. To understand why parties developed in the 1960s and not the 1860s, one has to consider a host of factors, including issues like the use of North Sea oil in Scotland and the failures of governments and established parties to respond to the minorities' new grievances (Gourevitch, 1977; Hechter, 1975). In other words, we have to push our analysis far beyond the cleavage structure itself.

Pinard (1971) and others have argued that it is the existence of a deep strain or divisive issue stemming from one of these cleavages that actually sets the stage for the development of a new party. Indeed, there is a sharper correlation between the existence of a burning issue and the development of a successful new party. New left parties may not have gotten off the ground in Canada, Belgium, or Sweden because there was no serious catalytic issue like the Vietnam War or university problems to touch off mass unrest.

Nevertheless, the correlation between strains and party formation is imperfect for many of the same reasons as those involving the two cleavages. For example, where have the strains underlying the new left been stronger than in the United States? But new left parties have rarely done worse than they have in this country. Similarly, where has the new right had a greater potential than in the United States among the white working and lower middle classes? Yet, the new right, epitomized by George Wallace, has had only the most fleeting success.

Again, we are not arguing that cleavages and strains are unimportant. They are critical, but their importance can be properly seen only when they are placed in perspective. In other words, we also have to consider the facilitating factors which, in fact, determine if and how cleavages and strains become the basis for the development of new political parties.

INSTITUTIONAL FACILITATORS

The institutional facilitators discussed above—electoral systems, electoral focus, and decentralization—have a privileged place in the literature on new parties. Our evidence does not indicate that these factors are unimportant. It does, however, cast doubt on the central role other scholars have given them.

One of the most controversial arguments in the study of political parties has revolved around the supposed failure of proportional representation to inhibit the development of new parties (Hermens, 1941; Duverger, 1954; Rae, 1971). Scholars, such as F.A. Hermens and Maurice Duverger, have claimed that under a plurality system a small emerging political party, whose support is distributed fairly evenly across a country, would receive a smaller proportion of the parliament's seats than of the nation's votes. Under proportional representation, on the other hand, its legislative representation would more closely approximate its proportion of the popular vote.

Because of the penalizing impact of the plurality system, potential leaders of new parties would be more reluctant to form one because their potential supporters would not be likely to cast what would amount to "wasted" votes. This does not mean that proportional representation encourages the formation of new parties or that it necessarily spawns multi-party systems. It simply means that proportional representation acts as a poor brake against the formation and growth of new parties.

In our countries, proportional representation does not seem to have aided new parties all that much. It is true that seven of the 11 parties in proportional systems have made at least some headway.[5] Also, in a case not included here, Wildgen (1973) has shown that the shift from a plurality to a proportional system allowed a regional party to supplant the Christian Democrats in provincial elections in the Val d'Aosta.

But new parties can and do prosper in plurality systems. Five (of a total of nine) parties have had at least temporary success under "first-past-the-post" electoral laws. The SNP, PQ, Social Credit, and NDP, for example, have won as large a share of the vote as any of the parties operating under proportional representation.

There is evidence that parties which did poorly under plurality systems would do better under proportional representation. Public opinion polls showed that George Wallace and the SNP (at least before its major breakthrough in 1974) would do far better than they actually did. In all likelihood, as the election neared, more and more people who might have voted for the new party were swayed by the wasted vote argument. Similarly, the parties that have done well in plurality systems have had highly concentrated support and have emerged as one of the two strongest parties in their regions, thereby minimizing the impact of the wasted vote argument.

The existence of a plurality system may well be an *arriére pensée* that has kept leaders and voters from supporting a party that is likely to have only a limited appeal. Even with these qualifications, however, a country's electoral system simply does not seem to have as great an impact on the emergence and development as changes in cleavage structures, strains, or the political facilitators we will consider in the next section.

The correlation between a nation's political focus, and the success or failure of new parties is also quite weak. Presidential systems have experienced some of the most successful new parties, including Wallace's AIP and the Gaullists. In fact, new parties enjoying at least a modicum of success are just as common in presidential as in parliamentary systems, even parliamentary systems which lack the stable "party government" focused on the prime minister and disciplined parties.

Electoral focus is probably not completely unimportant. The UDR and PSU both emerged and reached nearly their maximum support before the Fifth Republic's party system solidified and before the direct election of the president was instituted in 1962. Since then, the solidification of the party system into two blocks keyed on the presidency has perhaps been one of the factors keeping new parties from developing. Similarly, if the Wallace movement is any indication, new parties may not last long in a presidential system, if they do not quickly reach the difficult position of being a serious contender for the presidency. But these qualifications aside, electoral focus just does not seem to be all that important a factor in determining the fate of new parties. Like the electoral system, its effects seem only marginal.

Finally, it has been claimed that in a decentralized system new parties, especially those with a regional base, have a better chance of developing than in centralized countries. Success in important local or regional elections could be used to strengthen a party's organization and generally make it seem more credible. With that line of reasoning in mind, a minor party could throw a great deal of its resources into local elections in order to demonstrate its strength or even create "showcase" local governments to aid in the greater diffusion of party support.

Our evidence, however, does not indicate that decentralization facilitates the development of new parties. There have been many new parties in centralized systems, such as Belgium or Great Britain. And France, the most centralized of all, has had as many new parties as any decentralized country.

Similarly, not all decentralized countries have had to cope with a large number of new parties. There have not been any regionally based parties of any significance in the United States since the Populists in the 1890s, and, since then, new parties of all types have had at most a fleeting importance. Also, with the exception of the NPD, West Germany has not had any new parties since the political and party systems solidified in the early 1950s. In fact, it is only in Canada that new parties have fared well in a decentralized system.

It is true that Canada gives more power to its subnational units than any of the other federal countries we have considered. And new parties in Canada have used regional power bases as stepping-stones to broader national influence and as a refuge when that broader influence evaporated. Still, in comparative terms, decentralization is not the key to the development even of regionally based parties. Instead, concentration of the new party's target population, as we discussed in the last section, is the important factor. If enough people in its region feel dependent on and discriminated against by the national center, and if parties of the national center fail to respond to their discontents, a new party is likely to develop no matter what type of constitutional structure a country has.

POLITICAL FACILITATORS

New parties can form only after an issue like North Sea Oil, the Vietnam War, or inflation creates a mass of dissatisfied voters whose discontents are not being adequately addressed by established parties. These voters turn to new parties only if that discontent is politicized in certain ways. We have just seen that institutional facilitators have a marginal bearing on that process. We now turn to the political facilitators whose importance we believe is paramount in determining whether or not that discontent is expressed through new political parties.

Perhaps the most important of these is the behavior of existing parties. Quite simply, if they are doing their job well, it is all but impossible for new parties to succeed. Their failure makes it possible, though by no means certain, for new parties to prosper.

As we have seen, new parties develop when there is something wrong, that is, when a substantial number of people are concerned about a serious issue. New parties develop only when existing parties will not or cannot appeal to these discontented voters. In every case in which a new party has done well, even only as a flash party, we can see that existing parties were unable to make these appeals.

In Belgium, Canada, and Great Britain, ethnic self-identification became more and more important for the Québécois, Flemings, Walloons, Scots, and Welsh during the 1960s and 1970s. The existing national parties chose to ignore or proved unable to reach these new nationalists leaving the field open for the new parties which have done so well in the last decade.

Similarly, the PSU did best when other left wing parties failed to respond to discontented Communist and Socialist voters. In the early 1960s, the PSU attracted voters who opposed the French intervention in Algeria which the SFIO supported and the PCF only opposed halfheartedly. Unlike the Communists and the Socialists, the PSU supported the strikes and demonstrations in May 1968, and was far more successful than they were in attracting the *enragés* after the uprising ended. And the PSU benefitted from its support of "new left" issues like environmentalism, women's liberation, and worker self-management (*autogestion*), positions which the Socialists and the Communists either scoffed at or opposed.

Along these same lines, the Norwegian SEV prospered in the mid-1970s only because the Labor Party supported Norwegian entry into the Common Market, thereby making it possible for a new party to reach the leftist who wanted to stay our (Means, 1977; Tarschys, 1977). The NDP emerged and grew during the Depression (when it was known as the CCF) when the major parties were unable to cope with the economic issues of the day, particularly in the drought-ridden prairies, and seemed at the service of the more populous and prosperous center (Lipset, 1968). The NPD ended years of dismal failure for the German far right partially because it opposed the CDU-SPD grand coalition and benefitted from public discontent when the two large parties failed to solve economic problems in the late 1960s.

Finally, the French party system was a shambles in the late 1950s. No party or coalition of parties could form a stable government or solve the host of problems that ultimately toppled the Fourth Republic (Williams, 1964). As a result, the UDR could effectively refer to General de Gaulle's ideas about governing France, his leadership in the immediate postwar years, and, after 1958, its own accomplishments as the alternative to what the General referred to as the morally and politically bankrupt "parties of yesterday." As late as 1973, the Gaullists could still make headway, claiming to be the only party able to produce "change with order."

The failure of existing parties does not guarantee success for new parties. The Italian Communists and the Socialists have proved no more receptive to the new left than their French counterparts. Yet, the Italian new left has never had the electoral success of either the PSU or the Trotskyite sects in France. Still, one cannot discount the behavior of existing parties, for, if they do effectively respond to the new issues, that response seriously hinders a new party's development. An effective response may be more symbolic than real and may come before or after a new party is formed. But, if it comes, it can destroy the hopes of a new party.

The United States provides the best example of how even a minimal response by an existing party can forestall the development of a new one. No one can argue that the Democrats have met all the demands or needs of American blacks or radicals. Yet, the Civil Rights Acts of the mid-1960s and the symbolic commitment of many Democratic leaders to minority rights have helped keep blacks in the fold. Similarly, the tantalizing prospects of the anti-war candidacies of Kennedy, McCarthy, and McGovern kept many radical activists within the Democratic Party and limited the appeal of third party candidates who doubted that radical change could come through Democratic governments.

Similarly, the existence of the Tribune Group within the Labour Party and the *Jusos* in the SPD gave these basically reformist parties considerable legitimacy in the eyes of young radicals who might otherwise have been more willing to support new left parties. And the move of the Swedish Communist Party toward the new left—a move the Norwegian party failed to follow—goes a long way toward explaining the absence of a separate new left party in Sweden.

Existing parties can co-opt—even in watered down forms—the appeals of developing new parties and thereby hurt, if not destroy, them. This, of course, is the traditional way in which third parties in the United States (e.g., the Populists in the 1890s and the Socialists in the 1930s) have been dispensed with (Mazmanian, 1974). The decline of the AIP partially can be attributed to Nixon's use of a "southern strategy" in 1972 which appealed to the social groups which had provided Wallace with the bulk of his support four years earlier. The phenomenon is not, of course, strictly American. After François Mitterrand took over the Socialist Party in 1971, it began to support the PSU's causes, including women's rights and worker's self-management, and it began to cut into the PSU's support among young people, Catholics, and the radicalizing CFDT trade union confederation (Hauss, 1978, Chap. 2).

The emergence of regionalist sentiment within the traditional Belgian parties—the Social Christians, Socialists, and Liberals—in the 1960s and 1970s probably slowed the growth of purely regionalist or federalist parties (Rayside, 1976). And the willingness of the federal Liberal Party to adopt major portions of the CCF and later the NDP platforms has also limited the growth of that party, particularly its expansion into traditional liberal strongholds (Young, 1969).

The reader might object that we have skirted an important issue here: why existing parties behave as they do. The roots of their behavior, however, are not really very important for us here. We are not particularly interested in why established parties behave as they do, but in the impact of their behavior on a new party's chances. As such, we can take their behavior as given without worrying about its causes.

Next, the response of voters to a new party is nearly as important as that of the existing parties. Obviously, there has to be a public convinced of the need and potential for a new party, which has not always been the case for our parties. For example, despite the prominence of Breton nationalism in intellectual circles and the activities of the FLB, the Breton people do not appear to be all that interested in Breton nationalism as a political movement. More frequently, we found that there was a mass of discontented voters which had not been convinced of the desirability of supporting a new party. Certainly, that seems to be the case for radicals in the United States, Great Britain, West Germany, Italy, and Sweden as well as for American blacks.

There seems to be at least three reasons for rejecting a new party. First are tactical reasons, especially in plurality-based systems like the United States. In those countries, the argument that a vote for a new party is usually wasted and may even contribute to the election of the worst possible candidate has led many reluctant blacks and radicals to vote Democratic in 1968, 1972, and 1976, rather than for the hopeless candidacies of Dick Gregory, Eldridge Cleaver, Benjamin Spock, or Eugene McCarthy. Similar arguments have hurt other new parties, unless, as in the case of the SNP, the party can develop enough credibility and support to overcome the wasted vote argument.

Second, certain cultural values may keep people from supporting a new party whose values are quite close to their own. Americans, for example, prize their two party system, and that attachment has certainly not helped radicals who try to operate outside it. In the Bonn republic, there is a desire to avoid the "errors" of the past and to avoid voting for the sorts of extremist parties seen as responsible for Nazism, which has worked to the advantage of the three moderate parties and to the disadvantage of the NPD and APO.

Finally, the potential supporters of a new party may reject it because they have strong ties to one of the established parties. The Michigan Survey Research Center has shown that party identification can be very hard to erode, particularly among older voters (Converse et al., 1969). Burnham (1972) argues that subcultural and structural ties exerted through churches, unions, and other organizations can be even stronger and weld people even more unswervingly to their parties.

We find that, when such ties exist, new parties have made little or no progress. American blacks, for example, are unusually loyal to the Democratic Party, and it seems hard to imagine many blacks flocking to a new black party. Similarly, the SNP made little headway until large numbers of Scottish voters dropped their loyalties to existing parties, especially Labour. Finally, the Italian new left made few inroads into the mainstream of the working class because of the effective Communist subculture, based on its own party organizations and other interest groups.

Most parties which have done well have not had to cope with potential supporters already committed to other parties. Converse and Dupeux (1962) show how little the French thought of their party system in the 1950s and how few of them identified with any party. These attitudes facilitated the ephemeral success of the *Poujadistes* and the more permanent development of the Gaullists beginning in 1958 (Cameron, 1972). Generally speaking, the development of new parties is most common in places like Quebec in which partisan loyalties have been traditionally extremely weak (Pinard, 1971).

The importance of partisan attachments can also be seen in the unusual success that new parties enjoy among new voters who are normally not as committed to established parties as more experienced voters. Young people voted disproportionately for Wallace in 1968 (Converse et al., 1969). Immigrants have voted for Social Credit and the NDP in large numbers in the Canadian prairie provinces (Macpherson, 1962; Morton, 1960). And recently enfranchised women made up a large part of first the Christian Democratic (MRP) and then the Gaullist electorates (Cameron, 1972).

This is not to say that the new parties will necessarily develop or thrive in the absence of strong partisan commitments among their potential supporters. One has only to look at the failure of new parties in the United States since 1968, even though party identification has continued to erode, to see that this is the case. Nonetheless, an existing party is less threatened and probably needs to respond less fully to new issues if it has solid support, and no new party can hope to do well without a pool of available voters.

So far, we have said very little about the new parties themselves. We believe, in other words, that to a great extent they are not masters of their own destiny. They cannot do well if there is no divisive issue to crystallize public opinion. They cannot do well, either, if the existing parties respond to the new discontented voters or if ties to these parties are strong enough to overcome that discontent. And they cannot do well if voters are convinced that support for a new party is tactically dangerous.

However, we are not arguing that the fate of new parties is determined solely by forces beyond their control. In fact, what the parties and their leaders do is of critical importance and allows us to understand why they have not always done well, even though the preconditions for their success existed. It is the behavior of the leaders and the organizational base that they have to work with that explains why some new parties have prospered while others have not been able to exploit the opportunities available to them.

New parties need effective leadership. Those that have had highly visible and charismatic leaders have used that popularity to build at least their initial support. The *Poujadistes,* the early Gaullists, and the AIP of 1968 were little more then vehicles for the ambitions of Pierre Poujade, Charles de Gaulle, and George Wallace. The PSU, NPD, SEV, CCF, and Social Credit have profitted to a lesser extent from the popularity of their leaders.

These leaders provide new parties with a focus for their appeal. A new party often finds it hard to gain exposure, particularly through the mass media, exposure which can be more easily obtained if it has a "newsworthy" leader like George Wallace or General de Gaulle. More importantly, voters probably find it easier to learn about and support a new party if they can identify its cause with a popular and respected leader.

A party can do well without a charismatic leader. It does need, however, at least a unified core of leaders committed to the idea of developing the new party which includes most of those politicizing the issue that made the party possible in the first place. Thus, the early PSIUP was led by most of the old and new leftists who found the reformism of both the Socialist and the Communists unacceptable (Spini, 1972).

The importance of leadership can perhaps best be seen by examining the consequences of its absence. In six of our cases, the leaders of protest movements which could have become political parties disagreed about the value of a new party, and none developed. The fact that radical leaders in the United States, Great Britain, Sweden, and West Germany were not convinced of the need for and possibilities of a party robbed what attempts were made to form parties of much of their potential active support. Leaders of American blacks and French Bretons have by no means agreed on forsaking either existing parties or nonelectoral activity in order to work in a new political party.

Parties also suffer when they lose a unified, coherent leadership. Factionalism, and ultimately schisms, can directly lead to the loss of voters and members (Hauss, 1978, Chaps. 6 and 7). The defection of key leaders—such as Michel Rocard from the PSU and George Wallace from the AIP—has hurt their parties immeasurably. And a squabbling leadership can also present a poor image for a party and thus eat away at its support which seems to have been the case with the NPD, SEV, and UDR after Georges Pomipidou's death in 1974 (Macridis, 1975, Chap. 4).

When we began this project, we expected that our final facilitating factor—a party's organizational base—would prove to be extremely important. We felt that a party that could draw on an existing network of support through unions or other interest groups or which could quickly put together such a network on its own would do extremely well. This has not proved to be the case. At least initial success is not dependent on strong organizational support. While the UDR drew effectively on earlier Gaullist movements and the remnants of the resistance networks, the PSU had support in the left-Catholic milieux, and SEV in the forces that opposed Norwegian entry into the EEC, there are also two types of counter-examples that minimize our ability to generalize very broadly about the importance of an organizational base, at least in a party's early stages. First, there are parties that did well without much of an organization. George Wallace had almost no organization in 1968 and what support he did have was poorly coordinated. Second, many new left movements had large groups of activists, the presence of which does not seem to have appreciably helped the many radical parties which never really got off the ground.

An organizational base does seem to be important for the continued success of a party, especially one based initially on support for a popular leader. Against de Gaulle's better judgment, Pompidou built a strong Gaullist organization during the mid-1960s, which helped the party sink relatively deep roots and survive the General's departure in 1969 (Charlot, 1971; Cameron, 1972). In contrast, the AIP remained little more than a fund-raising device for

George Wallace and was devastated when Wallace decided to run as a Democrat in 1972.

In conclusion, our analysis of the political facilitators has been vague. We have not tried, because our sources have not permitted, to specify what constitutes successful and unsuccessful responses by major parties, how strong commitments to existing parties must be to forestall new party development, what good leadership entails, or what a solid organizational base is like. This shortcoming is serious because it tends to make our analysis retrospective and almost tautological. Still, the correlations between these political facilitators and the development of new parties, and the ways in which they help us understand why it is that cleavages and strains do not always produce new parties, are so strong and clear that they cannot exist simply because we loaded the dice in our favor.

CONCLUSIONS

Any explanation of the emergence of new parties in established party systems is necessarily complex, and the array of factors we touched upon in this paper evokes such complexity. Because we have had to rely on secondary sources, we have not been able to either marshall all the evidence we would have liked or to ferret out the independent effects of our many independent variables. Still, we believe we have made some progress in trying to understand the conditions under which new cleavages and strains become reflected through new parties.

We have tried to argue that, by and large, new party development is not simply a product of sharpening social cleavages or of strain. In virtually all of the countries we considered, one can find examples of intense divisions which fail to generate parties.

Nothing in our discussion of those variables, however, should detract from the argument that new party formation tends to indicate that something is wrong, and that some segment of society perceives that it is being unreasonably disadvantaged. We pointed to the importance of two cleavage lines in demarcating discontented sectors of the countries being treated here. One separated those occupational groups which are the product of the postindustrial era (essentially tertiary sector employees who had previously comprised only a small part of the work force) from the petite bourgeoisie whose social standing is rapidly deteriorating. Most of the Western world's party systems formed and solidified shortly after the major advances of the industrial revolution, and they have been slow to respond to the needs of postindustrialism. Several new parties, on the right and the left, have emerged to take up that ideological slack.

The other social division which seems important to us is that which Lipset and Rokkan (1967) call the center-periphery cleavage, separating a dominant political and social center and an often culturally distinct and geographically distant periphery. What those two authors underplayed was that this kind of cleavage line almost necessarily involves the coincidence of cleavages—the *segmentation* of one part of the population from another. As such, it is peculiarly difficult for established parties to successfully straddle and, therefore, peculiarly susceptible to new party formation. Most of the countries we considered have experienced partisan formation which could be styled "peripheral protest" of a regional or ethnic sort. Certainly in the case of Canada, Belgium, and, now, Great Britain, we are prepared to argue that peripheral alienation, fed in part by ethnic differentiation, has become sufficiently strong so that the presence or absence of political or institutional facilitators has not had all that much to do with the emergence of new parties.

But even in the case of center-periphery cleavages, there is a great deal of unpredictability in the link between the existence of a deep social or political division and the development of new parties. This unpredictability exists largely because of factors we have called political facilitators. The politicization of a cleavage into a new political party depends on the stability of voter attachments to existing parties, the inclination of elites to form new parties, their abilities, their organization, and the willingness or capacity of existing parties to respond even symbolically to the discontended group's grievances. Finally, we find that institutional facilitators, including the much ballyhooed electoral law, have little effect on the development of new parties.

These, of course, are not iron clad conclusions. More evidence on the parties we considered, let alone those we did not, could invalidate and certainly would refine what we have said. Perhaps, then, it is best for us to end by inviting our readers to take our conclusions and probe them further, precisely as we inend to do.

NOTES

1. We are restricting our attention to electoral parties. As a result, we are not considering groups, like the Black Panther Party, which have had considerable success though not in the electoral arena.
2. The Gaullists have a habit of changing their names before each election. We will use these initials for the Gaullists throughout, since they are the only ones the party ever used in two consecutive elections (1968 and 1973), although, of course, they stood for different names.
3. In West Germany, a party must win at least 5% of the vote in order to gain representation in the *Bundestag* through the proportional representation half of the electoral system.
4. Our concentration argument applies to the new left as well. They have done well in the United States only in university towns or in rural areas like Canaan, Maine, in which there are enough radical voters to make local success possible and the formation of a party worthwhile.
5. The four French cases have been excluded since the French have neither a plurality nor a proportional system. Their two-ballot system has intriguing implications of its own. See Milnor, 1969, Chap. 5.

REFERENCES

BOCHEL, J.M., and DENVER, D.T. (1972). "The decline of the Scottish National Party: An alternative view." Political Studies, 20:311-316.

BURNHAM, W.D. (1970). Critical elections and the mainsprings of American politics. New York: W.W. Norton.

——— (1972). "Political confessionalism and political immunization." Journal of Interdisciplinary History. 3:1-30.

CAMERON, D.R. (1972). "Stability and change in patterns of French partisanship." Public Opinion Quarterly, 36:19-30.

——— (1977). "The dynamics of presidential coalition formation in France: From Gaullism to Giscardism." Comparative Politics, 9:253-279.

CARMICHAEL, S., and HAMILTON, C.V. (1967). Black Power: The politics of liberation in America. New York: Random House.

CHAMBERS, W.N., and BURNHAM, W.D. (1967). The American party systems. New York: Oxford University Press.

CHARLOT, J. (1971). The Gaullist phenomenon. Chicago: University of Chicago Press.

CONVERSE, P.E., and DUPEUX, G. (1962). "Politicization of the electorate in France and the United States." Public Opinion Quarterly, 26:1-23.

CONVERSE, P.E., MILLER, W.E., RUSK, J., and WOLFE, A. (1969). "Continuities and change in American politics: Parties and elections in the 1968 election." American Political Science Review, 63:1083-1105.

CRIDDLE, B. (1971). "The parti socialiste unifié: An appraisal after ten years." Parliamentary Affairs, 24:140-165.

Critique Socialiste (1973). Numéro spéciale Bretagne. No. 15-16.

DAALDER, H. (1966). "Parties, elites, and political development in Western Europe." Pp. 43-77 in J. LaPalombara and M. Weiner (eds.), Political parties and political development. Princeton, N.J.: Princeton University Press.

DITTMER, L. (1969). "The German NPD: A psycho-sociological analysis of neo-Nazism." Comparative Politics, 2:79-110.

DUVERGER, M. (1954). Political parties. New York: John Wiley.

GOUREVITCH, P. (1977). "State building, industrialization, and the reemergence of peripheral nationalisms: Some comparative speculations." Unpublished paper, Harvard University, Center for European Studies.

GYLLENSTEIN, L. (1972). "Swedish radicalism in the 1960's." Pp. 279-301 in M.D. Hancock and G. Sjoberg (eds.), Politics in the post-welfare state. New York: Columbia University Press.

HANCOCK, M.D. (1972). Sweden: The politics of post-industrial change. Hinsdale, Ill.: Dryden Press.

HAUSS, C.S. (1978). The new left in France: The Unified Socialist Party. Westport, Conn.: Greenwood Press.

HECHTER, M. (1975). Internal colonialism. Berkeley: University of California Press.

HERMENS, F.A. (1941). Democracy or anarchy: A study of proportional representation. South Bend, Ind.: University of Notre Dame Press.

HIBBS, D. (1976). "Indistrial conflict in advanced industrial societies." American Political Science Review, 70:1035-1058.

HOFFERBERT, R.I., and CAMERON, D.R. (1973). "Continuity and change in Gaullism: The general's legacy." American Journal of Political Science, 17:77-98.

HOFFMANN, S. (1956). Le mouvement poujade. Paris: Armand Colin.

INGLEHART, R. (1971). "The silent revolution in Europe." American Political Science Review, 65:990-1117.

——— (1976). "The nature of value change in post-industrial society." Pp. 57-99 in L. Lindberg (ed.), Politics and the future of industrial societies. New York: David McKay.

IRVING, J.A. (1959). The social credit movement in Alberta. Toronto: University of Toronto Press.

JAENSCH, D.H. (1975). "The Scottish vote in 1974: A re-aligning party system?" Political Studies, 24:306-319.

KELLAS, J.G. (1975). The Scottish political system. New York: Cambridge University Press.

KIRCHEIMER, O. (1966). "The transformation of the European party systems." Pp. 77-101 in J. LaPalombara and M. Weiner (eds.), Political parties and political development. Princeton, N.J.: Princeton University Press.

LAUX, W.H. (1973). "The West German political parties and the German election of 1972." Western Political Quarterly, 26:507-525.

LIPSET, S.M. (1963). "The changing class structure and contemporary European politics." Pp. 337-362 in S. Graubard (ed.), A New Europe? Boston: Beacon Press.

——— (1968). Agrarian socialism. Berkeley: University of California Press.

——— and ROKKAN, S. (1967). "Cleavage structures, party systems, and voter alignments." Pp. 1-56 in S.M. Lipset and S. Rokkan (eds.), Party Systems and Voter Alignments. New York: Free Press.

MacPHERSON, C.B. (1962). Democracy in Alberta: Social credit and the party system. Toronto: University of Toronto Press.

MACRIDIS, R. (1975). French politics in transition. Cambridge: Winthrop.

MALLET, S. (1963) La nouvelle classe ouvriere. Paris: Editions du scuil.

MANSBACH, R.W. (1973). "The Scottish national party: A revised political profile." Comparative Politics, 5:185-210.

MARCUSE, H. (1968). An essay on liberation. Boston: Beacon Press.

MAZMANIAN, D. (1974). Third parties in American politics. Washington: Brookings Institution.

MEANS, I. (1977). "The Norwegian SEV." Paper presented at the annual meetings of the Canadian Political Science Association. Frederickton, New Brunswick.

MERRITT, R. (1969). "The student protest movement in West Berlin." Comparative Politics, 1:516-534.

MILLER, W., SARLVIK, B., CREWE, I., and ALT, J. (1977). "The connection between SNP voting and the demand for Scottish self-government." European Journal of Political Research, 5:83-102.

MILNOR, A.W. (1969). Elections and political stability. Boston: Little, Brown.

MORTON, W.L. (1960). The progressive party in Canada. Toronto: University of Toronto Press.

NAGLE, R. (1970). The National Democratic Party. Berkeley: University of California Press.

PINARD, M. (1971). The rise of a third party. Englewood Cliffs, N.J.: Prentice-Hall.

RAE, D. (1971). The political consequences of electoral laws. New Haven, Conn.: Yale University Press.

RAYSIDE, D.M. (1976). Linguistic divisions of the Social Christian Party of Belgium and the liberal parties of Canada. Unpublished Ph.D. dissertation, University of Michigan.

SALE, K. (1973). SDS. New York: Vintage.

SHELL, K.L. (1970). "Extra-parliamentary opposition in post-war Germany." Comparative Politics, 2:653-680.

SPINI, V. (1972). "The new left in Italy." Journal of Contemporary History, 2:1-31.

TARSCHYS, D. (1977). "The changing basis of radical socialism in Scandinavia." Pp. 133-154 in K. Cerny (ed.), Scandinavia at the polls. Washington, D.C.: American Enterprise Institute.

TOURAINE, A. (1969). La société post-industrielle. Paris: Editions Gallimard.

WALTON, H. (1969). The Negro in third party politics. Philadelphia: Dorrance.

———— (1972). Black political parties. New York: Free Press.

WARNECKE, S. (1970). "The future of right extremism in West Germany." Comparative Politics, 2:629-652.

WILDGEN, J.K. (1973). "Electoral formulae and the number of parties." Journal of Politics, 34:943-950.

WILLIAMS, P.M. (1964). Crisis and compromise. Hamden, Conn.: Archon Books.

WRIGHT, V. (1975). "Presidentialism and the parties in the French Fifth Republic." Government and Opposition, 10:24-45.

YOUNG, W.D. (1969). The anatomy of a political party: The National CCF. Toronto: University of Toronto Press.

ZAKUTA, L. (1964). The CCF: A protest movement becalmed. Toronto: University of Toronto Press.

ZUCKERMAN, A. (1975). "Political cleavage: A conceptual and theoretical analysis." British Journal of Political Science, 5:231-248.

Chapter 3

THE EMERGING TRANSNATIONAL PARTY SYSTEM AND THE FUTURE OF AMERICAN PARTIES

RALPH M. GOLDMAN

I. INTRODUCTION

Although political parties have been a special American contribution to human institutions for nearly two centuries, although the marxist internationals have existed for more than a century, and although transnational political parties have been an increasingly significant force in world politics for the last quarter century, United States scholars, party leaders, and foreign policymakers have paid transnational parties remarkably little heed.[1] Yet, transnational parties do exist, are active, and, in many settings, exercise substantial influence. It becomes a nicety of definition whether or not a transnational party "system" exists today; a very lively one, apparent to all, will surely exist within the next half century. The implications for United States political parties and foreign policy are likely to be far-reaching.

The Communist internationals are, of course, "old hat." Between world wars, they were a consuming concern of American politicians, numerous youth movements, American trade union leaders, governments-in-exile from Eastern Europe, scholars at the Hoover Institution on War, Revolution and Peace at Stanford, and the Central Intelligence Agency. The Cold War, the foreign policy of John Foster Dulles, the McCarthy investigations, Vietnam, and the popularity of Maoism among American youth and intellectuals have been some of the post-World War II reactions to the international Communist party movement. On the other hand, no American politician has suggested launching a Democratic International or a Republican International as a competing organizational weapon. Thomas Jefferson and James Madison would probably have no difficulty endorsing such a proposal if they were alive today.

Nor have American leaders and scholars taken serious notice of noncommunist transnational party organizations. The Christian Democratic International has affiliated parties on several continents. The Social Democratic, or Socialist, International thrives. The Liberal International, somewhat less successful than the others, has associated organizations in many countries. Other minor parties exist, e.g., the International Peasant Union or "Green International." Fellow-partisans in most of these internationals work together on a regular basis in the European Parliament, seek each other out in regional bodies, such as the Organization of American States, the Arab League, and the Organization of African Unity, consult and vote together at the United Nations, and lend each other political sustenance during elections and other partisan crises in their respective home countries. In short, there is a great deal of transnational party activity going on. Why have not Americans, the originators of modern party politics, become involved?

II. PERCEPTUAL HURDLES TO AMERICAN PARTICIPATION

There are significant perceptual, psychological, and political blocks to American involvement in the emergent transnational party system. They must be recognized before they can be dealt with. A brief examination follows.

Antipartyism in America is a strong tradition (Belloni and Beller, forthcoming). When the loyal opposition to the British king took the form of party organization in the mid-18th century, Lord Bolingbroke wrote critical tracts deriding the "heat and animosity" generated by party contests. In his message to the Third Congress, President Washington condemned the activities of "certain self-created societies," referring to the Democratic-Republicans. The Federalist leaders abhorred parties and factions, refused to co-operate with Hamilton's efforts to organize, and, as a consequence, disappeared from American politics. The press, an antipolitical academic community, reform politicians, and even corrupt politicians have developed an antiparty rhetoric that keeps in question the legitimacy of political parties. Thus, when the Bolshevik Communist International came into world affairs in the 1920s, with their express commitment to violence and subversion, most Americans were attitudinally prepared to respond negatively to the party of the "Red Terror" and to classify international party movements generally as another manifestation of evil. After World War II and McCarthyism, it seemed to most Americans quite appropriate to deal in kind with the subversion and "wars of national liberation" sponsored by international communism, i.e., covert operations by the C.I.A.

The time-honored American doctrine of nonintervention is another motivation for supporting covert responses to the Communists and another hurdle to future American participation in transnational party politics. One of the grand principles of United States foreign policy is self-determination: every people has the right to choose its own form of government and conduct its own domestic politics without interference from other nations. In an age when boundaries separated countries in a meaningful way and national sovereignty was a nearly sacred concept, self-determination and nonintervention were principles respectful of the equality and dignity of nations. But that age is passing. The globalization of world politics has been accompanied by new styles and techniques of intervention by one nation into the internal politics of others (Cottam, 1967). Here again American adherence to a principle compels it to engage in subterfuge in practice, e.g., $6,000,000 in U.S. aid to non-Communist parties in Italy, chiefly the Christian Democrats, channeled covertly through the C.I.A. (New York Times, 1976).

Most Americans believe, with some justification, that the American party system is, if not unique, quite distinct from those in other nations. Ours is a centrist, nonideological politics in which intraparty factions are able to come together into working coalitions for the great contest against the other major party. "Their" party systems are presumably composed of monolithic ideological parties in single-party or multiparty relationships. How could the Democratic Party, with its liberal and conservative wings, for example, affiliate with either the British Labour Party or the British Conservatives? Without public funds, how could our major parties, barely able to raise enough money for their own campaigns, engage the reportedly Moscow- or Peking-financed Communist parties throughout the world? As for the emergence of a global party system, such a hypothesis seems to many Americans to be an ill-founded analogy to our own domestic history. Federalists were similarly misinformed and unperceptive in 1800 and would never have believed that less than two centuries later some 500 political parties would be functioning in the more than 150 nations of the world.

Another hurdle, it must be said, is the fact that transnational parties, as a substantive concern of scholars or a policy concern of political leaders, are not yet in intellectual vogue in the United States. The "discovery" of multinational corporations (MNCs) during the early 1960s is an example of this phenomenon. Twenty years ago MNCs were practically unmentioned among scholars and politicians. In the last four or five years, scores of scholarly works have been published about the multinationals. According to one estimate, there are currently 10,000 MNCs with 50,000-70,000 foreign affiliates (Sauvant and Mennis, 1976). *Newsweek* (1976) recently reported that nearly 40 American MNCs have been accused of paying bribes to friendly politicians and others in foreign countries in order to win contracts. The total expended by 10 of the largest admitted spenders was about $250 million. Such scandals assure attention in the press and in Congress; the subject of MNCs, therefore will, be "in" among academics. Perhaps similar notoriety is needed in the field of transnational parties.

Thus, antipartyism, noninterventionism, noncomparability of party systems, and unfashionableness appear to be the main obstacles to an American appreciation of the growing role of transnation parties. As a consequence, the United States has neglected its favorite organizational weapon—the political party—in the conduct of its world affairs.

III. THE PRINCIPAL TRANSNATIONAL PARTIES

Transnational parties have the same general functional and structural characteristics of all political parties as a form of social organization.[2] Political parties are collaborations among political leaders seeking to mobilize legislators, electors, voters, and other participants in voting institutions with the object of getting the parties' leaders into public office, their programs adopted as public policies, and their status as a majority or a minority sustained and protected. Parties expound philosophies, ideologies, and symbols as justifications of programs and reinforcements of attitudes. Parties draw—or drive—the indifferent, the inert, and the unknowing into the arena of civic awareness and political action. Party leaders serve as brokers in a marketplace whose political currencies are often poorly understood and too often assumed to be counterfeit.

These are indeed familiar functions of national parties, but how and where are they pertinent to transnational parties? There is as yet no world government whose offices they may seek or world electorate whose votes they may try to mobilize. Can transnational parties really be counted as political parties within the meaning of traditional definitions? A brief survey of the history, activities, and programs of the principal transnational parties may, in part, provide a response to these questions.

COMMUNIST INTERNATIONALS

The oldest of the transnational parties have been the communist and socialist internationals. Sixteen years after the appearance of their *Communist Manifesto* in 1848, Karl Marx and Frederick Engels joined the International Working Men's Association, inaugurating what came to be known as the First International. The association was a joint effort, mainly among British and French trade union leaders, to promote unionism, which was still illegal in many countries, and to encourage working-class political action. The First International soon became embroiled in factional struggles between trade-union Marxists and anarchists led by Bakunin, but by 1869 it had been successful in promoting trade unionism and party affiliations in several countries. The Marx-Bakunin struggle led to the disbandment of the First International in 1877 (Cole, 1954).

In 1889, Marxist revolutionary groups from several nations and a group of trade unions and reformist parties merged to become the Second, or Socialist, International. This international included a broad political spectrum, the non-Marxist parliamentary British Labour Party on the one extreme and the Russian Socialist-Revolutionary Party on the other. The Second International held nine congresses before it discontinued meeting because of the outbreak of World War I in 1914. At the 1910 congress, for example, there were some 896 delegates representing 23 nationalities (Thomson, 1964). However, on the issue of how to prevent capitalist states from starting wars, the Second International could never come to a common course of action. This failure gave such Marxists as Lenin the opportunity to condemn "revisionism" as a betrayal of the masses and to organize a new movement emphasizing the "dictatorship of the proletariat" and the use of revolutionary violence to end "imperialist wars."

The first Communist-controlled government was created by the Bolshevik Revolution of 1917. In March 1919, the founding congress of the Third International convened in Moscow. The Comintern, as it was called, was joined by Communist parties from Eastern and Central Europe and by the Swedish, Norwegian, and Italian Socialists. The new International was to be a tightly run organization led by the party in Moscow.

There was little question that the Third International and its successors considered themselves "pregovernmental" parties, i.e., movements preparatory to the creation of a world-state (Goodman, 1960). Such a party goal, fundamental in the Marxist view of things, made the principle of nonintervention irrelevant, in fact, an obstacle to the party's goal. For a Communist party in one country *not* to help a Communist party in another is, in this perception, as though the American revolutionary committee of correspondence in

Boston had refused to lend assistance to the committee in Philadelphia, i.e., bad for the movement and the new political system
being created. Yet, when Lenin proclaimed that the first major
Bolshevik revolutionary efforts outside Russia would be concentrated in England and Germany, the West reacted in horror, helping
Tsarist generals try to overthrow the Bolsheviks and carrying on
deportations of "subversives" from their own countries.

The Bolsheviks themselves anticipated that the International
would become the means by which Communist parties and states
would eventually work jointly and contribute equally to the establishment of a Communist world order. That the Comintern became
an unofficial branch of the Russian government, responsible for
controlling Communist organizations abroad largely in the Soviet
Union's interest, was a later development (Hulse, 1964). Stalin came
to power in 1928, postponed the goal of world revolution, and
dedicated the Soviet Union to the task of "socialism in one country."

When Hitler invaded Russia in 1941, the Allies, in exchange for
lend-lease and other help to the Soviet Union, insisted upon an end
to the Comintern, which was dissolved in 1943. As World War II
drew to its close, however, a Communist Information Bureau
(Cominform) was established by representatives of nine Communist
parties, six from Eastern Europe and three from the West (France,
Italy, and Czechoslovakia). Organized in 1947, the Cominform was
assigned the tasks of exchanging information and coordinating
activities, which, in less ambiguous terms, meant unifying Marxist
parties, attracting peasants away from the peasant parties, and
eliminating bourgeois parties. This was accomplished speedily in all
but France and Italy, where Allied occupation forces protected the
revival of prewar party systems.

Thereafter, Soviet domination of world communism began to
suffer serious weaknesses. Tito of Yugoslavia spoke of an East
European or Balkan federation of Communist states outside the
Soviet Union and of "separate roads" to socialism. The Cominform
expelled Yugoslavia from its councils in June 1948. Titoism became
synonymous with nationalist communism (World Today, 1950).

In the same year, the Chinese Communist Party, under Mao
Tse-tung, came to power, having pursued a path relatively independent of Moscow. Mao's agrarian communism and strict ortho-
doxy was very different from Stalin's drive toward industrialization

and socialism-in-one-country. Later, Mao's theory of "wars of national liberation," i.e., the promotion of civil war in nations with Communist parties ready for violence, made Mao the hero of revolutionary movements in many of the new nations created out of the postwar disintegration of former colonial empires.

In 1956 the Cominform was dissolved as a tattered remnant of the Stalinist era. At the same time uprisings were being crushed in Poland and Hungary. A year later, 64 Communist parties, from all parts of the world, met in Moscow and issued a declaration reestablishing the Communist International (Comintern). The new Comintern, however, was a loose confederation whose internal politics grew more unruly each year. Perhaps the last show of Communist global unity came in 1960 when delegates from 81 parties met in Moscow, issued a statement reaffirming their Manifesto of 1957, and proudly reported party membership of 36,000,000 in 87 countries. The statement also condemned Titoism, asserted the equality and independence of all Communist parties, gave special kudos to the leadership of the Soviet Union, and looked forward to the ultimate victory of world communism (McNeal, 1967).

While the world watched the Cold War between the United States and the Soviet Union during the 1950s and 1960s, Peking became the new center of Communist transnational party achievements, particularly in Korea, Indochina, Tibet, India, Africa, and elsewhere in the Third World (Taylor, 1976). By the mid-1960s, international communism had three separate "headquarters": Moscow, Belgrade, and Peking.

Yet another factional center emerged in 1975: "the Eurocommunists." On November 17, 1975, Enrico Beringuer and Georges Marchais, leaders of the Italian and French Communist parties, respectively, the two largest in Western Europe, issued a communique pledging themselves to freedom of thought and expression, freedom of movement across borders, religious freedom, the right to privacy, multiparty politics, and the principle of nonintervention in the affairs of other nations. This "declaration of independence" from Moscow and endorsement of democratic institutions was intended not only to attract voters as these parties faced domestic elections but also to reassure voters that it would be "safe" to vote Communist in the first direct popular election of representatives to the European Parliament to take place in 1979. Eurocommunists could also expect future strength from the reemergence of the Communist parties of Spain and Portugal, an expectation indicated by the March 2, 1977, summit meeting of Eurocommunist leaders in Madrid as guests of Spanish Communist leader Santiago Carrillo. The meeting took place even before the Spanish party had regained legal status.

Whatever the factional condition of the Comintern as a transnational political party today, there can be no doubt about its presence and achievements. Communists now claim, with confirmation by objective observers, a total of 89 parties throughout the world, including 14 in control of their national governments, a world membership of more than 60 million, plus some 40 million supporting voters in capitalist states (Starr, 1976). None can deny the "globalizing" consequences of a century of Communist internationals (Modelski, 1968).

The eminent historian of the American frontier, Frederick Jackson Turner, in 1918 wrote a memorandum for President Wilson to take with him to the peace conference at which the League of Nations would be a key Wilsonian proposal. Discussing the advantages and disadvantages of bringing the Moscow-dominated Comintern into the League, Turner wrote:

> Is it better to try to exclude these international political forces from the organization of the new order, or to utilize their internationalizing tendencies by enabling them to operate upon an international legislative body, responsive to the play of parties? . . . In the reconstruction and the ferment which will follow the return of peace [1918], there will be doubts about the existence of Edens anywhere, and the Bolshevik serpent will creep in under whatever fence be attempted. May it not be safer to give him a job of international legislation rather than to leave him to strike from dark corners, and with no sense of responsibility? [Diamond, 1942]

What is the Communist program? Thousands of volumes have been written and billions of words spoken interpreting and reinterpreting the arcane jargon of the Marxist ideology. By comparison, the platforms of the Democratic and Republican national conventions seem to be models of specificity and clarity. A remarkable amount of Marxist political terminology refers to party organization (cadres, democratic centralism, dictatorship of the proletariat), party functions (agitation, propaganda), and party loyalty (revisionism, fractionalism, deviationism). But their political goals are typical party goals: establish new governments—world and national; place their leaders into the principal offices of established governments; promote particular public policies such as nationalization of industry, collectivization of agricultural enterprise, education of entire populations according to Marxist principles, and so on. However, a reading of any of the official programmatic statements of recent Comintern meetings would find ambiguities of language that, as is typical in all factionalized parties, conceal wide philosophical and policy disagreements.

The same variety also prevails in tactical approach, ranging from the brutal totalitarian terror of Stalin or the Khmer Rouge in Cambodia to the democratic style of the Italian and French Communists. It has, however, been standard practice for established Communist parties to train cadres—organizing teams—for party work in noncommunist nations, communities, and private organizations. The "curriculum" usually includes party history, Marxist ideology, principles of organization, preparation of propaganda, tests of party loyalty, and, significantly, the strategies and tactics of revolutionary and other forms of violence and subversion. From time to time Communists will call for "united front" collaborations with Socialists and other left-wing parties, often on a coordinated basis across several nations. The transfer of financial, military, propaganda, and other forms of aid, at one time covert, has in recent years become a more explicit function of Comintern activity. With the profoundly important exception of the Communist uses of terror, violence, and military means, most of the other tactical and organizational approaches are familiar features of political party effort everywhere.

SOCIALISTS AND SOCIAL DEMOCRATS

When the Second International called off its congress of 1914 because of the war, many of the affiliated parties, particularly the French and the German, were absorbed into the war efforts of their respective countries. Not until 1923 were these non-Bolshevik socialists sufficiently recovered to attempt a reestablishment of the Second International. Delegates from 43 countries met that year in

Hamburg. A Labor and Socialist International was declared heir to the Second International and held four congresses between 1923 and 1931. Most of these Socialist parties were closely associated with trade unions, particularly the International Federation of Trade Unions, and were dedicated to parliamentary means of change within the framework of democratic systems. The rise of fascism in Germany and Italy, however, drove most of the Socialist leadership on the Continent into exile.

In 1945, the British Labour Party called preliminary meetings in London to explore steps for reviving the Socialist International. Then, in 1946 in Clacton, England, delegates from 19 socialist parties from all parts of the world gathered to plan for the future. Some representatives came from countries with socialist governments, others from parties participating in democratic governments, still others working with Communists in coalition governments, and some functioning as the opposition. Three more conferences were held before a Committee of the International Socialist Conferences (Comisco) was created as a permanent agency of the conferences. Finally, in Frankfurt-am-Main in 1951, a conference, in which 22 national parties were represented, reconstituted the Socialist International.

The statute of the revived International established the customary organizational components: a congress, a council of all member parties, a ten-member executive bureau, a secretariat, and an "observer" status for such associated bodies as the Socialist Union of Central-Eastern Europe and the International Union of Socialist Youth. A Declaration of Aims and Tasks offered a critique of capitalism, an attack on communism, a commitment to the basic freedoms of political democracy, and the recommendation of public policies that would bring full employment, higher production, social security, a fair distribution of wealth, socialist planning, and so forth (Pickles, 1951).

In the annual and, since 1963, triennial congresses of the Socialist International, between 100-170 representatives from 30-50 countries on at least four continents have attended. As of the mid-1970s, the International claimed a membership of nearly 20 million in 57 Socialist parties in 50 countries across the world, with nearly 80 million voters supporting the affiliated parties in their home countries. Transnational organizations associated with the International include: the Asian Socialist Conference, the International Council of Social Democratic Women, the International Union of Socialist Youth, the Socialist Union of Central and Eastern Europe, and the International Union of Social Democratic Teachers. From the outset, the International advocated European union. During the mid-1950s, the International gave special attention to organizing efforts in Asia, Latin America, and Africa. In 1956, the International condemned Soviet suppression of protest in Hungary and rejected a Soviet invitation to confer in Moscow about "socialist unity." The rejection was advocated by Trygvie Lie, the Norwegian delegate whose term as Secretary-General of the United Nations had been harassed by the Soviet Union. In the mid-1960s, the International began taking strong stands in opposition to apartheid in South Africa, the Smith regime in Rhodesia, Portuguese control over Angola, the United States bombings of North Vietnam. It also began to hear proposals for the creation of a European Progressive Party to help distinguish the Socialists from Communists and to attract nonsocialist progressives; numerous Socialist national parties had already begun to call themselves Social Democrats or Labor parties.

The "united front" tactic continues to be attractive to some Socialist leaders, usually in specific political situations. In Italy, for example, the memory of the rise of fascism, as a consequence of the split in the Marxist left, for some time brought Communists and Socialists together; the tactic, it was argued, strengthened the Communists but also moderated and "democratized" them. Italian Socialists have most recently favored alliances with the Christian Democrats. In France, on the other hand, Socialists have occasionally drawn strength from Communist support, most recently in the 1974 election of Socialist leader Francois Mitterand as president. In England, the Labour Party has no such problem since its trade union base is strong and its Communist element small.

During the mid-1970s, the united-front tactical issue became aggravated by the emancipation of Spain and Portugal from totalitarian regimes. Discussion of possible future Socialist and Communist collaboration in southern Europe—Italy, Spain, and Portugal—has been vigorously opposed by such British and German Socialists as Harold Wilson and Helmut Schmidt. This question, however, seems more one of practical politics than ideology, i.e., how best a weak Socialist party can maximize its influence on a multiparty situation in which coalitioning is the principle procedure for winning a role in governments (Paterson and Campbell, 1974; Revel, 1976). Other considerations appear to be the relative strength of Socialists or Communists in a nation's trade unions, the extent to which Communists are willing to forego revolutionary for parliamentary approaches to change, and the acceptability of mixed economies—part capitalist, part nationalized—in the programs of either party.

CHRISTIAN DEMOCRATS

Although less tangible in the American mind than the Communists and the Socialists, the Christian Democratic International—more formally, the Christian Democratic World Union—has become a major political force throughout the world, particularly in Europe and Latin America, since the end of World War II. Christian democracy began in local and national politics in Europe during the 1850s in response to the development of party systems generally and the modernization of the political role of the Catholic Church. After World War II, the European Christian Democratic parties softened their strong Catholic orientation, broadened their appeal to farmers, professionals, and the middle class generally, and took successful steps to organize transnationally (Fogerty, 1957; Dechert, 1967).

The earliest initiatives for transnational organization came from Italian and German Christian Democratic leaders. In 1921, Don Luigi Sturzo and Alcide De Gasperi of the Italian People's Party and other associates began a series of meetings with Christian Democrats in Munich, Berlin, Cologne, Paris, and Vienna. The First International Congress of Peoples Parties was held in Paris in 1925, with delegations from France, Italy, Germany, Belgium, Poland, and Lithuania. Annual congresses were conducted until the early 1930s when the rise of fascism in Italy and Nazism in Germany destroyed the two principal centers of the transnational movement.

In 1936, Don Sturzo formed a People and Freedom Group in London which led to the establishment of the International Christian Democratic Union (ICDU) in 1940. ICDU served as a clearinghouse for Christian Democratic groups-in-exile and, working with

Communists and Socialists, coordinated militant Christian Democratic cadres as part of the Resistance in German-occupied countries. In 1945-1946, as European Christian Democratic leaders and parties began to reemerge, a Nouvelles Equipes Internationales (NEI) of the ICDU was formed as a coordinating and consultative body. The *equipes* were national political teams that were instrumental in establishing new governments during the Allied occupation and rebuilding the remnants of the prewar Christian Democratic parties.

The East and Central European Christian Democrats, because of Soviet control of their homelands, remained essentially parties-in-exile and developed their own Christian Democratic Union of Central Europe (UCDEC) in 1950, affiliating later with ICDU. In the early 1950s, UCDEC, under the leadership of Adolf Prochazka, a Czechoslovakian exile resident in New York, took the initiative to promote links between European and Latin American parties. By 1955, the first international congress of the Christian Democratic Organization of America (ODCA) was convened, with delegations from Mexico, Peru, Bolivia, Paraguay, Argentina, Columbia, and Cuba.

It was now evident that the energies and activities of the three organizations—ICDU, UCDEC, and ODCA—would need to be coordinated. The First World Conference of Christian Democratic Movements met in Paris in 1956, attended by 33 delegations from 28 countries. The conference set in motion plans for a single transnational organization. In 1960, a permanent headquarters and research center—Centre International Democrate-Chretien d'Etudes et de Documentation—was established in Rome (Dechert, 1967). The 1966 Fifth World Conference in Lima was the first really comprehensive gathering of Christian Democrats. There were some 350 delegates representing 44 national parties and affiliated groups. In the final plan of organization, CDWU emerged as a confederation of regional transnational parties, with a secretariat in Rome operating under the direction of a World Committee made up of the presidents and general secretaries of the three regional organizations and the affiliated youth organizations and the general secretary and the adjunct general secretaries of the CDWU. A decade later, some 60 Christian Democratic parties and movements sent delegations to the 1975 World Conference in Rome.

Programmatically, the postwar Christian Democrats have stressed the merits of personal freedom, the disadvantages of violence in all forms, the value of a pluralistic society, and cooperation among social classes. Private property is seen as a source of personal independence and entrepeneurial initiative, but cooperatives and credit unions are also thought to protect and maximize the worth of private property. National and international economic planning is seen as essential and best implemented by such indirect means as monetary and fiscal policy. Colonialism and war are condemned, free trade and economic unions encouraged. International order, the self-determination of peoples, cultural pluralism, and democratic institutions are strongly favored.

In technique and tactics, the Christian Democratic International pursues familiar party activities: exchanges of information about electoral organization, press, and propaganda methods; training of cadres of party organizers and prospective government officials; development of personal contacts through travel among fellow-partisans; maintenance of permanent representatives at the United Nations and other supranational organizations; the conduct of world conferences; and dissemination of Christian Democratic publications.

LIBERAL INTERNATIONAL

Liberalism, too, claims a long tradition in European thought and political action. Premised upon concepts of liberty from authoritarian control, freedom of choice, the right of private property, and the sanctity of contract, liberal philosophy has roots in the Protestant Reformation. Spiritual liberalism gave rise to religious freedom, freedom of conscience, and the notion that all men are endowed with inalienable natural rights. Economic liberalism sought an end to feudalism, protection of the right of free contract and private property, and a laissez-faire doctrine of governmental nonintervention in free enterprise. Civil liberties for the individual citizen, an 18th century development in liberal thought, emphasized natural rights, equality, liberty, property, security, and resistance to oppression. The American and French revolutions, based as they were upon these liberal doctrines, were also the occasions for the rise of the first pregovernmental, revolutionary political party movements in the world (Ruggiero, 1927).

By 1832, liberal doctrine was widely accepted in England and France, strong in Holland and Belgium, and active in the Rhineland cities of Germany, the northern provinces of Italy, and the coastal cities of Spain and Portugal (Neill, 1953). Thereafter, according to Harold Laski, the 19th century became the epoch of "liberal triumph. . . . From Waterloo until the outbreak of the Great War no other doctrine spoke with the same authority or exercised the same widespread influence" (Laski, 1936:270). It preached industrialism and transformed Great Britain into the "workshop of the world." Its exposition of free trade created a world market. Its advocacy of religious toleration broke the temporal power of Rome. Its respect for statehood brought nationalism to Italy, Greece, Hungary, and Bulgaria. It converted constitutionalism, parliamentarism, and universal suffrage into principles of natural law. American civilization was lauded as the fulfillment of the liberal ideal. The political awakening of the ancient East was also to its credit (Laski, 1936: 270-271).

However, with the coming of the 20th century, liberal political parties and movements went into retreat before the advances of expanding governmental organizations, new concepts of general welfare, trade unionism, socialism, and communism. Liberal parties diminished not only in size but began to split into factions that moved either to the left or the right. What often remained were minor liberal parties in search of a role in coalitions with larger parties. In the United States, liberals tended to find a place within the factional makeup of either the Democratic or the Republican party, each with different programmatic emphases.

The conclusion of World War II convinced liberal party leaders of the need for transnational collaboration. British liberals took the initiative in opening communication among prewar liberal leaders in many countries (MacCallum Scott, 1967). In April 1947, individuals from 19 nations met in Oxford, England, to found the World Liberal Union, or Liberal International. A Liberal Manifesto was adopted by the 19 participating delegations, subsequently endorsed by liberals in 22 other nations. The Manifesto was updated in a Declaration of Oxford in 1967. A secretariat was established in London. The International has conducted annual congresses.

Associated organizations include the World Federation of Liberal and Radical Youth and the Liberal Movement for a United Europe. The International hosts a semiannual School for Freedom for young liberals from different countries as well as annual international colloquia attended by legislators, government ministers, academicians, and others.

The Liberal International continues to be largely a European organization, although substantial efforts have been made to develop liberal activity and groups in the United States, Latin America, and the British Commonwealth. The most successful of the liberal parties has been the Canadian where Prime Minister Trudeau has been in power since 1968. In the European Community, liberal parties have attracted from 10% to 20% of the popular vote, come in third or fourth in national elections or parliamentary representation, and have, from time to time, been key factors in ruling coalitions, particularly in Germany and Switzerland. Unlike the leftist parties, liberals tend to eschew efforts to develop strong grass-roots organizations.

"MINOR" TRANSNATIONAL PARTIES

Other smaller transnational party organizations have been important in the past. Some continue to operate, usually based on parties-in-exile, regional collaborations, or revolutionary movements.

The economic despair and the Red Terror that followed World War I spawned international fascism, a transnational party movement that precipitated World War II. Mussolini's Fascisti won their first electoral victory in 1921: 35 seats in the Italian parliament. In 1923, the National Socialist Workers Party (Nazis) was founded in Munich. In 1936, Generalissimo Franco won control in Spain, with military aid from Hitler and Mussolini. During the 1930s, Fascist parties sprung up in France, Belgium, Holland, Austria, Norway, (made famous by the traitor, Quisling), Rumania, Czechoslovakia, Argentina, Chile, and even the Soviet Union. Only Allied victory in 1945 brought the fascist international collaboration, never a formal transnational organization, to an end. Since the end of World War II, however, there have been occasional reminders that tiny fascist and neofascist clubs continue to exist, usually as secret organizations, in France, Great Britain, the United States, Sweden, Italy, Argentina, Chile, and South Africa (Laqueur and Mosse, 1966; Boca and Giovana, 1969; Meynaud, 1961; Sugar, 1971).

The International Peasant Union, or "Green International," consists of 12 parties-in-exile, with current headquarters in New York. The member parties are entirely from Eastern Europe. During the 1920s, Eastern Europe was largely an agrarian society in transition. Peasant parties emerged to preserve many traditional features of peasant landholding and to promote a moderate development of industry. The Comintern, on the other hand, dedicated to the liquidation of small landholders and the rapid advancement of industrialization, came onto the scene at this time. The peasant parties, which were already prominent in Czechoslovakia, Bulgaria, Croatia, and Poland, began transnational consultations in an effort to counter the Comintern.

The Green International's first formal body was the International Agrarian Bureau created by these four national peasant parties in 1921. Two years later the Comintern formed the Red Peasant International, known as the Krestintern. In 1928, the Green International broadened its organizational base, achieving a membership of 17 peasant parties from most of the countries of Europe. This success was in part a reaction to Stalin's assumption of power in the Soviet Union and the Krestintern's readiness to employ terrorist methods to achieve its objectives. The success of communist takeovers in several East European countries, the rise of fascism, and the end of World War II drove most of the leaders of the Green International parties into exile. In 1947, the International Agrarian Bureau was reconstituted as the International Peasant Union, which conducts research, organizes lectures and congresses, and publishes a quarterly bulletin (Jackson, 1961; International Peasant Union Bulletin).

A similar tale may be told of the Aprista parties of Latin America. The Alianza Popular Revolucionara Americana (APRA—Popular Revolutionary American Alliance) began as a Peruvian student movement in the years 1918 to 1923. The Aprista demands initially sought greater educational opportunity for the growing middle class and the indigenous Latin American Indians. Victor Raul Haya de la Torre became the philosopher of the movement. Its programs favored political democracy, agrarian reform, comprehensive economic planning, industrial development, nationalization of industry, social security, education, nationalism, and interamericanism.

The first Aprista party was organized in Peru in 1931; subsequently, others emerged independently in Cuba, Venezuela, Costa Rica, Paraguay, and Haiti. The Popular Democratic Party of Puerto Rico, under the leadership of Munoz Marin, was essentially an Aprista party. During the 1940s, Aprista parties came to power on a number of occasions in most of these countries. Wherever they were active, the Apristas were closely associated with the labor movement and, in some instances, with indigenous socialist parties (Alexander, 1949, 1973). In 1950, while President of Venezuela, Romulo Betancourt was instrumental in founding the Inter-American Association for Freedom and Democracy (IADF) as a transnational coordinating body for Latin American Aprista and socialist parties and associated committees-in-exile. Headquarters have been in New York where a monthly magazine, *Hemispherica,* continues to be published.

Another regionally oriented transnational party, with continuing vitality, is the pan-Arab Ba'th Socialist Party, originating in Syria. After World War I, most of the former Ottoman Empire was administered by the French and the British under League of Nations mandates. Arab partisan movements emerged to organize a struggle for independence from mandate status. This process accelerated as World War II began and as the Allied powers became preoccupied with their own survival. During 1942 and 1943, Michel 'Aflaq and Salah al-Din Bitar, two Arab nationalists, teachers by profession, founded the Arab Ba'th (Resurrection) Party. By 1945, the Ba'th was a full-fledged party in Syria, with organization and influence spreading rapidly to Jordan, Lebanon, Iraq, Kuwait, and Saudi Arabia.

The Ba'th party adheres to a quasimilitary type of hierarchical organization: "circles" of three to seven members each, companies of three to seven such circles, divisions of two or more companies, branches of at least two divisions, and regions that are in effect entire countries under the direction of national commands. The transnational Ba'th organization consists of the national parties' representatives to its national convention. Membership figures have always been difficult to obtain, but, in 1966, one authority estimated

8,000 members in Syria, where the Ba'th is the governing party, 2,500 in Iraq, 1,000 in Jordan, 1,000 in Lebanon, and lesser numbers in other Arab nations and overseas in France, Great Britain, the United States, and elsewhere (Abu Jabur, 1966). In their public statements, however, Ba'th leaders have minimized the importance of numbers and stressed the quality of members. Since 1966, nonetheless, there can be little doubt that the numbers have multiplied— 20,000 members in Syria in the early 1970s (Ma'oz, 1975).

In 1966, a split occurred in the Ba'th party, resulting in separate headquarters in Damascus and Baghdad. The party remains active, however, and transnational in its operations, reaching into most Arab counties as the vanguard of pan-Arabism (Devlin, 1976).

RELEVANCE OF TRANSNATIONAL PRESSURE GROUPS

This survey would not be complete without a brief reference to transnational pressure groups, or nongovernmental organizations (NGOs). Organized interest groups, voluntary associations, and pressure groups have only recently been recognized as significant and legitimate components of national political systems, particularly those with guarantees of freedom of association. However, an ambivalence about pressure groups continues, particularly in the United States, that is similar to the antipartyism described earlier. Americans have treated transnational interest groups as an esoteric subject best left to academicians. Yet, the subject is hardly esoteric; the *Yearbook of International Organizations* lists approximately 2,500 transnational NGOs.

NGOs are nonprofit associations of individual members or confederations of national interest groups or voluntary associations organized around some common concerns of the members. The types are familiar to students of American pressure group politics. Business and industry NGOs, such as the International Chamber of Commerce, have paralleled the phenomenal growth of multinational corporations. One of the principal labor NGOs is the International Confederation of Free Trade Unions. Transnational religious NGOs abound, e.g., the World Alliance of Reformed Churches, the World Methodist Council, the International Council of Christian Churches, the World Jewish Congress, and so on. Technical and professional groups range through the entire gamut of medical, scientific, educational, legal, engineering, and similar organizations. Youth, women's, ethnic, arts, media, veteran, and other types of transnational interest groups are included among the 2,500 (White, 1951; Meynaud, 1961; Lador-Lederer, 1963; Feld, 1972; Feraru, 1974).

Whatever their campaign rhetoric about "selfish interests," practicing party politicians in the United States fully appreciate the intimate, even essential, relationship between pressure groups and political parties. In democratic politics, pressure groups are the building blocks of ever-changing coalitions with and within the parties. In the Communist lexicon, such groups, usually referred to as "front" organizations, are often creatures of party, designed to appeal to special publics. Whichever pattern of relationship, however, the existence of 2,500 transnational pressure groups must be counted as a practical reality of fundamental significance for the future development of transnational parties. It is a case of Madison's Federalist Paper Number 10 writ transnationally.

IV. WHERE THE ACTION IS

Political parties, whether local, national, or transnational, are organizations with real political objectives. Parties are created to promote attitudes and philosophies, to seek out and coordinate political leaders of like mind in legislatures and other political bodies, to mobilize voters in support of their goals, to design and implement public policies, and to promote civic loyalty to particular political systems. Party leaders may be neutral brokers or adamant ideologues, philosophers or propagandists, majority or minority spokesmen, representatives of their popular constituencies or manipulators in "smoke-filled rooms." Such are some of the functions parties serve and the roles party leaders play. These functions and roles, however, require some place or situation where they may occur, e.g., legislatures, elections, bureaucracies, revolutions, and so forth. In time, these places or situations become regularized and institutionalized. Where, then, do contemporary transnational parties carry on their activities?

IN NATIONAL DOMESTIC POLITICS

One such place is domestic politics within nations. National party leaders will accept help from whatever legitimate source they can. Usually, particularly in partisan politics, the question is: what is "legitimate"? The easy and often rhetorical answer is that, if the help is going to the opposition party, it cannot be legitimate. Until recently, too, if the help came from beyond a nation's borders, it must have illegitimate motives. During the 1920s, covert "Moscow gold" was seen in the West as the lifeblood of menacing national communist movements everywhere. After World War II, the Marshall Plan of foreign aid seemed a much more overt and elegant way of carrying on a transnational political campaign, i.e., fighting international communism and affording traditional party leaders of Europe an opportunity to reestablish themselves.

Examples of transnational party involvement in the politics of particular nations are readily available but usually denied by the principals. In 1975, for example, an emergency committee of the Socialist International was formed to lend aid to Mario Soares and his Portuguese Socialists who were then campaigning to win an electoral majority and establish Portugal's first democratic government. The emergency committee was chaired by former West German Chancellor Willy Brandt. The press reported that the committee had channeled several millions of dollars of aid to Soares; Brandt's staff denied the amount but not the fact of financial aid. After the Portuguese Socialists won 38% of the popular vote, their efforts to convene a constituent assembly to establish the new government continued to be vigorously opposed by the Portuguese Armed Forces and the Portuguese Communists. Brandt's committee sought to influence this process by inviting West European governments to provide economic aid to Portugal as soon as the new Socialist-run government could be inaugurated (Christian Science Monitor, 1975).

In a contrasting example, the partisan aid is covert. The Central Intelligence Agency, according to press reports, was authorized to give $6 million in covert aid to non-Communist political parties in Italy, chiefly to the Christian Democrats, in anticipation of the 1976 elections there. However, this amount was considered "small change" when compared to past contributions by United States corporations, labor unions, and other sources. For their part, Italian Communists have reportedly received $27 million from the Soviet embassy for campaign expenses in the 1972 general election alone (New York Times, 1976). Thomas Braden, the journalist, as chief of the International Organization Division of the C.I.A. in 1950, inaugurated a program to subsidize labor unions and student groups abroad in order to help countries from "going Communist." He estimated that the Soviet Union was then spending about $250,000,000 a year on transnational front organizations. Commenting in 1967 on these activities, Braden said: "We stepped in with this organizational weapon, and look at those countries today" (San Francisco Chronicle, 1967).

Whether covertly or overtly, transnational fellow partisans are accustomed to helping each other in their respective domestic struggles by sending money for organizational and campaign expenses, coordinating propaganda and policy lines, publishing political literature, providing moral support and endorsements by leaders, and engineering favorable visits or other events. This type of practical partisan aid is likely to be a powerful solvent of the concept of national sovereignty and the principle of nonintervention.

IN PREGOVERNMENTAL AND REVOLUTIONARY POLITICS

Revolutions and the creation of new governmental systems do not simply "happen," the belief of political romantics to the contrary notwithstanding. Both events require highly organized effort by highly motivated people, and such people are usually brought together by revolutionary political parties. Such parties are "pregovernmental" in the sense that they are instrumental—even essential—for the creation of new governments. Pregovernmental parties usually have a quasimilitary adjunct organization. A successful pregovernmental party usually becomes the governing party when the new political system is established. Pregovernmental parties also welcome "outside" help. In the latter respect, French aid to the American committees of correspondence and Continental Congress and Maoist aid to fellow Communists engaged in "wars of national liberation" are comparable.

Wars of national liberation in Indochina have been clear examples of transnational party collaborations between revolutionary pregovernmental parties and "outsiders," in this case the Communist Party of North Vietnam, the National Liberation Front of South Vietnam, the Neo Lao Hak Xat Party of Laos, and the Khmer Rouge of Cambodia on the one hand and Soviet and Chinese Communists on the other. These have not been local branches of any single transnational party. The "outsiders" have been suppliers of resources to the local parties and their respective military components. Typically, these pregovernmental parties have been as much involved in the conduct of violence, subversion, and espionage as in propaganda, electoral mobilization, and less war-like partisan activities. Even when there is no civil war going on, "outside" parties may offer support to illegal parties of otherwise friendly nations, e.g., the recent announcements of the Chinese Communist Party that it would support fellow Communists in Malaysia (via clandestine radio), the Philippines (where Communist Party activity is illegal), and so on (Christian Science Monitor, 1975).

The disintegration of former colonial empires and the creation of many new states after World War II have led to several divided nations (East and West Germany, North and South Korea, North and South Vietnam), civil wars (the Congo, Angola), and other occasions for pregovernmental struggle. In every case, one or more political parties, with or without quasimilitary components, have been the organizing agents of civil war and the new national government.

The number of sovereign nations has trebled in the last 25 years and a similar growth has occurred in the number of political parties in the world. As the process of nation-founding comes to a conclusion over the next decades, the pregovernmental parties that have been or will be the principal governing parties in the new states are likely to experience internal factionalism or competition from other domestic parties. The opportunities for transnational party collaborations are also likely to grow, in many cases replacing revolutionary with constitutional forms of party combat.

IN REGIONAL TRANSNATIONAL POLITICS

Sectional politics is a familiar phenomenon for Americans. The South has in the past been solidly Democratic, the Northeast Republican, the Midwest Republican, and so on. Sectional favorite-son candidacies have rested upon interest in helping the local boy make good or providing leverage in transactions with other sections in developing national coalitions. Examples of regionally oriented transnational party movements have been described in this survey: the Green International, the Aprista parties of Latin America, the Ba'th parties, and so on. The development in recent decades of regional associations of nations—the Organization of American States, the Arab League, the European Communities, the Organization of African Unity, for example—has provided another stimulus to the development of transnational parties.

Probably the most explicit example of the role of transnational parties in regional organization may be found in the European communities. There are three communities created by separate treaties: the European Coal and Steel Community (ECSC) established in 1951 to pool the coal and steel production of six original members (Belgium, France, West Germany, Italy, Luxembourg, and the Netherlands); the European Economic Community (EEC) or Common Market in 1957; and the European Atomic Energy Community (EURATOM) in 1957 to promote the growth of nuclear industries. In 1973, the original six were joined by Denmark, Ireland, and the United Kingdom.

The three communities share common political institutions: the commission, which formulates and implements policy; the Council of Ministers, whose consent the commission must receive before implementing policy; the European Parliament, which supervises the executive organs; and the Court of Justice, to interpret the relevant treaties. There are also numerous consultative bodies.

The European Parliament, which normally meets in Strasbourg, consists of 198 members chosen by the parliaments of the nine states, with membership apportioned as follows: 36 members each to France, Germany, Italy, and the United Kingdom; 14 each to Belgium and the Netherlands; 10 each to Denmark and Ireland; and 6 to Luxembourg. Each national delegation, in most cases, has been chosen by its own parliament from lists nominated by the political parties on a proportional basis reflecting party strengths in the domestic parliament. About 45% of the seats have been held by Christian Democrats, 25% by Socialists and Social Democrats, 15-20% by Liberals, and the remainder by parties of the extreme left or extreme right (Modelski, 1969).[3]

Each of these transnational parties in the European Parliament is formally constituted as a party "group" and provided with a secretariat staff (Fitzmaurice, 1975). The national voting cohesion of delegations has, over time, been diluted by a tendency toward transnational partisan cohesion in the Parliament's votes (Merkl, 1964). The debates on the annual reports of the three communities have less and less emphasized national interests and have generated a growing focus on partisan and European points of view. Pressure groups representing continental rather than national interests increasingly have presented their demands and proposals through friendly party groups at the Parliament.

In 1975, the European Parliament, under the provisions of the 1957 Treaty of Rome, assumed increased authority over the community budget; by 1978, the community is supposed to be fiscally autonomous. Also in June 1979, the first direct popular election of representatives to the European Parliament is scheduled to take place, an institutional development of profound importance for European integration. The number of parliamentary seats is to be raised from 198 to 410, with 81 each apportioned to Great Britain, France, Italy, and West Germany, 25 to the Netherlands, 24 Belgium, 16 Denmark, 15 Ireland, and 6 Luxembourg. As in the United States, the specific election procedure is left to each of the member states. To underscore the significance of the new European institution, former West German Chancellor Willy Brandt, French President Francois Mitterand, and Belgian Premier Leo Tindemans have announced their candidacies for seats. The first two are Socialists, the latter a Christian Democrat.

The transnational parties of Europe are already preparing for the 1979 campaign. In a move designed to assure European voters of their independence of Moscow and their loyalty to European democratic institutions, Italian and French Communist party leaders, as we have noted above, have issued a joint statement on these and related subjects; in other words, "Eurocommunists" are off and running. In sum, there is now an active regional transnational party system in Europe, and its evolution and experience is likely to serve as a model in other regional contexts. For example, from its inception in 1963, the Organization of African Unity (OAU) has heard proposals to establish a United States of Africa from such leaders as Kwame Nkrumah of Ghana or to pursue forms of functional cooperation—as in Europe or the United Nations—from men such as William V.S. Tubman of Liberia (New York Times, 1964). Since then, rival groups with different subregional and partisan affinities—Casablanca Group, Monrovia Group, etc.— have emerged within OAU, beginning what may become an African pattern of regional transnational party development.

IN GLOBAL POLITICS

If a world party system develops, it will, of necessity, be related to world governmental structures. To date, the United Nations and its affiliated organs are generally perceived as a feeble but durable start toward world government. While direct popular election of the officers and delegates of the United Nations may be generations away, the proposal, when it comes, it likely to be made meaningful by the support of one or more transnational parties. Meanwhile, in the manner of legislative parties, transnational partisan voting patterns have been discerned in the General Assembly and its committees. The partisan beginnings are there, overshadowed for the time by national and regional coalitions.

As might be expected, the earliest and most explicit manifestation of transnational party collaboration was among the Communists at the General Assembly. The "Soviet bloc," originally consisting of 10 nations governed by Communist parties, has voted in the General Assembly with remarkable cohesion (Hovet, 1960; Triska, 1969; Alker and Russett, 1965). During the 1950s and 1960s, voting blocs, other than the Communists, tended to be regional (Western Europe, Africa, Latin America, etc.) or subregional (at least six such blocs in Africa). What has not been investigated is the influence of regional transnational party movements within the various caucusing blocs in the Assembly. To the extent that such voting blocs and formal caucuses have developed, however, the basic institutional ingredients for transnational legislative parties in the General Assembly already do exist.

While formal acknowledgement of transnational parties has not yet occurred at the United Nations, formal recognition of pressure groups—international nongovernmental organizations (NGOs)— has. Of the more than 2,500 known NGOs, approximately 600 have been awarded formal "consultative status." Such status indicates that an NGO has established its credentials as spokesman of a specialized interest, has registered with the U.N., and may be called upon by a U.N. agency to render advice and assistance in the development of U.N. programs.

NGOs engage in the entire gamut of customary pressure group activities: technical information, proposals for programs or program changes, mobilization of public opinion, coordination of U.N. and country programs, participation in hearings and other inquiries, and so forth. It is but a matter of time before NGOs begin forming explicit coalitions for the promotion of specific U.N. programs and policies, and it is of such coalitions that political parties are made and maintained (Roosevelt, 1970).

Another factor relevant to the further development of the role of transnational parties in global politics need only be mentioned for its importance to be recognized, namely, the availability of world-wide media of communications. Satellites have made events anywhere in the world instantaneously observable to television viewers everywhere. Radio is a much-used instrument of the ideological wars across the Iron Curtain. A process of transnational newspaper ownership has begun and, together with the long-established international wire services and opinion-leading newspapers of certain major cities, is another step in the evolution of a world press. Weekly newsmagazines covering events in entire continents are another recent press innovation. It is only a matter of time before world politicians learn how to use these media resources for purposes of partisan leadership.

V. IMPLICATIONS FOR AMERICAN PARTIES

With all the activity just reported, it is indeed difficult to believe how little attention Americans have paid to transnational parties. The insurmountability of the perceptual hurdles suggested earlier—

antipartyism, noninterventionism, unwillingness to compare to American experience, disinterest among press and intellectuals—is all the more impressive. Reality, however, has many ways of making its presence known, and American awareness of and involvement in the emerging transnational party system is likely to appear soon, possibly with the focus and energy that so often characterizes American responses to competition, e.g., Sputnik. American attention to transnational party development is then likely to have important implications for the future of American foreign policy and the party system in the United States. Some of these are suggested in the pages that follow.

FOREIGN POLICIES

For Americans to appreciate the inevitability and practical utility of transnational parties in world politics and foreign policy formation may require that they discard old intellectual categories and accept new ones, never an easy process. It is admittedly premature to think of the world as a single nation, the United Nations as a world government, or the emerging transnational parties as a world party system. But *if* Americans were to think in these categories—world state, world government, and world party system— and *if* some single world official such as the U.N. Secretary-General were being chosen by direct popular election, Americans would have no difficulty understanding and using transnational parties. Obviously, the psychic leap over old and somewhat nationalistic intellectual categories is not likely to occur for Americans soon or easily, and this is perhaps why the Communists' conception of a future world state gives them substantial advantage in the practical uses of transnational party organization. Until Americans can more readily accept the global scope of contemporary international politics, however, they will probably respond to the emerging transnational party system slowly and principally as a matter of *foreign* policy.

There are, of course, a few specialists in the Department of State and the Central Intelligence Agency who follow closely the activities of foreign and transnational parties. They are, however, hoist upon two petards of the United States' own making: (1) the perception of the Comintern, and, by analogy, *all* transnational party activity, as conspiratorial and subversive; and (2) the perception of such transnational party activity as interventionist, hence contrary to American principle. As a consequence, there is a mirror-image effect: United States foreign policymakers deal with existing transnational parties conspiratorially and covertly. In the future, as American foreign policy leaders begin to judge transnational parties as a normal and legitimate feature of global political life, they may conclude that the conspiratorial and covert approach to transnational parties has been "un-American." Open politics and publicity—the noisier, the better—is the traditional American approach to party politics, and, as these policymakers may realize, a more valid approach to the American interest in world politics.

More specifically, encouragement of Democratic and Republican national party involvement in transnational party relations may add a powerful new tool to those now employed in the conduct of United States foreign policy. At present, the United States uses primarily military and economic techniques as instruments of influence in the pursuit of its foreign policy objectives, a "bomb 'em or buy 'em" approach. There are, on the other hand, partisan techniques that, when mentioned, will be recognized as familiar domestic activities almost directly applicable to the international context.

Perhaps the most comprehensive of party functions is the capacity to supplement and often circumvent the formal organizations and procedures of government; a Democratic president, with no formal party structure for consulting his party colleagues, will breakfast with Democratic leaders of the Senate and the House of Representatives to coordinate the party's policy agenda. In like manner, transnational parties already serve as vehicles of informal diplomacy at the United Nations, in regional organizations, and in other supranational bodies, facilitating cooperation for electing fellow partisans to strategic offices in these bodies or to coordinate and implement the party's programmatic agenda. The trend toward informal diplomacy will accelerate as the number, activity, and influence of nonstate actors (transnational interest groups, multinational corporations, etc.) grows. It is already the conclusion of many observers that most of the world's economic policies are today being formulated in the board rooms of multinational corporations rather than in national or supranational governmental agencies.

However, if Democrats and Republicans begin to develop ties with transnational parties or possibly inaugurate their own Democratic or Republican "internationals," it must be expected that partisan politics will no longer—if it ever did—"end at the water's edge" in the making of United States foreign policy. Just as issues before the European Parliament are becoming more "European" in scope and definition, so will American policy questions become increasingly "world issues." Transnational Democrats and transnational Republicans would, in time, be expected to share partisan views on "world issues" with their party colleagues abroad rather than with each other as Americans promoting strictly national policy.

A salutary domestic consequence of such a development may be the invigoration of popular domestic debate on foreign policy issues now too often left to experts and a small "attentive public." There are those who argue that American involvement in Vietnam would have been of an entirely different character if the political parties had debated the issue openly and vigorously during the mid-1950s (Broder, 1972). We might also speculate whether President Carter's campaign for human rights could not more appropriately, more relentlessly, and more effectively be carried forward in his role as head of a Democratic party with transnational partisan ties than as President of the United States whose principled words will inevitably be submitted to tests not always in the national interest or convenience.

Democratic and Republican national party involvement in transnational party politics is also likely to afford the United States a new source of international political intelligence. This intelligence responsibility is now assigned primarily to the Central Intelligence Agency and the Department of State. At the risk of overstatement, this assignment places political intelligence information excessively into a military and conspiracy-secrecy evaluation process at the C.I.A. and a diplomacy-oriented review at the State Department. The perspectives of political party professionals are thereby excluded from what are essentially political party questions. It is, after all, one of the oldest functions of political parties to flush out conspiracy, corruption, and subversion perpetrated by adversary parties. Parties are freer to gather political intelligence from open sources and to publicize unsupported hypotheses as well as confirmed facts about the behavior and intentions of an opposition. American politicians in a Watergate era know this. Yet, it is ironic that the point should be driven home by a Frankfurt "free socialist" underground weekly, *Information Service,* through its publication of the names of C.I.A. agents operating in several European countries. A spokesman of the weekly explained that "people who are affected by the C.I.A. have a right to know who they are and who appoints them. . . . The C.I.A. is a paramilitary organization and its agents are at least as responsible for the development of political policy as elected politicians" (Christian Science Monitor, 1976).

When it is recognized that the Central Intelligence Agency is not the best suited organization for finding and keeping political friends abroad, foreign policymakers may more seriously turn to transnational party relationships. To illustrate, Congress could possibly authorize and support certain types of open and legitimate *political development aid* to friendly party leaders abroad, i.e., to provide information regarding the principles and institutions that make the United States a constitutional democracy, explanations of current United States policies on world issues, assistance in the design of electoral systems, improvement of relations with the world press, and so on. Such a program could be financed through and administered by the Agency for International Development (AID), perhaps under Title IX of the Foreign Assistance Act, through contracts with the Democratic and Republican national committees. Each national committee could then develop its own distinctively Democratic or Republican approach to the program's objectives. Such a program of political development aid would undoubtedly result in a substantial savings of public funds, for it would in effect replace expensive covert C.I.A. activity with an open AID program, one that presumes that conversion rather than subversion is the more effective technique in transnational politics. This proposal simply illustrates that party operatives rather than intelligence operatives may have more suitable training for political intelligence work, at the same time reducing the conspiratorial features of international politics and promoting a more open world political process in which American political talents can more successfully flourish.

American participation in a world of transnational parties is also likely to require a reconsideration of the principle of nonintervention. Nonintervention has already been somewhat redefined in actual practice by the existence of United States economic and military foreign aid programs, Central Intelligence Agency operations, the recent United States role as the world's unofficial policeman, the 'Vietnam War, and other exercises in global *realpolitik*. There is hardly a nation in the world today that does not have some important interest in the domestic political affairs of other nations. Arabs and Israelis seek to influence public opinion in the United States. The United States endeavors to liberalize emigration and human rights policy in the Soviet Union. China invites the Nixons for a private visit and consequences follow in the 1976 presidential primaries. Such examples support the view that nonintervention is neither practical nor in many instances possible in contemporary world politics.

Yet, the policy persists as a premise in the formulation of United States foreign policy. As a consequence, the United States is compelled to do covertly what others do openly and even proudly, i.e., help political friends in whatever nation they exist. The policy of nonintervention has made the C.I.A. the United States' main channel of communication with party leaders and groups in other nations. Usually, too, this covert approach has put the United States on the side of conspiratorial elites rather than popular movements within other nations. Future attention to transnational party affairs is likely to raise important challenges to noninterventionism. In many respects, an analogous debate has already taken place in American domestic party politics on the issue of states' rights.

We have noted earlier the growing importance of nonstate actors, international pressure groups, and informal diplomacy. Such developments are still in their early stages. However, as Americans know so well from their own domestic political experience, a symbiotic institutional relationship arises between pressure groups and political parties. In the future, this type of relationship will have to be taken increasingly into account in American foreign policymaking. Already the scores of economic, professional, religious, social, and other types of international NGOs are active in the formulation of global policies in monetary affairs, trade, migrant labor, dissemination of technology, freedom of religion and press, crime, hijacking, and other equally significant world issues.

Here again current American attitudes create a hurdle for United

States foreign policymakers. Because Americans tend to distrust pressure groups and "interests," United States officials are likely to keep international pressure group leaders and opinions at arms' length. This official aloofness may, however, have the effect of pushing NGOs seeking levers of influence into closer contact with United States political parties, thereby nudging the parties closer to transnational alliances of their own. As NGOs and multinational corporations step up their efforts at group coalitioning and world opinion formation, United States foreign policymakers may, in fact, lose much of their official initiative in world politics unless they too begin to work through the political parties, both domestic and transnational, more systematically.

Transnational party development may be expected to have significant implications for two other areas of United States foreign policy: the promotion of American interests in regional organizations and the integration of the United Nations system. Regional organizations are, of course, formal associations of states. Whether other regional organizations such as the Organization of American States or the Organization of African Unity follow the European road to integration or not, these bodies are likely to become increasingly institutionalized and politicized. Members will tend to vote on issues according to the party complexion of their governments at the time, i.e., according to transnational party alignments. These alignments will undoubtedly seek out political friends in the United States, and American policy regarding the region will, as a consequence, be difficult to implement without "the partisan connection."

There is a similar prospect at the United Nations and its associated agencies. At this level, however, the United States' own domestic experience with the constitutionalizing influence of political parties may help generate greater American enthusiasm for transnational party collaborations in U.N. affairs. As this becomes the case, significant shifts in the focus of United States foreign policy leadership may accompany the trend, e.g., the emergence of the United States representative to the United Nations as a significant spokesman for United States policy, sometimes exceeding in visibility and influence the Secretary of State and, at times, possibly the President himself.

DOMESTIC PARTY POLITICS

With the tendencies and changes anticipated above, it is hardly likely that the domestic party system of the United States will remain unaffected. Greater awareness of and responsiveness to the emerging transnational party system may be expected to bring changes in the structure and operation of both major domestic parties. Some of these possibilities are suggested below.

Initially, the change may be modest, probably little more than the exchange of key personnel with other parties or the addition of a "transnational activities" staff to the national committee headquarters. Curiosity may be the principal stimulus for this development. The purpose of additional staff may simply be to inform the national party leadership about transnational party activities, interpret their impact on party concerns in domestic affairs, and arrange visits or participation as observers at transnational party conferences. A perceptive and persistent proponent of such transnational party conferences and leadership exchanges has been Representative Donald M. Fraser of Minnesota, chairman of the House Subcommittee on International Organization.

World issues, particularly those relating to war and peace, are becoming increasingly important to American voters (Harris, 1973). These world issues are formulated not only by what American politicians say and do but also by the behavior of political leaders abroad, particularly leaders of transnational parties. Future reactions of American party leaders to such external initiatives are likely to be of two kinds: first, to establish special party task forces, probably at the national or congressional committee level, to inform and coordinate their party's domestic responses to these external developments, and, second, to make responses that result in more partisan domestic debates about world issues. In other words, future transnational party developments are likely to influence increasingly the shape of United States foreign policy initiatives and debate and, as a consequence, probably make it increasingly difficult—as it already is on some issues—to have domestic political considerations end "at the water's edge" in foreign policy matters.

Future transnational party developments may tend to enliven factional and ideological divisions within the Democratic and Republican parties. For example, many Democrats of one factional orientation may be willing to associate with the Social Democratic International while others may prefer affiliation with the Christian Democrats. Many Republicans may feel more at home in the Liberal International while others favor a more conservative affiliation. If national factions within each of the major United States parties become increasingly organized and durable over the next several decades, as seems to be occurring, these factions, particularly if they assume ideological coloration, will make it difficult for each party as a whole to affiliate transnationally. However, this probably will not prevent factional organizations or coalitions from doing so. In the illustrations above, more leftist Democrats may decide to associate with the Social Democrats while more conservative Democrats may choose the Christian Democratic International. A similar process may take place among Republicans. The process as it unfolds is also likely to have the domestic effect of reinforcing factional divisions within the major parties, creating new challenges for domestic party management and cohesion.

Political scientists have in recent years reported an increase in the ideological orientations of American voters and party rank and file. A growing proportion of voters are responding to ideological appeals. Clusters of attitudes on issues have become more closely tied to ideological premises. There is some question, however, whether it will be the parties as a whole or their respective internal factions that become more ideological. Given the long-standing centrist and coalitional nature of American parties, the greater odds seem to favor ideological factions rather than ideological parties. However, it may surprise some American politicians to learn that similar factional processes inhabit the presumably monolithic ideological parties elsewhere in the world, including their transnational organizations. The principal ideological code words and statements of principle may be different from the American, but the factional disagreements about meanings, priorities, and applications to current situations are the same. The comparability between the "nonideological" content of American political discourse and the more "ideological" debates abroad is, it will be realized, much greater than Americans have believed. This realization will undoubtedly hasten the involvement of Americans in the transnational party process.

Future American interest in transnational parties is also likely to make American party politics more interesting for American youth as well as young people abroad. At present, one of the lowest rates of turnout at the polls in the United States is among voters between the ages of 18 and 25. On the other hand, observers of the political behavior of American youth have frequently commented upon the success with which the Marxist and other movements with strong world-system emphases have recruited many of the most idealistic and talented of young Americans. Such youthful political activists are notably interested in the global aspects of political as well as philosophical discussions that encompass humanity as a whole. They are, in recent years, also the most avid travelers to foreign shores—studying abroad, hitchhiking, hosteling, attending international youth rallies, and so forth. Hence, when the Democratic and Republican parties acquire transnational activities to a greater degree than at present, their capacity to recruit the idealistic and talented young is likely to experience substantial improvement.

Once they become part of the emerging transnational party system, the major parties of the United States are bound to remain influential in that system for generations to come. American party leaders will surely come to appreciate that success in their precincts at home may depend more and more upon their successes in "precincts" abroad. Those party leaders knowledgeable in the history of political institutions may also begin to recall that in many societies successful political competition within and between political parties has served as the institutional equivalent of civil and other forms of internal war. As these leaders search for means of worldwide political competition less destructive than war and less costly than arms races, they are likely to turn more and more to transnational parties in their pursuit of international influence and in their arrangements for civilian control over the future military institutions of global security. As this happens, the pace in the evolution of the transnational party system will undoubtedly speed up, but, most importantly, and for some, surprisingly, so will the prospects for arms control and nonviolent processes of elite contest over world policy and leadership (Goldman, 1974). In sum, the transnational party system will do globally what it had done so often nationally, provide the principal constitutionalizing and pacifying institution in the political system.

NOTES

1. Notable exceptions are Frederick Jackson Turner, Arthur N. Holcombe (1959), and George Modelski (1969). Turner's memorandum to President Woodrow Wilson is quoted elsewhere in this paper. Holcombe's observations are made in a chapter of a report of the Commission to Study the Organization of Peace. Modelski's article, in a collection of papers edited by Black and Falk, is the most systematic treatment of the subject. The present author noted that international parties are a gowing factor in international politics in the cited article in Vista (1967). On the practical side, Representative Donald M. Fraser of Minnesota has been particularly attentive to transnational party developments in recent years. George E. Agree, former director of the National Committee for an Effective Congress, has initiated a Freedom House Study known as "Transnational Interactions of Political Parties," one of whose objectives is to put United States party leaders into better touch with transnational party developments.

2. For a comprehensive review of functional and structural characteristics of political parties, see Sartori (1976).

3. Two European assemblies anteceded the European Parliament: the Consultative Assembly of the Council of Europe, founded in 1949 by 10 European nations interested in promoting European economic and social progress, and the Assembly of the Western European Union, established in 1954 as successor to the Brussels collective defense treaty among the six nations who later constituted the Common Market. The delegates to the WEU Assembly served in the CE Consultative Assembly and made up about two-thirds of the latter's membership. According to Haas (1960), between 1949 and 1958, the average party breakdown in the CE Consultative Assembly was 27% Socialists, 25% Christian Democrats, 16% Liberals, and 30% other parties.

REFERENCES

ABU JABER, K.S. (1966). The Arab Ba'th Socialist Party. Syracuse, N.Y.: Syracuse University Press.

ALEXANDER, R.J. (1949). "The Latin American Aprista parties." Political Quarterly, 22(3):236-247.

——— (1973). Aprismo: The ideas and doctrines of Victor Raul Haya de la Torre. Kent, Ohio: Kent State University Press.

ALKER, H.R., and RUSSETT, B.M. (1965). World politics in the General Assembly. New Haven, Conn.: Yale University Press.

BELLONI, F.P., and BELLER, D.C. (forthcoming). Antipartyism.

BOCA, A. del, and GIOVANA, M. (1969). Fascism today (R.H. Boothroyd, trans.). London: Heinemann.

BRODER, D.S. (1972). The party's over. New York: Harper and Row.

Christian Science Monitor (1975). Report on Socialists by David Mutch, September 9. Report on Chinese Communists by Mohan Ram, October 16.

——— (1976). Report by David Mutch, February 5.

COLE, G.D.H. (1954). A history of socialist thought (vol. II). London: Macmillan.

COTTAM, R.W. (1967). Competitive interference and 20th century diplomacy. Pittsburgh: University of Pittsburgh Press.

DECHERT, C.R. (1967). "The Christian Democratic 'international'." Orbis, 11(1):106-127.

DEVLIN, J.F. (1976). The Ba'th Party. Stanford: Hoover Institution Press.

DIAMOND, W. (1942). "American sectionalism and world organization by Frederick Jackson Turner." American Historical Review, 47(3):545-551.

FELD, W.J. (1972). Nongovernmental forces and world politics. New York: Praeger.

FERARU, A.T. (1974). "Transnational political interests and the global environment." International Organization, (winter):31-60.

FITZMAURICE, J. (1975). The party groups in the European Parliament. Lexington, Mass.: D.C. Heath.

FOGARTY, M.F. (1957). Christian democracy in western Europe. Notre Dame, Ind.: University of Notre Dame Press.

GOLDMAN, R.M. (1967). "The international political party." Vista, 3(3):35-42.

——— (1974). "The world is our precinct; world parties and the arms control process." Paper presented at Stanford Arms Control Conference, August.

GOODMAN, E.R. (1960). "The Soviet design for a world state." Current History, 39(228): 94 ff.

HAAS, E.B. (1960). Consensus formation in the Council of Europe. Berkeley: University of California Press.

HARRIS, L. (1973). The anguish of change. New York: W.W. Norton.

HOLCOMBE, A.N. (1959). Organizing peace in the nuclear age. New York: New York University Press.

HOVET, T., Jr. (1960). Bloc parties in the United Nations. Cambridge, Mass.: Harvard University Press.

HULSE, J.W. (1964). The forming of the communist international. Stanford, Calif.: Stanford University Press.

International Peasant Union. Bulletin.

JACKSON, G.D., Jr. (1961). "The Green International and the Red Peasant International." Unpublished Ph.D. dissertation, Columbia University.

——— (1966). Comintern and peasant in East Europe, 1919-1930. New York: Columbia University Press.

LADOR-LEDERER, J.J. (1963). International nongovernmental organizations. Leyden: A.W. Sythoff.

LAQUEUR, W., and MOSSE, G.L. (eds., 1966). International fascism. New York: Harper and Row.

LASKI, H.J. (1936). The rise of liberalism. New York: Harper and Row.

MacCALLUM SCOTT, J.H. (1967). Experiment in internationalism. London: George Allen and Unwin.

McNEAL, R.H. (1967). International relations among communists. Englewood Cliffs, N.J.: Prentice-Hall.

MA'OZ, M. (1975). Syria under Hafiz al-Asad: New domestic and foreign policies. Jerusalem: Hebrew University.

MERKL, P.H. (1964). "European assembly parties and national delegations." Conflict Resolution, 8(1):50-64.

MEYNAUD, J. (1961). Les groupes de pression internationaux. Lausanne: Etudes de Science Politique.

MODELSKI, G. (1968). "Communism and the globalization of politics." International Studies Quarterly, 21(4):380-393.

——— (1969). "World parties and world order." In C. Black and R. Falk (eds.), The future of the international legal order (vol. I). Princeton: Princeton University Press.

NEILL, T.P. (1953). The rise and decline of liberalism. Milwaukee: Bruce.

Newsweek (1976). February 23.

New York Times (1964). July 18-21.

——— (1976). January 7, 1:8 and 4:4.

PATERSON, W.E., and CAMPBELL, I. (1974). Social democracy in postwar Europe. London: Macmillan.

PICKLES, W. (1951). "The revived international." Political Quarterly, 22(3):335-345.

REVEL, J.F. (1976). The totalitarian temptation. Paris: Laffont.

ROOSEVELT, C. (1970). "The politics of development: A role for interest and pressure groups." International Associations, 5:283-289.

RUGGIERO, G. De (1927). The history of European liberalism (R.G. Collingwood, trans.). London: Oxford University Press.

San Francisco Chronicle (1967). May 7.

SARTORI, G. (1976). Parties and party systems. New York: Cambridge University Press.

SAUVANT, K.P., and MENNIS, B. (1976). Emerging forms of transnational community. Lexington, Mass.: Lexington Books.

STARR, R.F. (1976). Yearbook of international communist affairs, 1976. Stanford: Hoover Institution Press.

SUGAR, P. (1971). Native fascism in the successor states, 1918-1945. Santa Barbara, Calif.: ABC-Clio Press.

TAYLOR, J. (1976). China and southeast Asia: Peking's relations with revolutionary movements. New York: Praeger.

THOMSON, D. (1964). Europe since Napoleon. New York: Knopf.

TRISKA, J.F. (ed., 1969). Communist party-states. Indianapolis: Bobbs-Merrill.

WHITE, L.C. (1951). The role of international NGO's in world affairs. New Brunswick, N.J.: Rutgers University Press.

World Today (1950). "The evolution of the Cominform, 1947-1950." (May).

Chapter 4

STRUCTURES OF INEQUALITY:
TWO DECADES OF NEW YORK
BLACK REPUBLICAN POLITICS

M A R S H A   H U R S T

I. INTRODUCTION

When political scientists examine the politics of race in America, they tend to look at the obvious. We ask what party blacks align themselves with, what candidates they vote for, what issues are salient, and which blacks hold office. Moreover, we tend to answer these questions based on national politics. This type of analysis is necessary, but it is not sufficient. Race politics is often critically different at the local level than at the national; and, more importantly, the relationship of blacks to the political system can only be understood by examining not only the patterns of political behavior, but the structures of inequality which have characterized race politics in this country.

This paper will focus on the development of black party politics during the period from 1910 to 1930 in New York City. Although popular wisdom tells us that blacks in the United States were loyal

AUTHOR'S NOTE: I would like to thank Dr. Ruth Zambrana-Shojaei (Department of Community Medicine, Mt. Sinai School of Medicine) and Professor Michael L. Goldstein (Department of Political Studies, Pitzer College) for their professional criticism, Professor Louis Maisel (Department of Government, Colby College) for his editorial suggestions, and Richard J. Hiller and Elsie M. Hurst for their assistance with earlier drafts.

Republicans from the time they were granted the vote until the 1932 presidential election, in New York City the loosening of the Republican grip on the black ballot began almost 20 years earlier. The loss of federal patronage to the Democrats with the election of Wilson, the death of Booker T. Washington, and the demise of the national black Republican machine, the direct courting of the black vote through class and race-oriented appeals of certain New York City Democratic politicians, and the growth of Harlem as a potential political power base, all contributed to the realignment of the black vote.

Along with the realignment of the black vote, and integrally related to it, were changes in the structure of race politics. Between 1910 and 1930, the major change in black party participation in New York City was a change in the relationship between blacks and whites in the major parties. In 1910, each party was segregated, had two parallel (though not equal) party hierarchies, and the black party leader, chosen by the white party leaders, played a "buffering" role (see Halpern, 1969:63) between the white political system and his black followers. By 1930, black political leaders were community-based, dependent on the local black electorate, and were in the throws of overturning their dependence on local white party leaders. The following is a close look at the changes in race politics in the New York City Republican party, with particular attention paid to the structures of inequality that characterized the relationship of blacks to the party system.

II. THE SEGREGATED PARTY MACHINE

As the black population in the North increased, white politicians and party organizations began to view the black vote as useful in local and national elections. In order to gain black support, while limiting access of blacks to decision-making positions and without alienating the white party politicians by integrating party councils, the white parties created organizational linkages with black political leaders and black clubs which were responsible to white leaders. These linkages established buffering relationships between black politicians, the white party leader above, and the black party followers below. As long as black support could be harnessed into separate structures—auxiliaries to the regular party organizations—white politicians could benefit from the black vote without paying off their supporters in anything but symbolic recognition and minor patronage. These payoffs would reinforce the stakes black leaders had in maintaining segregated political structures. The major parties in New York both followed this practice. The Republican club network was informally tied in with the Tuskegee machine through Booker T. Washington and his New York lieutenant, Charles W. Anderson. The Democrats were linked to their black followers through the United Colored Democracy (UCD), a segregated auxiliary of Tammany Hall.[1] These linkages, established in the late 19th century, were critical in the determination of later political relationships. The buffering relationships between political race leaders within the major political parties established an informal quid pro quo, whereby white party bosses would be assured of black electoral support and, more importantly, black political quiescence. In exchange, certain middle-class black notables were guaranteed personal political advancement and some political influence in the form of partronage positions.

Those blacks who used political party structures to make political demands generally accepted the party machine ethic that loyalty and dependability would be appropriately rewarded by the white bosses. According to that ethic, blacks, like the ethnic groups involved in a political machine, should be paid in machine services. In an ideal-type machine relationship, a neighborhood boss controlled the votes of the members of his community in exchange for supplying services to that community (Bryce, 1961:186).[2]

In some ways, blacks had the same relationship to the party machines in New York as did other groups. There were black party organizations, black party bosses, and black patronage positions to be awarded for votes delivered. Crucial differences existed, however, between the black linkages with the machine and the linkages of other communal groups. In the first place, although white ethnic groups were organized on a community basis and were represented in the machine by ward captains and district leaders who lived within the community, blacks in New York City were organized in countywide auxiliary structures without an effective territorial base. Thus, from the beginning, blacks were treated as a separate category of voters.

Second, the black political bosses were selected and maintained in office by the machine rather than by their own communities. They were thus responsible only to the white machine leaders for their position, not to a local black constituency. This made black insurgency within the black neighborhood very common, for most voters owed their black party bosses precious little. On the other hand, these insurgency efforts had very little chance of success, for the white party leader, unmoved by these risings, determined who would lead the black voters.

Finally, there was little in the way of goods and services provided by the machine to the black community. Black patronage went to a few select middle-class blacks as a symbolic reward for the whole race. The Republican party felt it could count on the black vote without providing anything but recognition of its affinity with black Americans, and the Democratic party thought the black vote was too insignificant to expend energy or resources to attract it. In short, relationships established by the white party machines in New York City were buffering relationships in which the black community had access to political power only through intermediaries chosen from above. Further, these intermediaries were, on the whole, unrepresentative, unresponsive, and ineffective.

THE DECLINE OF THE BLACK REPUBLICAN PARTY MACHINE

The presidential election of 1912 and the following eight years of Woodrow Wilson's Democratic administration began the breakdown of black Republican allegiance and of the nationally controlled black Republican party machine. Blacks who joined the Democratic ranks in 1912 to support Wilson had little in common. August Meier (1963:189) has called them a "paradoxical union of office-seekers and anti-Bookerites, disillusioned Republicans and economic radicals." But those 15% (Miller, 1913) of the black voters who chose to believe that Wilson's reform orientation and vague campaign promises would be translated into enlightened race policy were to feel disillusioned and deceived.

President Wilson's treatment of blacks in the United States is well documented (see Wolgemuth, 1958, 1959). He did not discourage his first Congress from introducing the greatest flood of bills proposing discriminatory legislation against the black man ever presented in the Congress. Although most of those bills never passed, Wilson himself, by executive order, instituted segregation in federal offices, eating facilities, and rest rooms. "By putting certain bureaus and sections . . . in charge of negroes," rationalized Wilson, "we are rendering them more safe in their possession of office and less likely to be discriminated against" (Kruger, 1977:91). Many white reformers shared Wilson's views. "Segregation, carried out in a kind and considerate way," wrote Seth Low, a prominent New York reformer (February 26, 1914, Seth Low Papers), "is likely to prove an advantage rather than a disadvantage to the negro in the public service. . . . The plain truth is that neither in the North nor in the South do whites like to work in offices with negros."

When Wilson was first elected, black Democrats thought that they would step into the positions and powers occupied by Booker T. Washington's Republican followers during the previous administration. But Wilson, during his entire first term, made only three black appointments requiring Senate confirmation, one of which encountered so much opposition that the nominee withdrew.[3] Black Wilson supporters, led by such notables as W.E.B. DuBois, and white liberal Democrats, led by New York *Evening Post* publisher Oswald Garrison Villard, worked constantly to apply pressure on Wilson to nominate blacks to federal office. But the President, whose anti-black sentiments and actions later would be manifest, continued to plead powerlessness in the face of Senate opposition.

Fierce protests by black individuals and organizations mounted against Wilson's segregation policies and his failure to appoint blacks to federal positions.[4] Amid this flood of criticism there was one black voice in particular that was notably silent—Charles Anderson, leader of the New York black Republicans. As Booker T. Washington's New York lieutenant and a beneficiary of his political patronage, Anderson was, when Wilson came to power, Collector of Internal Revenue in New York. Anderson's position, a political plum, carried with it patronage of its own that enhanced his stature as New York's leading black Republican. But Booker T. Washington's national network of black power and patronage depended on a national Republican administration.

Anderson never openly criticized President Wilson or his administration, despite the concern he privately expressed to Washington

(April 4, 1913, Washington Papers). Anderson's public opposition to Wilson might have helped keep his Republican followers cohesive during the national Democratic administration, but, as was typical of black machine politicians during this period, Anderson owed his position not to his followers, but to his black political boss, and his boss's white political patron. Anderson's own job as Collector of Internal Revenue was in jeopardy, and his silence on race matters was an effort to save that job.

At first Anderson tried to work through the old channels to keep his position, relying on Washington's influential white contacts (Anderson to BTW, April 11, 1913; McAneny to McAdoo, July 9, 1913, Washington Papers). Anderson argued that segregation and discrimination were not the real problems of the Wilson administration. He criticized DuBois for sending a circular to the President about segregation in the Treasury Department, claiming that too big a fuss was being made out of the fact that blacks were required to go to a "separate toilet room on the top floor." To Anderson, the big issue was jobs for blacks: "Why was not something said about the number of men, holding presidential places, that have been separated from the service?" (to BTW, August 19, 1912). But the preservation of his job as collector was paramount.

Anderson's refusal to join in the criticism of Wilson was not the most controversial of his machinations to save his position. He also cut political deals. Rumors soon began to circulate in the black press that Anderson had made a deal with the Fusion mayoral candidate, John Purroy Mitchel. If Anderson could deliver the black vote in the city to Mitchel, Mitchel would use his influence with Wilson to save Anderson's job. Every other prominent black Republican had spoken out against segregation in federal offices, and Anderson was under pressure to do the same. One prominent New York black leader was quoted as saying:

> Collector Anderson is playing every card in the deck for retention. I know it, and every one in New York knows of the influence he has mustered to his support. The national administration has not made an appointment to his place in order to see if he can deliver the colored vote to Mitchel. Now that they are demanding this as a payment for retention for a few months longer, he ought to demand that segregation now in the departments here be stopped peremptorily. There has been considerable criticism from colored Republicans

aimed against colored Democrats willing to accept office in the face
of the prevalent segregation of the race here, but greater criticism
ought to be aimed at colored Republican officeholders who bring
influence to bear, indirectly or directly, for retention. [Unsigned
news release, Washington, D.C., Sept. 22, 1913, Washington
Papers][5]

Booker T. Washington supported Anderson's position, not
surprisingly, since the Tuskegee principal only spoke out against
segregation posthumously in an article published in 1916. Nor did
he seem, as was frequently his style, to be working privately to stop
Wilson's extension of segregation (Wolgemuth, 1959:172). Washington reassured Anderson that the charges against him were
unfounded since Anderson was powerless to stop federal segregation, and because segregation was not being enforced in the office in
which Anderson worked (October 4, 1913, Washington Papers).

Resisting the pressure of his fellow black politicians, Anderson
helped Mitchel win election as mayor in New York City. Mitchel,
true to his promise, urged the President to retain Anderson as
collector, which he did until 1915; and Anderson looked forward to
becoming the most important black politician in the Mitchel
administration (Scott to Anderson, n.d.; clipping, *New York
World,* n.d., Washington Papers).[6]

The collector, however, was becoming increasingly isolated from
other aspects of black politics, both nationally and locally. He had
not joined the protests against the Wilson administration, and,
more importantly, he did not join the efforts of the independent
Negro Civic League to nominate a black for alderman in the 31st
Harlem Aldermanic district in 1913.

Having failed to break into the Republican party ranks in the
Harlem districts in which blacks were fast becoming a Republican
majority, and facing further frustration by the refusal of the Progressives to nominate a black from one of the Harlem assembly
districts, black independent Democrats and Republicans organized
a political party to run their own nominees for local office (see
Goldstein, 1973:241-253). Anderson, very much the party regular,
was opposed to the Negro Civic League (later called the United
Civic League, or UCL) and the candidacy of its black aldermanic
nominee.

The collector argued that the UCL nominee had about as much chance to win the election as "I have to be made president of the Argentine Republic," or "as my chance of being elected to the United States Senate from the State of Alabama." Accordingly, the only accomplishment of the UCL campaign, he argued, would be to divide the Republican votes and thus to elect a Democrat. In fact, Anderson believed that the UCL campaign was financed by Tammany for that purpose. The Republican political leader insisted that political influence be achieved through the regular Republican party organization, and was convinced that independent electoral efforts would only alienate white Republican supporters (to BTW, Oct. 16; Nov. 14, 1913, Washington Papers).

Washington, also an opponent of independent black electoral efforts, was a more astute politician, and refused to speak out openly against a popular race movement. He did, however, console Anderson with the prediction that the UCL clearly would be defeated, and thus "within six months this organization will not be heard of." He further promised to try to convey to the parties concerned his opposition to their electoral politics (November 19, 1913, Washington Papers). Anderson and Washington had always worked behind the scenes in black Republican politics (see Meier, 1963:110-114). Their role in terms of their Republican followers was to keep blacks in line, not to mobilize them for political action. The death of Booker T. Washington in 1915 meant that Anderson had lost not only his patronage, but also his patron. While Anderson persisted in his machine politics style, he no longer had a real political organization within which to work.

Without the backing of Washington's power and prestige, and lacking sufficient patronage in New York during the Fusion and subsequent Democratic administrations, Anderson was vulnerable to challenge from below. In July of 1916, the *New York Age* ran lead articles criticizing the white dominated structure of the black Republican organization. The *Age* articles made a plea for new black leadership, noting that although the Republicans had been slow to realize it, the black voters in New York were not the blind party followers they had been in the past.

The rank and file of colored voters want new and capable leadership. They want leaders not totally eaten up with selfishness—leaders who are willing to secure a square deal for others as well as themselves. They want leaders who are not afraid to come out in the open and make an intelligent and aggressive fight for the political and civic rights of the race. They want leaders who, while astute politicians and men of·ability, must also be men of character. They want leaders whose influence with the race is not a negative quality and who command respect among all classes of Negroes. Last but not least, they want leaders who are made by Negroes and not by White people. [*New York Age,* July 20, 1916]

Having faulted the black Republican politicians in general, the *Age* proceeded to place specific blame on the Honorable Charles Anderson for holding back political progress of the race. Criticism of Anderson centered on five points: (1) he had opposed the black Regiment movement until he felt it was inevitable and then jumped on the bandwagon for political purposes; (2) he had opposed civic movements in Harlem, especially the election of blacks from the independent Republican United Civic League organization to positions as assemblyman and alderman; (3) he had not obtained positions for other blacks during the Mitchel years despite his personal influence and progress in the Mitchel-Fusion administration; (4) he had acted as if he believed that his own position with the white politicians was independent of black support; and (5) he had behaved as if he were the only black leader whom whites would recognize.

The most serious objection to Anderson was that he monopolized the attention of white politicians, convinced them that he was in control of the black Republicans, and pretended that all was peaceful in the ranks.

Mr. Anderson's position is peculiar in that he enjoyed the confidence and popular esteem of many white persons who labor under the opinion that he is all powerful among the members of his race. It cannot be denied that he could be had he pursued different tactics. But he does not seem to believe in the theory that the higher you get the more support you need to hold you up. [*New York Age,* July 27, 1916]

Washington, Anderson's mentor, had behaved similarly in his political role. He was able to monopolize the attention of the white

Republicans, and convince those men of that which they wanted to hear: that Washington was indeed the chosen leader of the large majority of blacks, that those who dissented from Washington's leadership were a small minority of black deviant troublemakers, and that all was quiet and under control in the black Republican rank and file. Washington, however, had complete control over black patronage during the Roosevelt administration and direct control over most of the black press. Anderson, on the other hand, without Washington's backing and prestige and without significant Republican patronage to distribute, was doomed. Although he remained an active Republican and a not-infrequent political appointee, Anderson lost his black following.

The machine-like structure of inequality that characterized race politics in the Republican party until Booker T. Washington's death controlled and directed black political participation, but it was too rigid and personalized. The segregated black machine network could not adapt. An opposition party occupied the White House; black pressure from below increased. Demands were made for political rewards other than symbolic patronage, and critical black "buffering" agents like Washington and Anderson, whose influence had depended exclusively on personal contacts with selected white party leaders, were dead or discredited. Blacks, supported by a rapidly growing urban electoral base, were demanding more than patronage crumbs. And whites, in order to keep their cake, were finally forced to restructure the nature of black participation in the party.

III. THE ROUTINIZATION OF BLACK REPRESENTATION

Beginning about 1912, this auxiliary machine structure of party politics confronted a formidable external challenge. The growth of Harlem provided resources for independent black politicians and interest group leaders to build political structures like the United Civic League that rested on support from below rather than pull from above. The new orientation was toward the black population rather than the white party, local district arenas instead of city, state, or national politics, and electoral rather than patronage types of political rewards. New black leaders felt that not only could the machine not deliver, but the paltry patronage benefits proffered were no longer satisfactory as the chief prize in the political contest. According to a 1916 Department of Labor report on black northern migration, 350,000 blacks were forced from the South over a period of 18 months (Bergman, 1969:378). Poor housing, inferior schools, injustice in the courts, and the horror of lynch law all contributed to the plight of the black man in the South. As if the disfigurement of the black body and spirit were not enough to drive blacks from the South, the boll weevil and major floods dropped farm wages to 75 cents or less a day by 1915, making bare subsistence almost impossible (Bergman, 1969:375). In the early wave of migration before World War I, over 450,000 blacks moved north. Then there was a relative lull until 1922, when the great wave of migration began again (Tatum, 1951:55).

In New York City, white middle-class Harlemites steadfastly resisted black migration and sought to contain it. Beginning in 1909, with the West Side Improvement Association, whites organized to restrict black residence in the upper West Side and Harlem. In 1911, 85% of the white tenants on West 135th Street between Seventh and Lenox Avenues pledged not to sell to blacks for 15 years (*New York Age,* February 23, 1911). Some of the white churches even joined the movement to stop blacks from invading Harlem (*Crisis,* January 1915:115). But all of this was to no avail. A 1911 report by the National League for the Protection of Colored Women found that in the two blocks where black enterprises were most heavily concentrated, there were ten real estate offices (*New York Age,* May 4, 1911). The pledge tactic of the whites proved ineffective because black real estate dealers were offering irresistibly high prices for Harlem property (*New York Age,* December 14, 1911). By 1917, the *New York Times* was calling Harlem the "black belt," and referring to it as "the Wealthiest Negro Colony in the World," where "there are those among its members who count their fortunes in six figures" (*New York Times Magazine,* September 2, 1917:10).

The growth of the black population and the shift of the population center to Harlem is most clearly demonstrated by comparing census data for 1910 and 1920. The 1910 census returns showed 91,709 blacks in Greater New York.[7] Only three census tracts in Manhattan had more than 50% black population: one in Harlem and two in the black belt of San Juan Hill.[8] The greatest concentration of blacks in any one assembly district in the city was in the 13th A.D. (San Juan Hill), which was 17.4% black, followed by the 21st A.D. in Harlem with 14.9%. By 1920, there were 152, 467 blacks in New York City—a 66% increase. Eight census tracts in the city had more than 50% black residents, only one in San Juan Hill, and seven in Harlem. Two of the Harlem tracts had more than 90% blacks. This meant that the 21st and the 19th A.D.s in Harlem had 48.6% and 34.8% blacks respectively, while the two San Juan Hill districts (gerrymandered since 1905 to split the black vote) had less than 10% black inhabitants each.[9] (See Table 1 and Figure 1.)

BLACK VOTING INDEPENDENCE:
THE 1917 NEW YORK CITY ELECTIONS

During the early years of Harlem's growth and the black party machines' decline, New York City was run by reformers. The good intentions of men like Seth Low, Woodrow Wilson, and New York City Mayor John Purroy Mitchel were directed at problems of political corruption and government efficiency, not at issues related to the rights and status of blacks. Mitchel, for example, filled his administration with technocrats, most of whom were middle-class WASPS and Jews, and thus cut off access to groups which had traditionally used political patronage as one of the few channels of upward mobility open to them. But mobility for black and immigrant groups was considered a small cost to pay by the reformers who aimed to use city hall to "make a demonstration of what a city government in New York can be if administered solely with a view of achieving continuous efficiency" (Lewinson, 1965:110).

Blacks made only one political breakthrough in New York between 1913 and 1917—a Mitchel appointment early in the 1917 municipal election year of the first black man to serve on the consolidated New York City Board of Education.[10] Otherwise, Mitchel kept his race activities to a minimum: Charles Anderson was placed on the highly visible Mayor's Committee to Receive Distinguished Visitors to the City, so that the Mitchel administration received favorable coverage in the black press. Even Roosevelt, who thought Mitchel's administration was the best in 50 years, recognized that the mayor was not popular, partly because he did not keep in touch with the voters, including blacks (Morison et al., 1951-1954:1249).

Table 1. BLACK POPULATION TRENDS IN HARLEM, 1910, 1920, and 1930 a

Tract (Map #)[b]	1910[c] % Black	1920[d] % Black	1930[e] % Black
212 (200)	50.5	96.3	99.2
226 (214)	36.5	68.8	96.6
210 (198)	30.7	74.8	96.0
228 (216)	17.6	77.2	99.0
208 (196)	15.9	44.0	93.1
206 (194)	15.3	31.4	62.2
222 (210)	9.6	12.8	58.0
214 (202)	5.5	93.3	99.0
232 (220)	1.7	65.1	99.0
224 (212)	1.2	12.4	93.2
230 (218)	0.2	88.5	99.4

a. Census tracts listed are those over 10% black by 1920.

b. The census of 1910 used a different tract notation (Map numbers in parentheses), but the tracts themselves are identical for all 3 decades.

c. Derived from Walter Laidlaw, compiler, Statistical Sources for Demographic Studies of Greater New York, 1910 (New York: New York Federation of Churches, 1913).

d. ____ , Statistical Sources for Demographic Studies of Greater New York, 1910 (New York: 1920 Census Committee, 1922).

e. ____ , Population of the City of New York, 1890-1930 (New York: Cities Census Committee, 1932).

During the 1917 mayoral election, Mitchel overestimated the anti-Democratic sentiment of the black community based on the overwhelmingly Republican vote blacks cast in the presidential election of 1916.[11] To his dismay, the mayor was confronted in Harlem by hecklers led by the black Socialists.[12] They demanded to know why Mitchel had not stopped the New York showing of "Birth of a Nation," the film masterpiece that glorified the Klan and debased the blacks. They denounced his introduction of the Gary system of industrial education—a class-based educational tracking system promoted by Rockefeller money— to the New York schools (Lewison, 1965:163-169; *New York Age,* October 1; *New York Times,* October 30:8; Clippings, XIII, *World,* October 30; Gumby Scrapbooks, *American,* October 30; *Messenger,* 1, November 1917).[13]

Mitchel's Democratic opponent, John Hylan, was an unknown Brooklyn judge and the candidate of the Brooklyn Tammany leader. Hylan campaigned on a platform of freeing the city schools from the mill and factory education imposed under the Gary plan. This was an issue with clear appeal to the black community where recent migrants would be the ones whose children would be most likely to be tracked into the vocational plan. Hylan was considered

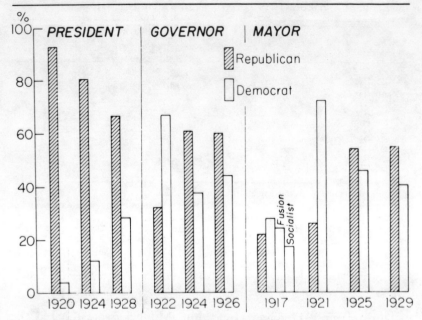

SOURCE: Returns taken from New York City, *City Record,* "Canvass of Votes," December of each election year.

a. The "black vote" is the vote from an election district partially or wholly included in census tracts over 50 percent black according to the 1920 census.

Figure 1: PERCENTAGE OF BLACK VOTES CAST IN HARLEM NINETEENTH AND TWENTY-FIRST ASSEMBLY DISTRICTS FOR PRESIDENT, GOVERNOR AND MAYOR, 1917-1929

a "man of vaguely radical political leanings" by Socialist candidate Morris Hillquit (Hillquit, 1971:182), and it seems to be these vague appeals to class interest and his political anonymity that helped him win the city election[14] and an extraordinary number of black votes.

Considering the strong pull to vote a straight Republican ticket because of the candidacies of the first two black Republican nominees in Harlem, the mayoral vote in heavily black districts[15] was surprisingly divided, with all four candidates running strong races. Taking the 19th and 21st assembly districts as a whole, Hylan edged out his Republican and Fusion opponents by capturing 28% of the black vote, and Hillquit won a substantial 17% (see Figure 1). The Democrats and Socialists together were a clear match for the traditional pull of Fusion and the Republicans. Black voters defied their black Republican establishment leaders and cast their ballots against incumbent Mitchel, "a servant of the special interests of the rich, who cared nothing about the ordinary people of the City." (Lewison, 1965:234).

The biggest block of black votes in the 1917 election went to the first black Republican nominees for representative office in Harlem. E.A. Johnson and J.C. Thomas (who was to lose) had been nominated by the United Civic League and were supported by the Independent Political Council led by the black Socialists. Johnson was nominated for assemblyman from the 19th A.D., and Thomas for alderman from the 26th Ald. D. For the first time since the UCL began running candidates for office in 1913, both black men defeated their regular Republican opponents (white) in the primary elections.

E.A. Johnson had been politically active in Raleigh, North Carolina, where he lived until he moved to New York in 1907. He was an assistant district attorney in North Carolina for eight years, alderman for two years, Republican delegate to three National conventions, and black chairman of his congressional district. Prior to his nomination for assembly, his only political involvement in New York had been as Republican Committeeman in the 19th A.D.

Thomas was best known for his wealth. He was an undertaker by profession and, in 1907, known to be the richest black in New York City. When he moved to Harlem, Thomas increased his holdings by buying property and becoming involved in the Afro-American Realty Company. Although Thomas had been active in the Colored Republican Club on San Juan Hill, he was known politically for his involvement in the Progressive party. In 1912, his funeral parlor became the center of black political debates, and, in later years, it became the headquarters of the Equity League which was lobbying for the establishment of a black regiment.

Not only did Johnson and Thomas represent "the best intellectual and business types of the race," as one white newspaper commented (Kilroe Collections, Clippings, XII, *Sun*, September 22, 1917), but they were both politically active and knowledgeable men not tainted by association with the black Republican or Democratic machine organizations. For the first time in the four years that the UCL had been running black insurgents in the primaries, the organization was successful. The Republican party organization in

Harlem was forced to admit the inevitability of black nominees in heavily black districts and was smart enough to accept these first successful black candidates as regular party nominees. Both men were endorsed by the Republicans for office, although the problem of mobilizing white support for their candidacies remained.

Fortunately for Johnson, the November race in the 19th A.D. for assemblyman was divided three ways. (A fourth candidate only received 44 votes in the entire district.) In 1920, the 19th A.D. was 34.8% black. Johnson received 88% of the vote in the election districts within the census tracts that were over 50% black in 1920, but won the election with only 44% of the total vote in the district. The total votes in those black election districts comprised only 13% of the total valid vote in the district, although those e.d.s accounted for 26% of Johnson's total. Clearly, the vote of the whites in the 19th was essential to Johnson's success.

J.C. Thomas, however, was not as fortunate. In the first place, the 26th aldermanic district was composed of parts of the 19th, 20th, 21st and 22nd assembly districts. The black vote in the 19th and 21st (48.6% black population) was very strong. Only one election district in the 20th was included in the 26th Ald. D., and that one had a significant black population. But in the election districts of the 22nd A.D., Thomas lost heavily. His percentage in those districts was 19%, compared to well over 50% in each of the other three districts. The 22nd A.D. election district votes were 45% of the total votes in the 26th Ald.D., so losing heavily in the 22nd cost Thomas the race. Second, the aldermanic contest in the 26th was largely a two-man contest, for the third candidate won only 7% of the vote. Thomas did, however, make a very strong showing. In the election districts in census tracts with over 50% black population, Thomas won 76% of the vote, but he won much less support from the white voters than Johnson, for those black district votes comprised 65% of Thomas's total vote (compared to 26% of Johnson's). Thomas did come very close to winning the election. He had 2,500 votes compared to the Democrats' 2,866. Despite his claims of irregularities, Thomas was forced to concede defeat. [16]

STRATEGIES FOR COOPTATION

The successful candidacies of Johnson and Thomas forced the white political parties in the city to acknowledge the growing, concentrated black voting strength. The majority Democratic party, least in need of the black vote, made occasional nominations of blacks to Harlem offices, but basically contined to relate to the black voter through the black boss of the Tammany-controlled United Colored Democracy. The minority Republican party reacted to black voting strength by co-opting the independent black party movement (the UCL)[17] and promising future black nominations in Harlem under the Republican party label. John Hylan, the new Democratic mayor, anxious to build a political base independent of Tammany, developed his own method of gaining and maintaining black support.

Without expending political resources, Hylan successfully used two strategies to relate directly to the black community. First, he paid off his black supporters with more city appointments in his first term of office than any of his predecessors had made (Brisbane, 1969:118; Katznelson, 1973:83); and, second, he was regularly attentive to his black constituents. Hylan had a feeling for the necessity of popular contact which his predecessor Mitchel lacked. He kept a separate "Negro folder" (No. 353, New York City, Municipal Archives, Mayors' Papers, John Hylan Papers) with records and correspondence on the black population, black political organizations, and black leaders. He often went to Harlem for public ceremonies, wrote an article for a book on Negro opportunity, welcomed black groups meeting in the city, and wrote letters opposing the Ku Klux Klan.

Hylan made political mileage out of his few black appointments: the head of the UCL was appointed assistant district attorney (at Tammany Boss Murphy's request); four blacks were elected to the medical staff of Harlem Hospital, which had been segregated; Charles Anderson was reappointed to the Committee to Welcome Distinguished Visitors; and more black police were added to the force. Before the 1921 election, Hylan secured funds and a site for an armory for the black 15th Infantry to help him with the black vote in his bid for reelection.

Hylan based his 1921 campaign on appeals to the "common man." He stressed his humble background and promised to maintain the 5-cent fare. Marcus Garvey is purported to have donated Liberty Hall to the Democrats for a large Harlem rally at which Hylan spoke, thus giving his tacit support to the Democratic candidate (Furniss, 1969:227-229). Hylan's class-based appeals and his first term record of cultivated concern for the black population won him over 70% of the black vote in Harlem, a significantly higher percentage than he won citywide (63.1%; see Figure 1).

Despite his popularity with the voters, Hylan never gained the support of New York Tammany Hall. In 1925, Governor Al Smith blocked Hylan's renomination and ended his political career in New York.[18]

Symbolic mayoral attention to the black community is now commonplace in New York as in many other cities. Equally routine today is the strategy adopted by the Republican party, which needed black support to win the Harlem districts, but was not willing to pay the price of integrating blacks into party councils. By formal arrangement with black leaders, the Republican party agreed to nominate a black for each aldermanic election in the 19th A.D. if the blacks would relinquish their claims on the assembly seat. The arrangement in the 21st A.D. was similar, but less formal, and thus occasionally blacks were able to gain Republican nominations for assembly as well.[19] The black vote was split between the two districts, and thus in both districts blacks needed white support to win office (see Figure 2). Unless district lines were changed to favor black voters, which white party leaders were careful not to do, blacks would have to adhere to white guidelines on party nominations.

Between 1917 and 1929 no black was elected to the assembly from the 19th A.D., and, although many black independent Republicans tried to defeat the white candidate in the Republican primary, only one black was nominated. J.C. Hawkins was elected assemblyman three years running from the 21st A.D. (1918-1920), but only one other black sat in the assembly between 1920 and 1929, and for only one year (1924).

The years 1919 and 1920 were high points of Republican strength in Harlem. The party won all the elected positions in the 19th and 21st in those years, and it won the congressional seat in the 21st C.D. for the last time. Eight years of the Wilson administration in Washington had created a strong anti-Democratic vote among black voters in 1920, and the national Republican ticket helped pull along local Republican candidates.[20] Registration in the Harlem districts for the 1920 election increased by 40%, most of which went to the Republicans who claimed 67.9% of the enrolled voters that year (Morsell, 1951:186).

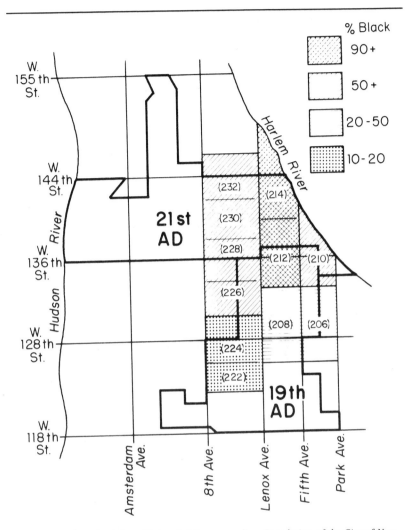

SOURCE: Derived from Walter Laidlaw, compiler, *Population of the City of New York, 1890-1930* (New York: Cities Census Committee, 1932).

Figure 2: BLACK POPULATION IN HARLEM, 1920

The Republicans, however, did not have long to savor their victory. In 1921, Republican registration dropped by 15% in Harlem. Although a decline was somewhat to be expected in this off-year election, the Democratic party in Harlem gained over 3,000 voters, probably because of Hylan's popularity. By 1922, Democrats claimed a majority (52.6%) of the enrolled voters in Harlem (see Figure 3). In 1922 and 1923, the Democrats won every office in the 19th and 21st assembly districts.

The strong black Democratic votes of 1922 and 1923 were radically reversed in 1924. Two factors caused the change. First, the pull of a presidential campaign: reluctance to risk another Democratic president drove many black voters to the Republican column.[21] Second, and perhaps more influential in the local elections, was the candidacy of black Republican Charles Roberts for Congress in the 21st C.D.

The movement for a black congressman had been growing for over six years. Blacks knew that they were the backbone of Republican strength in Harlem, and that their full strength was not being given commensurate political recognition. In 1918, a black independent Republican ran in the congressional primary. He lost. The same year, a Socialist, and the only black in the final election, won a surprising 14% of the vote in the most heavily black election districts.[22] In 1920, the former collector, Charles Anderson, together with the white leader of the 19th, placed in nomination the name of Wilford Smith, attorney for the late Booker T. Washington, but Smith failed to win the nomination (for details, see *New York Age,* August 14, 1920). Hope for a black congressman was lifted when Fiorello LaGuardia, at a 1923 meeting of the black Appomatox Republican Club, exclaimed that it would be a great day in his life if a black were elected to Congress (*Amsterdam News,* September 12, 1923). The following year, a Harlem delegation of black Republicans, buttressed by some white supporters, demanded from the Republican County Committee Chairman a black congressional nomination (*New York Age,* July 14, 1924). The chairman approved on the condition that incumbent Congressman Martin Ansorge would withdraw from the race (*New York Age,* July 26, 1924), which he did when confronted with a withdrawal petition and the promise of a judgeship. (Coolidge Papers, Reel 93; Martin Ansorge, Oral History).

The final selection of the candidate, however, still rested with white party leaders. Blacks did not hold leadership positions in the assembly districts comprising the 21st congressional district, and they had to submit, for final decision, a list of possible black candidates to a committee composed of leaders, associate leaders, and captains of the five districts making up the 21st C.D. The committee

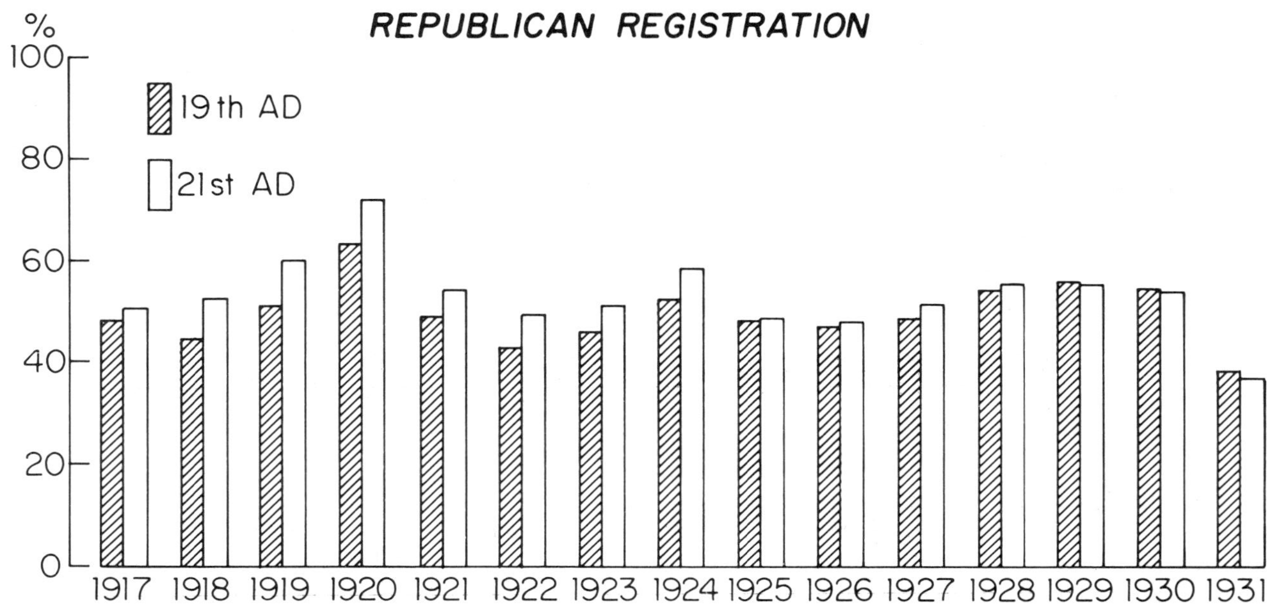

REPUBLICAN REGISTRATION

19th AD
21st AD

1917 1918 1919 1920 1921 1922 1923 1924 1925 1926 1927 1928 1929 1930 1931

% 100 80 60 40 20 0

SOURCE: Board of Elections, Annual Report (New York, N.Y.: 1917-1931).

Figure 3: REPUBLICAN REGISTRATION IN HARLEM DISTRICTS, 1917-1931

selected Dr. Charles Roberts, former alderman from the old 27th aldermanic district (*New York Age,* August 9 and 16, 1924).

The congressional district tended to be Democratic. The odds would be against Roberts. Suspicions rose that, although white leaders had yielded to pressure to nominate a black for Congress, they would not be willing to fight for his election. Knowing that the odds were long and the battle uphill, Harlem blacks were still determined to make a strong fight for the election of Republican Roberts.[23]

Despite the strenuous campaign efforts of black Republicans, Roberts was defeated. Yet, he won over 80% of the vote in the heavily black election districts and fared well in the 19th and 21st districts as a whole. But, in the white neighborhoods of the West Side and in the overwhelmingly white 13th, 22nd, and 23rd assembly districts, he was soundly trounced. The final tally showed Roberts with only 43.8% of the votes, while the white Democratic candidate garnered 53.4% (see Figure 4). The Republican party reverted to its old ways in the 1926 congressional elections and put forward a white nominee.. After their 1924 failure, blacks were easily rebuffed the next time around (*Amsterdam News,* July 18, 1926; *New York Age,* July 31, 1926).[24]

The white Republican running in 1926, however, did not do as well as Charles Roberts had done in 1924, and, with the increased black population in Harlem, a black congressional candidate seemed to have a good chance of being elected in 1928. And so, in that year, there was again a furor over nominating a black for Congress. A principal concern, expressed in the black press and among politicians, was the black voter turnout. The *Amsterdam News* reported that "Harlem's lack of representation in the legislature, on the bench, and in Congress is due to the people's failure to marshall their full vote." According to the *Amsterdam News,* there were 200,000 blacks living in Harlem, which should have meant at least 50,000 votes. Roberts could have been elected in 1924 with 44,000 votes (March 21, 1928).

Republicans needed only about 800 more votes in 1928 than they had received in 1926 to win the congressional election, and they projected that the strong black Republican vote in a presidential election year would help. The head of the Republican County Committee acquiesced easily to requests for a black congressional

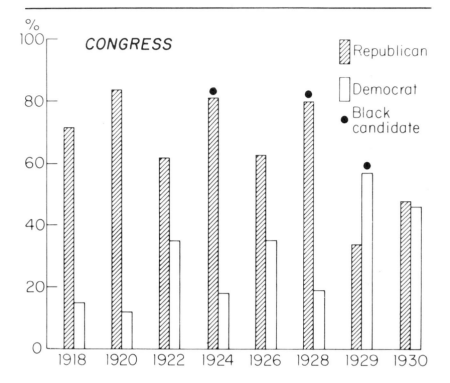

SOURCE: Returns taken from New York City, *City Record,* "Canvass of Votes," December of each election year.
a. The "black vote" is the vote from an election district entirely within census tracts over 50 percent balck according to the 1920 census.

Figure 4: PERCENTAGE OF BLACK VOTES CAST IN HARLEM NINETEENTH AND TWENTY-FIRST ELECTION DISTRICTS FOR CONGRESSMAN, 1918-1930

nominee, but the Harlem district organizations of both parties used this diversion of black concern from the local district elections to capture all the assembly nominations for whites. There was thus a strong feeling among blacks in the district that the white party leaders were "trying to hoodwink the Negro voters by offering them the congressional nomination," while keeping the safer seats for themselves (*New York Age,* September 1, 1928).

Although E.A. Johnson, who had been the first black assemblyman in New York and reputedly was a millionare (*Amsterdam News,* August 29, 1928; Gumby Scrapbooks, No. 90), was a popular candidate among blacks, there was less enthusiasm for the 1928 congressional campaign than there had been in 1924. Johnson was defeated by almost 11,400 votes, receiving about 10% less than his opponent. The black candidate polled about 75% of the vote in the heavily black election districts and did very well in the 19th and 21st A.D.s as a whole. But, like Roberts before him, Johnson was badly hurt by the white Democratic vote in the rest of the district.

The most critical factor in Johnson's defeat, however, was the blacks' lack of enthusiasm for Republican politics and their consequent failure to exercise the franchise. The national administrations of Harding and Coolidge gave blacks little recognition and less helpful legislation (Sherman, 1973:223). As a result, the percentage of blacks in Harlem who voted for Republican presidential nominees had declined drastically since 1920, dropping about 12% in 1924 and another 14% in 1928. Al Smith received almost 28% of the New York black vote in 1928, 16% more than his predecessor in 1924. Republican registration in the 19th and 21st Harlem districts had also fallen off. In 1920, there were almost 27,000 registered Republican voters in the two Harlem districts. In 1924 and 1928, there were about 19,000 and 20,000 respectively, and this despite the enormous growth of the black Harlem population during those years. For Johnson, the coattails of the national Republican ticket proved short indeed.

The Socialist vote in this election was higher in the black districts than in other districts, some indication of the political frustration blacks felt in 1928. No blacks that year were elected to office. The black press urged black readers to avoid the debacle of 1928 by choosing their own candidates in the future. This plea was the keynote for black political activity in the following year.

THE PRODUCTS OF COOPTATION: POLITICAL APATHY AND POLITICAL INDEPENDENCE

Between 1917 and 1920, black political party activity peaked in New York City. The pride of black participation in the War and the postwar promises of democratic treatment for all peoples fired enthusiasm and encouraged political assertiveness in Harlem. The real hope that a Republican administration would take over in Washington further encouraged black voters to work within the Republican party for more political rewards.

Black political enthusiasm for New York City politics, however, ebbed sharply after 1920. To be sure, voter apathy during this period was a national phenomenon, and black registration figures reflected the general Manhattan trend of low enrollment and low turnout throughout most of the decade. But the factors of a "return to normalcy" and general prosperity, which caused this trend elsewhere in the city, were only part of the reason for political indifference in Harlem. Disillusioned, disdainful, and somewhat despairing, black voters eschewed Harlem politics. Racial discrimination in the country as a whole seemed to be increasing. And acceptance by the local Republican party of black nominees turned out to be a minimal concession, not the first step in the achievement of black influence in the party.

Party registration in Harlem in 1920 was not equalled again in numbers until 1932, although the Harlem population was increasing throughout this whole period. The slight increases in enrollment in the 1924 and 1928 presidential election years and during the 1929 fight for black district control never brought registration back to the 1920 high point (see Figure 3). This apathy harmed the Republican party in Harlem, the traditional home for the black voter, more than the Democratic party. Democratic registration in the 19th and 21st A.D.s in Harlem increased, so that it equalled or exceeded Republican registration during most of the decade. Contributing to the rise in Democratic party registration was the considerable support among black voters for the class appeals made by John Hylan and Al Smith. Furthermore, Democratic hegemony in city and state meant that the Democrats had more patronage and other benefits to disperse and thus offered greater potential of reward for black support.

While Harlem was becoming increasing black, increasingly democratic, and increasingly disillusioned with electoral politics, the most marked trend in black voting during the decade was the consistency of the race vote. Blacks voted for blacks. Whatever the contest, whatever the party, the black nominee did dramatically better in the most heavily black election districts than the white nominee. On the district level, blacks still voted Republican. It was, after all, the Republican party that routinized black nominations, and it was in the Republican organization that blacks hoped to break the segregated party structure.

When two white candidates faced each other in Harlem elections for assembly, about two-thirds of the black voters consistently chose the Republican nominee. In the two instances of black Republican and Democratic assembly nominees contesting the same seat (1919 and 1924 in the 21st A.D.), the black Republican again won about two-thirds of the black vote. In aldermanic races after 1917, the Republican party routinely nominated a black in both Harlem districts; and in the 21st A.D., where Democrats were trying to use the black vote to shift the party alignment of the district, there were five contests in which blacks ran against each other. In these races the black vote was more evenly divided, in three cases (1921, 1923, and 1931) hovering around 50% for each party and, in the other two, giving less than 60% to the Republican nominee (see Figure 5).

In elections for city and state offices, black voters demonstrated their political independence and, to some extent, forecast their later Democratic sympathies. Frequently, it was the elections for mayor and governor in which positions on class-related issues were identified with particular candidates, generally with Democrats appealing to the lower income voter. As discussed above, John Hylan, who made an effort to attract the lower and working-class voters and, to some extent, the black voter specifically, clearly won the support of black Harlemites. In the 1925 election, blacks reacted strongly to the dumping of Hylan by voting Republican; and in the 1929 election, they not only voted against Walker, who had proven himself to be no friend to the race, but for LaGuardia, who made direct appeals to class and race (see Figure 1). Blacks also voted independently for governor, giving Smith 67% of the vote in 1922, but turning away from him in 1924 to cast 60% of their vote for Theodore Roosevelt, the son of the President who had invited Booker T. Washington to dine at the White House.

Republicans had attempted to restructure black party participation by narrowly incorporating demands for black representation in order to maintain the local black Republican vote, and yet continued to exclude Harlem blacks from leadership positions in the party councils where decisions were made. Blacks who voted during the low turnout years from 1921 to 1929 voted Republican on the local level, where they felt at least their vote would be heeded, even if their importance was not acknowledged. On the city and state levels, they cast their vote according to race and class appeal and the personality of the candidates (see Figure 1).

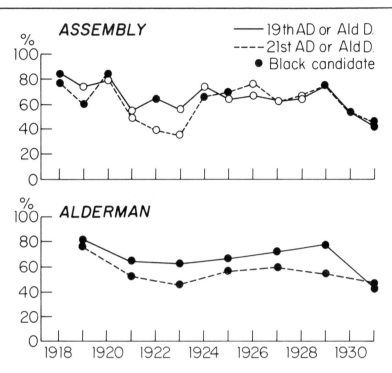

SOURCE: Returns taken from New York City, *City Record*, "Canvass of Votes" December of each election year.

NOTE: before 1920 the two Harlem Ald D.'s were the 27th and the 26th.

a. The "black vote" is th vote from any election district entirely within a census tract over 50% black according to the 1920 census.

b. The Twenty-seventh and Twenty-sixth aldermanic districts were redistricted after 1919 and changed to become the Nineteenth and Twenty-first aldermanic districts respectively, which were almost coterminous with the Nineteenth and Twenty-first assembly districts. Since the Nineteenth aldermanic district was not exactly coterminous with the Nineteenth assembly district, only those 'black' election districts that were in both the Nineteenth aldermanic and the Nineteenth assembly districts were used.

Figure 5: BLACK REPUBLICAN VOTE BY PERCENTAGE FOR ASSEMBLYMAN AND ALDERMAN IN HARLEM DISTRICTS, 1918-1931

IV. THE BLACK STRUGGLE FOR PARTY CONTROL

Between 1920 and 1930, the black population in New York expanded another 113% (from 152,467 to 327,706). In 1930, 21 census tracts in Harlem were over 50% black, 11 of these over 90% black (see Table 1). The 19th and 21st assembly districts were 70.2%

and 69.7% black respectively (Morsell, 1951:26). Clearly, Harlem was fast becoming a black community, but with few exceptions (its churches and fraternal lodges the most notable) its institutions were white controlled.

In the 1920s, when Harlem was a great social attraction for rich white New Yorkers, over 90% of the night clubs and speakeasies in that exotic black world were white-owned. Even the regular retail businesses in Harlem in 1930 were over 80% white-owned, most of them by European immigrants (B. Smith, "Harlem—The Negro City," Part I, *New York Herald Tribune,* February 10, 1930, Gumby Scrapbooks). An independent and progressive black columnist wrote in 1927 (*Amsterdam News,* March, 1927):

> There is no Negro-owned bank; a colored life insurance company has only recently arrived; not one colored man or [sic] other than churches, a theatre and a casino. There is only one resident of Harlem in the Fire Department; the 369th Regiment is still commanded by a non-resident of Harlem; white women still sit in the cashier's cage of the white business houses of the community and too many non-residents of Harlem are engaged as clerks in the stores in the community.

Black newspapers and magazines across the whole spectrum of political ideologies published lists of black businesses in Harlem and urged Harlem residents to "Patronize these Negro Enterprises: For Herein Lies the Strength and Sinews of the Race, with all the Possibilities of a Successful Future" (*Colored American Review,* October 1, 1915:8-9, 15).

Despite the entreaties of the black press, however, blacks remained the consumers, sometimes the laborers, but not the owners of Harlem businesses. Similarly, in the political arena, blacks were the voters, sometimes the candidates, but not the party leaders in Harlem politics. Blacks did not have the financial resources to control Harlem economically, but with their growing strength at the polls, they had the political resources to make a fight for party control.

In order to forestall a direct threat to the Harlem district leadership, white party leaders, in the early 1920s, began to gradually integrate their political clubs with a select group of black party politicians (Furniss, 1969:261).[25] The willingness of black politicians to work within a white dominated, but integrated, party structure depended on their own personal political status and ambitions, although their rationale was couched in terms of tactical advantages to the race. Black political aspirants without their own segregated base, or those who had no resources to build or sustain a separate black organization, stood to gain by cooperating with these white leaders.

Other black politicians opposed integrated clubs and refused to distribute party patronage to blacks who joined the whites (Furniss, 1969:272). The basis of patronage distribution for many of these black politicians had been their separate black organizations. Had these leaders acquiesced in the integrationist efforts of local white politicians, or supported black insurgent efforts to take over white orgnizations, their share of the spoils would have been less than they were getting under the dual club system. For example, in each election, the black clubs, in districts where the black vote might be important, were given a lump sum of money and campaign jobs to be divided among the black election workers. In a selectively integrated party organization, blacks would have been the minority members in numbers and status and would have been squeezed out of many of these patronage allotments.

Efforts of whites to tokenly integrate their Harlem clubs, and of some blacks to accept white leadership within an integrated structure, or, alternatively, to resist disbanding their segregated party base, did not keep black political insurgents from demanding black control of Harlem district politics. It did, however, keep black forces divided, and thus prolong the struggle for black party control.

By the 1920s, in the Republican party of New York, there was little remaining of the centralized hierarchical black machine built by Booker T. Washington and Charles Anderson. Black Republican party politicians could thus concentrate on district politics without being subject to sanctions or other controls from black party bosses. They also had the advantage of leading a crucial bloc of Republican votes which the city Republican party, hopelessly in the minority in citywide elections, could not afford to lose.

In 1930, the 21st and 19th assembly districts had almost equal percentages of black residents—69.7 and 70.2 respectively—and party affiliation was very similar; Democrats had a very slight edge in both districts. In the 19th A.D., blacks had taken control of the

Republican party organization, and, in the 21st, they were forced to settle for dual leadership—a white leader in charge of the white section (the "hill") and a black leader in charge of the black section (the "valley"). These two outcomes of black fights for party control reflected the methods employed by the white district leaders to maintain control of their districts. Black forces in the 21st were kept divided by the more astute tactics of the white leader in that district who held no political office himself and could concentrate on keeping two factions of black Republicans fighting against each other. As long as only one faction would benefit from blacks taking control of the district, the other faction would continue to support the white district leader's continuation in office. Black insurgents in the 19th were able to keep relatively united throughout the long struggle because of their common opposition to the district leader who insisted on keeping a safe Republican assembly seat for himself.

BLACK INSURGENCY: THE 19th A.D.

Three white Republicans held the district leadership position in the 19th A.D. between 1920 and 1929, when blacks finally took over: John J. Lyons, David Costuma, and Abraham Grenthal. Lyons faced insurgency efforts by the United Civil League in 1920. Over 75% of the black vote had gone for the white Republican assembly nominee the year before, and yet Lyons had yielded none of his party control to blacks and was hoarding all of his patronage positions. The UCL was particularly incensed because their candidate for assembly had lost the primary the year before to a regular white Republican.

Lyons withstood the UCL challenge to his leadership by widening the division between black Republicans. He accused the League of receiving $5,000 in campaign expenses from Tammany Hall and publicly announced that a vote for the UCL would be a vote for the Democrats (*Harlem Home News,* April 4, 1920, Scrapbook, Kilroe Collection).[26] All of the regular Republicans won in that 1920 primary and, as a reward for loyalty, Charles Anderson, black leader of the regular Republican forces, was elected alternate-at-large from the state to the national convention (*New York Age,* April 10, 1920). At-large positions had traditionally been the standard reward for black politicians because they carried symbolic recognition for the race without acknowledgement of accountability to black voters in any particular district.

The defeat of the UCL was a relief to the Republican County Committee.

> they ['the colored people'] will solve their problems with your assistance where principle must stand over treachery. John Royall and his methods should not be encouraged by the Republican leaders on one side and the Democrats with a slush fund on the other. He has tried to ride two horses going in opposite directions and has been caught with the goods. He should get the same consideration that any other criminal would get from the powers that be. [M.C. Brown to Herbert Parson, May 12, 1920, Parsons Papers]

Lyons' successor in 1921, David Costuma, was more attuned to the demands of the black Republicans in his district.[27] He agreed to continue to give blacks the nomination for alderman, and, in 1922, allowed a black UCL activist to run for assembly on the Republican ticket (probably because the white Republican had lost to a Democrat the year before with the help of 43% of the black vote). Costuma kept his district under control until he was replaced as district leader in 1927.

The precipitating cause of Costuma's retirement was his leadership of a revolt against county committee leader Koenig. Costuma carried on his attacks against Koenig in the name of his black constituents. He accused Koenig of blocking an assembly rent bill, which would have benefited poor blacks in the city, and of disenfranchising Harlem voters by the aldermanic reapportionment of 1921. According to Costuma, Koenig had promised that the aldermanic apportionment would be coterminous with the assembly apportionment, thus giving Costuma more power. Instead the aldermanic districts were mapped out in order to favor other leaders, practically disenfranchising 7,500 blacks outside of the new disctrict and allowing the Democrats to elect aldermen for three terms running. Another reapportionment was to take place in 1926, and Costuma wanted to prevent Koenig from further eroding his power.

Costuma's resolution against Koenig was defeated by an overwhelming vote for the chairman, and the district leader was censured by the committee. Koenig, however, did go to Albany to lobby personally for the rent bill, and its sponsor, Abraham Grenthal, became the next district leader of the 19th A.D. (*New York Age,* February 6 and 13; March 6 and 13, 1926; June 25 and July 2, 1927; Citizens Union Collection, Koenig, A-23; Samuel Koenig, 40-41).

Although Grenthal was a very liberal assemblyman and tried to keep in contact with his black constituents, he faced rising opposition from the black Republicans of his district. No black had been elected to office in the 19th since Charles Roberts was elected alderman from the old 27th in 1919. Many dissatisfied black politicians suspected that, although the white leadership was paying deference to the principle of black representation in the district, once the blacks were nominated, no support from the white party organization was forthcoming to help them get elected. Grenthal himself was elected three times on the Republican ticket while three blacks on the same ticket were defeated. The district was becoming more Democratic and many blacks attributed this to black disaffection with the Republican leadership.

Black suspicions were confirmed in 1926, the last year of Costuma's leadership. A black Republican from the 19th assembly district was nominated as State Senator for the 19th senatorial district, while Grenthal was renominated from the 19th assembly district for assembly. It was quite clear that a black could not win in the senatorial district, while a black nominee could probably have carried the assembly district. As was expected, the black lost and Grenthal won, causing one black columnist to comment:

> With all of these election casualties constantly occurring in respect to colored candidates, the conclusion seems inescapable that the colored men are placed on the ticket in that district as political baits or vote getters for the white candidates who run on the same ticket with them. [*Amsterdam News,* December 22, 1926]

Black groups organizing to overthrow the white leadership of the 19th viewed the 1926 election as further evidence that they were victims of white manipulation. Charges were leveled against Grenthal in 1927 accusing him of having made a deal with the white Democratic candidate from the 19th aldermanic district to shut out both the black Democratic candidate for assembly and the black Republican candidate for alderman (*Amsterdam News,* March 14,

1928). Both Grenthal and the black Republican aldermanic nominee won the 1927 election, but the feeling of resentment against the district leader was still strong.

Early in 1928, *Age* Editor Fred Moore, recently elected alderman from the 19th, inflated with his own success (see *New York Age,* October 29 and November 5, 1927) and probably desirous of the district leadership, became the self-appointed leader of a campaign against Grenthal (*New York Age,* February 25, March 10 and 17, July 14, 1928). When Grenthal ran again for reelection, he was opposed in the primary by an independent black Republican whose campaign was run by Moore. Grenthal won the primary because of the support of the black women's vote, and because regular black Republicans led by Charles Anderson were still supporting the white Republican leadership (*New York Age,* August 11; *Amsterdam News,* August 15, 1928). But Moore's candidate had demonstrated enough political strength to be appointed Assistant Attorney General of New York State (*Amsterdam News,* January 23, 1929).

Finally, in 1929, black insurgents gathered their forces in a drive to overthrow Grenthal and the white leadership of the 19th. They called in black Congressman Oscar DePriest from Chicago and former leader David Costuma for a pep rally in the summer and organized a registration drive among blacks in Harlem (*Amsterdam News,* August 28; *New York Age,* August 21, 1929). In 1927, the 19th district was slightly Democratic (48% to 46%, but, by the 1929 primary, registration had temporarily shifted to give Republicans a 12% edge over the Democrats (53% to 41%).

In the 1929 primary, the entire regular Republican organization ticket in the 19th was defeated. The insurgents elected 125 county committeemen, as opposed to Grenthal's 47. Grenthal himself was defeated by an insurgent Republican, and Fred Moore won the nomination for alderman against a black Republican supporter of Grenthal's. An elated *Amsterdam News* editor wrote, "Harlem voted black . . . not so much from choice as from absolute necessity" (September 25, 1929).

DUAL LEADERSHIP: THE TWENTY-FIRST A.D.

In the 21st A.D., as in the 19th, black Republicans opposed white control of the district, but blacks were also divided between "regulars" and "independents," dependent on their loyalty or opposition to the white Republican organization. The demands and strategies of the regulars and independents differed depending on their relative position of power and their immediate goal in the next election.

The most important black politicians in the district were J.C. Hawkins, three times elected to the assembly (1919-1921), George Harris, editor of the *New York News,* twice elected to the Board of Aldermen (1919 and 1921), both "independent" Republicans, and Charles Mitchell and Charles Roberts, both regular Republicans close to the white district leader. The white Republican district leader, Robert Conklin, was, however, in a good position to retain control of the 21st. He was secure in Republican party councils, blacks were hopelessly divided, and he co-opted the issue of securing a black voice in the Republican county committee.

In early winter of 1923, Conklin called a meeting of the warring black Republican clubs at his own Manhattan Republican Club (a prestigious and powerful Republican club which had for a number of years admitted a few high-status loyal blacks like Charles Roberts and J.C. Hawkins). The coalition of clubs issued a joint resolution to the county committee (*Amsterdam News,* February 28; *New York Age,* March 3, 1923) demanding more black representation in executive councils and district leadership.

In July, the county committee adopted one of the proposed resolutions, after both Koenig and Conklin spoke at meetings of the Appomatox Club during the spring, in favor of black representation on the executive committee (*Amsterdam News,* May 23, 30, and *New York Age,* July 7, 1923). Henceforth, two blacks—a man and a woman—chosen by the white leaders of the 19th and 21st A.D.s were allowed to sit on the Republican party executive committee. The other recommendation did not pass until 1926 when the committee recommended, but did not require, dual leadership for the Harlem districts.

Conklin could also count on the split in the black community to keep his position secure. Each black Republican faction claimed to represent the true interest of the race in establishing real black district leadership. In April 1923, the black county committee, dominated by the regular Republican Appomatox Club and supported by Conklin, voted to remove Harris and Hawkins from

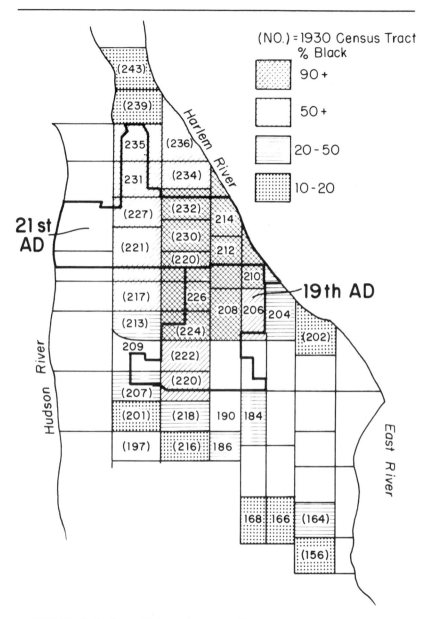

SOURCE: Derived from Walter Laidlaw, compiler, *Population of the City of New York, 1890-1930* (New York: Cities Census Committee, 1932).

Figure 6: BLACK POPULATION IN HARLEM, 1930

leadership in the district on the grounds that they were not chosen by the blacks themselves.[28] The committee chose Charles Mitchell as black leader and selected its own aldermanic nominee (*Amsterdam News,* April 18, 1923). The move really did nothing to change the status of black Republicans in the district. Even the regular black Republican nominee was subject to approval by the white Manhattan Republican Club (*New York Age,* July 21, 1923).

Conklin further secured his position by instituting a black associate leader for the district, a position first held by regular Republican Charles Roberts, then, with Roberts's and Conklin's backing, by J.C. Hawkins and, finally, by Charles Mitchell (*New York Age,* September 29; *Amsterdam News,* September 26, 1923). This not only served to give the appearance of equal black participation in the Republican politics of the 21st, but also created a useful focus for the conflict between black groups and put Conklin in a position to mediate or arbitrate these conflicts.

As was happening in the neighboring 19th, registration in the 21st was becoming increasingly Democratic. Black Democrats had won assembly seats in 1922 and 1923, running against white Republicans, and aldermanic positions in 1923 and 1925 against black Republicans. A black regular Republican[29] won the election for assembly in 1924 (*New York Age,* August 2, 1924), but was defeated in 1925 by a white Democrat. For the next three years, the white leadership of the district nominated white Republicans to try to win back the seat.

The black press reported great dissatisfaction among black Republicans and implied that blacks were switching to the Democratic camp (*New York Age,* June 13, 28, November 22, 1924). But black Republicans were still deeply divided, and the white leadership used this as the standard rationale for not giving blacks more recognition in the party.[30] Beginning in 1925, black factionalism focused on the issue of dual leadership versus attempts at black leadership for the district. Dual leadership would divide the district into white (the "hill") and black (the "valley") sections, with a white or black leader in charge of each section respectively. Although segregated party politics would have been reinforced by this plan, Charles Roberts, Charles Mitchell, and the regular Republicans who proposed the plan would have at least gained co-equal status. The plan, however, was defeated by a new coalition of black opponents led by Harris, Hawkins, and the leader of the black Republican women, Hortense Warner, who argued that dual leadership meant the acceptance of segregation which blacks should under no circumstances condone (*New York Age,* June 27, 1925). In practical terms, dual leadership would have shut out these black independent Republicans and solidified the positions of the regulars.

After the failure of the dual leadership proposal, the factions reversed their stand. Mitchell decided that if the white leadership was not willing to compromise, he would run against Conklin for control of the entire district, and the opposition coalition decided that white leadership was better than black leadership by the Mitchell faction. Conklin was reelected by a vote of 87 to 49 (*Amsterdam News,* September 30, 1925; *New York Age,* September 6, 1925). As a reward for his support, Conklin named his old enemy, George Harris, as associate leader in defiance of Conklin's own promise to allow blacks to select their own leader. Blacks rebelled, however, and at a meeting of the black county committee, they elected Mitchell as the rightful associate (*Amsterdam News,* October 21, 1925). Conklin had clearly overstepped his bounds. He had not only tried to blatantly ignore the blacks' own choice for leader, but had many of the insurgents running for reelection to the black county committee removed from the ballot. In an unprecedented effort, Mitchell and his followers printed up sample ballots and taught voters how to write in the candidates' names. All the candidates whose names were removed from the ballot were elected and the Mitchell faction won 55 of the 102 committee seats (*New York Age,* September 26, 1925).

Continual losses to the Democrats over the next two years and low black Republican voter registration kept the black Republicans demoralized and divided. In the summer of 1926, in remarks intended to be "off the record," Conklin told Appomatox Club members that whites in the district would never accept black leadership and that, since blacks were accustomed to white leadership, the status quo should continue (*New York Age,* July 31, 1926). This increased the defiance of Mitchell and the Appomatox Club. They blocked the nomination of Conklin's black candidate (Hawkins) for state senate, allowing the nomination of a white, and refused to serve on the state and judiciary conventions, threatening to put up their

own slate of minor offices, when Conklin appointed a state com-
mitteewoman (Hortense Warner) and an assembly nominee from
his own camp (*New York Age,* August 7, 1926). It took 11 ballots for
the deeply divided black forces to agree on a nominee for alderman
in 1927,[31] and soon after Conklin was once again reelected leader
over Mitchell (*New York Age,* August 3, 6, and October 8, 1927;
Amsterdam News, October 5).

Disputes over leadership in the 21st were overshadowed in 1928
by the presidential election, but in 1929, the Appomatox Club again
prepared to revolt (*New York Age,* June 2, 1929). Conklin seems to
have tired of the fight and was tentatively considering resignation.
He was also opposed by the white Republican assemblyman from his
district. As a last attempt to save himself, Conklin bid for black
support by reintroducing the idea of dual leadership. Mitchell and
his supporters, who had themselves proposed dual leadership when
it seemed the only way of gaining control of the District in 1925, now
opposed it as a "political confidence" game. Conklin's plan,
however, was passed after a long debate and Mitchell resigned himself to being the leader of the black section of the 21st, the "valley"
(*New York Age,* June 22, August 3 and 21, 1929).[32]

Despite the only partial success of blacks in the 21st A.D. fight
for party control, black Republican insurgents had proven they
could mobilize their forces and successfuly challenge white party
hegemony in Harlem. Black Republican insurgent candidates swept
the Republican primary in 1929 and won every district election.
Most significantly, they had maintained the majority Republican
registration gained during the previous presidential election year
and had brought out the black vote.

V. BLACK POLITICAL PARTICIPATION:
THE GROUND RULES

The fundamental assumption upon which structures of race
politics were built during the early decade of the century has changed
very little. The grounds for black participation in the political parties
are still racial. Although the basic rule that kept the boundaries of
black participation impermeable have begun to break down with

blacks winning more citywide and statewide offices, their exclusion or inclusion in the political arena is still a matter of race.

Between 1910 and 1930 in New York City, blacks did change the nature of their participation in the Republican party. But their participation continued to be a matter of color—blacks represented blacks and, if the party could help it, no one else. While blacks sought to maximize their influence by taking advantage of their expanding political base in Harlem, white party leaders tried to control these black influence attempts. Most frequently, this involved creating political party structures which channeled blacks in separate and subordinate political auxiliary organizations. When expedient, white political leaders tried to create other structural changes outside the political organizations to thwart black political participation, such as disenfranchisement, reapportionment, or political consolidation. If these means of containment were not sufficient, the authorities had to respond to the influence pressure itself. This response was designed to minimize the change in power distribution, and was manifest in attempts to co-opt certain black leaders, to make visible symbolic appointments, or to routinize black political participation in certain positions, while strictly confining the scope of power attached to that office.

The drama of black efforts to gain influence in New York City party politics was played out in a theatre which was directed and controlled by white political leaders. First, white leaders institutionalized a form of black political participation which could be easily manipulated through a powerful black broker responsible only to the white bosses. Next, when blacks proved that they could circumvent their white-appointed leaders by mobilizing the black vote in local elections, the party co-opted the black independent electoral movement by routinizing black Republican nominations for the lowest local office. Black attempts to gain higher office were thwarted by gerrymandered districts and lukewarm party support. Finally, as the Republican party was on its way to becoming a permanent minority in Harlem, white leaders caved in to black pressure for black district control, with the important qualification that whites on the "hill" in the wealthier neighborhoods along the Hudson would not have to be represented by a black from the "valley" below.

We take largely for granted the following political facts: that there is race politics in America; that black political participation is on the basis of color; that pigmentation determines who gets what, when, how. As some political scientists have noted (see Wolfinger, 1966; Melson and Wolpe, 1970), when political participation is based on race or ethnicity and political rewards reinforce group distinctions gaps between groups become wider. Bridges are harder to build. The bridge that might be built by common class concerns gives way again and again to barriers erected by the politics of race.

NOTES

1. Nationally, Democratic relationships with blacks would shatter the party which depended on Southern white support. Thus, blacks were largely ignored by the national Democratic party, although a number of independent black leaders worked for Cleveland during his three campaigns, and many supported Wilson in 1912.

2. Robert Merton, in his now classic piece, "Some Functions of the Political Machine" (1957:77), describes the prototype of a machine relationship and discusses some of the services the political machine supposedly rendered: dealing with private problems of constituents in a personal manner; providing services to individual legitimate and illegitimate businesses, which, in turn, serviced the community; and "providing avenues of social mobility for the otherwise disadvantaged." It has become part of American folklore to credit the urban machines of the late 19th and early 20th centuries with integrating the recent American immigrants into the political life of the country (see, for example, Cornwell, 1964) and structurally uniting the fragments of power scattered throughout communities within the city.

3. Bishop Walters of the A.M.E. Church, an active New York Democrat, was offered a position as Minister to Liberia, which he refused because of his church duties. (The post went to James Curtis, a New York attorney active in the UCD.) Robert Terrell was retained as a municipal judge in D.C., and A.E. Patterson of Oklahoma was nominated for Registrar of the Treasury. He withdrew because of Senate opposition.

4. The NAACP also proposed a National Race Commission to be modeled on Roosevelt's Country Life Commission and Taft's Industrial Commission to undertake a study of the Negro in America, especially socioeconomic aspects. Wilson refused to appoint the commission, claiming that he was blocked by Southern Senators, and that a number of blacks with whom he had spoken agreed with him about the advisability of segregation (see Villard, 1939: Chap. 14; Speeches, Proposal for a National Race Commission, Box 136, suggestions by J.E. Spingarn about Commission, Box 120, Villard Papers).

5. Anderson had never actually denied the charges made against him, but argued that none of his critics had seen fit to speak out on the subject until their own resignations were demanded. The implication was that Anderson's critics had violated the rules of the political game by exposing another party politician for behaving exactly as they themselves would have behaved under the circumstances (Anderson to BTW, Sept. 26, 1913; Anderson to Tyler, March 6, 1914, Washington Papers).

6. Two years later, when it became clear that Anderson would be replaced, Washington gave Anderson advice about who to contact in order to keep his position, where to apply political pressure to obtain another job, and how to stay in the good graces of the administration by thanking them for allowing him to stay in office for two extra years (January 25, March 5, 12, 1915, Washington Papers).

7. This was probably a gross underestimate because of the movement north and the high nonresponse rate. The 1910 census included a mulatto category and, since many blacks responded that they had foreign or mixed parentage, they were not counted in the black population.

8. San Juan Hill was the name commonly used for the west side of Manhattan, roughly from the 40's through the 60's. The black belt was between 58th and 66th Streets, from 10th Avenue to the Hudson River. For an account of black politics on San Juan Hill before 1910, see Hiller, 1972: Chap. 5.

9. Reapportionments kept the black vote split in San Juan Hill. In 1917 the black vote was split again—half going into a Democratic district and half into a marginal district—rendering it essentially insignificant.

10. Twenty years earlier, the last black man sat on the separate Brooklyn Board of Education. Since consolidation, no black was appointed to the board in New York. The appointment in 1917 followed reformist policy, and stayed as much as possible outside the realm of regular party influence. Dr. E.P. Roberts was recommended by the National League on Urban Conditions among Negroes (the Urban League), whose white members were leading reformers in the city. Roberts himself had a relatively apolitical background, although he had been Medical Inspector for the Board of Health and examiner for the public schools, in addition to his private practice in Harlem and his many civic involvements (Lowi, 1964:42-43; Roberts, Verticle File).

11. Although blacks voted overwhelmingly for Republican presidential candidate Charles Evans Hughes in 1916, there was little enthusiasm among black voters for the election. The Republican platform had no civil rights plank, and Hughes gave little indication of being interested in winning the black vote. Blacks did not really support Hughes with their vote; they opposed Wilson (Sherman, 1973:120-122).

12. The black Socialists were led by the Messenger group, referring to the magazine edited by Chandler Owen and A. Philip Randolph, which started publication in 1917 and would be the radical organ of the black Socialist movement for the next 11 years.

13. Charges of Rockefeller domination of the Mitchel administration's education policy stemmed from the fact that Abraham Flexner, a powerful Mitchel supporter on the Board of Education, was assistant secretary of the Rockefeller financed General Election Board. Mitchel had adopted the Gary education plan from an experimental vocationally oriented system of elementary education operating in Gary, Indiana, primarily because it promised to save money for the city.

14. Mitchel himself contributed to Hylan's popularity by accusing Hylan of being unpatriotic and, in fact, pro-German, a tactic which backfired (Lewison, 1965:230-233).

15. The black vote throughout this paper was estimated by using the recorded vote (*City Record* for December of the election year) of those election districts entirely within census tracts having 50% or more blacks in 1920. For more detailed tables and an analysis of the black vote in Harlem from 1917 through 1930, see Hiller (1972).

16. Thomas, claiming irregularities by the New York Board of Canvassers, demanded a recount. His opponent won a halt in the recount through the courts and counterattacked by claiming that the district had been gerrmandered by the Republicans so that a black Republican would win. The election itself was even more vicious, with Tammany handing out hand-

bills saying: "Do you want your alderman to be a Negro?" (*New York Times,* November 23, 1917; *New York Age,* December 8 and November 15, 1917).

17. The United Civic League continued to exist through the early 1920s, but most supporters were incorporated into Republican politics in Harlem. A small group of League activists attempted to organize against the Democrats, but without success (Goldstein, 1973: 253).

18. Smith accused Hylan of association with the KKK and of discrimination against Jews, Catholics, and Negroes. Hylan, however, continued to make periodic appearances at black political functions, usually to reaffirm his support for the black community or to urge blacks to vote Democratic. In 1929, at the height of the campaign among black Republicans to take control of Harlem district leadership, Hylan encouraged these efforts at a Harlem meeting (*Amsterdam News,* June 1, 1927; *New York Age,* January 12, 1929).

19. In the 19th A.D., the only assembly nomination given a black between 1919, when this arrangement was made, and 1929, when black insurgents swept the district primary, was in 1922, when regular black and white Republicans nominated Reverend Richard Bolden, probably because the white Republican running the year before had lost to a Democrat partly as a result of an exceptionally strong black Democratic vote.

20. In 1920, the black election districts in the 19th and 21st A.D.s voted 93% Republican.

21. In 1924, the black election districts in the 19th and 21st A.D.s voted 80% Republican.

22. Black Socialists running for assembly in the same election year against black Republicans received only 5-6% of the black vote.

23. A black NAACP activist declined the nomination to run in the district on the Progressive and Liberal tickets, so as not to risk dividing the black vote (letters from Pickens to editor of *New York News,* August 30, 1924, Box 7B, Category C, Pickens Papers, Schomburg Library). Exceptions to Roberts's supporters among blacks were the Messenger group, who felt Roberts had made no stand on issues, and some NAACP leaders, who continued to support Progressives.

24. Both J.C. Hawkins and Fred Moore ran for nominee at the party convention, but even combining their votes, the white nominee had 150 votes more.

25. Even those black politicians who were members of tokenly integrated white Republican clubs like the Manhatan Republican Club in the 21st and the Central Republican Club in the 19th were also leaders in segregated black clubs of their own.

26. Although the UCL admitted receiving these funds from Tammany, they claimed to have regularly supported Republican candidates, having 498 out of 500 of their members as Republican. Lyons had never given the league any Republican money. The $5,000 was to be used in support of three Democratic judges, and the Republicans themselves had put two Democratic judges on their own ticket. In addition, according to Furniss (1969:280), it was part of the league strategy to support some Democratic nominees in order to pressure the Republicans into giving blacks more electoral recognition.

27. The UCL revolt against Lyons probably added fuel to the dissatisfaction already existing in the county committee over Lyons' break with Koenig, the county committee chairman, over another issue.

28. In fact, in December 1923, Conklin actually published a statement in the *New York Age* (December 15:4) enumerating the objections he and his white associates had with Harris:

> That he refused to act with his party in the Board of Aldermen; that he has failed to support other local Republican nominees; that he has been an adherent of and had supported Hylan and his unsavory "gang"; that he is allied with Morton, the Tammany Hall representative in the colored district; that he is extremely selfish, has declined to do anything at any time for any Republican save those in his own club, and has sought to encourage and capitalize race hatred for his own advantage.

29. Pope Billups was nominated by Conklin without the consent of the black caucus led by Mitchell, but was generally felt to be a new political face acceptable to all factions (*New York Age,* August 2, 1924).

30. An example of shifting factional alliances is that, by July 1925, Harris was back in Conklin's good graces and was named by Conklin as the regular Republican nominee for alderman. But Harris was defeated in the district primary balloting by an independent black candidate (*New York Age,* July 25, 1925).

31. Hortense Warner, supported by her campaign manager, Edgar Grey, and a women's organization she had established to help her candidacy, came within five votes of the necessary 47 on the first ballot. George Harris, supported by Conklin, and Francis Rivers, backed by the Appomatox Club, split the remaining 50 votes almost equally. When the second and third ballots produced the same results, a conference committee was appointed to try to come up with a solution. After the fourth ballot deadlocked, the committee recommended the nomination of J.C. Hawkins as a compromise candidate and, on the fifth ballot, Harris withdrew in favor of Hawkins. The nomination finally did go to the former assemblyman, but not until the 11th ballot.

32. Hortense Warner, leader of the black Republican women, remained opposed to dual leadership because it was segregation institutionalized. She filed suit against Conklin, County Committee Chairman Koenig, and Mitchell on that basis, but lost. George Harris had switched over to the 19th A.D., where he was given the aldermanic nomination by Grenthal's organization. Hawkins was nominated alderman from the 21st.

REFERENCES

Amsterdam News, November 1922-December 1931.

Anderson,Charles W. Verticle File, Schomburg Library.

Ansorge, Martin. Oral History Research Office, Columbia University.

BERGMAN, M. (1969). The chronological history of the Negro in America. New York: Harper & Row.

BRISBANE, R. (1969). The black vanguard: Origins of the Negro social revolution, 1900-1960. Valley Forge, Pa.: Judson Press.

BRYCE, J. (1961). "Rings and bosses." Pp. 145-153 in E. Banfield (ed.), Urban government. New York: Free Press.

Citizens Union Collection. Special Collections, Columbia University.

Colored American Review, Vol. I, 1915-1916.

CONNABLE, A., and SILBERFARB, E. (1967). Tigers of Tammany: Nine men who ran New York. New York: Holt, Rinehart and Winston.

Calvin Coolidge Papers, Library of Congress.

CORNWELL, E. (1964). "Bosses, machines and ethnic groups." Annals, 153(May):27-50.

Crisis. November 1910-1929.

FURNISS, G. (1969). "The political assimilation of Negroes in New York City." Unpublished Ph.D. dissertation, Columbia University.

GOLDSTEIN, M.L. (1973). "Race politics in New York City, 1890-1930: Independent political behavior." Unpublished Ph.D dissertation, Columbia University.

Gumby Scrapbooks. Special Collections, Columbia University.

HALPERN, M. (1969). "A redefinition of the revolutionary situation." Journal of International Affairs, 23(winter):54-75.

Harlem Home News. 1910-1911.

HILLER, M.H. (1972). "Race politics in New York City, 1890-1930." Unpublished Ph.D. dissertation, Columbia University.

HILLQUIT, M. (1971). Loose leaves from a busy life. New York: DaCapo Press.

Hylan, John, Papers. Mayors' Papers, Municipal Archives, New York City.

KATZNELSON, I. (1973). Black men, white cities. London: Oxford University Press.

Kilroe Collection. Special Collections, Columbia University.

Koenig, Samuel. Oral History Research Office, Columbia University.

KRUGER, R. (1977). Simple justice. New York: Random House.

LAIDLAW, W. (compiler, 1913). Statistical sources for demographic studies of Greater New York, 1910. New York Federation of Churches.

——— (compiler, 1922). Statistical sources for demographic studies of Greater New York, 1920. New York: 1920 Census Committee.

——— (compiler, 1932). Population of the City of New York, 1890-1930. Cities Census Committee.

LEWINSON, E.R., (1965). John Purroy Mitchel: The boy mayor of New York. New York: Astra Books.

Low, Seth, Papers. Special Collections, Columbia University.

LOWI, T. (1964). At the pleasure of the mayor. London: Collier-Macmillan Ltd.

MEIER, A. (1963). Negro thought in America, 1880-1915. Ann Arbor: University of Michigan Press.

MELSON, R., and WOLPE, H. (1970). "Modernization and the politics of communalism: A theoretical perspective." American Political Science Review, 64:1112-1130.

MERTON, R.K. (1957). "Some functions of the political machine." Pp. 72-82 in Social theory and social structure. New York: Free Press.

Messenger. 1917-1928.

MILLER, K. (1913). "The Political Plight of the Negro." Kelly Miller's Monographic Magazine, 1(2), May.

MORISON, E., BLUM, J.M., and BUCKLEY, J.T. (eds., 1951-1954). Letters of Theodore Roosevelt. Cambridge, Mass.: Harvard University Press.

MORSELL, J. (1951). "The political behavior of Negroes in New York." Unpublished Ph.D. dissertation, Columbia University.

New York Age. 1910-1931.

New York City. City Record, 1917-1930.

New York State. Legislative Manual of the State of New York. Albany, 1918-1931.

New York Times. 1910-1930.

OSOFSKY, G. (1963). Harlem: The making of a ghetto. New York: Harper Torchbooks.

OTTLEY, R. (1968). New world a-comin'. New York: Arno Press.

Parsons, Herbert, Papers. Special Collections, Columbia University.

Pickens, William, Papers. Schomburg Library.

Roberts, E.P., M.D. Verticle File, Schomburg Library.

SHERMAN, R.B. (1973). The Republican party and black America: From McKinley to Hoover, 1896-1933. Charlottesville: University of Virginia Press.

TATUM, E.L. (1951). The changed political thought of the Negro, 1915-1940. New York: Exposition Press.

VILLARD, O.G. (1939). Fighting years: Memoirs of a liberal editor. New York: Harcourt, Brace.

Villard, Oswald G., Papers. Houghton Library, Harvard University.

Washington, Booker T., Papers. Library of Congress.

WOLFINGER, R.E. (1966). "Some consequences of ethnic politics." Pp. 42-54 in M.K.

Jennings and L.H. Ziegler (eds.), The electoral process. Englewood Cliffs, N.J.: Prentice-Hall.

WOLGEMUTH, K.L. (1958). "Woodrow Wilson's appointment policy and the Negro." Journal of Southern History, 24:457-471.

——— (1959) "Woodrow Wilson and federal segregation." Journal of Negro History, 64:158-173.

Chapter 5

CONSTITUTIONAL CHANGE AND
PARTY DEVELOPMENT IN FRANCE, NIGERIA,
AND THE UNITED STATES

KAY LAWSON

I. INTRODUCTION

What is the relationship between the development of political parties and the development of political systems? We know the relationship is necessarily reciprocal: parties help to form systems; systems help to form parties. Yet although the fact of reciprocal causation is acknowledged, most research on the subject has been limited to how system change causes party development, and in particular to how particular system changes have caused particular parties to be formed in the first place. There has been remarkably little effort, in this unsymmetrical study of causal relationships, to trace general patterns, or to construct a theory of party development.

A brief look at the literature confirms this impression of imbalance. Maurice Duverger (1951) suggested that parties begin either inside legislatures in response to the formation of factions and the siren call of the expanding electorate, or outside legislatures in response to the growing demands of the inadequately represented. The former tend to be cadre parties, loose coalitions of notables working comfortably and undemocratically together under the leadership of their elected representatives to maintain their privileges; the latter are mass parties, democratically organized down to the last *arrondissement,* bent on expanding their dues-paying membership to the utmost limits, and subjecting their elected representatives to the will of the party, as interpreted by the leaders of the party apparatus. Joseph LaPalombara and Myron Weiner (1966) believe that parties develop in response to crises: crises of legitimacy in which the new party challenges the right of those presently in authority to be so placed; crises of participation in which groups within the system but hitherto excluded from a part in the decision making organize in order to make more forceful assaults on the closed doors of politics; and crises of integration in which new parties form to wage the fight for inclusion in a system—or for separation from it into a new state. Samuel Huntington (1971) suggested that in developing systems parties are formed less to facilitate than to channel participation; parties are a response on the part of elites to the need for a place to put the mob, as its cries grow more strident and more disruptive to the serious business of development being carried on by the grown-ups. Most recently, Giovanni Sartori (1976:3-29) stresses the origins of parties in factions, political groups bent on "dire doings." Parties differ from factions, he says, in being "part of the whole" and not necessarily adverse to the whole, but "factionalism is the ever-present temptation of a party arrangement and its ever-possible degeneration."

All of these ideas of party formation are interesting, and the fact that we can find as many exceptions as examples of the rules proposed or that we find parties forming (our own, for example) in ways which cross categories meant to be mutually exclusive does not mean we should abandon the insights these propositions contain. It does suggest, however, that more work is to be done on the question of party origins.

However, far more woefully neglected are the questions relating to how parties, once created, develop and change over time in response to system change and/or their own internal dynamics. This is so despite the fact that parties are always changing, visibly and with profound impact, the systems in which they operate. Indeed, it might well be said that parties are the most unabashed accommodationists in the galaxy of political institutions. They exist, after all, in order to put people in office with some semblance, usually electoral in nature, of popular approval. They must therefore always be ready to follow where constitutions and statutory law shall lead: decentralize power and you decentralize parties; concentrate power and expect a concentrated attack upon it by a party well subordinated to its own leadership.

Furthermore, parties respond differently even to centralized political systems, depending upon *where* power is concentrated. In the days of strong legislatures, centralized parties not only placed their representatives in office, they placed them in power, able to advance their supporters' causes in rough proportion to their own electoral strength in parliament or congress. As power has shifted in centralized systems from parliaments to directly elected presidents, parties have been compelled to concentrate on presidential politics (Hill, forthcoming), but have as yet found no way to prevent a strong president from wresting a significant degree of independence from his party by turning to alternate sources of support, especially to the electorate at large, via the media. Furthermore, presidential politics is inevitably majority politics. When political power is concentrated in the presidency, the nation becomes in effect a single member constituency and the pressure on parties to consolidate forces in order to win that majority is likely to be irresistible.

There is another sense in which parties are accommodationist: when they do acquire a measure of power, they are seldom hesitant to exercise that power in ways to make institutions accommodate them. That is to say, elected representatives of parties, finding themselves in positions of real power (which is not always—or even usually—the result of successful electioneering; Rose, 1969) are always ready to change the system to make reelection easier, provided only that being seen to do so will not in fact make reelection harder.[1] Indeed, successful party politicians are so often ready to make political upward mobility easier for themselves and their cohorts that they lose sight of the fact that they *can* be seen doing so. Chinua Achebe (1967:82) applies an Ibo saying in his fictional account of this tendency in Nigeria: one should not steal so much that the owner will notice. It is a principle of universal applicability among the world's putative democracies.

Visibly stealing sovereignty back from the people is not the only error parties in power make in their manipulation of electoral laws and constitutional principles. Poetic justice can be found in political as well as personal relationships, and it is not at all unusual that the very "reforms" instituted to improve the status of those in power will have the opposite effect of that intended (Ranney, 1975:188-210). Changes designed to make life easier for a group of individuals united in a common view of the public good can have the surprising result of banishing them from office altogether. This may happen in various ways. Unanticipated responses on the part of the opposition to the reforms may make that group's standard-bearers electorally more appealing than those in power. Or the changes may be made too blatantly, undermining the legitimacy of those who made them. In severe cases, the legitimacy of the system itself may come into question, so that an elaborate program of counterreforms is undertaken, forcing further accommodation on the part of the parties. It is not even impossible in such cases that system and parties will tumble down together and be replaced by military coup or praetorian takeover.

There is, then, a remarkably dynamic relationship between parties and systems over the course of their respective development. Can such dynamism—or some selected aspects of it—be reduced to the cold language of testable hypotheses? On closer inspection, we find 10 propositions lurking in the discussion thus far. These may be grouped in two major categories:

I. Parties out of power accommodate themselves to political systems.

  (1) Decentralized political systems stimulate the development of decentralized parties.

  (2) Centralized systems stimulate the development of centralized parties.

  (3) Centralized legislative systems stimulate parties to focus on legislative politics to achieve and/or maintain power.

  (4) Centralized presidential systems stimulate parties to focus on presidential politics to achieve and/or maintain power.

  (5) Where parties pursue presidential politics, they are hampered in their efforts to exercise control over appointments and policymaking by the ability of the president to turn to alternate bases of support.

  (6) Where parties pursue presidential politics in multiparty systems, they are stimulated to build coalitions with each other in their efforts to win the majority necessary to elect the president.

II. The elected representatives of parties in power accommodate political systems to themselves.

(7) The elected representatives of parties in power seek to modify the system for their own electoral advantage.

(8) Parties in power, which have modified the system for their own electoral advantage, lose power when the opposition forces are able to respond to the changes in such a way as to make them more attractive to the electorate.

(9) Parties in power lose power when the party's elected representatives modify their system for their own electoral advantage in a fashion which undermines their own legitimacy.

(10) Parties in power, whose elected representatives have modified the system for their own electoral advantage in a fashion to undermine not only their own but also the system's legitimacy, will provoke further system change to counteract the effects of their actions.

These 10 hypotheses, once verified, or at least substantiated in a number of case studies and not refuted in any, may help us to understand something more about the nature of the interaction between parties and systems; they also suggest reasons for the present decline of parties, a question we will return to at the end of our discussion. At this point, it is necessary to offer some evidence of the probable truth of each. What follows is an effort to explore the recent history of political party development in three nations, France, Nigeria, and the United States, with a view to illustrating the truth or inadequacy of these propositions as they suggest themselves in the context of the political and constitutional developments of these three nations.

II. FRANCE

The relationships between system development and party development in France are particularly interesting. The French have been remarkably prone to constitutional experimentation, with profound effect on their parties, which, in turn, have played a major role in shaping further constitutional developments. Modern France is a unitary state, not a federal system, and, in keeping with the second proposition, its parties have always been centralized as well: policy stances, party finances, and nominees are determined in Paris. Some of the parties, particularly on the left, may permit expressions of grass-roots sentiment on these matters to travel upward through the party organization, but final decisions are made at party head-quarters. At the same time, divided popular opinion over the key issues of church-state relations, the role of France in the world, the distribution of wealth, and the form of government has contributed to the evolution of a multiparty system more fragmented and more given to ephemeral but powerful "flash parties" than most such systems in Europe (Avril, 1969; Thomson, 1969). The inability and unwillingness of such intransigeantly distinct parties to form ade-quately functiong coalitions contributed to the stalemate of Third and Fourth Republic politics, culminating in the Algerian crisis of 1958, the birth of the Fifth Republic, and a new constitution de-signed to foster a new relationship between government and parties (Berger, 1974; Blondel, 1974; Ehrmann, 1976).

The constitution, adopted in November 1958, changed the role of parties in several significant respects. Most important was the shift of power from the lower house of Parliament—the National Assembly—to the presidency. Under the new constitution, the presi-dent's power to appoint the premier has more than the merely cere-monial significance usually assigned such a function in parlia-mentary systems. The premier is in fact responsible to the president (as well as to the Parliament), and can be removed by him at will. The premier, in turn, maintains, with his cabinet, firm control over parliamentary proceedings: government bills have priority over those of private members, and the government may refuse amend-ments and demand that its bills be made subject to a single vote on the whole or a part (Articles 39, 41, 44, and 48). If the budget is not voted upon within 70 days of being submitted, the government may apply its provisions by ordinance (Article 47). Any matter not specifically reserved to Parliament for legislative action is con-sidered of "a regulatory character," to be ruled upon by executive decree (Article 37). If the government believes Parliament is legis-lating on a matter belonging to its realm it may appeal to the Consti-tutional Council (Article 41), but no such right is guaranteed should Parliament question the government's power to act. The govern-ment may make any of its bills a matter of confidence. Such a bill is considered as adopted, without a vote, unless one-tenth of the members of the assembly file a motion of censure within 24 hours of the bill's presentation (Article 49). If the motion of censure is then passed, Parliament is dissolved. The assembly may also file a motion of censure against the government at any time, but again must risk dissolution as the price of success.

The president's power is, as the above suggests, routinely exercised through his premier and the latter's cabinet. However, the president may also exercise power directly. Article 11 gives him the power to submit to the public for settlement by referendum matters which would otherwise be ruled upon by Parliament. Article 16 permits him to assume emergency powers when the institutions, independence, or integrity of France "are threatened in a grave and immediate manner," and, although he is required to "consult" with the premier, parliamentary leaders and the Constitutional Council, the decision as to when to assume such powers is his alone.

The exercise of such far-reaching powers requires a firm electoral base. In 1962, the new Constitution was amended to strengthen that base, when Charles de Gaulle, the leader for whom the new Constitution had been designed, asked the French people to approve a referendum calling for direct election of the president.

The net result of these changes was to make the presidency the focal position in a much more centralized system of government. No longer could the parties exercise their strength in powerful legislative committees and in playing musical chairs with rotating cabinet posts. Now the parties would have to turn to the presidency: *centralized presidential systems stimulate parties to focus on presidential politics to achieve and/or maintain power.*

What has happened in France in the first 20 years of the Fifth Republic lends both positive and negative evidence to support this proposition. Those parties which learned to play presidential politics have had increasing success; those which have not have progressively declined. France is also an excellent example of the ability of presidents to muster independence from party in such a system (proposition five), as we shall see.

The natural antipathy between strong presidents and political parties was heightened in France by the personal attitudes of Charles de Gaulle. De Gaulle had always been anti-party. He believed that the political machinations of the parties had destroyed his first efforts to guide France in the immediate postwar period, and, when he resumed power in 1958, he did so on the specific condition that he would not be required to negotiate with party leaders (de Gaulle, 1959). His determination to create a strong presidency was owed in large measure to his understanding of the capacity of presidents to move away from party, to be "above" party. In keeping with this philosophy, he refused to allow the Union pour la Nouvelle République, a new party formed from a coalition of various older Gaullist groups and new organizations devoted to keeping Algeria part of the French Empire, to say that they were "his" party. When the U.N.R. defied his wishes, announcing that "Voter U.N.R. c'est voter de Gaulle," and won a large plurality of seats, the party was still kept from power. Other parties were brought into the coalition, usually disproportionately to their strength, in order to weaken the U.N.R., a policy subsequently followed by de Gaulle's successor, Georges Pompidou, as well (Ambler, 1968; Wilson, 1973). Those who battled with Fifth Republic presidents over this reduced role for party went down to defeat: first, the militant Jacques Soustelle over the Algerian issue; later, Jacques Chaban-Delmas, the chief spokesman for reserving a role for party in domestic affairs.

Both de Gaulle and Pompidou were thus able to maintain independence from party by relying on popular support and the shifting assistance of other parties in the Gaullist coalition. But the U.D.R. was an able partner in its own suppression, and never mustered its forces for the games of presidential politics. The party was clearly hoist on its own petard: having campaigned on the basis of unadulterated loyalty to de Gaulle, it has to be loyal to his notions of leadership as well. This meant accepting the idea that leaders cannot be "nominated," that they must "emerge" self-nominated, and that all political parties can or should do is endorse that emergent candidate of whom they most approve.[2] The party has no nominating procedure as such; it merely endorses. Its failure to nominate a candidate upon Pompidou's death in 1974 proved disastrous; the candidate who "emerged" and had unavoidably to be endorsed, Chaban-Delmas, did *not* have to be voted for in the polling booth. Large numbers of U.D.R.[3] supporters shifted to his opponent, Giscard d'Estaing, following the heavy-handed hints of U.D.R. leader Jacques Chirac, who was duly rewarded with the prime ministership when Giscard won the presidency (Criddle, 1974; Hayward and Wright, 1974). As Chirac's own presidential ambitions brought him into closer and closer competition with the new president, his party was pushed further from the center of power, as witnessed by declining U.D.R. membership in the cabinet and finally Chirac's resignation as prime minister in 1976. An open break over the Paris mayoralty, which Chirac won over the competition of Giscard's hand-picked candidate, confirmed the breakup of the Gaullist right. The reorganization of the U.D.R. into the Rally for the Republic (R.P.R.), under the closer personal leadership of Chirac, makes clear the basis for a renewed onslaught on the presidency. But even if Chirac should one day succeed, there is no reason to imagine the R.P.R. will be better placed to control or guide him than it was, in earlier guises, to influence de Gaulle or Pompidou.

Thus, the constitutional changes made in 1958 and 1962 by the supporters of de Gaulle, which enabled many of them to ride his coattails into power, have had the longer range effect of weakening, not strengthening, their political party. To make the irony complete, these changes have had the effect of strengthening the parties of the left, to the point where they are now considered much more likely to be able to place their candidate in the presidency in the future. How has this reversal of fortunes come to pass?

In 1958, the Communist Party of France was the only party to vote unanimously against de Gaulle's return to power. The French Socialist party divided over the issue of support for the General, and those who opposed him formed the Parti Socialiste Unifié (P.S.U.). France's moderately progressive Christian Democratic Party, the Mouvement Républicain Populaire (M.R.P.), and the moderately conservative Radical Party both gave de Gaulle their support and, then, supplanted in their voters' affections by the new Gaullist movement they thus indirectly endorsed, plunged into a decline which was to prove fatal to the first and nearly so to the second.

However, parties *are* accommodationist, and the French example suggests accommodation can be found even among the most doctrinaire forces of the left. Their wits perhaps refreshed by the cold they were left out in, left-wing leaders soon recognized the need to focus on presidential politics. But presidential politics is majority politics, which meant the left could no longer afford the luxury of its own divisiveness.

The movement to left-wing unity has been long, slow, and uncertain. The struggle to overcome the old divisions began as soon as the referendum calling for direct election of the president had won the voters' approval. Gaston Defferre, the mayor of Marseilles, made an effort to rally all leftists except the communists into a new federation. His failure taught his successor some necessary lessons, and as the 1965 presidential elections approached, Socialist leader François Mitterrand was able to form a looser but somewhat more lasting electoral alliance, the Federation of the Democratic and Socialist Left, composed of the old Socialist Party (at that time still known as the Section Française de l'Internationale Ouvière), the Radical Party, and the Convention des Institutions Républicaines (C.I.R., an agglomeration of political clubs) (Ehrmann, 1971:218-219). Mitterand's strategy was sufficiently successful to force de Gaulle into an unexpected run-off election.

However, efforts to expand and strengthen the federation were not successful, particularly after the invasion of Czechoslovakia and the May 1968 disturbances in France provoked ideological conflicts among the ranks of those seeking grounds for unity. When de Gaulle resigned the presidency in 1969, the left fielded no fewer than five candidates.

But although the federation had dwindled away, the motives for the left to unite remained as strong as ever. In addition, several new developments provided new impetus. The French economy was beginning to falter, giving new life and attractiveness to the slogans of the left and augmenting the increasingly serious disagreements on the right (Bondy, 1973). The prospect of forming an alliance which would include the communists became more appealing and less alarming, with the emergence of "Eurocommunism." Most apparent in Italy, this new commitment to polycentrism (separate paths to socialism) suggested the possibility that the French Communist Party might also find a way to liberate itself from Soviet dominance and form credible new domestic alliances. Mitterrand, looking forward to his next bid for the presidency, provided tireless and enthusiastic leadership. In 1972, the Socialists, Communists, and Left-Radicals joined together to sign a Common Program. The new alliance differed from those in the past in that it was based on a detailed program of policies to be followed once power was won, rather than merely on a set of rules for dividing up the electoral turf

(Ehrmann, 1976:259). More than that, it achieved a significant measure of success: in the 1973 legislative elections, the left regained many of the seats it had lost in the debacle of 1968 (Goldey and Johnson, 1973; de Lacharrière, 1973); in 1974, Mitterrand came within a percentage point of winning the presidency; in 1976, the left made even more pronounced gains in municipal elections; and, by mid-1977, pollsters were freely and confidently predicting a leftist victory in the 1978 legislative elections, while analysts noted the increasing polarization in the French electorate (Campbell, 1976). Such predictions have proved premature. At present, the Communists and Socialists are once again disunited, having split apart in September of 1977 ostensibly over the question of what changes to make to update the Common Program (disagreeing in particular on the question of how many and which industries should be nationalized in the event of a leftist victory). However, both Socialists and Communists daily proclaim their willingness to reunite if only the other would take the "small steps" necessary. Furthermore, the split itself may be explained as a response to institutional change: the French electoral system was changed in 1958 to *scrutin majoritaire à deux tours,* i.e., single member constituencies in which only candidates with 12.5% or more of the first vote compete with each other (all others having been eliminated) in the second contest a week later. One effect of such a system is that the first election can become a double primary contest. Unless firm agreements are made in advance for dividing up the constituencies, candidates of different parties in each coalition will compete with each other in the hopes of being the alliance's standard-bearer in the second race. Further agreements must be made for the second race. Coalition partners must agree that they will, in fact, support the group's standard-bearer and not shift to the opposition candidate. Such an agreement is not always easily made. A moderate leftist may prefer to support a moderate rightist rather than an extreme leftist in his own coalition. In short, one effect of the electoral system is to operate contrary to the coalition-stimulating effect of the presidential system, i.e., to tempt coalition partners to split apart, at least for the first *tour,* and especially when (a) the programmatic and historical bases for alliance are fragile and unsure, and (b) the elections are for the legislature rather than for the presidency. But the fact that there *is* a second *tour* and that France has become a presidential system, eventually play their role, and some form of electoral cooperation remains probable. As Duverger (1977) commented only a few days after the rupture, "The union of the left goes on. Neither the Communists nor the Socialists can really change their strategy. In the absence of an electoral reform, both are obliged to unite at the second election, which compels them not to tear each other apart at the first."

In summary, it should be stressed that France has not become a two-party system. The right is deeply divided and all is far from well in the union of the left. Nevertheless, her parties have been pressured by institutional change to make more serious efforts at coalition politics. *Where parties pursue presidential politics in multiparty systems, they are stimulated to build coalitions with each other in their efforts to win the majority necessary to elect the president* (hypothesis 6). Furthermore, the attempt of the Gaullists to create a system in which their own power would be secure, particularly by making the presidency subject to direct election, has backfired: the opposition forces have gradually become more competent (although not yet fully expert) at building and maintaining the necessary coalition: *parties in power which have modified the system for their own electoral advantage lose power when the opposition forces are able to respond to the changes in such a way as to make them more atractive to the electorate* (hypothesis 8).

III. NIGERIA

Nigeria is a very different example of the interrelated roles of party and system development. A constitutional system bequeathed by the British in 1959 helped to stimulate the growth of political parties which are now credited by many with destroying the system and themselves and plunging the nation into civil war. The postwar period has been devoted to the quest for a constitution which will permit a return to civilian rule and the rebirth of political parties, while avoiding the disasters party politics brought to Nigeria in the past.

African nations' boundaries have been formed, in nearly every case, by the combined results of two sets of international struggle: the struggle between invading colonial forces and indigenous peoples, and the struggle between different colonial powers for the same African territory. These struggles were conducted both on the battlefield and at the negotiating tables. In both cases, their outcome depended on the levels of strength of the contesting parties, and the strength of the African contestants was never such as to ensure that the boundaries of the new colonies—which were, with minor adjustment, to become those of the new nations—would respect preexisting ethnic units or the geographic divisions they had established between themselves. As a result, African nations now include diverse people who were brought to share a common destiny against their will and have done so for a relatively short span of time. Nigeria is very much a case in point, composed as she is of over 200 different ethnic groups. Among these many and diverse peoples, three are most numerous and were dominant in Nigeria's early history: the Ibo people of the East, the Yoruba of the West, and the Hausa-Fulani of the North. (For general studies of Nigeria's pre-independence history, see Coleman, 1958; Hatch, 1970; Ostheimer, 1973). While still under British rule, each of these peoples (and regions) produced its own political party (Sklar, 1963).

In the East, the dominant party was the National Council of Nigerian Citizens (N.C.N.C.). Led by Nnamdi Azikiwe, the N.C.N.C. had its origins in early nationalist movements. Originally an umbrella organization of affiliated separate movements, the party had switched to individual memberships and become the strongest party in Nigeria at the time of independence. Its leader was widely respected for his role in hastening that independence. The N.C.N.C. adopted a moderately progressive program and worked more seriously than any of the other parties to build a following in all three regions. Its chief supporters, the Ibo people, were seen by themselves, by other Nigerians, and by the British to be among the most individualistic, aggressive, and achievement-oriented of Nigeria's peoples.

The Action Group of Western Nigeria evolved from a Yoruba mutual aid association, the Egbe Omu Oduduwa. Its organization was more hierarchical than that of the N.C.N.C., and its program was more carefully defined. The party was comitted to a mild form of socialism. Its leader, Obafemi Awolowo, was respected for his seriousness of purpose, but was less widely known and admired than Azikiwe. The Action Group was more limited to the Western

Region and to the Yoruba people than the N.C.N.C. was to its base, but it did make some efforts to become a national party.

The Northern People's Congress (N.P.C.) was a party for northerners. Led by the Sardauna of Sokoto, Sir Ahmadu Bello, the party made no effort to disguise its parochialism; quite the contrary (Bello, 1962). The Hausa-Fulani, unlike the Ibo and Yoruba peoples, are Muslims committed to highly centralized system of rule based on Islam, in which no sharp distinctions are made between the temporal and spiritual realms. This party also evolved from an ethnic association, the Jam'iyyar Mutanean Arewa (Dudley, 1968).

The distinctions among the three major ethnic groups and the political parties each maintained were heightened during the pre-independence period by the British system of ruling via "native authorities," a system in which British law was transmitted to subject peoples via their traditional rulers or, when these proved insufficiently cooperative, by British-appointed substitutes. This system meant that no uniform system of rule was adopted throughout Nigeria, and that each group, in fact, gained *greater* awareness of its distinctiveness from the others (Post and Vickers, 1973:21-25). The logical consequence of this policy, as independence approached, was to adopt a federal constitution, with many important powers delegated to the three regions. The national government was a parliamentary system, in which what powers remained would be concentrated in the legislature. However, the strength of the regions, and of the regions' separate parties, ensured that the legislature would be based on coalition politics and would be weak.

The north was Nigeria's largest region, both in land area and in population, and, as a consequence, the N.P.C. won a plurality of seats in the 1959 federal election. However, to ensure a legislative majority, one of the other parties had to be brought into the cabinet. Since the name of the game was regional politics and the parcelling out of national spoils rather than the building of a strong nation-state, the choice of a partner depended more on political bargaining than ideological sympathies. Nnamdi Azikiwe was more keen than Obafemi Awolowo to strike such bargains and helped form the coalition (winning for himself, not coincidentally, the position of Governor-General, later President, of Nigeria). Sir Ahmadu Bello of the N.P.C. took the premiership of the Northern region, and sent his second lieutenant, Sir Abubakar Tafawa Balewa, in as Prime

Minister of the new nation. In his view, well substantiated by careful reading of the constitution, the more significant role was that of leading the North (Bello, 1962:208). In sharp contrast and in what was to prove a vain effort to counter the constitutional thrust toward decentralized spoils system politics, Obafemi Awolowo of the Action Group decided it was more important to serve as leader of the opposition in the federal government, a position with only symbolic significance, than to take the premiership of the Western Region, which he left in the hands of his second-in-command, Samuel Akintola.

The new government was thus set up to pursue the struggle to maintain and increase regional powers and perquisites, and two of the three major parties quickly assumed appropriate roles accommodating the new arrangements. The failure of the third party to be accommodative produced a struggle within the party, and eventually within the entire nation, so severe in its consequences as to suggest that the hypothesis that decentralized systems lead to decentralized parties is in fact an iron rule, and that attempts to break it can lead to disaster for parties and for systems.

The only party where there was a meaningful effort on the part of some to fight the disintegrating impact of the new constitution was, as we have seen, the Action Group. But Obafemi Awolowo's certainty that the role of the Action Group should be to try to strengthen the federal government by setting up an opposition which would be both loyal and an attractive alternative to the present coalition was not shared throughout his party, particularly by the man he appointed premier of the Western Region, Samuel Akintola. Akintola saw only that the Action Group's intransigeance had disadvantaged the Yoruba people in the quest for regional spoils. The N.C.N.C.-N.P.C. coalition was an anomaly in the eyes of many. The personal and cultural conservatism of the Yorubas and the Hausa-Fulani gave these peoples—and their respective parties—more in common than could be found between easterners and northerners, particularly given the long-standing rivalry between the Ibos and all other Nigerian peoples for the choicest positions in the civil service and other jobs in the westernized sector of the Nigerian economy. Many members of the N.C.N.C. were uncomfortable in supporting the coalition; many Action Group members were uncomfortable in their exclusion from it. It was a situation which could not endure.

And it did not. Akintola soon began secret negotiations with the N.P.C. When Awolowo learned of his lieutenant's treachery, he called for his removal as Premier of the Western Region. Akintola was duly voted out of office by Awolowo loyalists, but refused to leave and, instead, petitioned the federal government to dissolve the Western House. The Action Group petitioned the Governor-General to dismiss Akintola, and this was done, but Akintola filed an action asking the High Court to declare him Premier and restrain the Governor-General from dismissing him. At this point the federal government took over the West with an emergency administration. Politicians were restricted to remote villages, but within two months the Akintola people were released while Awolowo and his supporters remained restricted. The N.P.C. was putting its power to work on behalf of those who supported it. (For a fuller description of the events of this period, see Post and Vickers, 1973:63-78.)

The tide had clearly turned against Awolowo. Akintola now formed a new party—the United Peoples Party. The Supreme Court declared that his dismissal from the premiership was invalid. A commission was set up by the federal government to inquire into the fiscal solvency of the West and found that the Action Group had been all too solvent indeed: serious accusations of graft and corruption were made, including the charge that the Action Group had used its position to build the party treasury from government funds. Furthermore, Awolowo and others (not including Akintola) were accused of treason, of setting up a tactical committee to buy arms, engaging in military training, and working toward the eventual overthrow of the government. On what was widely deemed to be very limited evidence, all were convicted and were forced—perhaps luckily so—to watch developments over the next few years of Nigeria's history from prison cells.

With Akintola's star clearly rising and their own party's fortunes likely to decline as its usefulness to the N.P.C. waned, the N.C.N.C. became as divided as the Action Group. Party realignment swiftly followed. Those N.C.N.C. followers who agreed with Akintola's pragmatism (and this included many of the western Yoruba followers of that party, the one party which had gained significant numbers of adherents outside its own region and dominant ethnic identity) now joined with him and the United Peoples Party to form a new alliance, the Nigerian National Democratic Party (N.N.D.P.).

On the other hand, N.C.N.C. loyalists were happy to welcome to their ranks the betrayed Awolowo loyalists from the old Action Group; together these two factions formed the United Progressive Grand Alliance (U.P.G.A.). Not to be outdone, the N.N.D.P. joined with the N.P.C. in the Nigerian National Alliance (N.N.A.), yet another electoral alliance (Ostheimer, 1973:135-136).

Thus at last, whatever the costs in national progress (and they were high) the constitutional and political structures of Nigeria were a fit: *decentralized political systems stimulate the development of decentralized parties.* Furthermore, the N.P.C., through its control of the federal government, had engineered the downfall of its only significant opponent, Awolowo, ensured the loyalty of most of the West by appropriately rewarding Akintola, and made itself independent of the support of unsure easterners in the N.C.N.C.

Unfortunately for its own interests, the N.P.C. did not stop there, and before long the party and its new allies had gone further. A government census, taken in 1962, showed rates of growth for the population in the north (from 16.8 million in 1952-1953 to 31 million in 1962) that were widely repudiated as impossible and patently falsified. The census was retaken in 1963, and the Northern figures dropped slightly, but not sufficiently to satisfy other Nigerians, particularly easterners (the West was apparently inflating its figures as well, although not so excessively) and particularly in view of the fact that census figures were used in the allocation of federal monies to the regions (Post and Vickers, 1973:81, 99). To make matters worse, the N.P.C. insisted that the forthcoming 1964 legislative elections would be based on these figures and then proceeded to turn a blind eye to the electoral corruption and violence which erupted in the course of the campaign. By now the manipulation of the system was becoming more and more blatant and intolerable to all Nigerians. At the last minute, the U.P.G.A. announced a boycott of the elections, which merely assured the N.N.D.P. victory.

The following year a very similar scenario was played out in Western Region elections, in which corruption, "thuggery," and outright falsification of ballots were widespread and apparent. Although Akintola's forces were declared victorious and he himself was reappointed premier, the parties in power had gone too far: *Parties in power, whose elected representatives have modified the*

*system for their own electoral advantage in a fashion to undermine
not only their own but also the system's legitimacy, will provoke
further system change designed to counteract the effects of their
actions* (hypothesis 10). The Nigerian fashion had very thoroughly
undermined the legitimacy of the leaders and of the Nigerian
political system in many Nigerians' minds, and the subsequent loss
of power was proportionately thorough: in January 1966, Prime
Minister Tafawa Balewa, Premiers Ahmadu Bello and Samuel
Akintola, and several others were killed in a coup d'etat which left
an Ibo soldier in power and all parties outlawed. A countercoup
six months later shifted power into new hands more sympathetic to
northern interests, although not overtly dominated by former
N.P.C. supporters. Large-scale battles between Ibos and Hausa-
Fulani erupted, and the failure of the military to control the situation resulted in the death of thousands of Ibos, which led in turn to
the decision of the East, newly aware of its vast oil reserves, to
secede. Civil war broke out in May 1967 and lasted until January
1970.

Now, one and a half more coups and two supreme military com-
manders later, political parties have still not been permitted to reform in Nigeria. At present writing (Summer, 1978), a Constituent
Assembly is working on a new constitution, one which will produce an entirely different political system and a new set of political
parties. A few words about this document and its implications for
parties are in order before we move on to the third and final case.

Despite the history we have briefly recounted, the new constitution will not outlaw political parties. It is clear that Nigerians
want the freedom of expression associated with a multiparty
system.[4] They do not want a single party, and especially not one
imposed by the military. They believe the base for national parties
does exist in Nigerian popular opinion, and they believe the political
system can be so structured as to encourage future politicians to
respond to that opinion (Lawson, 1976).

The attempt to create such a system is clearly visible in the new
constitution. The Constitution Drafting Committee recommended
that when Nigeria returns to civilian rule (now scheduled for October 1979) she should have a centralized presidential system of
"the American type" but with "overriding Nigerian features,"
and the Constituent Assembly has agreed. It now appears certain

Nigeria will have a directly elected president, serving a four-year term, whose powers, although limited, will nevertheless be extensive. To ensure his being the leader of all Nigerians, the president will have to win majorities in a specified number of states (the number varies according to the number of candidates involved). In short, Nigeria will have a centralized presidential system. Such a constitution would be in keeping with changes already instituted under the military regime. A military government is, of course, always a highly centralized system of rule, but in some cases the apparatus of the soliders' government is a thin veneer, easily scraped away by returning civilians. In Nigeria, this process of concentrating power at the top has extended into virtually every domain: the public service has been subjected to a massive purge of employees, state marketing boards have been abolished, the federal government finances and supervises local government bodies, the states have been subdivided into smaller and weaker units, and the central government has taken direct control of activities in education, agriculture, and road building (*West Africa,* 1976a:1130).

Once Nigeria's government is fully centralized, what kind of parties are expected to form? Clearly, Nigerians hope that the system will be conducive to the evolution of national, centralized political parties focused on presidential politics, and that the divisive battles of regional or state-based politics will not be repeated. The clauses in the draft constitution which deal specifically with political parties are patently intended to foster this development. Thus, although anyone "may form or belong to any political party, trade union or other association for the protection of his interests," membership in any party must be open to every citizen, and the party's name, emblem, or motto must have "no ethnic or religious connotations" and must not "give the appearance that the association's activities are confined to a party only of the geographical area of Nigeria." All parties must have constitutions providing for democratic elections to all offices, and membership in any party's executive committee must "reflect the federal character of Nigeria." Party programs must conform with the "fundamental objectives" of the national constitution, although parties are free to advocate changes in the constitution. No party may receive funds from abroad nor train or employ people to use coercion. All parties must register with the Electoral Commission, which may set up penalties for contravening the constitutional provisions regarding parties, and is to report to the National Assembly on party finances (*West Africa,* 1976b:1521).

Obviously, the authors of Nigeria's new constitution have considerable faith in the efficacy of constitutional engineering for producing political parties of the desired type. The faith has been shared by the present military regime which will lift the ban on political parties in advance of the return to civilian rule, because "the formation of a democratic government presupposes virile political parties." On the other hand, when elections were held to fill new local government posts, the ban on parties was enforced: candidates were not allowed to issue manifestos or organize meetings; all campaigning had to be done on a door-to-door basis by the candidate himself.[5] It has been suggested by one author (Panter-Brick, 1977) that when parties do form they are likely to be "parties of opinion," organized around the continuing debate over the new constitution once the draft has been accepted or modified by the Constituent Assembly (which began its deliberations in late 1977).

In any event, the capacity of Nigerians to maintain at least some commitment to the rights of parties to exist and contest freely for public office is impressive, given the past tendency of Nigerian party leaders to set aside national interests in pursuit of partisan and personal gain with disastrous results for the nation. An equivalent capacity to distinguish between the errors of individual leaders and the free play of partisan competition essential to democratic politics has not always been shown in the nation whose parties we will next consider: the United States.

IV. THE UNITED STATES

The United States began its history as a thoroughly decentralized political system. Indeed, the powers of nationhood were so widely distributed under the Articles of Confederation that it was soon recognized that no effective national entity had been created. We have grown so accustomed to deriding the articles that we often overlook the fact that the state of affairs they created was exactly what many of the revolutionaries had battled for. However, such a degree of freedom from the dictates of powerful government seemed excessive to those whose interests (the collection of private debts, the making of economic pacts with other nations, the redemption of i.o.u.'s issued by the revolutionary government) required the backing of a stronger public force (Beard, 1913). It was not long before this troubled elite (otherwise known as the founding fathers) was able to rally sufficient support for creating a stronger union of the states, through the work of the Constitutional Convention of 1787.

Although the new constitution created a stronger national government, and thus began a drive toward centralization of power which has been going on ever since, the revolutionary impulse toward a safely divided system of rule was still very strong. The authors of the new constitution carefully divided the powers of government between states and nation and among the three branches of government. Their awareness of the connection between institution building and political development was acutely expressed in the Tenth Federalist Paper: the new system was expected to force such a variety of political combinations for the pursuit of the various state and federal offices that national parties (factions, they called them) would prove impossible to form, and the nation would thus be kept secure from control by the representatives of any single special interest. With hindsight we may say they were trying to work out a corollary to the hypothesis that a decentralized system will stimulate decentralized parties: they hoped a *thoroughly* decentralized system would prevent parties altogether.

Of course they did not succeed. Although they repudiated the appellation, they themselves formed the first party as they organized for ratification of the constitution and the filling of the new offices with their own men. And the Federalists, as they came to be known, soon stimulated the emergence of the Anti-Federalists, the progenitor of today's Democratic Party. When the Federalists faded they were replaced, after a brief and probably misnamed "Era of Good Feeling," by the National Republicans, a schism from the Anti-Federalist group which had by now assumed the name of Democrats. The National Republicans evolved into the Whigs, who were replaced in the days preceding and during the Civil War by the Republican Party as the nation's second party (Binkley, 1965:3-119).

But although parties emerged, they remained, like the system in its early years, thoroughly decentralized. Although some argued that the system was made to work at all only by the integrating effects of national political coalitions, all agreed that such coalitions were sporadic and fragile (Schattschneider, 1942; Key, 1964; Hofstadter, 1969). The Democratic Party in Alabama bore little resemblance to its namesake in New York; South Dakota and California Republicans may have had more in common, but they operated with equal independence from each other.

At the same time, however, the nation was changing. Territorial expansion, the resolution of the issue of slavery, the growth of corporate power, and increased involvement in foreign affairs were key developments in the 19th century provoking the shift to a more centralized political system. The constitution had to be made to fit the new realities. But by now that document, preserved through the bloodshed of civil war, had achieved so great a sanctity in the American consciousness that it was itself one of the strongest symbols of centralized national power: to jettison it in the name of increasing that power would have been as counterproductive as it was politically impossible to achieve (Dahl, 1959). The answer was to proceed by constitutional amendment and changing judicial interpretation.

Although the precedent for strengthening the national government by judicial interpretation had been set in the first years of the new republic by establishing the principle of judicial review (*Marbury* v. *Madison*), the trend of judicial decision making during the first century was to increase the powers of the state governments over their citizenry rather than to increase the powers of the national government over the states. A turning point came in 1937, when the Supreme Court reluctantly agreed that President Franklin Roosevelt's New Deal legislation was a proper exercise of national power. Since then the courts have tended, although certainly not without important exceptions, to ratify increased exercise of national power, first in the realm of economics, then in that of civil rights. Furthermore, judicial interpretation has increasingly ratified the expansion of the powers of one branch of the national government, the executive.

Constitutional amendments have also played an important part in the process. The first 10 amendments—the Bill of Rights—

originally had the opposite effect of limiting the power of the national government, but many of the subsequent amendments have moved the system toward more centralized power. The 12th amendment, separating the elections for President and Vice President, strengthened the power of the presidency by virtually eliminating the possibility that his second in command would be of a different party. Amendments 13 through 15—and the 24th nearly one hundred years later—provided the grounds for increased national power in the domain of civil rights. The 16th Amendment gave Congress the power to "lay and collect taxes on incomes," perhaps the most significant expansion of national power found in any of the amendments. The shift to direct election of Senators (Amendment 17) gave those national officers the increased power of a popular base, and that base for all government officials was widened by the passage of the 19th Amendment, extending the right to vote to women, and the 26th, lowering the voting age to 18. The 21st Amendment, repealing the 18th Amendment, showed that there *were* limits to the expansion of national power: the right to the consumption of alcoholic beverages could not be safely invaded. The 22nd and 25th Amendments worked against increased centralization in more serious fashion by limiting the term of office of the President and ensuring his replacement when unfit for duty.

In sum, constitutional change, by judicial interpretation and by amendment, has been marked by ambiguity—by steps taken first in one direction and then in the other—but the net result, particularly within the second half of the nation's history, has been to extend the powers of the national government—and particularly of its chief executive—to control the lives of the citizenry of the United States.

These changes took place painfully and slowly, long after the need for increased federal power was widely felt and acknowledged. Nevertheless, the shift was made, and as the power in the nation's political system became more and more concentrated at the top, the decentralized parties became more and more anomalous.

State and local parties had battened on the very weaknesses of the federal government. The government's inability to meet the growing demands of the citizenry for social assistance had left an important lacuna which machine politics attempted to fill: jobs and welfare assistance had been provided by the parties in exchange for votes.

The system was thoroughly corrupt, but a means of survival was at least provided. However, with the extension of the civil service system and New Deal programs of welfare assistance, the parties lost this important function. Furthermore, once they no longer offered serious rewards, the disadvantages and dishonesty of the old system somehow seemed much more apparent. Reform movements mushroomed. The parties struggled to keep control over the reformers' favorite device, the presidential primary, by a variety of tactics designed to keep actual control of the nomination in the hands of the party leadership and its most loyal (and often its most affluent) supporters. (For the history of nomination procedures and attempts at reform, see Crotty, 1977:193-237, and Keech and Matthews, 1976:91-156.) But doing so was possible only so long as they could count on the partisans to rally to their choice, however excluded they, the rank and file, might feel from the selection process.

Such loyalty was less and less forthcoming. An increasingly mobile population, dependent now directly on government rather than party economic support and increasingly open to the blandishments of political campaigns conducted by well paid public relations firms, had less and less reason to offer loyalty or even much attention to the parties (Nimmo, 1970:34-68). A decentralized system had produced decentralized parties; a centralizing system left those parties stranded in 50 irrelevant fragments. Local parties no longer controlled the voters, and the traditional interest groups could not be counted on to deliver the votes of a majority of the citizens or even of their own memberships. Americans were becoming free agents, free to respond to the candidates and to the issues (Nie, Verba, and Petrocik, 1976; Miller and Levitin, 1976). Ticket splitting, independent registration and just plain nonvoting (especially in nonpresidential elections) were all increasing dramatically (Crotty, 1977; DeVries and Tarrance, 1972). The electorate focused on the man, not the party, and the man they focused on was the president, in whose hands more and more of the nation's power was concentrated. What could the parties do?

Not surprisingly, the party out of power was the first to accommodate itself to the new distribution of power. The debacle of 1968, first at the convention in Chicago and then at the polls, made clear to the Democratic party leadership that they were not only losing adherents, as Democratic registrations declined, but they were also losing the support of those who called themselves Democrats. Party supporters could no longer be secured by local machines or local interest group leadership: the party would have to reach out to its supporters the same way presidents reached out to citizens—from the top and directly to the individual. And, also like the president, the party would have to reach out to as many individuals as possible, with little concern for the increasingly superficial quality of such contacts.

In short, what was required was strong national organization, capable of creating structures which would rebuild grass-roots participation and loyalty. In 1968, the party created the McGovern Fraser Commission, and that body's "guidelines," endorsed by the National Committee, were surprisingly well followed in the selection of delegates for the 1972 convention. The results of that year's election suggested that, in its efforts to include those hitherto largely excluded from the nominating process—the blacks, the young, and women—the party had shifted the balance in the other direction, particularly angering its white labor constituency. The Mikulski Commission produced the apparently necessary compromises and modifications. Meanwhile the party adopted its first charter, and held its first mid-term convention. The charter contributed to a further strengthening of the national organization by expanding the National Committee to 225 members and setting up an Executive Committee (elected by the National Committee) to meet at least four times a year to carry out the business of the committee. The committee has, by the terms of the charter, more business to carry out: three potentially very powerful Councils have been established. The Judicial Council supervises the delegate selection process. The National Finance Council has general responsibility for the finances of the party. The National Education and Training Council sets up educational and training programs. The charter also attests to the strengthening of the central apparatus of the party by asserting that state parties are expected to "take provable positive steps to bring state laws into conformity with national party dictates" (Article Two, Democratic National Committee, 1975). Finally, the charter states that the party "may" hold a national party conference between conventions (Article Six), and one is to be held in 1978.

The mid-term convention reinforces the image of a party open to all, or at least to the delegates selected by the grass-roots membership. Currently the party is struggling with further reform issues: should the mid-term convention be devoted to a serious discussion of national issues, with votes taken and a mid-term platform devised? Are futher modifications in delegate selection processes in order? How can the party adjust to the effects of public financing of campaigns?

There is, however, a certain air of futility about these efforts. Reform may prove to be the Laetrile of party politics: it makes the patient feel better for a while, but its capacity to cure the ravaged organism is dubious indeed. To understand why this is so, it will be helpful to consider two other aspects of the relationship between system change and party change in the United States. The first has to do with what happens when the party in power abuses that power; the second with the difficulty all parties face in pursuing presidential politics.

The elections of 1968 and 1972 persuaded the Democrats of the importance of creating a stronger national party, in direct if superficial contact with the mass of its supporters. They had, however, no such effect on the victorious Republicans, particularly those who joined Richard Nixon in the offices of the executive branch. Their emphasis, like that of most parties in power, was to be less on party change than on system change. Despite the party's image as the opponent of big government, the presidency became, under Nixon, even stronger than heretofore. The president and his aides had no compunction about modifying—perverting, many would say—the practices of that branch of the government in a way to serve their own electoral advantage. Government favors were distributed to reward political contributors, and executive agencies were encouraged to exercise their sanctions in ways designed to harass, punish, and spy upon political enemies. Eventually, some of the worst abuses became known, were labelled Watergate, and forced the President and eventually his party from office. *Parties in power lose power when the party's elected representatives modify the system for their own electoral advantage in a fashion which undermines their legitimacy* (hypothesis 9).

The dismay over Watergate produced a wave of political reforms, particularly in the area of campaign financing (Crotty, 1977:139-188). Limitations were placed on campaign contributions: the names, addresses, and occupations of all those making contributions above a very minimal level were to be fully disclosed; and public financing was to be provided presidential candidates, with the stipulation that those accepting such funds were to abide as well by limitations on spending (Federal Election Commission, 1977). Although none of these changes have been made via constitutional amendment, they have been ratified by the processes of judicial review as constitutionally correct.[6] And these changes will have an impact on the parties. On the one hand, a party may now receive, contribute, and spend money more freely than may a candidate, and, in that respect, the parties' role in the electoral process has been strengthened. On the other hand, the idea of public financing has been introduced and accepted, and, in that respect, the parties' role has been weakened. The 95th Congress has filibustered to death a bill extending public financing to congressional campaigns, out of concern not for the parties but rather for maintaining their own pecuniary advantages as incumbents able to attract and spend more than their challengers. However, public sentiment in favor of such a move is strong and growing stronger. If the day comes when all campaign expenses are paid by the government, the effect in eliminating monied control of elected representatives may be entirely salubrious; the effect on the parties' capacity to hold those representatives to any party program may well be otherwise. *Parties in power, whose elected representatives have modified the system for their own electoral advantage in a fashion to undermine not only their own but also the system's legitimacy, will provoke further system change designed to counteract the effects of their actions* (hypothesis 10).

At the same time that Republican abuses of power (preceded by Democratic abuses somewhat less odious and considerably less apparent) have provoked system changes probably detrimental to party fortunes, the nation's shift to a far more centralized political system, with power ever more concentrated in the presidency, has hampered the ability of the party in power to exercise control over policymaking. President Carter proved to be a master in the art of maintaining party support without becoming dependent upon it. He campaigned as an outsider, not caught up in the discredited games of party politics, and then proceeded to anger Democratic party leadership, both in and outside of Congress, by failing to consult them regarding his policies and his appointments to the extent they desired. He let it be known that he would prefer a mid-term convention which would offer support rather than guidance to his administration. He consistently appealed directly to the people via the media and town meetings and to various interests, via public addresses, for support unmediated by party. The Democratic Party was helpless to prevent these tactics: *Where parties pursue presidential politics, they are hampered in their efforts to exercise control over appointments and policymaking by the ability of the president to turn to alternate bases of support* (hypothesis 5).

Furthermore, such tactics were successful and are likely to be so in the foreseeable future. Parties have lost control over campaigning and are, as Pomper (1977:39) points out, "little more than another private association or interest group" in the electoral process. The parties are becoming more centralized and somewhat more democratic in their internal processes at the same time that they are becoming less and less meaningful.

V. CONCLUSION

The three case studies we have explored suggest not only the plausibility of the 10 propositions offered at the outset, but suggest as well some futher explanations for the contemporary decline of political parties (Burnham, 1975; Dennis, 1975; Pomper, 1977). All three cases have two factors in common. First, all three systems have recently become more centralized, with power concentrated in the hands of the chief executive. Under such circumstances, parties have been (or will be) forced to modify their tactics. In doing so, they lose the forms of control formerly theirs, and there is little possibility they will be able to wrest an equivalent amount of power in the new system: presidents are well placed for sidestepping the demands of party. Second, in all three systems, the elected representatives of parties in power have proved unable to resist the opportunity to try to make the system more accommodative of their needs and interests, and in all three systems this effort has had a negative effect: in France, the opposition parties have been able to respond to the changes somewhat more successfully than the Gaullists; in

Nigeria, manipulation of the system led to a general collapse in which the house of government crushed the party Samsons along with everything else; in the United States, the effort to accommodate the system to Nixon's electoral needs brought the downfall of one party and a form of system change likely to worsen the lot of all parties. In sum, these three cases strongly suggest that parties will continue to decline so long as the forces making for strengthened chief executives continue and the parties conceive of no means to prevent their elected representatives from manipulating the political system in ultimately dysfunctional ways. Is such decline inevitable?

The parties, as we have said, are power-seeking accommodationists. At present, they are learning how to accommodate to presidential politics, and to expect them to do otherwise is not realistic. However, there are other forces at work within such systems which suggest some grounds for hope that in the not too distant future the nature of presidential politics—and thereby of party accommodation to presidential politics—will undergo significant change. The hope for the regeneration of parties, admittedly a slim one, can be found in the very conditions that presently are cause for despair. A review of these conditions is in order.

In contemporary centralized presidential systems, presidents monopolize power and maintain access to their electoral base in a direct and unmediated fashion. Such an arrangement encourages voters to develop awareness of the man and his policies, but only to a limited extent. It offers no guarantee that the president, once elected, will be informed about and responsible to the will of the electorate. The television screen is a one-way window. Polls may inform, but they cannot command compliance. Hopes of reelection may rest more on plans for demagogic campaigning than on pride in a record of meeting the people's wishes. Interest groups pressure the president and his aides on behalf of their own interests (sometimes very surprisingly defined by the group's leadership), and parties are becoming more and more like interest groups themselves. In short, the general citizenry are left with no means to hold their elected representatives accountable, on a day-to-day basis, to the programs on which they campaigned. Increasingly better educated populations become more and more concerned about the issues and less and less able to command that responsible attention be paid to them. The grievances of those populations vary from nation to nation, but their intensity increases as their expectations are repeatedly disappointed by the failure of those they elected to carry out campaign pledges.

However, the accumulation of those grievances represents a force which must ultimately find expression. The promise of democracy is an old one, and the failure to fulfill that promise is ever more apparent to increasingly alert and knowledgeable electorates. It seems possible that demands will be made for more accountability on the part of those elected, and that structures will be created to institutionalize that accountability. If so, then the usual relationship between system change and party change could be expected to prevail. Parties would change their own structures, perhaps involving the membership more closely in the creation of party platforms and the choice of nominees. They would endeavor to hold candidates much more accountable to party programs, during the campaign *and* during the term of office, by threatening irresponsible incumbents with loss of support. Having regained the loyalty of their membership by involving them more meaningfully in party processes, the parties would be in a better position to make good on such threats. Parties might even develop the power to ensure that public financing of campaigns would be channelled *through them,* giving them greater control over their candidates.

At present, such hopes are reasonably seen as utopian by party enthusiasts and dangerous by the far more numerous enemies of party. They may well never be fulfilled. Publics and parties may continue to acquiesce in the aggrandizement of presidential power, seduced by short-run advantages, real or imaginary, and blind to the dangers involved. But the dangers are very real indeed: "The ultimate cost of the decline of parties is the loss of popular control over public policies and the consequent inability of less privileged elements to affect their social fate" (Pomper, 1977:41). Modern democracies cannot depend exclusively on the occasional and imbalanced demands of special interest groups (including today's truncated parties) to keep government responsive to the needs and wishes of all its citizens. But perhaps "modern democracy" is itself a contradiction in terms. If so, let us say so and be done with it. If not, there is much work to be done.

NOTES

1. President Carter's proposal to make registration a matter easily accomplished at the polls, facilitating thereby greater turnout by those most likely to vote Democratic, is only the latest case in point—which is not to say the idea lacks merit.
2. Interview with Nicolas Pilliet, U.D.R. headquarters, August 27, 1974.
3. The party has undergone several name changes, most recently to *Rassemblement pour la République* (R.P.R.).
4. Statements regarding "what Nigerians want" are based on interviews conducted by the author in Nigeria in 1974 and reported in Lawson, 1974.
5. It was interesting to note, however, that many former politicians won election to these posts, considered by many to be the first jumping-off spot for the return to civilian politics *(West Africa,* 1977:53). For an interesting discussion of the difficulties of linking local officials to public opinion without benefit of party, see Jibo (1976).
6. The changes discussed here have been ratified by Buckley versus Valeo, 1975. A further change—to limit spending in campaigns not involving public financing—was ruled unconstitutional by the same court decision.

REFERENCES

ACHEBE, C. (1967). A Man of the People. New York: Doubleday.
AMBLER, J.C. (1968). "The Democratic Union for the Republic: To survive de Gaulle." Rice University Studies, Papers in Political Science, 54(summer):1-51.
ARNOLD, G. (1977). Modern Nigeria. London: Longman.
AVRIL, P. (1969). Politics in France. Baltimore: Penguin.
AWOLOWO, O. (1960). The autobiography of Chief Obafemi Awolowo. London: Cambridge University Press.
BEARD, C. (1913). An economic interpretation of the constitution of the United States. New York: Free Press.
BELLO, A. (1962). My life. London: Cambridge University Press.
BERGER, S. (1974). The French political system (3rd ed.). New York: Random House.
BINKLEY, W. (1965). American political parties: Their natural history (4th ed.). New York: Knopf.
BLONDEL, J. (1974). The government of France (4th ed.). New York: Thomas Y. Crowell.
BLONDEL, J., and GODFREY, D. (1968). The government of France. New York: Thomas Y. Crowell.
BONDY, F. (1973). "New society, old politics." Encounter, 40(5):53-54.
BURNHAM, W.D. (1975). "American politics in the 1970's: Beyond party?" Pp. 238-277 in L. Maisel and P. Sacks (eds.), The future of political parties. Beverly Hills, Calif.: Sage.
CAMPBELL, B. (1976). "On the prospects of polarization in the French electorate." Comparative Politics, 8(2):272-290.
COLEMAN, J. (1958). Nigeria, background to nationalism. Berkeley: University of California Press.
Constitution Drafting Committee (1976). Report of the Constitution Drafting Committee (vols. 1 and 2). Lagos: Author.
CRIDDLE, B. (1974). "The French presidential election." World Today, 30(6):231-238.

CROTTY, W. (1977). Political reform and the American experiment. New York: Thomas Y. Crowell.

DAHL, R. (1959). Political oppositions in western democracies. New Haven, Conn.: Yale University Press.

De GAULLE, C. (1959). The complete war memoirs. New York: Simon and Schuster.

De LACHARRIERE, R. (1973). "Gaullism Mark II: The elections of 1973." Government and Opposition, 8(3):280-289.

Democratic National Committee (1975). Charter of the Democratic Party of the United States. Washington, D.C.: Author.

DENNIS, J. (1975). "Trends in public support for the American party system." British Journal of Political Science, 5(April):187-230.

De VRIES, W., and TARRANCE, V.L. (1972). The ticket-splitter: A new force in American politics. Michigan: William B. Eerdmans.

DUDLEY, B.J. (1968). Parties and politics in Northern Nigeria. London: Frank Cass.

DUVERGER, M. (1951) . Les partis politiques. Paris: Librairie Armand Colin.

——— (1977). "L'union sans programme commun," Le Monde, September 29, p. 1.

EHRMANN, H. (1971). Politics in France (2nd ed.). Boston, Little, Brown.

——— (1976). Politics in France (3rd ed.). Boston: Little, Brown.

Federal Election Commission (1977). Campaign guide: The 1976 amendments. Washington, D.C.: Author.

HAMILTON, A., MADISON, J., and JAY, J. (1961). The Federalist papers. New York: Mentor Books.

HATCH, J. (1970). Nigeria, the seeds of disaster. Chicago: Henry Regnery.

HAYWARD, J., and WRIGHT, V. (1974). "Les deux France and the French presidential election of May 1974." Parliamentary Affairs, 27(3):208-236.

HILL, F. (forthcoming). "People, parties, politics: A linkage perspective on Africa party-states." In K. Lawson (ed.), Political parties and linkage: A comparative perspective. New Haven, Conn.: Yale University Press.

HOFSTADTER, R. (1969). The idea of a party system. The rise of legitimate opposition in the United States, 1780-1840. Berkeley: University of California Press.

HUNTINGTON, S. (1971). Political order in changing societies. New Haven, Conn.: Yale University Press.

GOLDEY, D.B., and JOHNSON, R.W. (1973). "The French general elections of March, 1973." Political Studies, 21(September):321-342.

JIBO, M. (1976). "Elections without politics." West Africa (3103): 1933.

KEECH, W., and MATTHEWS, D. (1976). The party's choice. Washington: Brookings Institution.

KEY, V.O., Jr. (1964). Politics, parties and pressure groups (5th ed.). New York: Thomas Y. Crowell.

LaPALOMBARA, J., and WEINER, M. (1966). Political parties and political development. Princeton, N.J.: Princeton University Press.

LAWSON, K. (1974). "Nigeria's future constitution: Academic hopes vs. military intentions." Journal of African Studies, 3(1):1-33.

——— (1976). The comparative study of political parties. New York: St. Martin's Press.

MIKULSKI, B., HATCHER, R., and SEITH, A. (1973). Democrats all: A report of the Commission on Delegate Selection and Party Structure. Washington, D.C.: Democratic National Committee.

MILLER, W., and LEVITIN, T. (1976). Leadership and change: The new politics and the American electorate. Cambridge: Winthrop.

NIE, N., VERBA, S. and PETROCIK, J. (1976). The changing American voter. Cambridge: Harvard University Press.

NIMMO, D. (1970). The political persuaders: The techniques of modern election campaigns. New Jersey: Spectrum.

OSTHEIMER, J.M. (1973). Nigerian politics. New York: Harper and Row.

PANTER-BRICK, K. (1977). "Nigeria's great debate." West Africa, (3108):190-191.

POMPER, G.M. (1976). The election of 1976. New York: David McKay.

——— (1977). "The decline of the party in American elections." Political Science Quarterly, 92 (1):21-41.

POST, K.W.J., and VICKERS, M. (1973). Structure and conflict in Nigeria 1960-65. London: Heinemann.

RANNEY, A. (1975). Curing the mischiefs of faction: Party reform in America. Berkeley: University of California Press.

ROSE, R. (1969). "The variability of party government: A theoretical and empirical critique." Political Studies, 17(December):413-443.

SARTORI, G. (1976). Parties and party systems (Vol. I). London: Cambridge University Press.

SCHATTSCHNEIDER, E. (1942). Party government. New York: Holt, Rinehart and Winston.

SKLAR, R. (1963). Nigerian political parties. Princeton, N.J.: Princeton University Press.

THOMSON, D. (1969). Democracy in France since 1870 (5th ed.). London: Oxford University Press.

West Africa (1976a). August 9, p. 1130.

——— (1976b). October 18, p. 1518.

——— (1977). January 10, p. 53.

WILSON, F. (1973). "Gaullism without de Gaulle." Western Political Quarterly, (September):485-506.

Chapter 6

PARTISAN CHANGE IN THE SOUTH, 1952-1976

RAYMOND WOLFINGER
ROBERT B. ARSENEAU

The Solid South is at least a generation in the past, but political scientists still do not agree about what has happened, and why. What are Republican prospects? Is the Republican party gaining adherents, or is it just that the Democrats are losing them? What sorts of people are contributing to the change? What issues lay behind the loss of the old Democratic monopoly?

Our attempt to answer these questions begins with a detailed examination of the circumstances in which Republican candidates, primarily for the House of Representatives, have been most successful since the 1950s. We then explore alternative ways to measure the changes in partisan identity that have occurred in this period. After this extended prologue we approach the topics where most other analyses have begun: the kinds of people responsible for the shift and the effect of issues. Unlike other contemporary

AUTHORS' NOTE: An earlier version of this article was delivered at the 1974 Annual Meeting of the American Political Science Association. We are grateful to James L. Sundquist for his helpful comments on that paper. Our research was supported by grants from the Academic Senate Committee on Research and by funds made available by the Department of Political Science of the University of California, Berkeley.

studies, we have been able to make use of the recently released survey data on the 1976 election. This advantage is partly responsible for many of our different conclusions.

I. MEASURES OF PARTISAN CHANGE

The 1944 election was the last time a Democratic presidential candidate could take the South for granted. President Roosevelt easily carried every southern state and held Governor Dewey to just a quarter of the region's popular vote. In 1948 Dewey improved his performance slightly, particularly in urban areas. The main southern problem for the Democrats that year was the States' Rights Democratic candidacy of J. Strom Thurmond. Truman lost four states to the Dixiecrats and failed to win as much as two-thirds of the popular vote in any southern state. Eisenhower carried four states and received fully 46% of the southern popular vote, just nine percentage points below his nationwide total. He did a bit better in 1956. Nixon's share of the southern vote was almost as high, only 3.5% below his nationwide percentage. In 1964 Goldwater carried five deep southern states, four of which had not voted Republican since Reconstruction, and did substantially better in the South than in the country as a whole. Humphrey won only Texas, with the rest of the South divided between Nixon and Wallace. In 1972 Nixon completed the Republican surge by winning every state and capturing 70% of the region's popular vote, nine percentage points above his national average. The Democrats recovered somewhat in 1976, but the results were a far cry from the old days of the Solid South. Jimmy Carter lost Virginia and won more than 57% of the vote in only two southern states.

Southern presidential voting is summarized in Figure 1, which shows the Republican share of the popular vote in the South and in the country as a whole from 1948 through 1976. In 1964 and in 1972 the Republicans did better in the South than nationwide. In 1976, confronted with a candidate from the deep South, they still received 45% of the region's popular vote.

This growth in Republican presidential votes is the most apparent and commonly cited evidence that the two-party system

Percentage of the
total popular vote
won by Republican
presidential candidate

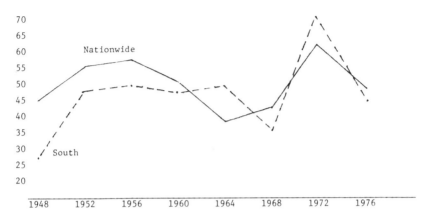

SOURCES: *Guide to U.S. Elections.* Washington: Congressional Quarterly Inc. 1975. *Statistical Abstract of the U.S.* 1976, 97th ed. Washington: Bureau of the Census.

Figure 1: REPUBLICAN PERCENTAGE OF THE PRESIDENTIAL VOTE NATIONWIDE AND IN THE SOUTH, 1948-1976

has come to the South, at least in national elections. There are, however, drawbacks to using voting returns as the dependent variable. Short-term forces strongly affected southern voting patterns, producing big fluctuations from one election to the next (Phillips, 1970:187-285; Strong, 1963; Sundquist, 1973, chap. 12). Thurmond ran best in areas with large black populations, who could not vote in those days. Eisenhower, on the other hand, was popular in the more modern urban areas where the Dixiecrats had been less successful. No state that he carried in 1952 had given Thurmond as much as a sixth of its vote. The same was true in 1956, except for Louisiana. But Eisenhower's vote fluctuated enormously from 1952 to 1956 in many counties with black majorities whose white voters, presumably attuned primarily to the race issue, were horrified by the 1954 school desegregation decision. Nixon generally ran well where Eisenhower had, and also reaped the benefit of another short term factor—disproportionate southern Protestant alarm at Kennedy's Catholicism. Goldwater's appeal, on the other hand, was strongest in the black belt where Thurmond had done best; he lost the states that Eisenhower and Nixon carried. The 1968 election provided two alternatives to the Democratic candidate. Nixon was the choice of the metropolitan South, while Wallace had special appeal to the black-belt counties that had been Thurmond and Goldwater strongholds.

Some observers felt that Republican gains from 1948 through 1964 reflected little more than a succession of short-term forces that had no lasting significance for partisan realignment: Eisenhower's extraordinary popularity, Kennedy's religion, and Goldwater's southern strategy. The most influential of these skeptics were the students of voting behavior associated with the University of Michigan's Center for Political Studies (Converse, 1966; Converse et al., 1965). The 1972 and 1976 elections leave little doubt that the two-party South is here to stay.

A second drawback to presidential voting as a measure of southern realignment is the persistence of red herrings that are possible sources of distraction both to voters and to political scientists. For example, Thurmond was on the ballot as the official Democratic candidate in four states—the only states he carried. (Truman was not even on the ballot in Alabama, and citizens there who wanted to vote for him had to write in his name.) Elsewhere the Dixiecrats had to run as third-party candidates, and they fared rather badly. Thus the election presented varying and confusing stimuli, since it seems reasonable to expect that many of Thurmond's southern votes were affected by the party label under which he ran.

In 1956 there were States' Rights electors on the ballot in many states. Motivated by doubts about Eisenhower's and Stevenson's commitment to total segregation, these electors received almost as many votes as Eisenhower in Mississippi and somewhat more than he did in South Carolina. They probably cost him enough votes in Tennessee to keep him from winning the state, as he had in 1952.

Similarly, Wallace's candidacy in 1968, which earned him more than 30% of all votes in the South, muddied the water for analysts trying to discern long-term partisan trends.

During the first part of the postwar era, evidence of Republican strength in the South did not extend beyond presidential elections.[1] Evidently this state of affairs was not wholly uncongenial to many Republican politicians. Writing more than 20 years ago, Alexander Heard (1952:97) observed that

the most signal characteristic of the [Republican] party's southern "leadership" has been a lack of interest in winning elections. . . . Republican officials in the South by and large have not wanted to build a party worthy of the name. They have been big fish in little ponds and they have liked it. . . . Republican officials have not sought to disrupt their closed corporation by electing candidates.

Part of this reluctance reflected the understandable desire of "post office Republicans" to minimize the number of people with whom they had to share federal patronage. Doubtless other reasons were simple discouragement and the traditional role of the Democratic party as the sole channel for ambitious candidates, activists, and campaign contributors. During the 1950s, when Eisenhower made such deep inroads on Democratic votes in the South, Republicans held only 7 of 106 southern House seats and no Senate seats. During the 1952, 1954 and 1956 elections they contested only half of the 22 southern Senate races and about a third of the House seats.

In the next decade, the realignment began to affect congressional elections. From 1961 through 1972 Republicans won 7 of the 22 southern Senate seats. In the same period, their strength in the House grew from 7 to 34. The Democratic tide of the mid-1970s cost southern Republicans two senators and seven representatives by 1976.

It was not until 1962 that Republicans contested as many as half the southern House seats, and they still concede almost a third of the districts to Democrats, as Table 1 shows. This failure to enter candidates has cost the Republicans congressional seats. In 1964 the Mississippi Republican "candidate selection committee" decided not to run congressional candidates for fear of offending conservative Democrats and thus jeopardizing Goldwater's chances (Ripon Society, n.d.:80). One Republican defied his party's leaders and was carried into the House on the coattails of Gold-

Table 1. CONTESTED, UNCONTESTED, AND OPEN SOUTHERN HOUSE
SEATS, 1954-1976

Year	Uncontested Seats Won by		Contested Seats[a] Won by		Percent of[b] Open Seats Won by	Total
	Democrats	Republicans	Democrats	Republicans	Republicans	Seats
1954	68	--	31	7	10	106
1956	64	1	35	6	--	106
1958	83	--	16	7	--	106
1960	64	2	35	5	14	106
1962	49	--	46	11	23	106
1964	33	--	57	16	33	106
1966	46	1	37	22	33	106
1968	38	4	42	22	33	106
1970	42	1	37	26	60	106
1972	35	3	39	31	41	108
1974	37	--	44	27	33	108
1976	28	4	53	23	9	108

a. Seats contested by an independent or third-party candidate were included in the uncontested category, as were a few elections in which the Republican candidate won less than 200 votes.
b. Except for 1976, data in this column are from Hutcheson, 1975.

water's 87% of the vote. If others had followed suit, the rest of the Mississippi congressional delegation would surely have been in serious trouble.

Uncontested House districts often have considerable Republican potential and therefore one should be wary about concluding that the absence of opposition reflects negligible Republican strength. The recent history of the Fifth Mississippi District illustrates the extraordinary Republican potential of uncontested seats and also shows how strongly incumbency can muffle underlying popular trends. The district was represented for 40 years by William M. Colmer, an ultraconservative Democrat, who generally was challenged neither by primary contenders nor Republicans. When Colmer announced his retirement in 1972, his young administrative assistant switched parties and was easily elected as a Republican. In 1974 and 1976, he turned back Democratic challengers by more than two-to-one ratios and now seems as safe as Colmer ever was.

The inertial power of incumbency has been established conclusively by Hutcheson's (1975) analysis of the Democrats' ability to hold on to their southern House seats. Examining separately the Democratic seats contested by their incumbents and those without an incumbent, Hutcheson found that southern Democratic congressmen were almost invulnerable to Republican challenges. Their worst year was in 1966, when 5 of 76 were unseated. Otherwise, they have had an almost perfect survival rate. Open seats were another story, however. Most Republican gains in the House were achieved in contests without an incumbent. As Table 1 shows, Republicans did fairly well in such elections, winning at least a third of all open southern seats in every election from 1964 through 1974.

Thus, Republican gains in southern congressional elections, although substantial, fall short of the party's underlying popular support for two reasons: the failure to contest all Democratic seats and the importance of incumbency as a factor in individual voting decisions (Nelson, 1978). For the same reasons, researchers would be imprudent to rely on voting choice in House elections as an index of party realignment. Indeed, the large number of uncontested elections reduces to a perilous level the number of survey respondents available for analysis.

Accordingly, we will use party identification as our measure of party realignment, thus conforming to the practice of other recent students of partisan change in the South (Beck, 1977; B. Campbell, 1977a, 1977b; Gatlin, 1975; Sundquist 1973).[2] Our data are from the national election studies conducted by the Michigan Center for Political Studies (formerly Survey Research Center) in 1952 and then biennially from 1956 through 1976— 12 in all. We define the South as the 11 former Confederate states, and the North as the rest of the country.[3]

Survey research has certain disadvantages for studying southern electoral patterns. It does not provide enough cases to differentiate various important subregions: the black belt, metropolitan areas, and the "upcountry," not to mention such strategic groups as Texas Chicanos, Louisiana Cajuns, South Florida Jews, Appalachian hillbillies, and so on. As the more intricate aggregate data analyses demonstrate (Phillips, 1970), all these varieties of southern voters often march to different drummers. In the old days, when one could safely assume that few southern blacks voted, aggregate data analysis had a lot to recommend it. But by the 1970s southern blacks were voting fully as much as whites of similar education (Wolfinger and Rosenstone, 1977).

This development makes aggregate data analysis considerably more risky. Survey research provides a solution to this problem and also lets the analyst take into account northern migrants, an increasingly important feature of the southern political scene. While there are not enough cases to permit differentiation among the migrants (senior citizens in Florida, junior executives in Atlanta and Dallas, space technicians on the Gulf Coast, and so on), we can at least remove them in order to analyze the native Southerners.

One often hears the argument that "southern Democrats are different" and, therefore, party identification is a misleading variable for studying that part of the country. This viewpoint has several facets, some of which are more compelling than others. From a strictly technical frame of reference, there is no doubt than when everyone belongs to the same party, the absence of any variance robs the concept of meaning. But as variance develops, with increasing Republican affiliation, one can at least expect to find meaning in the concept of party identification.

A more substantive objection is that many southern Democrats are loyal essentially to their "state party" and distinguish between this entity and a national Democratic party toward which many have distinctly cool feelings. Converse has effectively disposed of this argument, demonstrating that party identification does not have one meaning for Southerners and another for other Americans (Converse, 1966:216-219).

We might also consider whether party differences are meaningful among southern politicians. The conservative sympathies of many southern Democratic congressmen are a well-known feature of American politics, forming the basis for the alliance with Republican legislators that is generally called the "conservative coalition" (Manley, 1973). There is no doubt that as a group the southern Democrats on Capitol Hill are considerably to the right of their northern colleagues, and some are fully as reactionary as the most right-wing Republicans. This is not, however, tantamount to saying that party makes no difference among southern congressmen. In fact, southern Democrats are considerably more liberal than southern Republicans. One way to show this is with the ratings of congressional votes by the Committee on Political Education (COPE) of the AFL-CIO. In COPE bookkeeping, 100 is a perfect score and zero represents complete disagreement with the labor movement. In 1973, the 34 southern Republican representatives had a mean COPE score of 11, compared to a mean of 52 for the 74 southern Democrats. The corresponding scores for southern senators were 23 for the Republicans and 47 for the Democrats (C.Q. Weekly Report, 1974).

Finally, we should consider the contemporary refrain that party identification has lost its meaning for most American voters. If this is true, or true for the South, then paying much attention to shifting party identification is little more than studying the irrelevant. The short answer on this point is that the refrain is wrong; party identification remains an important determinant of voting in the South. It is easier to elaborate this assertion in the course of addressing a related controversial issue: is the change in the South essentially a *realignment,* in which many Southerners are becoming Republicans rather than Democrats, or a *dealignment,* in which the alternative to Democratic affiliation is lack of identification with either party? It is to this question that we now turn.

II. REALIGNMENT OR DEALIGNMENT?

One preliminary step is consideration of blacks. Their exodus from the South continued during almost all the period we are studying. While they were becoming a smaller fraction of the southern population, their share of the electorate increased dramatically, a result of heightened political consciousness and the removal by federal legislation of impediments to registration and voting. Table 2 shows that blacks, only 6% of the southern electorate in 1952, accounted for nearly a fifth of those going to the polls 24 years later.

Blacks have not shared in the region's trend toward Republicanism; indeed, they have moved in the opposite direction. During the 1950s, nearly a third of black Southerners professed to be apolitical when asked about their party identification, about a fifth were Republicans, and less than half claimed Democratic allegiance. By the 1970s, black disengagement had virtually disappeared, and only vestiges of Republican affiliation remained.

Table 2. CHARACTERISTICS OF THE SOUTHERN ELECTORATE, 1952 and 1976

	1952		1976	
	Presidential Voters	Sample[a]	Presidential Voters	Sample[a]
Native whites[b]	87%	70%	56%	57%
Migrant whites[c]	7	5	25	22
Blacks	6	25	19	21
	100%	100%	100%	100%

a. Excludes respondents for whom data are missing about either turnout in the presidential election or where they grew up.
b. People who grew up in the South.
c. People who grew up outside the South.

More than two-thirds of all southern blacks called themselves Democrats. For obvious reasons, our analysis henceforth will concentrate on whites.

Table 3 depicts the party identification of white Southerners in every presidential election year from 1952 through 1976. The most striking and unambiguous trend is the pronounced decline in Democratic identification. This is most noticeable in the case of strong Democrats, who fell from 38% of the group in 1952 to 16% in 1976. Weak Democrats went from 40% to 30%. All told, the explicitly Democratic share—78% in 1952—dropped to 46% in the latter year.

At first glance, Republicans seem to have picked up virtually none of the Democratic losses. Strong and weak Republicans amounted to 22% as long ago as 1960, and had not done better than that as late as 1976. Most writers on southern political change have drawn attention to this finding, generally coming to conclusions similar to Sundquist (1973:347): "most of the new GOP voters in the South still have not crossed the realignment threshold. As noted, in their own eyes they are only 'independents,' not yet 'Republicans'" (Beck, 1977; Gatlin, 1975:43; Ladd and Hadley, 1975:144).

This interpretation is based on the assumption that everyone who initially identifies himself as an Independent should be classified that way, thus ignoring responses to the follow-up question which asks such people whether they are closer to one or the other

Table 3. PARTY IDENTIFICATION OF WHITE SOUTHERNERS, 1952-1976

	Strong Dems.	Weak Dems.	Indep. Dems.	Pure Indeps.	Indep. Repubs.	Weak Repubs.	Strong Repubs.
	(%)	(%)	(%)	(%)	(%)	(%)	(%)
1952	38	40	7	2	3	7	4
1956	33	36	4	6	7	10	6
1960	25	35	4	12	3	10	12
1964	36	30	6	8	6	7	8
1968	20	30	11	14	12	8	5
1972	13	33	9	15	10	11	8
1976	16	30	9	16	9	14	8

party (see Note 2). This has been the orthodox way to analyze data on party identification. It has been challenged recently by a paper (Keith et al., 1977) showing that self-professed Independents, who admit being closer to a party and whom we will call "Independent Democrats" and "Independent Republicans," are different in almost every respect from those Independents denying such partisan leanings, whom we will call "pure Independents." Most important, the partisan Independents are as likely to vote for the presidential candidate of the party toward which they lean as the weak partisans of that party. Independent Democrats are as likely to vote for Democratic presidential candidates as are weak Democrats, and likewise for Republicans. In short, partisan Independents are really closet Democrats and Republicans, not people without attachments to a party.

These findings by Keith et al. were for white Northerners, but they are almost equally applicable to white Southerners, as Table 4 shows. For present purposes, the most interesting figures are those on the presidential choices of southern Independent Republicans. Since 1952, they have equalled weak Republicans in their loyalty to Republican presidential candidates. Their mean level of support has been 90%, compared to 90% for weak Republicans and 98% for the strong Republicans. This group, accounting in recent elections for about a tenth of all white Southerners, clearly has not adopted the "stance of neutrality toward the two-party system" that Beck (1977:484) ascribes to southern Independents.

Since southern Independent Republicans are so strongly Republican in their voting choices, we will include them with the weak and strong Republicans when talking about partisan change in the South. Using this definition in analyzing Table 3 produces quite different conclusions about trends in Republican affiliation. Counting all three kinds of identifiers, we see that in 1952 just 14% of all white Southerners could be considered Republicans. This proportion jumped to 23% in 1956 and, with one exception, continued to grow, reaching 31% in 1976. The only exception was in 1964, a very bad year for Republicans everywhere, when the party's share fell to 21%.

Another way to look at the issue of realignment or dealignment is to see where Republican votes come from in the South. To what extent does electoral support for Republican candidates come from Republicans, and how has this pattern changed over time? Table 5 answers these questions, displaying the proportions of the vote received by each Republican presidential candidate that have come from each of the seven categories of white southern party identifiers. In 1952, only 27% of the southern Republican presidential vote came from Republicans. This rose to 61% in 1976. The increase was steady over the seven elections except for 1972, when Democratic defections to Nixon—high everywhere—were highest in the South. At the beginning of this period, Eisenhower's strong showing in the South was based principally on his ability to attract Democrats, who comprised fully 70% of his total support. This has become increasingly less the case since 1952. Although Democratic defectors still make up an important part of the Republican electoral coalition, they no longer are its major component. Pure Independents are a relatively minor part of that coalition. If we are to explain the Republican party's growing strength in the South, we must focus our attention on those people who account for a progressively larger majority in that coalition: whites who identify with the Republican party or admit that they lean toward it.

We raised earlier the question of whether party identification is still a meaningful factor in explaining southern voting behavior. One way to examine this point is by comparing rates of defection, i.e., votes by party identifiers for candidates of the other party, among northern and southern voters. In each of the seven categories

Table 4. WHITE SOUTHERN VOTE FOR REPUBLICAN PRESIDENTIAL
CANDIDATES, BY PARTY IDENTIFICATION, 1952-1976

	Strong Dems. (%)	Weak Dems. (%)	Indep. Dems. (%)	Pure Indeps. (%)	Indep. Repubs. (%)	Weak Repubs. (%)	Strong Repubs. (%)
1952	23	55	75	100	80	100	100
1956	17	43	50	82	100	95	100
1960	14	47	11	68	100	96	89
1964	13	40	67	43	92	85	100
1968	8	24	33	64	81	85	100
1972	47	80	82	77	96	90	100
1976	6	40	32	55	81	79	100
MEAN	18	47	50	70	90	90	98

Table 5. SOURCES OF REPUBLICAN PRESIDENTIAL VOTES AMONG WHITE
SOUTHERNERS, 1952-1976[a]

	Strong Dems. (%)	Weak Dems. (%)	Indep. Dems. (%)	Pure Indeps. (%)	Indep. Repubs. (%)	Weak Repubs. (%)	Strong Repubs. (%)
1952	20	39	11	4	5	11	11
1956	13	31	5	9	8	19	14
1960	9	35	1	11	4	17	23
1964	14	23	5	4	15	15	23
1968	4	17	8	18	27	14	14
1972	9	34	8	9	11	15	14
1976	2	21	4	12	16	23	22

a. The entry in each cell designates the proportion of the total Republican presidential vote
cast by the indicated category of party identification.

of party identification, Southerners are less likely to vote for the
Democratic presidential candidate.[4] With rare and trivial exceptions, probably due to sampling error, this has been true in
every election since 1952. In other words, southern Democrats are
less loyal and southern Republicans are more loyal than their
northern counterparts. Party identification is related to southern
voting choice, but the scale is tilted toward the Republicans.

It appears that party identification is becoming *more* important in southern elections. With the exception of 1972, those Southerners who remain Democrats are less and less prone to defect. Together with the consistently very strong party loyalty of southern Republicans and their increasing importance to Republican candidates, these findings lead us to two conclusions: (1) party identification is more important than ever in southern voting decisions; and (2) Republicans are the crucial group to study if we are to understand southern partisan change.

III. MIGRANTS AND NATIVES

As most writers have observed, partisan change in the South can result from three processes: (1) *conversion*—change from Democratic to Republican identification by people already in the electorate; (2) *generational replacement*—arrival at voting age of young people with new political perspectives, accompanied by the death of oldsters with earlier loyalties; and (3) *migration*—changes in the population through movement to and from the North. One aspect of population movement—the black exodus to the North—need not concern us further. Its contribution to the weakening of the Democratic party is obvious and requires no further exploration.[5]

The same is not true of the other side of the ledger. In the 1960s, about 400,000 more whites moved into the South from the rest of the country than blacks who went in the opposite direction (Song, 1974:94). The northern influx continued in the early and middle 1970s. As Table 2 shows, in 24 years white migrants increased from 5% to 22% of the South's population. Compared to native white Southerners, the migrants are considerably younger, better educated, better off, and concentrated in urban areas. As we would expect from these demographic differences, the migrants vote at a higher rate than the natives. They are, therefore, somewhat more important politically than their share of the population would suggest. In 1976 a quarter of southern voters, and nearly a third of all white voters, grew up in the North.

The migrants are considerably more liberal on racial issues. This pattern, observed consistently on a number of questions, is illustrated by Table 6, which depicts the responses of migrants and native Southerners to the question, "Are you in favor of desegregation, strict segregation, or something in between?" In 1964, when most natives favored "strict segregation," this position was advocated by less than a quarter of the migrants. Both groups had moved toward more tolerant positions by 1976, although the greater shift by the natives still had not closed the gap with the migrants. Differences between the two groups were by no means explained wholly by the migrants' greater education.

As all students of this subject have noted, the migrants have very different political affiliations than the natives. For the past generation they have been one of the few substantial population groups in which Republicans outnumber Democrats. In 1976, fully 43% of the migrants were Republicans, compared to 39% who identified themselves as Democrats or Independents "closer to" the Democratic party. They include slightly more pure Independents than the natives, 18% as opposed to 15%.

It might be thought that we have discovered the principal cause of the Republican trend in the South: an influx of prosperous Northerners. This is the position expressed in the past by the Michigan researchers. In his most recent discussion of southern realignment, based on data through the 1968 election, Converse (1972:313-314) reported that about 80% of the changes in party identification among southern whites were due to migrants from the North. More recent studies, based on data through 1972, have come to opposite conclusions (Beck, 1977; Campbell, 1977a, 1977b).

This question cannot easily be resolved, and even the most rigorous treatment must be severely timebound. Within this restriction, however, we can provide a more satisfactory and contemporary answer than those cited above. Adequate analysis of this topic requires recognition that: (1) the migrants' share of the southern population continues to increase; (2) they comprise a larger share of the voters because of their higher turnout; (3) Republicans, whether migrant or native, vote more than Democrats and therefore are a disproportionate share of voters; and (4) southern Independent Republicans should be classified as Republicans rather than put in an inclusive category called, misleadingly, "Independent."

Table 6. SUPPORT FOR SEGREGATION BY WHITE SOUTHERN NATIVES AND MIGRANTS, 1964 and 1976

"Are you in favor of desegragation, strict segregation, or something in between?	1964			1976		
	Natives	Migrants	All Whites	Natives	Migrants	All Whites
Desegregation	5%	23%	9%	21%	33%	25%
In between	36	53	40	56	56	56
Segregation	59	23	52	22	11	19
	100%	99%	101%	99%	100%	100%
N	223	60	283	381	152	533

Table 7. THE COMPOSITION OF WHITE SOUTHERN VOTERS BY PARTY AND MIGRATION STATUS, 1952, 1972 and 1976 [a]

	1952			
	Democrats	Pure Independents	Republicans	All Voters
	(%)	(%)	(%)	(%)
Migrants	6	--	2	8
Natives	79	2	12	93
	85	2	14	101
N	139	3	23	165
	1972			
Migrants	9	2	13	24
Natives	49	7	19	75
	58	9	32	99
N	170	28	96	294
	1976			
Migrants	11	4	16	31
Natives	43	8	19	70
	54	12	35	101
N	162	37	107	306

a. The entry in each cell is the proportion of all white southern voters in that year composed of the indicated category.

We have approached this problem differently than other scholars dealing with this subject. Looking only at whites who voted in presidential elections, we have ascertained what proportions of this population were comprised of migrant and native Republicans, pure Independents, and Democrats in 1952, 1972, and 1976. These tabulations are displayed in Table 7. It shows that Republicans— just 14% of white voters in 1952—accounted for 32% 20 years later and 35% in 1976. A mere 2% of all white voters at the beginning of the period, Republican migrants had grown to a 16% share in 1976. The total Republican proportion of voters increased 21 percentage points from 1952 to 1976. The migrants accounted for 14 percentage points or more than half the total increase in Republican voting strength in the South. This gain did not stop in 1972, but continued through 1976, in contrast to Beck's (1977:481, 495) predictions.

In the past 40 years, the South exceeded the rest of the country in rate of economic growth. The historic regional gap in almost every index of prosperity has been closing for much of this period. The unemployment and business stagnation that afflicted most of the country during the 1970s had least impact on the South. Indeed, much of the South continued to enjoy a business boom. It seems reasonable to expect, then, that transplanted Northerners will comprise more and more of the southern population. If these newcomers are as Republican as the people whose footsteps they are following, the ranks of southern Republicans will continue to swell.

IV. GENERATIONS OF NATIVE SOUTHERNERS

The migrants are one source of southern realignment, but they are by no means the only one. Republican affiliation among the natives has grown, lagging a few percentage points behind the figures for all whites. If we were to remove the migrants from the tabulation of party identification presented in Table 3, the table would look much as it does now, but at a slightly lower level of Republican identification. In 1952, 13% of the natives were Republicans, compared to 14% of all whites. As the figure for the latter increased, that for the natives followed at a discount of a few percentage points. By 1976, 25% of natives were Republicans, compared to 31% of all whites. In other words, identifying the importance of the migrants leaves unexplained the parallel growth in Republican strength among whites who were raised in the South.

Our native respondents in 1976 do not, of course, represent the same population as the corresponding subsample from the 1952 survey. Millions of people in the 1952 population have died. A considerably larger number of native Southerners have reached voting age since then. The changes in native party identification may be a product of this generational replacement. Voters in the 1950s learned about politics in a world where the Democratic party stood for defending the southern way of life. Their partisan attachments firmed by generations of experience with the one-party politics of the old South, these old-timers would be unlikely prospects for conversion to Republicanism.

In the spirit of Converse's (1966:226) observation that "the younger generation often serves as the leading edge of change," we have explored differences in party identification among cohorts of native white Southerners. This endeavor involves the thorny problem of establishing some strategic dates in southern political history. It is easy enough to talk about political developments that crumbled the political assumptions of the old South. The problem is that one can plausibly argue that such a revolutionary change first became manifest in almost every election from 1948 onward. Was it in 1948, when the Democrats first could not count on the South? In 1952, when a Republican presidential candidate won several southern states? And so on.

A particularly strong case can be made for the importance of 1964, on the assumption that civil rights politics had a lot to do with the realignment. Until the early 1960s, the public did not see much difference between the two parties on race relations (A. Campbell, 1966:267-268; Converse et al., 1965:329). Both parties presented sufficiently diffuse and ambiguous records to permit individuals to come to whatever conclusion was most congenial. Supporters of segregation or integration affiliated with either party had no trouble with dissonance between their racial attitudes and party loyalties. The Civil Rights Act of 1964 and the subsequent presidential campaign dispelled this ambiguity. The bill was proposed by one Democratic President, enacted by a Democratic Congress, and signed into law by another Democratic President. Whatever identification with civil rights that might have affected the Republicans from their vital role in passing the legislation was quickly lost by the presidential nomination of Barry Goldwater, who made no secret of his intention to write off blacks and go hunting for votes in the South "where the ducks are." The vast majority of the public knew about the new law, President Johnson's support of it, and Goldwater's vote against it, perhaps the best-known vote by a senator in the history of the Republic (A. Campbell, 1968:29). The result was a sharp and durable shift in popular impressions of the parties' civil rights positions; the Democrats assumed a liberal image on this issue and the Republicans a conservative one (A. Campbell, 1966; Boyd, 1972:444-445; Pomper, 1972:420-425).

With this rationale, we picked 1964 as one cutting point for our analysis of political generations. Since 1952 was the occasion for a substantial increase in Republican fortunes in the South, we used it as another boundary, thus creating three cohorts of native white Southerners: (1) those of an age to vote before 1952; (2) a middle group composed of people whose first elections were those of 1952 through 1960; and (3) youngsters whose first election was 1964 or later. Unlike Beck (1977), whose two cohorts are defined by the New Deal, we were more concerned with events that, at least hypothetically, affected the South differently from the rest of the country.

Our preliminary analysis showed that the middle group, those who were first eligible to vote in the 1952, 1956, or 1960 elections, were usually not more Republican than older natives. Whatever the effect on southern politics of events in those years, they seem not to have left a lasting distinctive mark on people who came of political age in the years between Thurmond and Goldwater. Therefore we reduced our cohorts to two: native whites who reached voting age by 1960 and everyone younger.

Comparison of the trends in party identification of these two groups show how the younger Southerners are leading the way toward two-party politics in the South. This was not apparent in 1964, perhaps because there were only 18 respondents in the young cohort that year. This group grew to an adequate size for

Table 8. REPUBLICAN IDENTIFICATION IN TWO COHORTS OF NATIVE
WHITE SOUTHERNERS, 1960-1976 [a]

	1960		1964		1968		1972		1976	
	Young	Old	Young	Old	Young	Old	Young	Old	Young	Old
Percent Republican	--	18	22	13	40	20	31	22	32	19
Number of cases in cohort	0	331	18	201	40	206	154	275	168	231

a. The young cohort includes respondents who reached voting age in 1961 or later. All other
respondents are in the old cohort.

Table 9. PARTY IDENTIFICATION OF WHITE SOUTHERNERS BY MIGRATION
AND AGE, 1976

	Migrants	Natives Aged 18 to 36	Natives over 36
Strong Democrats	11%	13%	20%
Weak Democrats	20	27	37
Independent Democrats	8	10	9
Pure Independents	18	18	13
Independent Republicans	10	13	5
Weak Republicans	20	12	10
Strong Republicans	13	7	4
	100%	100%	98%
N	155	168	231

analysis in subsequent years. The Republican identification of the
two cohorts since 1964 is displayed in Table 8. The old-timers,
those who reached political maturity before the civil rights movement of the 1960s, have resisted the appeal of Republican affiliation. In 1960 only 18% of them were Republicans. This proportion shrank in 1964, increased in 1968 and again in 1972 to a peak
of 22% and then dropped back to 20% in 1976.

It is difficult to avoid the conclusion that some of these older
Southerners move into and out of the Republican party in response

to short-term forces. Thus Nixon's appeal in the South brings a few of them toward the GOP, while Carter's candidacy has the opposite effect. If the 1972 data had been the latest we analyzed, we might have concluded, along with Bruce Campbell (1977a, 1977b), that a fair amount of partisan conversion had occurred among older natives. While some of the differences we observe may reflect instability in party identification, some may also be due to sampling error. Some of the subsamples we are analyzing are not terribly large, and therefore our findings should be regarded as somewhat tentative.

Table 9 compares the party identification in 1976 of the three groups of whites: migrants and the two generations of native Southerners. The ever-more-numerous migrants are the most Republican of the three. They are 11 percentage points more Republican than the young natives and 24% more than the older ones. The older natives have almost as many Independents as the other two groups. In this respect, they have come a long way from the 1950s, when only about 5% of them were Independents. The amount of change in their Republican identification has been much smaller, however. They remain strongly Democratic, despite all the social and political changes of the past generation.

V. CAUSES OF THE SOUTHERN REALIGNMENT

One major source of increasing southern Republicanism can readily be identified: the continuing movement to the South of predominantly Republican northern whites. As we have seen, native Southerners are also becoming more Republican. It might be thought that our cohort analysis points the way to an explanation along these lines: Most white Southerners disliked the Democratic party's identification with civil rights in the 1960s. The partisan habits of a lifetime sufficed to keep most older natives in the Democratic party but the younger generation, with less experience as Democratic partisans, were freer to bring their party identification into line with their racial attitudes and thus the segregationists among them tended to become Republicans.

This hypothesis, often stated without reference to generations, has been examined by most writers on southern realignment.

Analysis of aggregate voting patterns through 1968 led Kevin Phillips (1970:205-212) to conclude that the Republicans were indeed benefiting from white backlash. Sundquist (1973:347-350) presented some survey findings consistent with this position. However, other more detailed analyses of survey data (Beck, 1977; B. Campbell, 1977b; Trilling, 1976) provide several reasons for doubting that the realignment has much to do with civil rights. Our own analysis leads to the same conclusion.

We begin by taking a closer look at the shift in party images on civil rights. In 1960 scarcely a third of native Southerners who saw a difference between the parties on school integration picked the Democrats as the more liberal party. This figure jumped to 77% in 1964 and stayed at the same level in 1968. In both of these later years, however, only half the respondents ascertained a difference between the parties, less than in 1956, when a substantial majority considered the Republicans more liberal on this issue. Including people who said the parties were alike on school desegregation or that they did not know if there were differences, only 39% of native Southerners judged the Democrats more liberal in 1964, and 41% in 1968. These findings are in Table 10. (Unfortunately, the same question was not asked after 1968.) Thus, although many southern whites did indeed come to think that the Democrats had become the party more favorable to civil rights measures, they nevertheless had in the late 1960s a fuzzier picture of the two parties' stands than they had had ten years earlier. These data lead us to conclude that the number of native Southerners who might be affected by changing party images is limited and that the change itself might be neither durable nor salient.

Nevertheless, there *was* a shift in party image on civil rights, no matter how widespread or durable, and this may explain Democratic losses in the South. Accordingly, we examined relationships between party identification and respondents' own attitudes toward desegregation. If the Sundquist-Phillips proposition were correct, we would expect Democrats to be more hostile to integration than other Southerners before 1964 and less so after this presumed watershed. We found, however, that Democrats invariably were more conservative on this issue from 1956 through the 1970s. The gap ranged from 2% to 11%, but always in the same direction and with no discernible pattern. The only trend was a

Table 10. NATIVE WHITE SOUTHERNERS' PERCEPTIONS OF THE PARTIES'
POSITIONS OF SCHOOL INTEGRATION, 1964 and 1968

Which party is more liberal on school integration?	1964	1968
Democrats	39%	41%
No difference	36	37
Republicans	12	11
Don't know	13	10
	100%	99%
N	184	214

gradual diminution of hostility to integration among all partisan groups. Reversing the independent and dependent variables produced the same result. Native white Southerners who expressed a preference for segregation were the most heavily Democratic, those favoring "something in between" were less likely to be Democrats, and integrationists were least inclined toward the Democrats and most likely to be Republicans. The Republicans were a decided minority in all three groups, most of all among the segregationists.

Since most of the Republican gains occurred among the younger natives, we compared the party identifications of respondents with different attitudes toward segregation in our two cohorts. In the older cohort, integrationists were twice as likely as segregationists to be Republicans in 1968, somewhat less likely in 1972, and equally so in 1976. In all three years Democrats comprised equal proportions of the two groups. The tiny subsamples of young natives in 1964 and 1968 do not display any coherent pattern. In 1972, young segregationists were a bit more Republican than the other two groups, but in 1976 they favored the Democrats and almost half the integrationists were Republicans. Moreover, there were no indications that Independents were more likely to take an "in between" position on segregation or to be a halfway house for segregationists fleeing the Democratic party. The small numbers of cases in these subsamples should make one cautious, but there clearly is precious little evidence that the race issue is making

Republicans out of young or old Southerners, and at least as many straws are blowing in the other direction.

The partisan direction of racial issues can be explored with a considerable body of other data. For example, we examined partisan variations in ratings of blacks on the "feeling thermometer." The results do not display any consistent tendency for Republicans to be more or less hostile to blacks. Similarly, other data show no consistent links between party and racial prejudice.

The strongest evidence about relationships between attitudes and partisan change would reflect not only the direction of respondents' opinions, but also their salience. We assume that changes in party identification are more likely to result from beliefs that are important and central in the individual's political perspectives. One way to approach this is through responses to the question about "the most important problem(s) facing this country" that the Michigan researchers have asked since the 1960s. Thirteen percent of native Southerners thought that topics explicitly concerned with race relations were most important in both 1964 and 1968. People in this group were slightly *less* likely than anyone else to be Republicans. The same was true for the somewhat smaller number of natives who considered civil disorder the most important problem. The number of native Southerners who mentioned race relations in the 1970s shrank almost to nothing. Only 17 respondents in 1972 and five in 1976 considered it the most important problem.

Another measure of the importance of racial matters also lets us see to what extent this issue plays a part in individual images of the two parties. In addition to questions explicitly asking respondents about party differences on selected issues, there is a series of open-ended items that allows respondents to provide their own portraits of the parties. The series begins with "Is there anything in particular that you like about the Democratic party?" Three other queries solicit dislikes about the Democrats and likes and dislikes about the Republican party. Analysis of the responses reveals the salience of any issue area in the images of the two parties and the parties' comparative popularity with respect to any issue.

Trilling (1976:165) reports that "southern white party images are less partisan with regard to the racial issue after 1964 than before, and by 1972 had become virtually neutral." Since migrants are more liberal on racial issues, we analyzed the racial images of the two parties among native Southerners only, with the thought that this group would be most likely to base its views of the two parties on race issues. Our findings confirm Trilling's position. Few natives ever mentioned civil rights or racial issues as reasons for liking *either* party, and after 1964 this trickle dwindled to 1% or less of all respondents. From 1956 through 1964, anywhere from 10% to 14% of the natives disliked the Democrats for racial reasons. In 1956 and 1960, the Republicans were unpopular on this score with a similar proportion of natives. Racial matters became less important in 1968, and by the 1970s the issue had almost disappeared as a component of either party's image. Only one respondent thought that racial matters were reasons to dislike the Democratic party, and three mentioned them as reasons to like the Republicans.

Southern realignment does not seem to be motivated by white backlash. We come to this conclusion for two reasons: (1) Compared to integrationists and people opting for a middle position, native segregationists are more likely to be Democrats. There is no evidence that those who dislike racial equality are becoming either Republicans or Independents as a result. (2) Although the decline of the Democrats and the growth of Republicans continues in the 1970s, racial issues have faded from the forefront of public attention.

This conclusion threatens the rationale for defining our two cohorts of native Southerners, the change in the parties' racial images that occurred in 1964. But although our assumption is ill-founded, nevertheless it "works." Something happened in the 1960s to produce a very different and continuing pattern of party identification among native white Southerners. If not the civil rights movement, what?

VI. CLASS POLARIZATION IN THE SOUTH?

Discussing various possible trends in southern politics, Converse (1966:213) suggested the likelihood of "a convergence outcome" in which the region's sociopolitical alignments came to resemble those elsewhere. One major feature of such convergence would be a stronger relationship between social class and party identification, as in the North. Such a relationship was nonexistent in the 1950s. If anything, middle-class Southerners were a bit *more* Democratic than members of the working class.

What we have seen already about southern demographic and political trends would lead us to expect stronger relationships between class and party in the 1970s. For one thing, the large black population, concentrated in lower status jobs, has become increasingly Democratic. Second, the numerous northern migrants are disproportionately middle class and Republican. Our present concern, however, is not with characterizing the entire southern electorate. Rather, we are interested in the causes of the move toward Republican identification of native white Southerners. We have, therefore, compared the partisan identifications, in the 1950s and in 1976, of four occupational levels of native white Southerners. In order to accumulate enough cases for analysis from the smaller Michigan samples of the 1950s, we combined the natives in the 1952 and 1956 samples for comparison with their counterparts in 1976.

These data, presented in Table 11, illustrate the slightly positive relationship between occupational status and identification with the Democratic party of a generation ago. In the 1950s, blue-collar workers were most likely to be Republicans, closely followed by farmers and people with upper-middle-class jobs. People in the lower middle class—clerks and salespeople—were by far the most Democratic. These relationships were reversed in 1976. In that year, people in all middle-class occupations were by far the most Republican, while the proportion of workers and farmers who were Republicans had changed only a couple of percentage points in two decades. The latter two groups were now the most Democratic, although appreciably less than they had been in the 1950s. The number of pure Independents had increased substantially in all categories, most of all in the workers and the upper middle class.

These data strongly contradict Gatlin's (1975:45-47) finding that "in the South, however, status has had only the faintest relationship with party identification among whites," and his consequent rejection of "the convergence model's assumption of an increasing

Table 11. PARTY IDENTIFICATION BY OCCUPATION OF NATIVE WHITE
SOUTHERNERS in 1952-56 and 1976 [a]

	Professional and Managerial		Clerical and Sales		Blue Collar		Farmers	
	1952/ 1956	1976	1952/ 1956	1976	1952/ 1956	1976	1952/ 1956	1976
Democrats	81%	52%	94%	58%	75%	60%	81%	71%
Independents	3	15	2	7	6	19	3	10
Republicans	16	33	4	35	18	21	17	19
	100%	100%	100%	100%	99%	100%	101%	100%
N	135	91	54	39	205	192	113	24

a. Occupation is for respondent's head of household. The 1952-1956 column combines
respondents in the 1952 and 1956 surveys.

status differentiation in party orientations in the South." This
change in the South is in the opposite direction from trends in
the North, where the relationship between class and party is
weakening. The search for an explanation, therefore, would focus
on regional rather than national causes.

Writing in the early 1960s, Donald S. Strong (1963:174-175)
suggested one reason for the partisan realignment that was to
come: "When the Democratic party ceased to be the champion of
white supremacy, southern whites began to act like other Americans
and vote in harmony with what they perceived to be their economic
interest." Among those natives who thought the two parties' racial
policies were similar, or that the Democrats had embraced civil
rights, the economic conservatives who were also segregationists
would therefore be "freer" to become Republicans. The logic
of this argument would also require that the less numerous economically liberal integrationists would be equally likely to switch
in the opposite direction.

Unfortunately, no questions were asked by the Michigan researchers, in either the 1950s or 1970s, that would let us see
whether native Democrats are more liberal on economic issues
vis-à-vis the Republicans now than they were 20 years ago. To
put it more precisely, we cannot compare the extent to which
economic or racial attitudes, then and now, predict party identi-

fication. A 1964 change in the format of the Michigan questions on issue attitudes would also cause difficulties for such an analysis.

One possibility is to see what sorts of natives were most concerned with the welfare state and government interference in the economy—the issues that presumably are drawing conservative Southerners into the Republican party. Virtually no native white Southerners thought that these were "the most important problem" until 1976. In that year, the 84 respondents who mentioned these topics were a bit *less* Republican than the 310 respondents who were more worried about other issues.

In short, political polarization along class lines is increasing in the South. Unfortunately, we do not have data that will let us test this proposition directly by examining relationships between attitudes on economic issues and party identification.

VII. CONCLUSIONS AND PROSPECTS

The increase in Republican strength in the South is less apparent in congressional elections because of Republican failure to contest many seats and the inertial power of incumbency. Although the number of Independents is growing, the more substantial and significant development is the continued increase in the number of white Southerners who identify with the Republican party and whose loyalty to Republican presidential candidates belies the claim that party ties have dissolved in the South.

One major factor in this realignment is the continuing influx of prosperous, politically active northern Republicans. The other principal source of Republican strength is a new generation of native whites who seem fairly unconstrained by their ancestors' traditional loyalty to the Democratic party.

The causes of this shift in party identification are more mysterious. We could find little evidence that native whites have become Republicans because of the changed images of the two parties on civil rights. Indeed, the realignment persists although racial issues have lost most of their salience. There is some relationship between occupation and party identification, a relatively new development for the South. But our preliminary examination did not unearth more direct evidence that the basis of southern political cleavages has shifted from racial to economic issues.

What about the future? Unlike Beck (1977:495) and Sundquist (1973:365-366), we think that the Republican party has a bright future in the South. Two important demographic factors favor the Republicans: (1) The actuarial odds are all on their side. Older Southerners are more likely to be Democrats, younger ones to be Republicans. If the only influence on southern population composition were the normal pattern of death and maturation, every passing year would help the Republicans. (2) The most consequential outside influence is the northern migration. Newcomers keep streaming into the South, the fastest growing, most economically dynamic part of the country. Younger, better educated, and more prosperous than the natives, they are also more Republican and more active in politics.

The political forces encouraged by these demographic trends are likely to produce further Republican gains. In his theoretical discussion of American realignments, Sundquist (1973:239-244, 263-269) formulated an explanation that seems perfectly appropriate to the contemporary South. He argued that a change in party identification, as opposed to a temporary deviation in voting choice, requires attractive local candidates and party leaders who really want to win elections, not just secure patronage when their party wins the presidency. As we have seen, this is just beginning to happen in the South. In some states, Republicans still avoid challenges to conservative Democrats that might dilute their presidential candidate's appeal and confound comfortable alliances with businessmen. In 1972, Gil Carmichael, who persisted in running against Mississippi's ultraconservative Senator Eastland, found himself something of a Republican stepchild but still won 39% of the vote.

Vigorous electoral opposition to the traditionally dominant party is most likely when there is a chance of victory. When a party has no hope of winning state or local elections, even the most fervent true believers or ambitious candidates will not toil indefinitely in barren fields. The party is likely to fall into the hands of listless functionaries devoted to patronage and inhospitable to newcomers, whom they view as competing claimants for the spoils won by their allies in other parts of the country. The prospect of winning a nearby election holds out hope to potential candidates, activists, and contributors. It encourages them to organize, contribute, and campaign. While the power of incumbency in congressional races therefore retards the growth of Republican identity, it cannot do so indefinitely. The eventual availability of open seats gives local Republicans their chance. An open seat is not a guarantee of Republican success, but, as we have seen, it is a powerful help.

Every open seat is an opportunity for aspiring Republican candidates to make their appeal without having to overcome the almost insuperable obstacle of incumbency. It offers a new situation for local contributors to reconsider their past alliances and perhaps to conclude that their needs will be better served by a Republican—if he has a chance to win. As Republicans become a viable alternative they draw off some conservatives from Democratic ranks, thus helping the chances of liberal contenders in the Democratic primary. The ability of blacks to vote in Democratic primaries is also likely to help liberals, a factor that was not present when many older incumbent Democrats first won their seats. These leftward shifts within the Democratic party increase the chances that its nomination will be won by a liberal who will offend conservative voters in the general election. This process explains many of the Republican congressional successes of the past dozen years.

If our samples were several times larger, we could test the proposition that contested elections for open seats hasten the trend toward Republican alignments in the South. As it is, we conclude with the prediction that time is on the side of the Republicans, and wait for the evidence of the next few elections to see if we are right or wrong.

NOTES

1. We except from these remarks the well-known persistence of Republican loyalties in mountain regions like eastern Tennessee and southwestern Virginia, not to mention such exotic enclaves as the Alabama county that refused to join the Confederacy and has been a Republican stronghold ever since.

2. Party identification is measured with this question, asked by the Michigan researchers

since 1952: "Generally speaking, do you usually think of yourself as a Republican, a Democrat, an Independent, or what?"

If the respondent answers "Republican" or "Democrat," the interviewer follows up with: "Would you call yourself a strong Republican (Democrat) or a not very strong Republican (Democrat)?"

If the respondent answers "Independent," the interviewer probes: "Do you think of yourself as closer to the Republican or Democratic party?"

3. The Center for Political Studies data used in this paper were made available through the Inter-University Consortium for Political Research. We are solely responsible for analysis and interpretation of the data.

The most recent CPS codebooks define the South as the Confederacy less Tennessee. Some earlier codebooks define the region as the "Census South": the Confederacy plus four border states and the District of Columbia. Sampling information about regions is absent from codebooks before 1964. In view of this array of alternative definitions, we decided to base our definition on the unique historical experience of the former Confederate states, since any other choice would also have involved problems about whether the subsamples were self-representing.

4. Two problems interfere with confident analysis of voting in southern House elections: (1) The large number of uncontested races drastically reduces the number of cases available for analysis. (2) The strength of incumbency mediates the relationship between party identification and voting choice, but we lack enough cases to control for this variable.

5. A great many whites also moved north, of course. Bruce Campbell (1977a:48) estimates that this white emigration slightly favored the Democrats, but warns that this datum should be interpreted with caution. We make no assumptions about the effects of this migration, since there is no comfortable way to calculate how the migrants would have behaved if they had remained where they were born.

REFERENCES

BECK, P.A. (1977). "Partisan dealignment in the postwar South." American Political Science Review, 71(2):477-496.

BOYD, R.W. (1972). "Popular control of public policy: A normal vote analysis of the 1968 election." American Political Science Review, 66(2):429-449.

CAMPBELL, A. (1966). "Interpreting the presidential victory." Pp. 250-273 in M. Cummings, Jr. (ed.), The national election of 1964. Washington, DC: Brookings Institution.

———— (1968). "Civil rights and the vote for President." Psychology Today, (February):28-34.

CAMPBELL, B.A. (1977a). "Change in the southern electorate." American Journal of Political Science, 21(1):37-64.

———— (1977b). "Patterns of change in the partisan loyalties of native southerners: 1952-1972." Journal of Politics, 39(3):730-761.

Congressional Quarterly Weekly Report (1974). March 31, pp. 813-828.

CONVERSE, P.E. (1966). "On the possibility of major political realignment in the South." Pp. 212-242 in A. Campbell et al., Elections and the political order. New York: John Wiley.

———— (1972). "Change in the American electorate." Pp. 270-336 in A. Campbell and P.E. Converse, The human meaning of social change. New York: Russell Sage Foundation.

CONVERSE, P.E. et al. (1965). "Electoral myth and reality: The 1964 election." American Political Science Review, 59(2):321-335.

GATLIN, D.S. (1975). "Party identification, status, and race in the South: 1952-1972." Public Opinion Quarterly, 39(1):39-51.

GREELEY, A.M., and SHEATSLEY, P.B. (1971). "Attitudes toward racial integration." Scientific American, (December):13-19.

HEARD, A. (1952). A two-party South? Chapel Hill: University of North Carolina Press.

HUTCHESON, R.G. (1975). "The inertial effect of incumbency and two-party politics: Elections to the House of Representatives from the South, 1952-1974." American Political Science Review, 69(4):1399-1401.

KEITH, B.E. et al. (1977). "The myth of the independent voter." Paper presented at the annual meeting of the American Political Science Association, Washington, D.C., September 4.

LADD, E.C., Jr., with HADLEY, C.D. (1975). Transformations of the American party system. New York: W.W. Norton.

MANLEY, J.F. (1973). "The conservative coalition in Congress." American Behavioral Scientist, 17(4):223-247.

McKINNEY, J.C., and BOURQUE, L.B. (1971). "The changing South: National incorporation of a region." American Sociological Review, 36(2):399-412.

NELSON, C.J. (1978). "The effect of incumbency on voting in congressional elections, 1964-1974." Political Science Quarterly, 93(4).

PERKINS, J. (1974). "Bases of partisan cleavage in a southern urban county." Journal of Politics, 36(1):208-214.

PHILLIPS, K.P. (1970). The emerging Republican majority. Garden City, N.Y.:Doubleday.

POMPER, G.M. (1972). "From confusion to clarity: Issues and American voters, 1956-1968." American Political Science Review, 66(2):415-428.

Ripon Society (n.d.). "Election '64." Cambridge, Mass.: Author.

SCHREIBER, E.M. (1971). "'Where the ducks are': Southern strategy versus fourth party." Public Opinion Quarterly, 35(2):157-167.

SONG, Y. (1974). "Political trends and the non-southerner in the South: A study in North Carolina." Politics 74. Greenville, N.C.: East Carolina University Publications.

STRONG, D.S. (1963). "Durable Republicanism in the South." Pp. 165-184 in A. Sindler (ed.), Change in the contemporary South. Durham, N.C.: Duke University Press.

SUNDQUIST, J.L. (1973). Dynamics of the party system. Washington, D.C.: Brookings Institution.

TRILLING, R.J. (1976). Party image and electoral behavior. New York: John Wiley.

——— (1975). "Party image, party identification and party realignment." Unpublished manuscript.

WOLFINGER, R.E., and ROSENSTONE, S.J. (1977). "Who votes?". Paper presented at the annual meeting of the American Political Science Association, Washington, D.C., September 4.

Chapter 7

PARTY, BUREAUCRACY, AND POLITICAL CHANGE IN THE UNITED STATES

MARTIN SHEFTER

I. INTRODUCTION

Over the past 180 years, five or six distinct party systems have emerged, developed, and decayed in the United States. These successive systems have been distinguished from one another by the issues dividing the major parties, the proportion of the vote each party normally received, and the social composition of each party's electoral base. Equally important, changes have occurred from one party system to the next in the strength of political parties relative to other public institutions and political actors in the United States (Burnham, 1970).

Among the most important institutional changes that have accompanied the emergence of new party systems in the United States have been shifts in the power of political parties relative to public bureaucracies. The relationship between these two institutions is of great significance for a number of reasons. First, it has major consequences for the structure of political parties and for the electoral strategies they are able to pursue. If political parties are the stronger institution, they will be in a position to extract patronage from the bureaucracy and to distribute it to the cadre who conduct their campaigns and the voters who support their candidates; if parties are weaker than bureaucracies, they must find some alternative means of mobilizing popular support (Shefter, 1978a). Second and more generally, the strength of parties relative

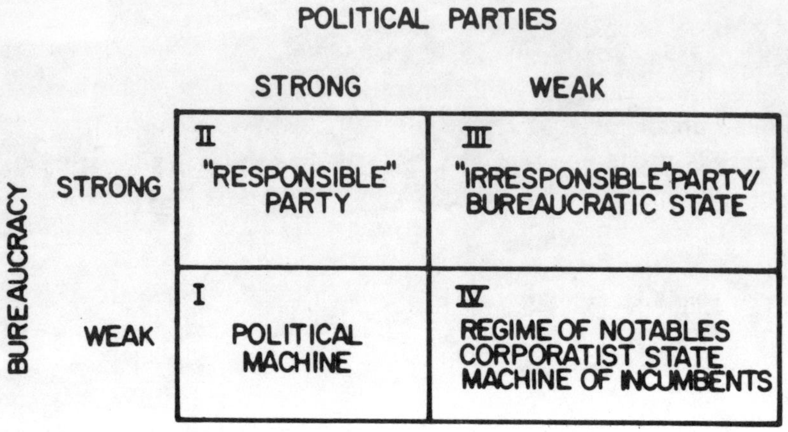

POLITICAL PARTIES

	STRONG	WEAK
STRONG	II "RESPONSIBLE" PARTY	III "IRRESPONSIBLE" PARTY/ BUREAUCRATIC STATE
WEAK	I POLITICAL MACHINE	IV REGIME OF NOTABLES CORPORATIST STATE MACHINE OF INCUMBENTS

(left axis: **BUREAUCRACY**)

Figure 1

to bureaucracies has an important bearing upon the character of the political system as a whole, as Figure 1 indicates.

Figure 1 is a simple typology of the relationships that may exist between the power of parties and bureaucracies. Where parties are strong and the bureaucracy is weak (cell I), parties will be in a position to dominate both the electoral and administrative arenas, and, as just noted, to use their power to generate patronage (Tolchin and Tolchin, 1971). Such political systems can be said to be governed by "political machines." Where parties and bureaucracies are both strong (cell II), each institution will be able to dominate its respective arena, to exert some discipline over its members, and to protect its boundaries from lateral penetration. In this situation, parties will not find it possible to obtain patronage from the bureaucracy for distribution to voters, but will be in a position to deliver on whatever promises they make concerning the general policies they intend to enact. Borrowing a term that was popular a generation ago, one can label these "responsible parties." Where the bureaucracy is strong and parties are weak (cell III), executive agencies may be able to resist not only lateral penetration, but also control from above. In this situation, parties will be able neither to extract patronage from the bureaucracy nor to deliver on any promises they may make concerning the implementation of public policy; all they can do is offer voters empty rhetoric or appeal to their supporters' racial, ethnic, or national sentiments. These can be called "irresponsible parties" and a regime governed in this way can be termed "bureaucratic state."

The final category (cell IV) is the most complex. If both parties and bureaucracies are institutionally weak, the locus of power depends upon which particular political actors, organizations, or institutions dominate in their stead. Where local dignitaries dominate the electoral arena and use their influence to extract patronage from the bureaucracy for distribution to their personal clients, one may speak of a "regime of notables." Where interest groups have influence over the bureaucracy and are able to help candidates win elections to public office, one may speak of a "corporatist state." Finally, where professional politicians secure elective office by constructing personal campaign organizations and remain in power by intervening before the bureaucracy on behalf of their constituents, one may speak of a "machine of incumbents."

Since the emergence of the first American party system in the 1790s, the power of party relative to bureaucracy in the United States has changed dramatically a number of times, and the American political system could aptly be characterized, at least in part, in each of these ways. In this essay, I seek to account for these patterns of institutional development, transformation, and decay.

My argument, briefly stated, is that changes in relative power of party and bureaucracy in the United States are intimately related to the process of critical realignment in American politics. Critical elections bring to power new political coalitions, some or all of whose members wish to use public authority for new purposes. By altering the relationship between, and the internal structure of, party and bureaucracy, elements of the new majority coalition seek to undermine the position of politicians who held power during the earlier party system, to seize control over the government, and to turn it to the purposes they want it to serve. Or to phrase this in somewhat greater detail, by restructuring the party and the bureaucracy, various contenders for power seek to create an institutional order which will enable them to (1) defeat their opponents in the other party, or in other factions of their own party; (2) subject voters to their discipline; (3) control the use of public authority; and (4) have the structural and technical capacity to perform those functions which the group in question wants the government to serve. Whether reformers in the wake of any given critical election will seek to strengthen or weaken the party as an institution, and to defend or to undermine the autonomy of the bureaucracy, depends primarily upon the structure of the antecedent regime and the nature of the resources they command.

In the sections below, I will indicate how the major changes that have occurred from one party system to the next in the structure of, and relationship between, party and bureaucracy in the United States can be understood in these terms.

II. THE REGIME OF NOTABLES:
THE FEDERALISTS AND JEFFERSONIANS

The first political parties in the United States—the Federalists and the Jeffersonian Republicans—were coalitions of notables. During the period extending from the emergence of the two parties in the 1790s through their collapse in the 1820s, the level of political participation in most areas of the country was low, party organizations were weak or nonexistent, elective offices were monopolized by local notables, and these officials appointed their associates and clients to positions in the bureaucracy.[1] There were, however, some differences between what the Federalists and the Jeffersonians sought to accomplish, the opposition they had to overcome to do so, and the resources they commanded, and these shaped their orientations toward party and bureaucracy.

The Federalists spoke for a rather narrow segment of the American upper class. The central policies of the Washington and Adams administrations (Hamilton's financial program, the pro-British tilt in foreign relations, and policies with respect to public lands and Indian removal that retarded settlement of the West) served the interests of the nation's mercantile elite, a sector of the economy which had commercial ties with Britain and little geographic presence apart form the coastal regions of New England and the Middle States. Because this sector encompassed such a small proportion of the nation's population (at most 10%), the ideology the party professed and the political techniques upon which it relied were necessarily antidemocratic (Ellis, 1971: Chap. 17).

Though there were some important exceptions, the Federalists, as Ellis (1971:279) observes, "publicly denied the ability of the people to govern themselves, stressed the need for elitist guidance, and never were able to successfully practice the art of popular politics" (cf., Fischer, 1965). Washington, in his farewell address, formulated the classic conservative critique of party, and one element among the Federalists was prepared to use the army, rather than to engage in countermobilization, in order to cope with the Republican opposition. Similarly, the bureaucratic appointment practices of the Federalists were narrowly elitist in their orientation. In selecting individuals to serve in the departments and agencies of his administration, President Washington chose men who in his words were "esteemed and honored by their neighbors," that is, local notables who "placed at the disposal of the [new government] a system of social relations in which they were already superiors, independently of their official tenure."[2] As opposition to Federalist policies congealed, the Washington and Adams administrations, if anything, narrowed their political base, and their patronage practices became more restrictive: they appointed only those notables who supported the administration in its conflicts with the Republicans (Van Riper, 1958:21). This culminated in Adams's midnight appointments. By packing the federal bureaucracy and judiciary with Federalists, Adams sought to ensure that these institutions would remain bastions of Federalism despite the party's repudiation by the majority in the election of 1800.

The majority which supported the Republicans in the critical election of 1800 was composed of two major groups. The first were subsistence farmers who opposed the administration both because they stood outside the market economy and, therefore, could only be injured by Federalist economic policies, and because they were radically democratic in ideology. This group formed the radical wing of the Republican Party. The second was composed of commercial farmers who would profit from trading in a larger market than Britain alone provided. This group, the Republican moderates, was led by planters such as Jefferson and Madison who, because they opposed Federalist policies on behalf of the nation's agricultural majority, were democratic in ideology and were able to successfully play the game of popular politics.

Although radical and moderate Republicans shared an antipathy to the mercantile, pro-British, and antidemocratic orientations of the Federalists, the economic and political orders they favored were not in the least similar. The moderates, unlike the radicals, wanted to build a commercial society and to have the government foster economic development through internal improvements and the chartering of banks. (The Republican moderates differed from the Hamiltonians to the extent that they wanted to develop the economy on an agricultural base and by strengthening the national market, rather than on a mercantile base and by tying the American economy to the British market.) And in the realm of politics, the moderates, unlike the radicals, regarded as dangerous all forms of political activity conducted apart from the established institutions and leaders of society; they were aghast at the Whiskey Rebellion, uncomfortable with the Democratic-Republican societies, and opposed to constitutional reforms which would radically democratize and decentralize the government.

To implement their program, the moderate Republicans sought to drive from the political arena extremists of both the right and the left—the High Federalists and the Old Republicans—and to construct a coalition of moderates from both parties who favored a republican polity, a market economy, and an ordered society. Jeffersonian practices with respect to party and patronage can be understood in light of this goal as well as the resources the Republican moderates were able to command, and the opposition they had to overcome to achieve it. When the Federalists, during the Adams administration, were preparing to use the army to crush opposition (or so it appeared), Madison and Jefferson were willing to ally with the radicals and to mobilize mass support—a strategy which involved creating the Republican Party (Cunningham, 1957). After gaining power, however, the moderates slowly turned away from their alliance with the radicals and sought to conciliate the moderate Federalists. The Republican Party was permitted to decay once its function of defeating the "monarchists" had been fulfilled. As Richard Hofstadter (1969:Chap. 5) has documented, Jefferson, Madison, and Monroe did not regard the Republican Party as a permanent institution, but rather as a temporary expedient to rout the enemies of republicanism and, thereby, to establish the preconditions for a partyless regime.

In a similar vein, Jefferson refused, in the face of substantial pressure, to purge all Federalists from the bureaucracy and judiciary, for fear of alienating those he wished to conciliate. He sought to give the Republicans proportional representation in, rather than total dominance over, the bureaucracy. During his first two years in office, Jefferson replaced somewhat over half the officials appointed by his predecessors—186 of 316 presidential appointees—and then he stopped. In selecting officials to be removed, Jefferson sought in particular to frustrate Adams's effort to turn the judiciary and bureaucracy into a Federalist power base. He refused to recognize the commissions of the midnight appointees, removed Federalist marshals and district attorneys to ensure that Republican suitors would enjoy access to the federal courts, and fired field administrators who used their positions in ways which helped the Federalists and injured the Republicans. Jefferson appointed only Republicans to the vacancies thus created, but not just any Republicans. In choosing whom to appoint, Jefferson canvased the Republican notability in the locality in question, and individuals who wished to secure appointments from him submitted petitions and letters attesting to their good character and their acceptability to the respectable men of the community (Cunningham, 1963: Chaps. 2-3; White, 1951, Chap. 24).

The Jeffersonians, then, were very much a party of notables. Where they differed from the Federalists was that their regime was grounded upon a much larger segment of the nation's upper class and that, in order to defeat their opponents, they were prepared to appeal mass support—a strategy which led them to build the world's first modern party organization (Chambers, 1963). Once their position was secured, however, the Jeffersonians mobilized their followers and recruited public officials through the informal community networks commanded by members of the patriciate and gentry who were loyal to the administration, rather than through a well organized party structure.[3] This system enabled the classes for which they spoke to gain privileged access to public benefits and to use public authority to discipline the groups that were excluded from the Jeffersonian regime. (During the Jeffersonian era, for example, public lands were sold only in large lots to commercial farmers, and federal marshalls appointed by Republican presidents evicted subsistence farmers who were squatting on the public domain.) And because the Jeffersonian notability was rather well educated (it is not coincidental that Jefferson founded a university), the state they staffed in this way was quite competent to administer the mildly mercantilist policies the regime pursued (Aronson, 1964: Chap. 6).

III. PARTY, PATRONAGE, AND POLITICAL MACHINES: THE JACKSONIANS

The system led by the Jeffersonians was overthrown following the election of 1828 by the Jacksonians. The politicians of the Jacksonian Era initiated a process which Luigi Graziano (1978), in a different context, has termed "the emancipation of the state from civil society." They established a party system and a system of public administration which were independent of the informal social hierarchies upon which the Jeffersonians had relied. They did this by creating mass based party organizations, reorganizing the bureaucracy, and perfecting the spoils system.

The Jeffersonian political economy had excluded, or at least disadvantaged, a rather heterogeneous collection of social groups. Chief among these were businessmen seeking to break into the existing order of limited mercantile privilege (the classic example is Wall Street's opposition to the Philadelphia-based Second Bank of the United States); farmers who faced competition in the local markets they once had monopolized from grain transported on government-subsidized canals; master mechanics being squeezed out by merchant-capitalists who were able to obtain credit from publicly chartered banks; and marginal farmers and laborers hurt by the price inflation caused, at least in their view, by the issue of currency by those banks (Lebowitz, 1969; cf. Gatell, 1966). The members of religious and ethnic minorities who were discriminated against by legislation enacted at the behest of more established groups also had reason to be dissatisfied with the prevailing regime.

This heterogeneous collection of social groups was available for mobilization by anti-administration politicians and by political movements which argued that the common source of all their problems was a regime which granted favors to those who occupied privileged political positions and which, in the process, intervened so actively in society that it upset the natural order of things. The Jacksonians proposed a dual remedy for these problems: open up the political system to the people; and limit the powers of government. They sought to implement this program by appealing for popular support apart from established leadership channels (Marshall, 1967). The reforms they sponsored in the electoral and administrative arenas were part and parcel of this effort to overthrow the notables' regime.

The Jacksonians sponsored a number of reforms in the procedures governing the conduct of elections and the recruitment of public officials which made it difficult for local notables to dominate these processes. Under the old regime, restrictions on the franchise, large election districts, the absence of a "top of the ticket" as a focus for popular enthusiasm (presidential electors and governors often were appointed by state legislatures), and, of course, the absence of an organized opposition, together limited the size of the active electorate. The restricted scope of the political universe in conjunction with viva voce voting enabled the leading men of the country to send one of their number to the state legislature. And because state legislatures or their appointees (governors, councils of appointment) commonly selected the heads of state executive departments, judges, and county officials, it was only necessary for the notability to dominate state legislative elections in order to dominate the entire governmental apparatus. The electoral reforms of the Jacksonian Era—white manhood suffrage; the paper ballot; small polling districts; direct election of governors, presidential electors, heads of state executive departments, and local government officials; and short terms of office—swamped the older, elite-dominated mechanisms of election management and political recruitment (McCormick, 1975).

After coming to power by overwhelming their opponents in the electoral arena, the Jacksonians sought to extend their sway over the bureaucracy. The doctrine of rotation-in-office, as is well known, legitimized this effort to expel their predecessors from positions in the bureaucracy. Somewhat less well known are the other moves the Jacksonians made in their effort to sever the ties between the notability and the bureaucracy and to extend their own control over it. In point of fact, the Jacksonians were responsible for the first major episode of administrative reform in American history. Though they were not at all self-conscious about what they were doing, they sought to transform the federal bureaucracy from a structure which operated according to the principles of personal organization into one which operated according to the principles of formal organization. Jacksonian officials such as Amos Kendall drafted administrative reorganization plans that specified the responsibilities attached to positions within the bureaucracy (rather than to the persons occupying these roles); established bureaus organized along functional lines within the executive departments; assigned officials to perform staff (as distinguished from line) responsibilities; created elaborate systems of inspection, reporting, and accounting to monitor departmental field offices; promulgated codes of official ethics; and insisted that officials distinguish sharply between their private funds and public accounts. Matthew Crenson (1975), who describes these reforms in an important recent book, argues, mistakenly in my view, that the Jacksonians established formal bureaucratic structures because rapid social change in the early 19th century had undermined traditional social institutions—the bar, the business community, the local community—and made it impossible to rely on them any longer to enforce standards of probity and good behavior upon bureaucrats.[4] I would argue, rather, that the Jacksonians established formal bureaucratic procedures instead of relying on these informal institutions to control the behavior of subordinate officials because these institutions (which continued to flourish well beyond 'the 1820s and 1830s) were controlled in the main by their political enemies. By removing the bureaucrats appointed by their predecessors, the Jacksonians sought to sever the ties between the bureaucracy, and these traditional social structures; and by re-organizing the bureaucracy, they sought to subject it to the control of the officeholders whom they had elected, the institutions (especially the party organizations) which they commanded, and the social groups for whom they spoke. In other words, the bureaucratic reforms the Jacksonians sponsored served to "emancipate" the output institutions of the state from the informal social hierarchies that an established class of notables controlled, just as the electoral and party reforms they sponsored served to emancipate the input institutions of the state from this segment of civil society.

The electoral and administrative reforms of the Jacksonian Era, then, were part and parcel of the realignment process: they were efforts by a new majority to drive from power the elites who had dominated the earlier regime. As such, they could be supported by all, or at least most, elements of the new majority coalition. Once enacted, however, these reforms had consequences for the distribution of power *within* the majority party. The expansion of the number of public offices subject to popular election, and the shortening of the terms of public officials, made legislators, executives, and judges dependent upon the politicians who organized the enlarged electorates of the period, and turned party management into, if not a full-time profession, then at least a vocation that demanded far more time and attention for its successful performance than had been devoted to it by the gentlemen dilettantes of the earlier regime. At the same time the expulsion of the notables from institutions of policymaking and administration, and the subjection of these institutions to party influence gave middle-class lawyers, editors, and businessmen an incentive to devote themselves to the tasks of party management, because these developments made it possible for such men-on-the-make to live off politics by serving as agents for private interests in their dealings with government (the Jacksonian period saw the rise of the lobby), by moving into and out of public office, and by making personal contacts and obtaining public contracts (e.g., printing contracts) that were useful in their private careers. The Jacksonian reforms, then, placed at the very center of the political system a group of middle-class professional or semiprofessional politicians (Hofstadter, 1969: 240-242; cf. Weber, 1958).

The leadership of this group did not go unchallenged. The Jackson coalition, as mentioned above, was extremely heterogeneous. It included elements of the business community and the middle class that wanted, as Carl Degler (1956: 216) terms it, to "liberate the expanding American economy from the fetters of a dying mercantilist approach to business enterprise," by permitting anyone to obtain a bank or corporate charter (free banking and general incorporation), and by expanding the supply of money and credit. It also included marginal farmers, mechanics, and laborers who wanted to contract the money supply, who regarded all banks and corporations as chartered monopolies, and who supported other policies equally antipathetic to the interests of the first group, such as the 10-hour day and the right to strike. Many of the spokesmen for this position, especially in the larger cities, were affiliated with the fledgling trade unions of the Jacksonian Era, organizations that were seeking to establish their political hegemony over the working classes. At different times these leaders worked through third parties—organizing the workingmen's parties of the period—or through the Democratic Party—forming its radical wing. To the extent that these leaders mobilized their supporters through craft organizations, their challenge to the professional party politicians of the period was as backward looking as that of the early Whig Party; it harked back to 18th century patterns of working-class political activity (Bridges, 1977).

The middle-class professional politicians in the Democratic party responded to this challenge in a number of ways. They came out in support of some of the policies advocated by the radicals. Such concessions, however, alienated the party's wealthier supporters (Gatell, 1967). It was possible, however, to appeal to the rank-and-file supporters of the radical factions without splitting the Jacksonian movement along class lines by pursuing two alternative strategies. Democratic politicians appealed to working-class voters by stressing the party's stance on religious and cultural issues—its defense of immigrants and Catholics against the attacks of nativists and evangelical Protestants (Montgomery, 1972). And Democratic politicians attempted to steal away the supporters of the radicals by pursuing a strategy of counterorganization. Whereas the radicals sought to organize their followers along craft lines or, more exactly, to politicize preexisting labor organizations, the professional politicians organized their followers along residential lines (in ward and town committees) and politicized preexisting recreational organizations, such as volunteer fire brigades and militia companies (Katznelson, 1975; Bridges, 1977).

The control that politicians established over the organs of administration and policymaking in the United States during the Jacksonian Era contributed to the success of this strategy of party building. The access they acquired to the bureaucracy enabled them to distribute patronage to the cadre who staffed the party apparatus, as well as to gang leaders, fire captains, and saloon keepers who enjoyed followings among the working classes.[5] Party politicians thereby provided these leaders with a stake in the success of the party organization and with an incentive to bring their followers into its camp. And the influence they enjoyed within city councils and state legislatures enabled party politicians to obtain public subsidies for militia and fire companies and for sectarian charitable institutions with similar consequences.

The party organizations that Jacksonian politicians built, and the bureaucratic reforms they simultaneously sponsored, then, were the means by which a particular political class squeezed out its competitors and came to power in the United States. The construction of a mass-based, geographically organized, and patronage-fueled party apparatus enabled professional politicians who were drawn from, or had ties to the middle class, to establish their hegemony over the working class and to triumph over leaders who depended on two older structures and traditions of political organization—namely, the elite networks of the notables and the autonomous craft organizations of the mechanics. And the building of this apparatus was linked to the bureaucratic reforms of the Jacksonian Era. The cadre who worked for the party organization were compensated for their labors with appointments to positions in the bureaucracy. And the activities of the organization were financed by political assessments levied on the salaries of civil servants.

In the dozen years between 1828 and 1840, the political forces which opposed President Jackson underwent a similar transformation. As had been true of the Jacksonians before them, they were transformed from a diffuse political movement, important elements of which were committed to earlier modes of political organization, into a political party that (a) was mass-based, autonomously organized, and patronage-fueled; (b) appealed to its supporters by focusing as much on ethnocultural concerns as on economic issues; and (c) was led by a corps of semiprofessional politicians drawn chiefly (though not exclusively) from the middle class. This metamorphosis was especially striking in the case of the Whigs because the very animus which had led to the party's formation had been its founders' opposition to the mode of political organization that the Jacksonians employed and the pattern of political activity in which they engaged, namely appeals to a mass public apart from established social hierarchies (Marshall, 1967). However, the imperatives of electoral law and political competition, and the availability of state patronage, enabled the Thurlow Weeds and William Sewards to seize the leadership of the anti-administration forces and to subject the old notability to their discipline, just as these imperatives and resources had enabled the Van Burens and Marcys to squeeze out competitors for leadership of the Jackson movement.

In meaningful sense, then, a new political class came to power in the United States as the second party system emerged. The leaders of the Democratic and Whig parties resembled each other— in terms of their origins and career patterns, the organizations they constructed and the political techniques they employed, and the relations they established with the bureaucracy—more than either resembled the notability that ruled the nation prior to the Jacksonian realignment.[6] There was, moreover, a community of interest within this political class that united it across party lines. As Martin Van Buren recognized, such a leadership group could best maintain control over its followers if an opposition party existed (Hofstadter, 1969:249). The general acceptance by 1840 of the "idea of a party system," to use Hofstadter's phrase, was the ideological expression of the hegemony of this political class, just as the general triumph of the party organizations these politicians constructed over alternative political formations was the institutional expression of its hegemony.

In sum, the electoral and administrative reforms of the Jacksonians emerged out of the efforts of a middle-class leadership group to overturn a previously dominant class of notables by pursuing a strategy of mass mobilization. The party organizations Jacksonian politicians constructed enabled them both to overwhelm these notables and to exert discipline over their political allies. The bureaucratic reforms they sponsored—the spoils system and administrative reorganization—enabled them to drive their opponents from the bureaucracy and to subject it to their own control. The Jacksonians were free to use bureaucratic appointments as a reward for party service to the extent that they wanted the state to perform only a limited range of functions—chiefly, delivering the mails, distributing public lands, collecting tariff revenues, and driving the Indians further west—and these did not require most civil servants to have skills and training beyond those which ordinary citizens possessed, as President Jackson himself observed in his first inaugural address.[7]

IV. THE ATTACK UPON PATRONAGE AND PARTY ORGANIZATION: THE MUGWUMPS

The dozen years which followed the realignment of 1860 were a turning point in American politics: they belonged both an earlier era and to a later one. Upon coming to power, the Republicans, as had the Jacksonians before them, sought to extend their control over the entire governmental apparatus, and to use the patronage they extracted from the bureaucracy for the purposes of party building. Within a decade, however, an important group of Republicans launched an attack upon the party organization and spoils system, and formulated what would prove to be one of the modern alternatives to that system.

The Republicans who came to power in 1860 were a heterogeneous collection of radicals who wanted to abolish slavery, farmers who supported homestead legislation, manufacturers and workers who wanted tariff protection, and voters who had toyed with nativism in the mid-1850s. They were bound together by the ideology of free labor and by the conviction that the construction of a society organized around this principle was threatened by the "slavepower," which sought to control the western territories and the national government in order to build a society based upon entirely different principles (Foner, 1970). During the 1860s the Republican Party was beset by factionalism; the issues which divided the party's radical, moderate, and conservative factions, however, did not center around questions of patronage and party organization. Thus, upon entering the White House, President Lincoln conducted the most thorough purge of the bureaucracy in the nation's history, and he used the patronage thereby generated to build a party committed to the unionist cause (Carman and Luthin, 1943). This endeavor was supported by radicals, moderates, and conservatives alike.

The very vigor with which the Republicans generated and used patronage for the purposes of party-building in the 1860s, however, had consequences by the 1870s for the character of the party and for the distribution of power within it. It transformed the Republicans from a political movement into a political party and advantaged the professional politicians within it. As Morton Keller (1977: 238, 255) notes:

> Party leaders and political organizations hardly were unknown in ... the 1860s. Nevertheless during the 1870s the character of American politics sharply changed. The passionate, ideologically charged political ambiance of the Reconstruction years gave way to a politics that rested on the perpetuation of party organization rather than the fostering of public policy. . . . These shifts of tone were accompanied by changes of party leadership. In state after state men who placed greater weight on organization than ideology came into or retained power.

The leaders who were squeezed out by these developments—journalists, ideologues, clergymen, and professional men—came to regard the political practices that were responsible for their undoing (to which they formerly had not objected) as profoundly illegitimate. This group of Republicans (who were known at various times as Liberals, Independents, or Mugwumps) was distressed not simply because they had lost influence within the movement they had helped to found, but also because they disagreed with many of the policies enacted by the politicians who belonged to the party's dominant factions, the Stalwarts and the Half Breeds. The leading Liberals and Mugwumps were ardent advocates of hard money, strong proponents of free trade, and hard liners on labor issues (Sproat, 1968). Also as labor conflicts grew more intense in their own communities during the 1870s, they increasingly came to regard as dangerous to property and good order the effort to build a Republican Party in the South on the basis of black votes and in opposition to local elites (Montgomery, 1967). The Stalwarts and the Half Breeds, on the other hand, as professional politicians, sought to fashion compromises on at least the first three of these issues (they did disagree on the Southern question), compromises with which all elements of the party could live, and which would alienate the fewest voters. The Mugwumps labelled such behavior unprincipled.

The Liberals and Mugwumps were the leading advocates of civil service reform in the United States in the 1870s and 1880s: it was they who placed this reform on the political agenda. And, as they themselves explained, their chief motive for so doing was their desire to purify American politics.[8] They argued that if bureaucratic positions were distributed not as a reward for party service, but rather according to merit as indicated by performance on an open, competitive examination, political competition no longer would center around a struggle for the spoils of office; rather, it would involve the clash of principles. Politicians no longer would be able to entrench themselves in power through what amounted to a system of organized bribery; they would instead have to pay heed to public opinion. Or, to translate this into slightly different language: the party organizations which sustained the incumbent leadership would crumble if deprived of access to patronage, and the politicians affiliated with them would be replaced by the journalists, patricians, and professional men who were opinion leaders in their communities.

In addition to attacking the patronage system, the Mugwump reformers opposed the highly disciplined, "militaristic" pattern of party organization that developed during the 1870s and 1880s (Jensen, 1971). In contrast to the Progressives of the early 20th century, however, they were not opponents of party per se; they were advocates not of *nonpartisanship,* but rather of *bipartisanship* and political *independence.*[9] Indeed, on the individual level, the defining characteristic of an Independent or Mugwump was his willingness to support whichever party nominated the best man. On the organizational level, as well, the Mugwumps sought to break the monopoly that party organizations had on the political loyalties and activities of citizens. They founded one of the first interest groups in American political history, the National Civil Service Reform League, an organization which worked outside party channels to secure the enactment of the policy it advocated, and which was prepared to endorse candidates regardless of party who pledged to vote correctly on this single issue. Finally, on the institutional level, the Mugwumps advocated bipartisan representation on commissions and boards as a solution to the problems of corruption and misgovernment.

The structure of political competition in the United States during the period of the "third party system" makes intelligible both the orientation of the Mugwumps toward political parties, and their ability to secure enactment of the Pendleton Act. During the third party system, the division between the two major parties was the closest it ever has been in American history. The Democrats and Republicans, moreover, were evenly balanced on the state level, as well as nationally, in at least the larger states of the Union. This enabled the Mugwumps to play balance-of-power politics quite successfully, especially so after the last Southern states were "redeemed" in 1877. The Republicans won the White House in 1876, after losing the popular vote, only because they secured a majority on the commission which certified disputed electoral votes; the switch of fewer than 2,000 votes in New York would have reversed the Republican victory in the 1880 presidential election; and in the elections of 1882, the Republicans suffered serious losses, especially in the states where the Mugwumps were strongest. By supporting the Pendleton Act in the short congressional session of 1882-1883, the Republicans hoped to keep the Mugwumps from deserting the party in 1884. Moreover, they calculated that if the Democrats did win the presidency, the incumbent Republican president could take advantage of the new procedures by freezing Republican patronage appointees into the classified service before the new president was inaugurated.[10]

Although the Mugwumps managed in this way to secure enactment of the Pendleton Act, civil service reform did not alter the structure of party politics in the United States in the direction the reformers desired, at least not during the 19th century. During the 20 years following the passage of the Pendleton Act, the federal bureaucracy grew more rapidly than did the number of positions in the classified civil service, and most of the positions that were placed in the classified service were technical in character, and hence not especially useful for patronage purposes (Sageser, 1935). Moreover, civil service reform made little headway in the 19th century on the state level, the genuine locus of power in the decentralized party system. Only two states (New York and Massachusetts) adopted civil service statutes in the 19th century, and the merit systems in these states were quickly emasculated (Hoogenboom, 1961:260). Consequently, the parties had no less federal or state patronage available to them in 1900 than they had had in 1883. Indeed, the very reason the parties were prepared to live with civil service reform was that it imposed no present costs on them, while it enabled the government to responde to technological change and it defused the opposition of some disgruntled elites. In other words, it permitted the parties to maintain their positions as the central institutions of the American political system through the end of the 19th century.

In sum, the movement for party and bureaucratic reform in the third party system was spearheaded by a political class *manqué* which attacked the patronage system in an effort to deprive the politicians in the dominant party factions of the resources they used to fuel their organizations. Because the major parties were well organized, broadly based, and evenly matched, the reformers pursued their goals by playing balance-of-power politics. Given these structural characteristics of the third party system, all alternative strategies—outmobilizing the dominant party factions, converting their supporters, or demobilizing them—would have been far more difficult, even impossible, to pursue. But for the very reason that the reformers did not acquire for themselves a broader mass base than the factions they opposed, they were not strong enough to defend the entire governmental apparatus against the patronage-seeking politicians who sought to extract resources from it. Only after the realignment of 1896 transformed the structure of party politics in the United States were the opponents of the patronage system able to enjoy greater success.

V. TOWARD A BUREAUCRATIC STATE? THE PROGRESSIVES

In the history of American politics two periods stand out for their institutional creativity—the Jacksonian and Progressive eras. The Jacksonians sponsored a set of institutional reforms which, as noted above, created a party-centered political system in the United

States. Following the realignment of 1896, the Progressives launched an attack upon the institutions of Jacksonian democracy and sought to establish in their stead an executive-centered political system.

There is a direct relationship between the realignment of 1896 and the emergence of the Progressive movement. Prior to 1896 the American political system was characterized by high levels of party competition both nationally and in most of the larger states of the Union. The 1896 realignment created a party system that was both regionally based and highly unbalanced. Consequently, in its wake, the great majority of states, and the national government as well, came to be governed by one-party regimes.[11]

This development provided a windfall for the incumbent leadership of whichever was now the dominant party in these one-party states. Moreover, since party politicians in turn-of-the-century America characteristically furthered their careers and strengthened their factions by drawing upon the resources of a major corporation or servicing a major economic interest within their state or city (e.g., the Southern Pacific Railroad in California, the Louisville & Nashville in Kentucky, traction and elevated railway companies in New York City), these developments provided a windfall for the sector of the business community that happened to be allied with the incumbent leadership of the locally dominant party (Mowry, 1951: Chap. 1; Woodward, 1951:377ff.; Shefter, 1976a:37f.).

What is a windfall for one set of political leaders and economic interests can be a disaster for other leaders and competing interests. The emergence of one-party regimes after the election of 1896 rendered the minority party useless as a vehicle through which individuals and groups that did not enjoy preferential access to the dominant party could challenge those that did; it made it impossible for them to pursue a balance-of-power strategy akin to the one the Mugwumps had employed. The political actors who found it impossible to advance their interests *within* the party system were joined together by the Progressives in an attack *upon* the party system.

The Progressive movement, far more than the supposedly boss-dominated party machines it attacked, was closely associated with the careers of individual politicians, such as Robert La Follette of Wisconsin, Hiram Johnson of California, Albert Cummins of Iowa, William U'Ren of Oregon, and Theodore Roosevelt in national politics. These political entrepreneurs commonly had found their personal careers frustrated by the leadership of the dominant party or had been recruited into politics entirely outside party channels (e.g., Thelen, 1976: Chap. 2; Mowry, 1951:106-113). They drew their political following from among those groups that did not enjoy privileged access to the locally dominant party—among shippers in states where the party was tied to a railroad, among firms that sold in national markets in cities where the machine was tied to businesses which sold in local markets, among the native middle classes where the party drew support from the ethnic working classes.[12] The ideology that bound the movement together was formulated by a class of intellectuals and professionals who argued that a government which was dominated by a party machine, and which consequently enacted only those policies which served the interests that were tied to the machine, was both corrupt and irrational. Not only did such a government benefit some groups at the expense of others, it also failed to intervene in the economy and in society when such intervention would serve the long-run interests of all groups (Wiebe, 1967: Chap. 7). In lieu of such a regime, the Progressives proposed to create a set of institutions that would respond directly to the voice of the people, rather than filtering it through party, and that would pay heed to the dictates of science (Haber, 1964).

Once the ideology and the institutional reforms of the Progressives had been developed in this core setting—in one-party states and cities—they were picked up by politicians and businessmen who found them useful in their struggles against incumbent party leaders in other cities and states, and in national politics. (Significantly, many Progressive reforms were labelled by their state or city of origin: the "Oregon idea," the "Des Moines plan.") The diffusion of the Progressive program was so rapid and widespread because the reformers established a network of organizations, such as the National Municipal League, and publications, such as the *National Municipal Review,* for this very purpose, and they were linked to others (namely, professional associations and national magazines) in whose interest it was to advance the cause. In all settings, however, the central thrust of Progressivism was an attack upon the political party—which since the Jacksonian period had been the central institution of American government—and an effort to create an executive establishment to supplant the party in this pivotal position in the American political system.

For each of the major institutional reforms of the Jacksonian era, the Progressives sponsored an equal and opposite reform. The Jacksonians had increased the number of executive offices subject to popular election; the Progressives sought to reduce that number and to create the position of chief executive through such reforms as the short ballot and the strong mayor plan of municipal government. The most extreme version of this strand of reformism—the city manager plan of government—removed even the position of chief executive from direct popular election. The Jacksonians extended the franchise; the Progressives contracted it through registration, literacy, and citizenship requirements (Burnham, 1970:76-79). The Jacksonians established party conventions to nominate candidates for elective office; the Progressives replaced them with primary elections. The Jacksonians created a hierarchical structure of party committees to manage the electorate; the Progressives sought to destroy these party organizations or at least to render their tasks more difficult through such reforms as nonpartisan municipal government, and the separation of local, state, and national elections. Finally, the Jacksonians established a party press and accorded influence to the political editor; the Progressive movement was linked with the emergence of a self-consciously independent press (magazines as well as newspapers) and with muckraking journalists.

The bureaucratic reforms of the Progressives were part and parcel of this more general program of institutional destruction and creation. Civil service reform was the Progressives' effort to destroy the spoils system of the Jacksonians. The Jacksonians had subordinated the bureaucracy as an institution to the political party. By appointing individuals to public jobs in exchange for party service, they were violating the institutional integrity of the bureaucracy for the purposes of strengthening the party. A major reason why the Progressives advocated the creation of an autonomous mechanism and set of procedures for recruiting personnel into the bureaucracy—namely, a civil service commission which would appoint candidates to positions on the basis of their performance on competitive examinations—was to deprive incumbent party leaders of access to the bureaucracy. Deprived of access to the resources necessary for their maintenance, the locally dominant party organization would crumble, and the field would be clear for the reformers to assume power by relying on the organizations and institutions which *they* controlled—the nonpartisan press, chambers of commerce, civic associations, and so forth. To this extent, the Progressive attack upon patronage resembled the one launched by the Mugwump reformers a generation earlier.

In addition, however, there was an affirmative component to the bureaucratic reforms of the Progressives, a component which had not been present in the earlier Mugwump movement for good government. The Progressives sought not simply to destroy the political party, or even to reduce radically the role it played in American government; they sought to create in its stead an administrative arm of government that would be subject to the authority of a chief executive. Toward this end, administrators and professors who were affiliated with the Progressive movement formulated the principles and practices of what came to be called "personnel administration": position-classification plans, career and salary plans, uniform promotion regulations, retirement and pension plans, efficiency reports, and so forth (Van Riper, 1958:191-198). They also formulated the doctrines and techniques of what came to be known as "administrative management." The Committee on Department Methods (Keep Commission) appointed by President Roosevelt in 1905 was the first task force or agency in American history commissioned by a president to inquire into, and recommend improvements in, federal administrative practices (Kraines, 1970; Pinkett, 1965). In Herbert Emmerich's words (1971:39), it "stimulated management improvements in bureau after bureau in such varied fields as accounting and costing, archives and records administration, simplification of paper work, use of office machinery, personnel administration, procurement and supply, and contracting procedures." Roosevelt also was the first president to request from Congress authority to reorganize administrative agencies by executive order. And the Commission on Economy and Efficiency (Taft Commission), appointed by his successor, recommended among other things the creation of a central budget bureau to prepare an executive budget and of a central personnel bureau to develop efficiency records, position classifications, and rules governing the discipline of civil servants that would extend over all federal administrative agencies and employees (Van Riper, 1958: 219-223). On the city and state levels, the Progressives sponsored a parallel series of reforms in an effort to create a unified executive branch out of the dozens of commissions and departments that floated somewhere between the city council and the mayor or the state legislature and the governor (Schiesl, 1977).

These reforms, when fully implemented, were to have major consequences for the political influence of various groups in American society, for the relative power of the nation's governmental institutions, and for the strength of the government and for the role it was able to play both in the domestic and international arenas. These consequences were closely intertwined, and can scarcely be discussed apart from one another. Consider first their political implications. An executive establishment which stood outside the domain of partisan conflict would be in a position to exercise stewardship over the economy as a whole, and would also be in a position to advance the national interest (as that interest was understood by whomever controlled the executive) in the international economy and state system. An executive with such responsibilities would be compelled to pay heed to various interests as much in proportion to their importance in their economy, as in proportion to their weight in the electorate (cf. Maier, 1975:9-15). Such a view of presidential responsibilities was expressed by Theodore Roosevelt in his well known stewardship theory of the presidency. And significantly, it was during the administrations of Roosevelt and his two successors, and with their full cooperation, that the first institutions of functional (or corporatist) representation developed in the United States (McConnell, 1966; Weinstein, 1968). In a similar vein, it was during their administrations that universities, professional associations, and Wall Street law firms and investment banks took their place beside the party as a channel for recruitment into the executive branch, and that the in-and-outer (e.g., Clifford Pinchot, Henry Stimson, James Garfield, Felix Frankfurter) made his appearance beside the patronage appointee in high level government positions

(Van Riper, 1958:206). The construction of an executive branch, then, was the work of men who commanded the great national institutions that were coming to play an increasingly important role in the American economy and society, and it provided a channel through which these men could influence public policy. Or to phrase this in slightly different terms, it was during the Progressive era that the executive acquired a constituency among the nation's "cosmopolitan" elite which, as Samuel P. Huntington notes, was to sustain it for the next 50 years, and, correlatively, that the Congress became the refuge of the nation's "parochial" elites (Huntington, 1973).

The administrative reforms of the Progressives increased the control that the president, and the groups which enjoyed access to the presidency, were able to exercise over the administrative apparatus of government, at the expense of the institutions and groups that competed with them for influence over it—the Congress, the political party, and most importantly, the bureaucrats themselves. Administrative reform involved the imposition of uniform procedures upon the bureaucracy—procedures, as mentioned above, governing accounting, records keeping, employee evaluation, promotions, salary scales, and so on. What these reforms meant concretely was that agency heads, chief clerks, and lower level bureaucrats no longer would have as much control as they formerly had over how their office accounts would be kept, which records would be retained, how the work of their subordinates was to be evaluated, who would be promoted, and over the salaries that individual bureaucrats would receive. At the same time, Presidents Roosevelt and Taft promulgated a series of executive orders—the most famous of which were Teddy Roosevelt's "gag orders"—which sought to restrict the lobbying and campaign activities of civil servants, as well as some more conventional union activities, that is, which sought to limit the ability of bureaucrats to win salary increases by working through the Congress, political parties, or labor unions, rather than by conforming to the uniform rules and standards the administrative reformers were seeking to impose on them.[13]

Finally, the administrative reforms of the Progressives increased the technical competence and the organizational coherence of the bureaucracy, and thereby endowed the government with the capacity to intervene far more actively in the economy and society. The Progressives, to be sure, were not New Dealers, and there were substantial disagreements among them (especially between the Western insurgents who rallied behind La Follette and the Easterners who looked to Teddy Roosevelt for leadership) concerning the policies the government should pursue. Nonetheless public officials who were commonly identified as Progressive generally sought to extend the sway of governmental regulations over the economy, and to implement "reforms" in the areas of public health, education, welfare, and morals, and in the management of the public domain.

In conclusion, then, Progressivism was a movement of political leaders and groups who did not enjoy privileged access to the one-party regimes that emerged in the wake of the 1896 realignment. As had been true of the Mugwumps before them, the Progressives attacked the patronage system and political machines in an effort to dry up the resources and destroy the organizations that incumbent politicians used to maintain themselves in power. There were important differences between the Progressives and Mugwumps, however, which enabled the latter movement to be more successful than the earlier one. The Mugwumps had been closely associated with one segment of the nation's upper class—the mercantile and financial elite of the Northeast—and their reformism was in part an attack upon the politicians who played a mediating role in conflicts between this elite and other sectoral and sectional interests over monetary and trade policy (Sharkey, 1959: Chap. 7). The Progressives, by contrast, did not play the role of intransigent ideologues in such intraclass conflicts. To the contrary, by attempting to create an executive branch which was insulated from partisan influences and the vagaries of electoral competition, they were seeking to establish a governmental institution which would be in a position to take account of all major interests within the economy, and which could supplant the party as the central mediating institution of American government. In addition, the advisory commissions and legislative reference bureaus and municipal research bureaus the Progressives established provided the professional and managerial classes with channels of access to the government; and the civil service reforms they sponsored advantaged the middle class in the competition for positions on the public payroll. Taken together, the managerial and personnel reforms of the Progressives endowed the government with the capacity to administer the regulatory and social overhead programs whose enactment was supported by many of the nation's major business leaders, as well as by groups further down the social scale (Hays, 1958; Lazerson, 1971; Weinstein, 1968). In other words, it was the political genius of the Progressives to discover the terms upon which some of the economic and regional cleavages that had divided the American upper classes in the 19th century could be overcome, and some popular backing could be acquired for an attack upon entrenched political machines.

The Progressive attack upon existing party and bureaucratic institutions, however, encountered substantial resistance. On the national level, the defenders of existing administrative arrangements, by working through the Congress, were able to defeat, or at least to delay, enactment of the major reform proposals of the Keep and Taft commmissions. On the state and local levels, the Progressives enjoyed considerable success in those states and cities, chiefly in the West, where the locally dominant parties did not rest on a broad and well-organized popular base. Where the incumbent leadership had mobilized such support during the previous party system, however, it was able to survive the challenge of the Progressives with only temporary losses (Shefter, 1976b).

VI. TOWARDS A RESPONSIBLE PARTY SYSTEM?
THE NEW DEAL

The second major wave of party and bureaucratic reforms in this century occurred in the aftermath of the New Deal realignment. On the national level, Franklin D. Roosevelt, in 1937, asked Congress to enact the most comprehensive package of administrative reforms since the proposals of the Taft Commission in 1912. And on the state level, as James Sundquist (1973: Chap. 11) has noted, struggles between reform Democrats and the regular or machine faction of the party erupted in dozens of states as "aftershocks" of the New Deal realignment. Moreover, the number of states adopting merit civil service systems shot up dramatically following the realignment. In the 16 years following 1933, 11 states enacted civil service statutes, whereas in the 16 years preceding the realignment only one state had done so.[14]

The relationship between the New Deal realignment and the party and bureaucratic reform movements which followed it is broadly similar to that between the realignment of 1896 and the reform struggles of the Progressive Era. In both cases, reform movements were spearheaded by elements of the new majority party who wanted to turn the government to new purposes, and who sought, by attacking the patronage system and reorganizing the bureaucracy, both to undermine the politicians who opposed them and to extend their own control over institutions of government. There were, however, some important differences between the New Dealers and Progressives. Most importantly, New Deal liberals were prepared to pursue a strategy of mass mobilization and popular organization in order to overwhelm their rivals. In addition, on questions of political and administrative organization, F.D.R., as the conventional wisdom asserts, was a thorough pragmatist. He was, for example, quite willing to collaborate with machine politicians who supported his administration. These considerations— the quest for power and control, the strategy of mass organization, and political opportunism—explain variations through time and across space in the party and administrative reforms the New Dealers pursued.

On the national level, administrative and political reform was of little concern to F.D.R. during the period of the "first" New Deal. To the contrary, positions in 60 of the 65 new administrative agencies created during the president's first two years in office were exempted from the classified civil service, and many of these new agencies were located outside the departmental structure of the executive branch (Van Riper, 1958:320). The president's associates frankly admitted that administrative reorganization was too touchy a problem to tackle prior to F.D.R.'s reelection, for, as they correctly predicted, it would generate furious opposition on the part of the interests threatened by it (Polenberg, 1966:10). F.D.R. only appointed a commission to study executive reorganization in 1936, and he only submitted a reorganization bill to Congress in January 1937, after he had won his second term (Karl, 1963).

Chronologically and politically, F.D.R.'s administrative reforms belonged to the second phase of the New Deal—the phase extending from the Wagner Act and Social Security Act of 1935, through the court packing and reorganization bills of 1937, to the congressional purge of 1938—and were part and parcel of an effort to institutionalize both the programs of the New Deal and the power of the New Dealers. The Reorganization Act would institutionalize the *programs* of F.D.R.'s first term by creating two new cabinet departments to administer the public welfare and the public works programs that had been enacted from 1933 to 1936, and by granting the president the authority to integrate other New Deal programs into the existing departmental structure. As the conservative opponents of the reorganization bill well recognized, these provisions would transform programs that had been enacted as emergency measures into permanent features of the American governmental system (Polenberg, 1966:167).

The reforms of 1935-1938 would institutionalize the *power* of the New Dealers by establishing a set of institutions which would link the administration to a mass constituency, and would enable it to assert its control over the entire governmental structure; that is, would perform for the administration precisely those functions served by the party organization in cities and states governed by centralized political machines (Merton, 1957:70-81). The first of these purposes was served by the National Labor Relations Act, which established procedures for organizing the industrial working class into unions that, as could be anticipated, were to become staunch supporters of the administration responsible for their creation, and by the Social Security Act, which established a bureaucracy to provide benefits to the poor and working class in times of need—assistance that formerly had been provided, if at all, only by political machines (Greenstone, 1969: Chap. 2). Significantly, under amendments to the Social Security Act enacted in 1939, the Social Security Board required states to establish merit systems covering the employees who administered the program on the state and local level, a requirement which was policed by a Division of State Merit Systems and which led to the creation of the first civil service systems in most states of the union (Civil Service Assembly, 1940). In this way, the framers of the act sought to ensure that locally dominant political forces would not gain control of the administration of the program and be strengthened by it. Rather, they wanted the flow of these new benefits to be controlled from the center, and the political advantages of the program to accrue to the administration which enacted it.

The second of the abovementioned purposes—the creation of a set of institutions that would enable the administration to extend its control over the entire administrative apparatus—was served by the Executive Reorganization Act of 1937. The Reorganization Act would expand the White House staff; extend the merit system and replace the Civil Service Commission with a single personnel director appointed by the president; transfer the preauditing function from the Comptroller-General (and the Congress) to the Budget Bureau (and the President); create a central planning agency in the Executive Office; and place all administrative agencies, including the independent regulatory commissions, under one of the cabinet departments (Emmerich, 1971: Chap. 3). Together these reforms would endow the administration with the institutional capacity to control the initiation, coordination, and implementation of public policy—a capacity whose only precedent in the political experience of the United States, again, was the control exercised by the party apparatus in cities ruled by centralized machines.

On the state and local levels, the New Deal realignment generated major struggles for control over the Democratic party between political forces committed to the programs of the national administration and the party's incumbent leadership. These after-shocks of the New Deal realignment occurred in some states while F.D.R. was still in the White House, while in others they did not erupt until 15 or 20 years after his death (Sundquist, 1973: Chap. 11). The timing and the character of these struggles for power depended upon the stance the incumbent Democratic leadership took with respect to the national administration and the techniques it employed to maintain itself in power. Where incumbent machine politicians supported the New Deal (e.g., Chicago, Pittsburgh) F.D.R. was perfectly willing to use the patronage generated by New Deal programs to strengthen local party machines (Stave, 1970). Where the incumbent Democratic leadership was hostile to the national administration and commanded a broadly based, patronage-oriented party machine (e.g., Tammany Hall in New York City), the liberals organized through third party organizations or reform clubs (e.g., the American Labor Party and later the

Democratic reform movement in New York). In these cities, the conflict between insurgents and incumbents resembled the battles between reformers and political machines during the Progressive era: the insurgents attacked the patronage system in an effort to dry up the resources upon which their opponents relied; they challenged the legitimacy of the party organizations their opponents led, accusing them of "bossism"; and they sought to demobilize their opponents' followers more than to bring new groups into the electorate (Wilson, 1962). Finally, where the incumbent Democratic leadership was hostile or indifferent to the New Deal and did not command a mass-based party organization (e.g., Michigan, Minnesota), the liberals were able with little difficulty to take over the Democratic caucus structure by allying with labor unions and farm organizations that had benefited from New Deal programs. In these states, factional struggles within the Democratic party took the form of a straight ideological conflict between liberals and conservatives; the issues of "bossism" and corruption did not occupy center stage (Fenton, 1966: Chaps. 2-3). Indeed, for the very reason that in these states liberals in the New Deal era (unlike the Progressives 30 or 40 years earlier) were able to gain power *through* the existing party system and party structures, they were not (again in contrast to the Progressives) opponents of party per se. To the contrary, they became advocates of party government, by "responsible," issue-oriented parties (Sawyer, 1960).

In states and cities, then, attacks upon the patronage system and efforts to construct issue-oriented party organizations in the wake of the 1932 realignment were led by New Deal liberals who sought in these ways to undermine the incumbent party leaders who opposed them and to gain power locally. In addition to these short-run political considerations, there were several long-run considerations which led the middle-class liberals who played such a prominent role in the New Deal coalition to favor bureaucratic and party reform. New Deal liberals wanted the government to play a rather active role in society, and a "modern personnel system" (competitive examinations, educational requirements, in-service training) was more likely than a patronage system to recruit civil servants who had the technical proficiency to perform the tasks they wanted the government to perform. It also should be noted, however, that these recruitment procedures would skew the distribution of public jobs to the advantage of the upwardly mobile semiprofessionals—teachers, social workers, etc.—who were an important element of the liberal constituency. And these personnel practices were a means of ensuring that the civil servants who administered New Deal programs at the grass roots would be socialized into the values and doctrines of the professionals who had initially drafted them, rather than the values of old-line politicians or "parochial" elites in local communities throughout the nation. Moreover, the greater the scale of government, the more compelling are arguments for administrative "coordination" and "rationalization," and the administrative reorganizations proposed by bureaucratic reformers during the New Deal era would, indeed, achieve gains in these respects. It must also be noted, however, that these reforms would transfer the tasks of coordination (and the power that inevitably flows to whomever coordinates the work of others) from politicians and political brokers to professional public administrators.

In addition, the long-run political interests of middle-class liberals would be served if America's decentralized, patronage-oriented party organizations were replaced by more disciplined, issue-oriented parties. Candidates who appeal for votes by promising to enact new programs, and incumbents who campaign for reelection by pointing to the new policies they have enacted, have need for the advice of professionals, technocrats, and administrators who are the most fertile source of ideas for new public policies. Presidential or mayoral "task forces" (the President's Committee on Income Security, which drafted the Social Security Act, was one of the earliest examples) accord far more influence to these groups than had the traditional mechanisms of policy formation in the United States, which were centered in legislatures and staffed by politicians. And to the extent that liberals were confident that the policies they favored enjoyed the support of a majority of the national electorate, they lamented the absence in the United States of a "responsible party system"—one which would enable a president elected by that majority and by virtue of his supporting those policies to extend his sway over the Congress.

In politics, the pursuit of short-run gains commonly prevails over long-run strategic considerations. Although the long-run interests of middle-class liberals would be served by the implementation of a full-scale program of bureaucratic and party reform, skilled political brokers during the postwar decades were able to integrate them into regimes that gave them something of what they wanted, but not everything. Mayors such as Richard Lee in New Haven, Robert Wagner in New York, and Richard Daley in Chicago were able to construct remarkably stable political coalitions, and to win reelection for term after term in the 1950s and early 1960s, by dividing the municipal government into "islands of functional power," and granting the party organization access to the patronage of only certain municipal departments, while the agencies and programs that were of greatest interest to would-be reformers (urban renewal, education, social welfare) were placed under the control of professionals, civil servants, civic leaders, and the downtown business community (Lowi, 1967). It is little wonder that the three seminal studies of urban politics published in 1960-1961—the books by Robert Dahl (1961), Edward Banfield (1961), and Wallace Sayre and Herbert Kaufman (1960)— found the pluralist framework so useful! In the mid-1960s, however, these coalitions fell apart.

VII. THE NEW POLITICS MOVEMENT

The third major movement for party and bureaucratic reform in this century, the New Politics movement, emerged during the 1960s and has had repercussions down to the present day.[15] Like its predecessors, the New Politics movement has sought in a number of fundamental ways to reform the procedures governing the selection of candidates for elective office and the recruitment of administrative officials; to alter the structure of authority within parties and bureaucracies; and to bring about changes in the way elected officials, bureaucrats, and private interests deal with one another. In contrast to the party and bureaucratic reform movements which preceded it, however, the New Politics movement did not emerge in the wake of a critical election. Nonetheless, I would argue that the reform movement of the 1960s can be understood in terms similar to those I have used to analyze earlier movements for party and bureaucratic reform. The difference between the New Politics movement and its predecessors with respect to the timing of its emergence is a function of the distinctive character of the post-New Deal party system—one in which the role of political parties and elections was rather circumscribed. This will become clear, I trust, as I describe the way the New Politics movement unfolded in the 1960s.

The reform movement of the 1960s was initially triggered by the Democratic victory in the 1960 presidential election. The election of 1960 was *not* a realigning election. The coalition which placed John Kennedy in the White House was very much in the New Deal mold; he was supported disproportionately by union members, city dwellers, Catholics, blacks, and Southerners (Axelrod, 1972:14). In organizational terms the Democratic party of 1960 also conformed to the pattern that had been established under FDR: its cadre were an amalgam of old line politicians, union leaders, and upper-middle class liberal activists.

This influence of this last group was greater at the peak of the political system than at its base. If for no other reason than to retain the loyalty of this element of their constituency, Presidents Kennedy and Johnson were constantly in the market for "program material," proposals for new programs and policies. As a number of scholars have noted, the major urban programs of the New Frontier and Great Society were drafted not in response to demands from their presumed beneficiaries—black slum dwellers—but rather on the initiative of presidentially appointed task forces (Marris and Rein, 1973; Piven and Cloward, 1971). The members of these task forces were in the main "professional reformers"—academics, foundation officials, senior civil servants, representatives of professional associations, and so forth (Moynihan, 1969: chap. 2; Beer, 1973:75).

On the local level, the picture was quite different. As mentioned above, in most large cities after World War II a rather stable accommodation had been achieved among the major contenders for local power—party politicians, businessmen, union leaders, newspaper publishers, middle income homeowners, the ethnic working classes. Writing at that time, Robert Salisbury (1964) described this pattern of accommodation as "the new convergence of power," and roughly speaking these forces converged around a program of urban renewal in the Central Business District for the business community and construction unions, low taxes for homeowners, and secure jobs in the municipal civil service for the lower-middle class and upwardly mobile members of the working class. Upper-middle class professionals had some influence over municipal agencies, but this was sharply constrained by the desire of mayors to keep taxes low, and of the municipal civil service to control its own work routines and to determine the standards which would govern the hiring, promotion and firing of public employees (Sayre and Kaufman, chap. 11).

Upper-middle class liberals sought to use the access they enjoyed to the Kennedy and Johnson administrations to circumvent these local accommodations and to extend their influence over the agencies of municipal government. The presidential task forces that drafted New Frontier and Great Society legislation argued that municipal bureaucracies did not command the resources, the talent, or the initiative that was necessary to solve the "urban crisis." To deal with this problem, they proposed to extend federal grants-in-aid to local governments to support "innovative" programs. To obtain these grants, cities found it necessary either to establish independent agencies under the control of the local counterparts of the officials in Washington who dispensed this money, or to have existing municipal departments contract with consulting firms or hire administrators who shared the outlook and knew the vocabulary of the dispensers of the federal grants. The "grantsmen," who were most successful in obtaining federal funds, naturally were those whose educational backgrounds, social origins, and institutional affiliations were similar to the federal grant givers, and who proposed to spend federal monies for purposes their Washington counterparts favored. In other words, the grant-in-aid programs of the Kennedy and Johnson administrations were the means by which upper-middle-class professionals—and their political allies—used their access to the White House to extend their control over the policies, programs, and hiring practices of municipal agencies.[16]

Blacks were useful allies in the endeavor. The attack upon municipal bureaucracies was justified, in part, by the assertion that they were "insensitive" and "unresponsive" to the needs of the black community. Blacks had strong reasons to join this attack because the mechanisms of community participation that were attached to

Great Society programs provided them with channels through which they both could influence the way municipal departments distributed their benefits and could obtain access to the patronage that was directly controlled by federally funded community action agencies, model cities boards, neighborhood service centers, and community development corporations. These mechanisms of community participation furthermore legitimized federal intervention in local affairs apart form elected local governments, and they provided an institutional framework through which blacks could be organized to provide local political support for these programs.

The attack upon municipal bureaucracies conducted through the Great Society programs of the 1960s, then, was an effort by one segment of the old New Deal coalition—upper-middle-class liberals and blacks—to extend its control over the institutions of local government at the expense of other segments of that coalition. It was through this struggle for power at the periphery of the political system that the elements of the upper middle class which were to rally behind the New Politics movement—the "new class" or the "conscience constituency"—first became aware of themselves as a distinctive political force.[17]

The second phase of the New Politics movement was triggered by President Johnson's escalation of the war in Vietnam. Vietnam turned upper-middle-class liberal Democrats against their party's national leadership, and at that point the struggle for influence at the periphery of the political system became an all-out battle for control at the center. The New Politics movement sponsored a series of party and bureaucratic reforms which were part and parcel of this effort to undermine the power of its erstwhile allies, and to construct a regime that the social forces for which it spoke could dominate.

The party reforms sponsored by the New Politics movement following the defeat of the antiwar candidates at the 1968 Democratic National Convention were the most comprehensive since those of the Progressive Era. Chief among them were rules requiring that delegations to future national conventions be composed of blacks, women, and youths in a "reasonable relationship to their presence in the population of the State"; encouraging states to select convention delegations through primary elections or open caucus procedures; and discouraging the slatemaking efforts of party organizations (Ranney, 1975). Organizations such as Common Cause also sponsored a number of reforms in the area of campaign finance: public subsidies to candidates, limitations on individual contributions, public disclosure of the names of contributors. Through these reforms the New Politics movement weakened the position of its major competitors for influence within the Democratic Party—big city party organizations, labor unions, business— and enhanced the importance of middle class issue-oriented activists, and the influence of three of the major movements with which it was allied, namely, the civil rights movement, the women's movement, and the youth movement.

In addition to reforming the parties, the New Politics movement also sought to bring about changes in the structure of the federal bureaucracy and the conduct of administrative agencies. Indeed, as James Q. Wilson has noted, the "bureaucracy problem," which since the New Deal had been a concern of the Right, became in the 1960s, a concern of the Left (Wilson, 1967). Practices that formerly had been the subject only of academic analysis became matters for journalistic exposure—the interchange of personnel between administrative agencies and the industries they regulated; the cocoon of minimum rates, entry restrictions, public subsidies, and tax benefits that had been placed around one sector of the economy after another since the New Deal; the mutually beneficial relationships that had developed between executive agencies, congressional committees, and private interests. Common Cause, the Nader organization, and various groups in the consumer and environmental movement have attempted to put an end to these practices by sponsoring sunshine laws, inserting strict standards in regulatory statutes, subjecting administrative agencies to close judicial supervision, and by providing for "consumer" or "public" representation in the administrative process.

Finally, the New Politics movement launched a full-scale attack upon the national security establishment as well as upon agencies in the domestic sector. As in that sector, practices which previously had aroused little journalistic attention or public opposition now were labelled as improper: the Pentagon's tolerance of cost over-runs in weapons procurement contracts, the public relations campaigns and lobbying efforts of the Pentagon, the hiring of retired military officers by defense contractors, the failure of Congress to monitor the activities of the CIA and other intelligence agencies. The New Politics movement sought to subject the "military-industrial complex" to stricter external control, and more generally to reduce its size (by "reordering national priorities") and limit the role it had come to play in the nation's life during the Cold War years.

By attacking these practices, the New Politics movement was attempting to disrupt the structure of accommodations through which the New Deal coalition had come to terms with the major established social forces in American society in the 1940s. This grand coalition was initially forged by F.D.R. in order to mobilize the entire nation behind the effort to win World War II; F.D.R.'s part of the bargain was to transform himself from Dr. New Deal into Dr. Win-the-War. After Germany and Japan had been defeated, however, the wartime coalition was subject to enormous strains: conservative, isolationist Midwesterners fought bitterly with moderate, internationalist Easterners for control of the Republican party; and the New Deal coalition split into a left wing, center, and a right wing faction (i.e., Progressives, Fair Dealers, and Dixiecrats). In order to cope with the Soviet threat to American interests in Europe in the late 1940s, Truman, with the support of liberal and moderate internationalists in both parties, sought to reconstitute the bipartisan coalition (Westerfield, 1955). By the early 1950s, the moderates had emerged on top in both parties and a bipartisan consensus on national security issues came to prevail in American politics, but only after major concessions were made to the conservatives (left wingers were purged from the bureaucracy and the labor unions, the Democrats abandoned their efforts to revive the New Deal, the civil rights issue was dropped), and of greatest relevance here, after NSC-68 was implemented and a massive and permanent military establishment was created (Huntington, 1961: 47-63). The creation of this military apparatus, and the development of all the practices to which the New Politics movement later objected, made it possible to give all the major actors in American politics a stake in the nation's national security policies, and therefore in its postwar regime. Elected officials were given access to a huge pork barrel, which incumbents could use to enhance their political security (Dexter, 1963). National defense made it politically possible for public expenditures to be maintained at a level which kept unemployment reasonably low, wages reasonably high, and labor reasonably happy. And through the procurement of weapons and supplies, those elements of the American business community which had been most strongly identified with the isolationist wing of the Republican Party—namely, Midwestern industrialists as opposed to Eastern financial and commercial interests—were reconciled to internationalism and big government.[18] In other words, the attack which the New Politics movement launched against the military-industrial complex in the late 1960s was the institutional variant of its challenge in the ideological realm to the Cold War consensus on foreign policy: by attacking the military-industrial complex, the New Politics movement was seeking to undermine the agencies and the organizational patterns through which the grand coalition behind that consensus had become institutionalized.

In the area of domestic policy, a rather similar pattern of accommodations between the New Deal coalition and its erstwhile opponents emerged during the postwar period, and the persistent charge made by the New Politics movement, that agencies in the domestic sector were serving "private interests" rather than the "public interest," can be understood as an effort to disrupt these accommodations. The regulatory and expenditure programs enacted by Democratic congressional majorities during the postwar decades, as studies by economists and political scientists have repeatedly demonstrated, generally redistributed income to the more established or wealthier members of each of the major segments of American society and each of the major sectors of the American economy (Boulding and Pfaff, 1972; Banfield, 1974: Chap. 1; Ross and Passell, 1973:61-89). On the local level, federal redevelopment and highway programs financed the grand political coalitions that enabled Democratic mayors to secure reelection term after term. On the national level, their effect was quite similar. As David Mayhew's (1966) study of roll-call voting in the postwar congresses indicates, what distinguished Democrats from Republicans was their willingness to enter into logrolling arrangements to pass legislation of this character across a broad range of issue areas. This enabled the Democrats to become a permanent majority party (indeed, the regime party) during the postwar era, and it enabled individual Democratic congressmen to acquire an extraordinary measure of political security. Or perhaps it might be more accurate to say that the Democratic party became the institution through which a "machine of the incumbents" emerged in American national politics during the postwar era. In recent decades, congressmen from both parties have secured reelection by entering into logrolling deals, negotiated by the Democratic congressional leadership, to pass legislation which serves the major producer interests in their constituencies, and by interceding before executive agencies to obtain "particularized" benefits for individual firms and voters in their districts (Mayhew, 1974; Evans and Novak, 1971). It is, of course, precisely this pattern of political behavior—logrolling; alliances between congressional committees, executive agencies, and producer interests; the receipt of campaign contributions for favors rendered—that the New Politics movement considers to be antithetical to the "public interest." By attacking these arrangements and the agencies implicated in them, the New Politics movement was seeking to undermine the practices and institutions which sustained its opponents in power.

If the political accommodations and the institutional arrangements underlying America's postwar regime can account for the *targets* the New Politics movement chose to attack, the composition of the coalition the movement assembled can account in large measure for the *content* of the administrative reforms it proposed. A comparison between the New Politics movement and the reform movements that immediately preceded it is instructive in this regard, because the administrative arrangements the movement endorsed are substantially different from those advocated by Progressive and New Deal administrative reformers. First, the New Politics movement has severely criticized the public personnel system established at the behest of earlier administrative reformers, one built around competitive examinations and a career civil service. As an alternative to the former the movement has advocated various mechanisms of affirmative action and community control. And as an alternative to the latter, the movement has advocated that the performance of many public tasks be delegated to nongovernmental institutions whose employees are not career civil servants. Second, the New Politics movement has challenged what has been *the* central tenet of administrative reorganization throughout this century: unity of command. It has opposed presidential efforts to centralize control over the bureaucracy, and has supported efforts to extend the influence of Congress, the judiciary, and the press (Glazer, 1975; Tugwell and Cronin, 1974; Wise, 1973).

These differences between the bureaucratic reforms advocated by the New Politics movement and those endorsed by earlier administrative reformers are to be explained to a considerable degree by differences in the social and institutional bases of these movements. In contrast to the Progressives and New Dealers, who drew mass support from a middle class and upwardly mobile working class whose members could expect to secure civil service jobs through competitive examinations, the New Politics movement sought to win support of blacks, who were excluded from public jobs by such examinations, and from members of the upper middle class who had little interest in moving slowly up the ladder in career civil service systems. The black members of this coalition would benefit in obvious ways, however, from the explicit racial criteria in affirmative action programs, and from the implicit ones in community control plans. And upper-class members of this coalition would benefit quite directly if public responsibilities were delegated, and public monies allocated, to the institutions with which they were affiliated—alternative schools, consulting firms, legal services clinics, public interest law firms, and so forth.

In a similar vein, bureaucratic reformers who were associated with the Progressive and New Deal movements sought to increase the administrative powers of chief executives because both movements (by pursuing rather different strategies, to be sure) reasonably could hope to elect presidents, governors, and mayors. The New Politics movement, by contrast, rarely could command a majority of votes in general elections, and it was either unwilling or unable to do what was necessary to acquire additional support—as the drubbing the McGovernites received in the 1972 presidential election indicates, and as the extremely low rates of turnout in antipoverty elections also suggest. (Indeed, the very demand for guaranteed representation through racial or sexual quotas is an indication that the movement was not prepared to secure representation by seeking to win more votes than its rivals). Because the movement rarely was able to elect chief executives, it opposed reforms—such as those proposed by the Ash Council in 1970, or the ones President Nixon sought to implement by fiat in 1973—that would increase their administrative powers. To the contrary, the New Politics movement sought to reduce the powers of the presidency, and to increase the influence within the administrative process of the institutions with which the movement was allied or to which it enjoyed access. Thus, the movement has sought to subject the bureaucracy to increased public scrutiny, and to influence its behavior through "investigative reporting" and Naderite exposés, because it is closely associated with an important element of the national press (Weaver, 1974). Civil rights, environmental, and consumer groups have attempted to subject the bureaucracy to tighter supervision by the courts because they command considerable legal talent, and because the federal judiciary (in *its* search for a constituency) in recent years has loosened requirements for standing, considerably narrowed the scope of the doctrine of political questions, and enriched the range of remedies it is prepared to consider in class action suits (Orren, 1976). And after decades of seeking to limit the powers of Congress, liberals recently have sought to expand Congress's powers over the administration—especially in the areas of budgeting and impoundments, investigations and executive privilege— because over the past 10 years increasing numbers of senators and representatives have associated themselves with the issues and political orientations of the New Politics movement (Fiorina, 1977).

Finally, the New Politics movement has sought to deal with the problem of administrative clientelism—the "capture" of regulatory and administrative agencies by producer interests—not by increasing the president's authority over "the headless fourth branch of government," which was the solution proposed by New Deal administrative reformers, but rather by establishing various mechanisms to represent the "consumer interest" or the "public interest" in the administrative process. In practice this means they have attempted to secure appointments to administrative positions for representatives of public interest groups, and they have sought to create new administrative agencies (e.g., a Consumer Protection Agency) which will serve as official spokesmen for their groups. That is, unable to defeat in the electoral arena the productive coalition which served as the constituency for America's postwar regime, they have sought to deal the social forces for which they speak into the pluralist game.

In conclusion, then, there are certain broad similarities between the contemporary movement for party and bureaucratic reform and the movements which immediately preceded it. Like its predecessors, the New Politics movement was led by a coalition of groups (the upper middle classes and their black allies) within the majority party (the Democrats) that sought to extend its influence over the institutions of local and national government at the expense of the political forces (producer interests, including organized labor) that previously had been dominant. And the reforms the New Politics movement advocated, like those sponsored by its predecessors, would deprive the previously dominant political forces of some of the resources (e.g., the military pork barrel) that had sustained their power; would enhance the influence of the organizations (e.g., public interest groups) the reformers established and the institutions (e.g., the press) with which they were allied; and would provide these organizations and the social groups for whom the reformers spoke with privileged access to public authority (e.g., through consumer representation) and to public resources (e.g, through the "social" park barrel) (see Stockman, 1975).

The distinctive characteristics of the recent wave of reformism can be understood in light of the distinctive characteristics of America's postwar, pluralist regime. As mentioned at the beginning of this section, the New Politics movement, unlike the other movements discussed in this essay, did not erupt in the wake of a realignment in the party system. It did not conform to this pattern because political parties have played a far less significant role in American government and politics in recent decades than at any time since the Jacksonian Era (Burnham, 1975:305f.). This in part was a tribute to the success of earlier bureaucratic reform movements, which had succeeded in creating an executive establishment largely insulated from the influence of party politics and directly linked to other major national institutions. This transformation in the institutional substructure of American politics explains how upper-middle-class liberals, who were affiliated with some of these institutions, could seek to use the national government to extend their influence over local bureaucracies in the early 1960s, even though they had little in the way of a local electoral base. And it explains how a full-scale struggle for control of the federal government could erupt in the mid-1960s when a number of national institutions, beginning with universities and the press, turned against the war in Vietnam, and sought to drive from power the incumbent leadership of the Democratic party, and to contain the power of the national security establishment. The party and bureaucratic reform movements of the past 15 years, as I have argued, emerged from, and were part and parcel of, these struggles for power (Hodgson, 1973).

VIII. CONCLUSION

As the analysis above indicates, the relationship between political parties and public bureaucracies in the United States, and the structure of these two institutions, has changed substantially a number of times over the past two centuries. The explanation most commonly offered for these institutional developments is that they are responses to changes in American society: shifts in the percentage of the population engaged in agriculture, industry, and the professions; the influx of European immigrants and then their assimilation into the middle class; the increasing scale and complexity of the tasks government must perform, and so forth. It would be follish to deny that social changes such as these have played a role in the institutional transformations described in this essay. But they constitute at most half the story. For, as I have argued, changes in the structure of party and bureaucracy, and in the relationship between these institutions, have had major implications for the distribution of power in the United States. And the groups sponsoring institutional reforms, as well as those who resist them, have not been unaware of these implications.

There is no need to repeat here what I argued above. Suffice it to say that my central theme has been that efforts to reform the structure of party and bureaucracy have been part and parcel of the struggle for power in American politics. These reform movements cluster in the wake of realigning elections as elements of the new majority party seek, in the first place, to deprive the politicians who had played a major role in the earlier party system of access to the resources upon which they had relied to maintain themselves in power, and in the second place, to build an institutional order which they (the reformers) can dominate.

In other words, the emergence, development, and decay of the successive American party systems has involved not only fluctuations in the relative strength of the two major parties, but also in the relationship between political parties and other institutions: as one party system is succeeded by another, changes occur both in the balance of power *within* the party system, and in the balance of power *between* parties and other public institutions. And this finding leads to the following general conclusion: *In American politics institutional conflicts are the functional equivalent of party conflicts.*

In asserting this proposition, I mean not only that controversies over the structure of institutions and conflicts between institutions are an integral part of the cycle of party realignment in the United States, but also that the outcome of these controversies and the very way they are resolved have their equivalents in the way governmental authority is allocated through a party system. Political institutions, as I have stressed in this essay, inevitably favor some interests over others: they elevate one set of spokesmen for a social group in preference to competing leaders; they skew the distribution of public benefits to the advantage of some segments of the population and the disadvantage of others; they give some interests preferential access to public authority at the expense of competing interests. This means that efforts to alter the relative power of different institutions (such as parties and bureaucracies), or to reform their structure so they will embody a new set of interests, can have consequences for the distribution of political power and public benefits as great as those occurring when one party trounces its rivals in the electoral arena.

Reform movements, however, rarely enjoy victories of this magnitude: institutional reformers generally are compelled to enter into compromises with their opponents, or at least to resign themselves to less than a total victory. For example, the Mugwumps succeeded in placing certain federal agencies under the jurisdiction of the Civil Service Commission, while others continued to serve as sources of party patronage; the Progressives triumphed in some states, but failed completely in others; during the post-New Deal period middle-class liberals enjoyed a measure of influence over certain municipal agencies in most large cities, while others remained under the control of old-line politicians; and, most recently, the New Politics movement has enjoyed remarkable success in opening up some federal agencies (e.g., the FCC) to the influence of public interest groups, while others (e.g., the Agriculture Department) continue to operate pretty much as before. Or to describe these outcomes in more general terms, in the aftermath of critical elections and of the institutional conflicts which follow them, the governmental structure of the United States has been divided along functional (and/or geographic) lines, different government agencies (and/or state and local governments) have been parcelled out to various contenders for power, and a coalition regime has been established. The process through which this has occurred in the United States is different in form, but not entirely different in substance or outcome, from the bargaining process which occurs in fragmented multiparty systems, where *after* elections have been conducted, the political parties and political factions jockey for advantage, seek to gain control of important government ministries, and ultimately resolve their differences by forming a coalition government. Thus, not only are institutional conflicts an integral part of the cycle of party realignment in the United States, but the process through which they are resolved and the regime which is established in their wake is equivalent to the way public authority is allocated through party systems that, on their face, do not resemble the American.

This last observation indicates that institutional conflicts can serve not only as a continuation of party warfare by other means, but also as a substitute for it. Groups which are unable to gain political power by seizing control of a political party or constructing a new one, and using it to overwhelm the incumbents at the polls (a strategy of *mobilization*) can adopt two alternative strategies. They can pursue a strategy of *demobilization:* sponsoring electoral reforms which effectively disenfranchise the voters who are likely to support their opponents, or sponsoring bureaucratic reforms which deprive the incumbents of the resources they use to link themselves to a mass base. Alternatively, they can pursue a strategy of *circumvention:* outflanking incumbent politicians by establishing executive agencies which stand outside the domain of electoral and party politics, and which provide the reformers with privileged access. The conflicts generated by mobilizing strategies are conducted within the party and electoral system; those generated by demobilizing or flanking strategies take the form of institutional conflicts—either disputes over the proper structure of institutions or conflicts between political institutions.

With the partial exception of the New Deal, reformers over the past century have pursued the second and third of these strategies to a greater extent than the first, and consequently, the locus of political conflict—and of the bargaining and the accommodations which resolve these conflicts—increasingly has moved outside the party system in the United States. Nothing illustrates the extent to which this trend has progressed quite so clearly as Watergate. President Nixon, claiming a mandate from his landslide victory in the 1972 election, sought at the beginning of his second term to centralize his control of the entire administrative apparatus of the federal government, at the expense of the institutions with which his opponents were affiliated—the congress, the press, and the bureaucracy itself (Nathan, 1975; Aberbach and Rockman, 1976). These institutions and political forces launched a counter-attack; they argued that the president's efforts to centralize power violated the constitution. Assisted, to be sure, by Nixon's having clearly broken a criminal law, they were able to secure his removal from office. A number of aspects of this struggle for power are especially noteworthy: it was conducted almost entirely outside the realm of electoral politics; political parties played at most a secondary role in it; it took the form in large measure of an institutional conflict; and the institutions opposing the president, by driving him from office, proved themselves to be powerful enough to reverse a decision (tainted though it might have been) made earlier in the electoral arena.

Only time will tell whether the Watergate episode signals the emergence of yet another American party system—one in which political parties and elections play a smaller role than ever before.

NOTES

1. On the "gentlemen freeholders" of Virginia, see Sydnor (1952); on the "patriciate" of New Haven, see Dahl (1961: Chap. 2). New York and Pennsylvania were, to some extent, exceptions to this pattern: party organizations were somewhat stronger and a partisan spoils system was more fully developed than elsewhere in the country. See Hofstadter (1969: 213) and Fish (1905: Chap. 1).

2. Dibble (1965:884f), cited in Crenson (1975:171). Dibble is speaking here of the Justices of the Peace in Elizabethan England, but, as Crenson observes, the same can be said of the notables appointed to office by Washington.

3. Indeed, Presidents James Monroe and John Quincy Adams even reappointed civil servants who were politically hostile to their administrations, although they could have been replaced under the Tenure of Office Act of 1820. See White (1951: Chap. 26).

4. Crenson's explanation for "the rise of bureaucracy in Jacksonian America" is rather similar to the explanation for the contemporaneous "discovery of the asylum" proposed by David Rothman (1971). Rothman's analysis has been criticized tellingly by Christopher Lasch (1974:316), and I draw upon Lasch's argument in my remarks below.

5. Ward heelers, gang leaders, and saloon keepers were "natural leaders" within the city's immigrant and working-class districts, and their rise to positions of power during the Jacksonian Era thus has been attributed by many scholars to the parochial and ethnic loyalties of the city's lower classes. They were not, however, the only leaders: the city's patriciate long had claimed that title, and in the 1820s and 1830s trades union leaders and even some radical intellectuals (e.g., Robert Dale Owen, George Henry Evans) sought to assert such a claim. Why did the former set of leaders prevail and the latter lose? To say that this occurred because ethnic loyalties were more salient to voters than class identifications, or that the American political culture was becoming less "deferential" and more "participant" during this Age of Egalitarianism (as do Lee Benson [1961], Ronald Formisano [1974], and other scholars of the "ethnocultural" school) is simply to describe the phenomenon that requires explanation, rather than to offer an explanation for it. A genuine explanation would have to consider the way in which changes in formal electoral arrangements, the availability of organizational resources, the behavior of elites, and the social structure worked to the advantage of one set of leaders and to the disadvantage of others. The excellent studies by David Montgomery (1972) of Philadelphia, and Amy Bridges (1977) of New York are exemplary in this respect. I am suggesting that the availability of patronage and public subsidies helped sustain the organizations led by one type of working-class political leader, while at the same time changes in the economy and social structure were undermining the organizations led by competing leaders, as Montgomery and Bridges indicate.

6. As White (1954: Chap. 16) points out, the spoils system became increasingly extensive during the years of the second party system regardless of the party in power.

7. Even at its height, the spoils system did not extend to the more technical branches of the civil service, and a system of examinations was instituted to fill some of these positions. See White (1954: Chap. 19).

8. My argument in this paragraph and the ones following concerning the politics of civil service reform in the late 19th century draws heavily upon the as yet unpublished work of Stephen Skowronek on this topic. Skowronek's work promises to be extremely important, and I am grateful to him for graciously sharing his ideas with me.

9. See the statement of George William Curtis, the president of the National Civil Service Reform League, quoted in White (1958:300).

10. Two other conditions contributed to the willingness of the major parties to enact the civil service reforms the Mugwumps advocated. First, the parties were coming to rely more heavily upon contributions from businessmen, and less heavily upon political assessments levied on the salaries of civil servants, to finance their campaigns. Second, the Pendleton Act received the support of merchants who wished to increase the efficiency of the largest post offices and customs houses. Significantly, the only positions outside Washington mandated for inclusion in the classified service by the act were those in post offices and customs houses employing more than 50 persons.

11. In cities where centralized one-party regimes were established before 1896, opposition to the locally dominant political machines took the form of an antiparty or nonpartisan reform movement prior to that date. On the emergence of the nonpartisan reform movement in New York City following the critical municipal election of 1888, see Shefter (1976a) and Shefter (1978b).

12. Scholars who have attempted to provide a sociological rather than a political analysis of Progressivism assume a priori (and incorrectly) that the same social groups rallied behind the movement in all areas of the country. Because the Progressives generally drew their support from among groups that did not enjoy privileged access to the locally dominant regime, it has been possible for historians studying different cities, states, and levels of government to find data supporting such divergent conclusions as that Progressivism was fundamentally a movement of a declining upper class, a rising business and professional elite, or of the working class. See, e.g., Hofstadter (1955), Hays (1965), and Rogin and Shover (1970).

13. In this respect, the administrative reforms of the Progressives were parallel to the managerial reforms that the Taylorites were advocating in private industry. As Christopher Lasch (1974: Chap. 7) has argued, these new managerial techniques enabled the directors and executives of corporations to extend their control over the organization of production and the pacing of work, an effort which entailed the destruction of older craft modes of organization and the defeat of the union efforts to assume these prerogatives. Moreover, the very groups that sponsored this effort in the private sector—an emerging *national* upper class and an increasingly self-confident professional class—advocated, and would benefit from, administrative reforms in the public sector. To this extent, the administrative reforms of the Progressives can be understood as an effort by a would-be governing class to assume control of the means of administration as well as the means of production, divesting in the process the groups that formerly had exercised this control. In the private sector, those who were squeezed out through this process attempted to protect themselves through strikes, an effort which generally failed. In the public sector, they sought to protect themselves by appealing to the Congress or to old-line party organizations, an effort which met with far greater success. (Congress, for example, refused to establish a Bureau of Efficiency under the control of the president, as the Taft Commission had requested, and it did not pass the Classification Acts until the White House was occupied by a conservative Republican.) Through this process, Congress came to represent the interests of "parochial" elites and social groups, and social conflicts came to be expressed as institutional conflicts. It is in *this* context that the "institutionalization" of the House of Representatives occurred. Cf., Huntington (1973) and Polsby (1968).

14. The contrast between the number of states adopting the merit system in 1933-1949 and in 1917-1933 cannot be attributed to the various social changes that supposedly render the patronage system obsolete and reduce its popular appeal (e.g., the increasing complexity of government in the modern era, the assimilation of immigrants) because more states (namely, six) adopted the merit system during the still earlier period, 1900-1916, than during 1917-1933.

15. In speaking of the New Politics movement, I am referring to the congeries of groups that took the liberal position on "the social issue" and on foreign policy questions during the

1960s and 1970s—in particular, the antiwar, civil rights, environmental, consumer, and women's liberation movements—as well as organizations, such as Common Cause, concerned more narrowly speaking with questions of electoral and administrative reform. Its boundaries on both the left and right can roughly be delimited by support for George McGovern's bid for the 1972 Democratic presidential nomination. I fully recognize that defined in this way the New Politics movement was extremely heterogeneous and did not speak with a single voice. (The same can be said, of course, of the Jacksonian movement or the Progressive movement, for this is one of the characteristics that distinguishes a political movement from a political organization.) Nonetheless, most of the groups and individuals falling within my definition supported each of the reforms I discuss in this section. On "movement politics," see Lowi (1971).

16. My argument here is consistent with that offered by Piven and Cloward (1969: Chap. 9). My interpretation of the Great Society differs from theirs, however, in two respects: they speak of the national administration as a unitary force; and they assume that the payoff which the proponents of the Great Society expected to reap from its programs was electoral support in national elections. But as Marris and Rein (1973:246 n.7) correctly observe, they offer no evidence to support their supposition that votes were central in the minds of those who planned these programs. I am suggesting, rather, that at least after 1965 the grant-in-aid programs of the Great Society were pet projects not of *the* administration (the president increasingly found them an embarrassment) but rather of the administration's liberal wing. These programs were a sincere effort on the part of upper-middle class liberals to assist the poorest city dwellers, namely blacks. What this entailed, in their understanding, was getting city bureaucracies to adopt the latest and best ideas, that is, their own ideas. And what this meant in practice was extending their own influence, and the influence of their local political allies, over municipal agencies and governments.

17. Although there are many insightful observations on the "new class" in the social science literature, to my knowledge there has yet to be published a scholarly analysis of the social bases of the New Politics movement. I would hypothesize that at the core of the movement stood upper-middle class professionals and young people who were affiliated with institutions in the "grants economy"—universities, government agencies, foundations, consulting firms, churches, charitable institutions, and so forth. This collection of individuals became self-conscious in the course of fighting against the domestic and foreign policies which tied together the coalition of producer interests (including labor) which, as I will note below, played a central role in American politics in the post-New Deal era. The New Politics movement's efforts to "reorder national priorities" (e.g., by reducing the size of the military establishment, enacting a "Marshall Plan for the cities," protecting the environment even at the cost of industrial growth) would reallocate political power, public benefits, and the use of the public domain to the disadvantage of the industrial sector and to the advantage of the institutions with which the members of the new class were affiliated. These policies could also be supported by members of the upper-middle class who worked for profit-making institutions (e.g., newspapers, law firms, financial institutions, advertising agencies) but whose livelihood was not tied in immediate and obvious ways to the prosperity of the industrial sector and to public policies (e.g., weapons procurement, highway construction, the licensing of power plants) contributing to that prosperity. For a compelling general statement on the role of political conflict in the process of class formation, see Lasch (1972:48 n. 1); on the "grants economy," see Boulding (1973). For analyses of the "new class" and its politics see Bazelon (1967) and Apter (1964).

18. A major scholarly debate has arisen concerning the politics and diplomacy behind American policy in the early years of the Cold War. For a review of the controversy, see Smith (1976).

REFERENCES

ARONSON, S. (1964). Status and kinship in the higher civil service. Cambridge: Harvard University Press.

ABERBACH, J., and ROCKMAN B. (1976)."Clashing beliefs within the executive branch: The Nixon administration bureaucracy." American Political Science Review, 70(June): 456-468.

APTER, D. (1964). "Ideology and discontent." Pp. 15-43 in D. Apter (ed.), Ideology and discentent. Glencoe, Ill: Free Press.

AXELROD, R. (1972). "Where the votes come from: An analysis of electoral coalitions 1952-1968." American Political Science Review, 66(March):11-20.

BANFIELD, E.C. (1961). Political influence. New York: Free Press.

——— (1974). The unheavenly city revisited. Boston: Little, Brown.

BAZELON, D.T. (1967). Power in America: The politics of the new class. New York: New American Library.

BEER, S. (1973). "The modernization of American federalism." Publius, 3(fall):49-95.

BENSON, L. (1961). The concept of Jacksonian democracy: New York as a test case. Princeton, N.J.: Princeton University Press.

BOULDING, K. (1973). The economy of love and fear. Belmont, Calif.: Wadsworth.

BOULDING, K., and PFAFF, M. (eds., 1972). Redistribution to the rich and the poor. Belmont, Calif.: Wadsworth.

BRIDGES, A. (1977). "The working classes in ante-bellum urban politics, New York City 1828-1863." Unpublished paper. University of Chicago Department of Political Science.

BURNHAM, W.D. (1970). Critical elections and the mainsprings of American politics. New York: W.W. Norton.

——— (1975) "Party systems and the political process." Pp. 277-307 in W.D. Burnham and W.N. Chambers (eds.), The American party systems: Stages of political development (2nd ed.). New York: Oxford University Press.

CARMAN, H.J., and LUTHIN, R. H. (1943). Lincoln and the patronage. New York: Columbia University Press.

CHAMBERS, W.N. (1963). Political parties in a new nation. New York: Oxford University Press.

Civil Service Assembly (1940). Civil service agencies in the United States, A 1940 census. Pamphlet No. 16. Washington, D.C.: U.S. Government Printing Office.

CRENSON, M. (1975). The federal machine: Beginnings of bureaucracy in Jacksonian America. Baltimore: Johns Hopkins University Press.

CUNNINGHAM, N. (1957). The Jeffersonian Republicans, The formation of party organization, 1789-1801. Chapel Hill: University of North Carolina Press.

——— (1963). The Jeffersonian Republicans in power, 1801-1809. Chapel Hill: University of North Carolina Press.

DAHL, R.A. (1961). Who governs? New Haven, Conn.: Yale University Press.

DEGLER, C.N. (1956). "The Locofocos: Urban 'agrarians'." Journal of Economic History, 16(September):322-333.

DEXTER, L.A. (1963). "Congressmen and the making of military policy." Pp. 305-324 in R.L. Peabody and N.W. Polsby (eds.), New perspectives on the House of Representatives. Chicago: Rand McNally.

DIBBLE, V. (1965). "The organization of traditional authority: English country government, 1558-1640." Pp. 879-909 in J.G. March (ed.), Handbook of organizations. Chicago: Rand McNally.

ELLIS, R.E. (1971). The Jeffersonian crisis: Courts and politics in the young republic. New York: W.W. Norton.

EMMERICH, H. (1971). Federal organization and administrative management. University: University of Alabama Press.

EVANS, R., and NOVAK, R. (1971). "The Johnson system." Pp. 225-241 in R.E. Wolfinger (ed.), Readings on Congress. Englewood Cliffs, N.J.: Prentice-Hall.

FENTON, J. (1966). Midwest politics. New York: Holt, Rinehart and Winston.

FIORINA, M. (1977). Congress: Keystone of the Washington establishment. New Haven, Conn.: Yale University Press.

FISCHER, D.H. (1965). The revolution of American conservatism: The Federalist Party in the era of Jeffersonian democracy. New York: Harper and Row.

FISH, C.R. (1905). The civil service and the patronage. New York: Longmans, Green.

FONER, E. (1970). Free soil, free labor, free men: The ideology of the Republican Party before the Civil War. New York: Oxford University Press.

FORMISANO, R. (1974). "Deferential-participant politics: The early republic's political culture, 1789-1840." American Political Science Review, 78(June):473-487.

GATELL, F.O. (1966). "Some sober second thoughts on Van Buren, the Albany Regency, and the Wall Street conspiracy." American Historical Review, 53(June):19-40.

——— (1967). "Money and party in Jacksonian America: A quantitative look at New York City's men of quality." Political Science Quarterly, 82(June):235-252.

GLAZER, N. (1975). "Towards an imperial judiciary?" Public Interest, 41(fall):104-123.

GRAZIANO, L. (1978). "Center-periphery relations and the Italian crisis: The problem of clientelism." In S. Tarrow et al. (eds.), Territorial politics in industrial nations. New York: Praeger.

GREENSTONE, D. (1969) Labor in American politics. New York: Knopf.

HABER, S. (1964). Efficiency and uplift: Scientific management in the Progressive Era, 1890-1920. Chicago: University of Chicago Press.

HAYS, S.P. (1958). Conservation and the gospel of efficiency. Cambridge: Harvard University Press.

——— (1964). "The politics of reform in municipal governments in the Progressive era." Pacific Northwest Quarterly, 55(October):157-169.

HODGSON, G. (1973). "The establishment." Foreign Policy, 10(spring):3-40.

HOFSTADTER, R. (1955). The age of reform: From Bryan to F.D.R. New York: Knopf.

——— (1969). The idea of a party system: The rise of legitimate opposition in the United States. Berkeley: University of California Press.

HOOGENBOOM, A. (1961). Outlawing the spoils: A history of the civil service reform movement. Urbana: University of Illinois Press.

HUNTINGTON, S.P. (1961). The common defense. New York: Columbia University Press.

——— (1973). "Congressional responses to the twentieth century." Pp. 6-38 in D. Truman (ed.), Congress and America's future (2nd ed.). Englewood Cliffs, N.J.: Prentice-Hall.

JENSEN, R. (1971). The winning of the midwest. Chicago: University of Chicago Press.

KARL, B. (1963). Executive reorganization and reform in the New Deal. The genesis of administrative management, 1900-1939. Cambridge: Harvard University Press.

KATZNELSON, I. (1975). "Community conflict and capitalist development." Paper presented at annual meeting, American Political Science Association, San Francisco.

KELLER, M. (1977). Affairs of state: Public life in late nineteenth century America. Cambridge: Belknap-Harvard University Press.

KRAINES, O. (1970). "The president versus congress: Keep Commission 1905-1909. First comprehensive presidential inquiry into administration." Western Political Quarterly, 23(March):5-54.

LASCH, C. (1972). "Toward a theory of post-industrial society." Pp. 36-50 in M.D. Hancock and G. Sjoberg (eds.), Politics in the post-welfare state. New York: Columbia University Press.

——— (1974). The world of nations. New York: Vintage.

LAZERSON, M. (1971). Origins of the urban school. Cambridge: Harvard University Press.

LEBOWITZ, M.A. (1969). "The Jacksonians: Paradox lost?" Pp. 65-89 in B. Bernstein (ed.), Towards a new past. New York: Vintage.

LOWI, T. (1967). "Machine politics—old and new." Public Interest, 9(fall):83-92.

——— (1971). The politics of disorder. New York: Basic Books.

MAIER, C. (1975). Recasting bourgeois Europe. Princeton, N.J.: Princeton University Press.

MARRIS, P., and REIN, M. (1973). Dilemmas of social reform (2nd ed.). Chicago: Aldine.

MARSHALL, L. (1967). "The strange stillbirth of the Whig Party." American Historical Review, 72(January):445-468.

MAYHEW, D. (1966). Party loyalty among congressmen. New Haven, Conn.: Yale University Press.

——— (1974). Congress: The electoral connection. New Haven, Conn.: Yale University Press.

McCONNELL, G. (1966). Private power and American democracy. New York: Knopf.

McCORMICK, R.P. (1975). "Political development and the second party system." Pp. 90-116 in W.D. Burnham and W.N. Chambers (eds.), The American party systems. New York: Oxford University Press.

MERTON, R. (1957). Social theory and social structure. New York: Free Press.

MONTGOMERY, D. (1967). Beyond equality: Labor and the radical Republicans 1862-1872. New York: Knopf.

——— (1972). "The shuttle and the cross: Weavers and artisans in the Kensingston riots of 1844." Journal of Social History, 5(summer):411-446.

MOYNIHAN, D.P. (1969). Maximum feasible misunderstanding. New York: Free Press.

MOWRY, G.E. (1951) The California progressives. Berkeley: University of California Press.

NATHAN, R.P. (1975). The plot that failed: Nixon and the administrative presidency. New York: John Wiley.

ORREN, K. (1976). "Standing to sue: Interest group conflict in the federal courts." American Political Science Review, 70(September):723-741.

PINKETT, H.T. (1965). "The Keep Commission, 1905-1909: A Rooseveltian effort for administrative reform." Journal of American History, 52(September):297-312.

PIVEN, F.F., and CLOWARD, R.A. (1971). Regulating the poor: The functions of public welfare. New York: Pantheon.

POLENBERG, R. (1966). Reorganizing Roosevelt's government: The controversy over executive reorganization, 1936-1939. Cambridge: Harvard University Press.

POLSBY, N. (1968). "The institutionalization of the U.S. House of Representatives." American Political Science Review 62 (March):144-168.

RANNEY, A. (1975). Curing the mischief of faction: Party reform in America. Berkeley: University of California Press.

ROGIN, M.P., and SHOVER, J. (1970). Political change in California. Westport, Conn: Greenwood.

ROSS, L., and PASSELL, P. (1973). The retreat from riches: Affluence and its enemies. New York: Viking.

ROTHMAN, D. (1971). The discovery of the asylum: Social order and disorder in the new republic. Boston: Little, Brown.

SAGESER, A.B. (1935). The first two decades of the Pendleton Act. Lincoln: University of Nebraska.

SALISBURY, R. (1964). "Urban politics: The new convergence of power." Journal of Politics, 26(November):775-797.

SAWYER, R.L. (1960). The Democratic State Central Committee in Michigan, 1949-1959: The rise of the new politics and the new political leadership. Ann Arbor: University of Michigan Institute of Public Administration.

SAYRE, W., and KAUFMAN, H. (1960). Governing New York City. New York: Russell Sage.

SCHIESL, M.J. (1977). The politics of efficiency: Municipal administration and reform in America: 1880-1920. Berkeley: University of California Press.

SHARKEY, R. (1959). Money, class and party: An economic study of civil war and reconstruction. Baltimore: Johns Hopkins University.

SHEFTER, M. (1976a). "The emergence of the political machine: An alternative view." Pp. 14-44 in W. Hawley and M. Lipsky (eds.), Theoretical perspectives in urban politics. Englewood Cliffs, N.J.: Prentice-Hall.

——— (1976b). "Party organization, electoral mobilization, and the conditions of reform success." Unpublished paper. Cornell University Department of Government.

——— (1978a). "Party and patronage: Germany, England, Italy." Politics and Society, 7(Winter):403-451.

——— (1978b). "The electoral foundations of the political machine: New York City, 1884-1897." In J. Silbey et al. (eds), The history of American electoral behavior. Princeton, N.J.: Princeton University Press.

SMITH, G.S. (1976). "'Harry, we hardly know you': revisionism, politics and diplomacy, 1945-1954. A review essay." American Political Science Review, 70(June):560-583.

SPROAT, J. (1968). The "best men": Liberal reformers in the gilded age. New York: Oxford University Press.

STAVE, B. (1970). The New Deal and the last hurrah: Pittsburgh machine politics. Pittsburgh: University of Pittsburgh Press.

STOCKMAN, D. (1975). "The social pork barrel." Public Interest, 39(spring):3-30.

SUNDQUIST, J. (1973). Dynamics of the party system. Washington, D.C.: Brookings.

SYDNOR, C.S. (1952). Gentlemen freeholders: Political practices in Washington's Virginia. Chapel Hill: University of North Carolina Press.

THELEN, D.P. (1976). Robert M. LaFollette and the insurgent spirit. Boston: Little, Brown.

TOLCHIN, M., and TOLCHIN, S. (1971). To the victor . . . political patronage from the clubhouse to the White House. New York: Random House.

TUGWELL, R., and CRONIN, T. (1974). The presidency reappraised. New York: Praeger.

VAN RIPER, P. (1958). History of the United States civil service. Evanston, Ill.: Row, Peterson.

WEAVER, P.A. (1974). "The new journalism and the old: Thoughts after Watergate." Public Interest, 35(spring):67-88.

WEBER, M. (1958). "Politics as a vocation." Pp. 77-128 in H. Gerth and C.W. Mills (eds.), From Max Weber. New York: Oxford University Press.

WEINSTEIN, J. (1968). The corporate ideal in the liberal state: 1900-1918. Boston: Beacon Press.

WESTERFIELD, H.B. (1955). Foreign policy and party politics: From Pearl Harbor to Korea. New Haven, Conn.: Yale University Press.

WHITE, L.D. (1951). The Jeffersonians: A study in administrative history, 1801-1829. New York: Macmillan.

——— (1954). The Jacksonians: A study in administrative history, 1829-1860. New York: Macmillan.

——— (1958). The Republicans: A study in administrative history, 1869-1901. New York: Macmillan.

WIEBE, R.H. (1967). The search for order, 1877-1920. New York: Hill and Wang.

WILSON, J.Q. (1962). The amateur Democrat: Club politics in three cities. Chicago: University of Chicago Press.

——— (1967). "The bureaucracy problem." Public Interest, 6(winter):3-9.

WISE, T. (1973). The politics of lying. New York: Random House.

WOODWARD, C.V. (1951). Origins of the new South, 1877-1913. Baton Rouge: Louisiana State University Press.

Chapter 8

GREAT BRITAIN: THE DEATH
OF THE COLLECTIVIST CONSENSUS?

W A L T E R   D E A N   B U R N H A M

> The crisis consists precisely in the fact that the old is dying and the new cannot be born; in this interregnum a great variety of morbid symptoms appears.
>
> > Antonio Gramsci,
> > *Selections from the Prison Notebooks*

I

For a considerable time after the end of World War II, British politics appeared to form a model for Americans to emulate. Following the Labour landslide of 1945 and the introduction of its comprehensive semisocialist programs for reformation and steering of the political economy, the Conservative opposition also came to accept the permanence of this substantially expanded governmental role (Beer, 1965). This "collectivist consensus" reached its apogee during the late 1950s, with the phenomenon of "Butskellism"—named for the revisionist social-democratic Labour leader, Hugh Gaitskell, and the leader of the Tory Progressives within the Conservative party, R.A. Butler. It was given concrete form by Labour's implementation of the wartime Beveridge Report on social-welfare responsibilities; an intellectual basis through the reception of Keynesian economics; and its legitimation both by the convergence of major-party leadership on the basics of the postwar political settlement and by its administration through 13 years of Conservative rule.

All of this was in a setting most congenial to American liberals. Britain had a party system with only two major components. The parties differed at the margins (e.g., over steel nationalization) but shared a broad consensus on the collectivist political settlement. Political leadership had created an apparently working welfare state in which the health and material well-being of the population was better provided for than at any previous time in history. But the parties did differ, they stated their differences before the electorate, and they carried out these statements when they won a majority in the House of Commons. In short, they were responsible parties, and as such formed a model of contrast with American parties.

But this political settlement, like others, did not come down from the skies. It was fashioned under specific historical circumstances by specific leaders. It was maintained so long, and only so long, as the contexts were favorable. Even in Britain, political settlements can and do degenerate when these contexts change and political leaders attempt to grapple with the steering mechanism under new circumstances. When this occurs, traditional political cues and formulas tend to break down, and politics often develops an unwontedly extreme ambience. Such episodes are well known to the historian of British politics, from the Reform Bill crisis of 1832 to the Home Rule crisis of 1885, the general constitutional crisis of 1910-1914, and the rupture of the Labour party in 1931, to the peaceful but very real displacement of the old order which occurred in 1945.

The movement toward the "new political economy" was quite general throughout the Western world during the postwar era. It was, fundamentally, a movement to restabilize and reinstate the capitalist mode of production in such a way as to exorcise the specter of the 1930s. It is often forgotten today how deep the worry was among elites in the West in the middle 1940s that economic slump would soon return and that any such return would surely threaten to create severe political instability—in the immediate wake of war's devastation, to create the possibility of overthrow of the political economy itself, no doubt with the help of the Soviet Union. Generous as the Marshall Plan and American aid flowing thereafter may have been, they were also designed to promote the most important external state interests of the United States itself.[1] The indispensable condition for the long-term success of the restabilization was, however, a long-term sustained economic growth in the West, a conjuncture which unfolded with a length and a vigor quite undreamed of by most leaders in 1945. This conjuncture was dependent, as we now know, on the abundance of very cheap sources of raw materials—especially energy—for the industrialized West, upon the stimulation of the conditions for high mass consumption, upon the short-term (but important) stimuli given European economies during the reconstruction period following the war, and upon breakthroughs of various kinds on the technological-marketing frontier.

The importance of this conjunctural context in promoting consensus in the political economy has become increasingly clear as the great boom of 1945-1969 recedes into history. A growing pie of disposable income provides, in the first place, increasing resources available to governments through taxation to support extensive systems of benefits to the population in education, housing, food-price supports, health, and other areas. Second, the harsh edges of class conflict are progressively eroded by the shift to high mass consumption of cars, television sets, and so on, while at the same time the basic class structure—the structure of differential status, ownership, and reward—remains substantially intact. This happens for many reasons. Among the most important are the evident atomizations of earlier affective solidarities which occur pari passu with the development of the "affluent society"—much discussed by theorists of "mass society" and of the incipient "Americanization" of European politics (see, for example, Epstein, 1967) —and the increasing apparent irrelevance of leftist political appeals based on arguments that the current politico-economic regime leads to increasing misery and deprivation.

In Britain, all these trends may be said to have reached their political apogee in the 1959 general election (see Butler and Rose, 1960). The incumbent government was headed by Harold Macmillan, leader of the "Right Progressives" and, along with R.A. Butler and others, a chief architect of the Tory version of the postwar welfarist consensus. His opponent, Hugh Gaitskell, was leader of the right-center forces in the Labour party's coalition. Very much an Adlai Stevenson figure, Gaitskell was unsble to avoid Stevenson's fate. The Labour party in 1959 lost its third election in a row, and lost electoral ground—something which had not occurred in British two-party electoral politics in the whole period since the creation of mass parties three-quarters of a century before. Moreover, as contemporaries clearly saw, 1959 was an archetypal "affluence" election. The winning Conservative strategy was candidly, if somewhat crassly, based on the slogan "You never had it so good." This, in turn, was grounded upon a growing affluence which permitted Britons not merely to dream of, but in unprecedented numbers to acquire, the mass-consumption durable goods of the new society. It was in this period that pundits began writing of the "end of ideology," and British analysts of politics wrote books with titles such as *Must Labour Lose?* (Abrams, 1960). Indeed, for a short time it seemed that the Conservatives had firmly reestablished themselves as the "party of the nation," as the normal governing party presiding over an adequately functioning mixed political economy. It seemed as well that Labour had little to say to the new affluent order. Memories of Tolpuddle and Jarrow appeared less and less relevant to a political economy in which unemployment was below 3% and in which the real income of workers continued to increase year after year. As ideology "ended," Labour's relevance to the new dispensation became harder to perceive, as—for many—did its future.

But, while the Great Boom after 1945 conjured away the worst fears for the survival of capitalist democracy among American and West European elites, it brought two other major problems in its wake. One of these problems—the growingly obvious relative malfunction of the British economy—was specific to the United Kingdom and will be discussed later. The other was that the boom, linked with the deeply echeloned defenses against mass poverty which were fashioned by the postwar welfare state, served to politicize the political economy to a degree never before approached in any earlier era of capitalist development.

Under classical capitalism and its neo-laissez-faire successors, matters were relatively straightforward. The state did not attempt to "command" the political economy except in major war. The economy itself operated anonymously as well as autonomously—no one in particular could be blamed for economic malfunction. Balance-of-payments problems were automatically dealt with by the international gold standard. If a nation ran deficits, it would lose gold reserves. To stop the gold drain, policies had to be implemented to "deflate" the relative position of the country in the international trade arena, which of course meant slowdown and unemployment in the domestic political economy until the imbalance was adjusted. Similarly, governments had—and, by the overwhelming majority of voters, were expected to have—no comprehensive responsibilities for social welfare beyond the rudiments existing after the Education Act of 1902, the poor laws, and the like, modified after World War I by a social-insurance "dole" based on demonstrated need (i.e., the prior exhaustion by the unemployed claimant of all personal assets). Obviously, this system could not last indefinitely. For if no one in particular was responsible for what happened in Stepney or Durham during the Depression and World War II, "the system" as a whole could be—and increasingly was—called to account for its inadequate performance after the great crash of 1929 and the war. But so long as it lasted, this regime ensured that effectively organizable demand on government tended to be both limited and diffuse.

With the rise of the new collectivist consensus after World War II, this convenient "wall of separation" between the state and the political economy progressively disappeared. The market power of the trade unions grew, and was extended (as, later, in the United States) to the substantial part of the labor force working in the public sector. The growth of the welfare state involved the growth of clientele groups and of "entitlement." The fact that the political state was now explicitly responsible for "managing prosperity" meant that governments and parties became widely perceived as accountable for decisions which affected the political economy. No longer was it a question of "the nature of the times," or things in general, but of concrete decisions which were made by sets of identifiable individuals, and which could be unmade by themselves or by another set of individuals.

One primary consequence of this, noted by a growing number of conservative analysts on both sides of the Atlantic, was the development of a politically linked "ratchet effect" involving wages and social-welfare expenditures (cf. Buchanan and Wagner, 1977). Keynes's original model of state involvement in the management of a mixed political economy had provisions for deflationary action as well as "pump-priming" through deficit spending, but only the latter in the main turned out to be politically feasible. There can be little doubt that this politicization of the political economy cut in a variety of ways not originally contemplated either by Fabians or by Tory Progressives. It ensured—or seemed to ensure—that never again would the nation return to the bad old days of the capitalist boom-bust cycle, with slump and the dole in its train. But it also guaranteed the growing proliferation of organized sectoral groups, all oriented around protecting and if possible expanding political claims on their share of the gross national product. It guaranteed an increasingly explicit struggle in the political arena among those groups, a struggle which came to involve debate over the foundations of the political economy itself.

More broadly, it can be said that this well-known malaise of mixed-economy pluralism involved what might be described as the "secularization" of political authority in our time. From this process arose a whole series of intractable legitimacy problems for the regime as a whole.[2] Without doubt, as Christopher Hill's or Eric Hobsbawm's studies of social rebellion in earlier British history should remind us, it is far too easy to elaborate a picture of "perfect" hierarchical order during the heyday of aristocratic rule: "The Lord bless the Squire and his relations, / And teach us to keep our proper stations." And yet accepted hierarchy and social deference in British political history was once an essential, immensely important part of a political formula which, skewing "acceptable" political demands far upwards in the social structure by definition, kept the political arena relatively simple, highly cohesive, and essentially undemanding. Classical laissez-faire capitalism—economic development and social change for which no one in particular was responsible—served similar skewing and demand-limiting purposes. This it did quite satisfactorily, and, considering the development of a mass political market in the meantime, for what is in retrospect an astonishingly long time.

One may suspect that two factors contributed to this: first, the survival of neo-feudal deference patterns well into the capitalist epoch, as well as the physical proximity in the same family circles of aristocrats and industrial/financial magnates; and second, the growth of the Empire during the 1880s and after, and with it the growth of a "sacral" mystique around the King-Emperor which could and did appeal to all classes. Clearly, as Andrew Gamble (1974) has shown, the Empire and its related mystique remained important to the Conservative party long after the Imperial heartland had lost its very independence to the United States during and after World War II. It is not difficult to suppose that its near-total evaporation after the Suez affair of 1956 had more than a little to do with the Conservative party's loss of clear self-identity as the "party of the nation." In any event, the self-destructive cultural trends of capitalist society—first hinted at by Marx and Engels in the Communist Manifesto, elaborated quite fully by Joseph Schumpeter (a non-Marxist) nearly a century later, and back again in discussion in the governability debate of the 1970s[3] —did seem to be well contained in the British context for an exceptionally long time. But the disappearance of mystiques of the King-Emperor variety, as well as the progressive disappearance of the social conditions supporting older deference patterns in and after two world wars, eliminated these constraints on "secularization" of political power.

Even so, the whirligig of secularized politics is much less likely to revolve at a disturbing pace if the political economy continues to grow in size. The fact that this occurred in Britain through the early 1960s did much to mask the extent of secularization and politicization from plain view. The new political market became increasingly similar to the economic market at the mass (or micro) level: oriented toward marginal differences, brand names, and advertising campaigns. So long as the economic market continued to deliver the goods, consensus tended to prevail. The collectivist political settlement of the postwar years ordered elite behavior and mass expectations more or less comprehensively. The problem was that the economy failed to stay the course, to an extent unmatched in any other part of industrial Europe.

II

Probably the most striking comparative feature of the evolution of West European political economy since the end of the immediate postwar reconstruction period has been the rapid relative decline of Great Britain. The basic facts are not in dispute, and oceans of ink have been spilled by economists and politicians in attempting to account for them. As Table 1 reveals, British per capita gross

Table 1. THE DECLINE OF BRITAIN: PER CAPITA GNP IN SELECTED YEARS*

	1939			1960			1970			1974	
1.	U.S.	2,163	1.	U.S.	3,737	1.	U.S.	4,886	1.	Switz.	5,478
2.	U.K.	1,778	2.	Canada	2,681	2.	Sweden	4,109	2.	Sweden	5,436
3.	Germany	1,768	3.	Sweden	2,470	3.	Canada	3,884	3.	U.S.	5,265
4.	Sweden	1,568	4.	Switz.	2,066	4.	Switz.	3,194	4.	Canada	5,109
5.	France	1,518	5.	France	1,953	5.	Denmark	3,159	5.	W. Ger.	4,900
6.	Norway	1,512	6.	U.K.	1,910	6.	W. Ger.	3,095	6.	Denmark	4,759
7.	Canada	1,502	7.	W. Ger.	1,850	7.	Norway	2,875	7.	Norway	4,604
8.	Switz.	1,493	8.	Denmark	1,707	8.	France	2,777	8.	Belgium	4,309
9.	Denmark	1,324	9.	Norway	1,691	9.	Belgium	2,652	9.	Neth.	4,039
10.	Neth.	1,073	10.	Belgium	1,632	10.	Neth.	2,429	10.	France	4,006
11.	Ireland	858	11.	Finland	1,478	11.	Finland	2,251	11.	Finland	3,720
12.	Austria	854	12.	Neth.	1,270	12.	U.K.	2,184	12.	Austria	3,464
13.	Belgium	826	13.	Austria	1,180	13.	Austria	1,932	13.	Japan	3,282
14.	Italy	670	14.	Italy	1,045	14.	Japan	1,887	14.	U.K.	2,668
15.	Finland	507	15.	Ireland	841	15.	Italy	1,727	15.	Italy	2,139
16.	Spain	329	16.	Japan	682	16.	Ireland	1,331	16.	Spain	1,919
17.	Japan	291	17.	Greece	558	17.	Greece	1,133	17.	Ireland	1,720
18.	Greece	257	18.	Spain	452	18.	Spain	1,089	18.	Greece	1,692

*1970 dollars. Basic sources: Brian R. Mitchell, *European Historical Statistics, 1750-1970* (New York: Columbia University Press, 1975); United Nations, *Yearbook of National Accounts Statistics,* 1970-75 (New York: UN, 1971-76). Conversion to 1970 from current dollars through implicit price deflators presented in U.S. official data, *e.g., The Economic Report of the President, 1977.*

national product—one measure of national power and well-being —has declined sharply since 1939, and even more sharply since 1960, relative to other European states and Japan. By this measure, Britain, which was arguably second to the United States among the industrial nations in 1939, fell to sixth place in 1960; 12th place in 1970; and 14th place by 1974. While per capita GNP in 1970 dollars had risen between 1960 and 1964 by 382% in Japan, 165% in West Germany and 105% in France, the increase was only 40% in Britain (and, for that matter, 41% in the United States). Put another way, while in 1952 the West German GNP per capita was not much more than two-thirds the British (72%), by 1974 the British was scarcely half the German (54%). The Japanese per capita GNP was one-quarter of the British in 1952; by 1974, Japan had forged ahead to such an extent that Japanese per capita GNP was now nearly one-quarter higher than British (123%). It was now widely predicted that per capita GNP in Britain, the "sick man of Europe," would fall below those of Italy and even Spain by the end of the century (Bellini et al., 1974).

Explanations for this tremendous deterioration in the relative economic position of Great Britain have been almost infinitely varied, ranging—according to the commentator in question—from problems of the British national character to the evils of socialism, or the peculiar status which the City of London and sterling had in international finance for more than a quarter-century after the war. It would seem reasonable to suppose, however, that there is a convergence on a number of key points. Probably the most universally accepted is that the roots of the current British plight go back a very long way before the creation of the welfare state or the rise of the unions. Correlli Barnett (1972:83-112) documents the utter inadequacy of British industry to cope with the demands of modern war during World War I, compared with German or American industry.[4] In key sectors of the economy, no basis existed for mass production and it was obvious that in a number of other key sectors (such as optics or dye-stuffs) no significant investment had been made at all in research and development. It seems rather clear that the norms of British managers were considerably more genteel-amateur than those of their German or American counterparts. It also seems clear that the financial ascendancy of the City of London played a significant role, among other things by attracting capital away from industrial development through higher and more certain rates of return in property and financial instruments. Barnett argues, in essence, that the British educational system—while perhaps suited to the training of administrators and soldiers of the Empire—was wholly inadequate to the creation of outlooks (scientific, entrepreneurial) needed for the management of a competitive industrial society; and it is hard not to agree with him.

With relative stagnation in industrial investment went a relative lack of productivity per worker—a continuing problem. With lack of incentives to rationalize went a relatively great overmanning of enterprises and the preservation of small shops and small plants as part of the British scene. With the rigidity of the class system separating managers from workers, and with the lack of modernization of industry, emerged the pattern of mutual estrangement in the plant which characterizes industrial relations in Britain; and, indeed, which forms the "basement" of the class polarization in British politics as a whole.

The need in so vulnerable an economy to maintain Britain's exports—to "defend sterling" under the fixed-exchange rate conditions set up by Bretton Woods—produced the first symptoms of political crisis: the "stop-go" policies pursued by the treasury. During the "go" phase, the economy was reflated; employment and wages rose, as did mass consumption (especially of imports). But this also tended to produce inflation and a growing loss of competitiveness for British exports. Hence, at some point the Chancellor of the Exchequer found it necessary to apply the brakes through raising taxes, imposing "pay pauses," and the like. The economy then stagnated until the balance-of-payments position improved, the pressure on sterling abated, and unemployment reached levels then considered dangerously high. At that point, reflation would resume. To a very real extent, the domestic economic problem was systematically exacerbated by the continuing illusions of empire—now in their "commonwealth" variant. The existence of the City of London as a world financial center was in large part a creation of the Empire; the continued existence of sterling as an international reserve currency, and of an international "sterling bloc," tremendously reinforced the pressures on governments to adapt their policies of growth and retrenchment to these ex-imperial financial obligations.

As is now well known, a chief feature of Western industrial regimes over the past generation has been continuous—and, more recently, radically accelerating—inflationary pressure. Without doubt, the long-term inflation owes a good deal to the existence of administered prices in the oligopolistic sector of the private political economy. Rather by the same token, the growth of the postwar interventionist state has played no small role in this inflation, particularly in view of the fact that the proportion of the gross national product funneled through public-sector expenditures—in the United States as in Britain—has tended to grow over the long term, and to grow especially rapidly since the early 1960s.

But in the United Kingdom, with its markedly stagnant economic performance, the problem of inflation surfaced earlier and more severely than in most of the rest of Europe, or in the United States. In the 1961-1964 period, for example, the average annual inflation rate in Britain was 3.1%, compared with an American average of 1.4%. By 1970-1973—the last pre-OPEC years—the average rates had climbed in Britain to 8.0%, compared with 5.1% in the United States. This was nothing, of course, to what happened afterwards, as the retail price inflation in Britain reached an annual average of nearly 30%—a truly Latin American figure—at one point in 1975. But it was quite sufficient to give rise to a major and continuing political upheaval.

Essentially, as Andrew Gamble (1974:127) has correctly observed, inflation rots the social order of "capitalism," i.e., of any political economy which is largely dependent upon voluntaristic exchange for the allocation of scarce resources.[5] Among many other things, it reinforces the tendency—already a notoriously chronic, long-lived problem in Britain—for capital to move toward speculation in property, shares, or other high-yield or high capital-gain ventures. Likewise, it tends to undermine all elements of predictability of the stable ordering of expectations and relationships among classes and sectoral groups in the society.

It is not unreasonable to suppose that, under normal circumstances, most elements in the society will be interested in getting only what they (and often others) regard as their "fair share." In any class society, the boundaries of that "fair share" tend to be more or less fixed by the norms which grow out of the reproduction of the class structure itself. Hence, in more or less normal circumstances—and particularly, of course, if the real standard of living is growing—we do not usually find violent collisions over "shares" even in a country like Britain, where trade-union leadership has far less enthusiasm for private enterprise than is the case in the United States. Similarly, strikes and other confrontations tend—apart from more or less routinely expressed worries by businessmen and conservative writers—to be regarded as particularistic struggles to redefine the marginal boundaries of "fair shares," and not as threatening the foundations of the juridical order.

This state of affairs tends to disintegrate under inflationary conditions. For inflation—at some as yet ill-defined stage of acceleration—produces what social psychologists would describe as an "unstructured situation." The precise problem becomes the definition of what "fair shares" mean. This particular inflationary sequence, both in Britain and in the United States, has been associated, for example, with a striking decline in the rate of profit which corporate enterprise enjoys.[6] But it also necessarily involves

for trade unions the clear and present danger of loss of relative—
and perhaps even absolute—income shares. For the unorganized
middle classes between the hammer and the anvil, the threat of
loss can become overwhelming reality under extreme circumstances:
the spectre of Weimar Germany's short, unhappy existence and
tragic end is still very much with us.

III

So long as government exists, in the last analysis, to uphold the
essential integrity of the dominant mode of production in the given
society, inflation-related public policy will inevitably tend to be
primarily oriented toward improving the profitability of enterprise
and maintaining the competitiveness of the national political economy in the international marketplace. At the same time, democratic governments find themselves limited by the requirements
of the current domestic electoral marketplace from going too far
in this direction. The lower classes now have unprecedented expectations of public-sector performance, and have unprecedented
organized capacity to articulate interests, both as clients of public
welfare bureaucracies and as organized workers. The politicized
public sector's share of the GNP tends systematically to grow over
time (O'Connor, 1973:236-243). By doing so, it contributes to
inflation, since this growth appears never to be fully matched by
taxation to pay for it. As profitability tends to fall, the size of
public-sector activity and the number of "entitlement" claims tend
to rise. Industrial actions thus tend to raise basic questions about
the future of the political economy itself, and politics tends to take
on a zero-sum character. The graver the crisis, the more governments will look to means of explicit intervention to check those
components of inflation which are apparently within their reach.
This will mean, in a country like Britain, that politics in the crisis
stage will involve confrontation sooner or later between the government and the trade unions. At an even later stage, the crisis will
involve a confrontation between the government and those who
benefit from the welfare state and its entitlements, whether or not
these beneficiaries are also organized in trade unions. And this will
happen *irrespective of the party in power or the manifest electoral*

ideologies which its leaders offer to the party militants or to the voters at large.

As this process occurs in the secularized political context mentioned above, it becomes visible to the extent that the crisis deepens, and the primary responsibilities of the political state to the dominant mode of production are overtly engaged in policy-making.[7] It is entirely consonant with the argument made here that the first effort to construct a statutory incomes policy (i.e., controlling downwards the factor cost of labor in the economy) was made not by the Conservatives but by the Labour government in 1968-1969. This attempt, keynoted by the paper *In Place of Strife*, turned out to be a "scandalous" failure. The negative response of the party's left wing—and more importantly of the TUC leadership—to this effort to involve pay policies in formal legal (hence governmental) process was too great for the government to sustain. Put another way, the needs of the state and of the political economy in general, as defined by the government, were in direct conflict with the electoral need to manage the Labour party's coalitional elements. The latter, particularly in view of the fact that the overall crisis of the British economy had not yet matured, required abandoning *In Place of Strife* and the legislation proposed on its basis (Jenkins, 1970).

The effort to create a statutory incomes policy was resumed rather promptly by the Heath government following the Conservative electoral victory of 1970. This was part of a comprehensive if ill-executed and ill-fated effort by the Conservatives to break out of the stop-go cycle once and for all into a sustained growth which could compete with that of the Europe which Edward Heath had committed the nation to join. The Industrial Relations Act of 1972 was adopted without difficulty in Parliament: Heath did not have the trade-union leadership to contend with as coalitional partners. But he did have them to contend with as opponents. From their point of view, this was not "ordinary" legislation but misuse of the coercive power of the state to promote capitalist class interest.[8] They rejected its legitimacy accordingly. From the government's point of view, this rejection raised a fundamental constitutional issue. If organized groups outside the machinery of state could refuse to obey the state's commands and reduce those commands to nullity through their industrial action, then government, as traditionally understood, was at an end.

So, what began as a growing conflict over scarce resources in a stagnant inflationary economy had now escalated into a general crisis of the regime. The point of confrontation, as it turned out, involved the pay claims of the mineworkers.[9] The result was a slowdown in the production of coal, the three-day week during the winter of 1973-1974, and Heath's call for a general election on February 28, 1974. The issue, as framed by the Prime Minister and his lieutenants, was "Who Governs Britain?" The government had adopted legislation in the national interest, and very much in the post-1945 tradition of interventionist public policy. The miners' union had refused to abide by the provisions of that legislation. A sectoral interest with a stranglehold over the national economy had challenged the authority of government itself.

The February 1974 election was one of the most peculiar, and perhaps one of the most important, in British electoral history; it will be discussed more fully in the following section. It was called as a referendum on a specific policy issue for the first time since Stanley Baldwin did so—also unsuccessfully—over the tariff issue in 1923. As all know, the election not only stimulated the highest voter turnout since 1951, but also a mass exodus from both major parties—toward the Liberals in England and the Scottish Nationalists north of the Tweed.

But these were not the only signs of disintegration. Since 1969, the situation in Northern Ireland had also broken out of the frozen mold established half a century earlier. This, no less than the extraordinary rise of Scottish Nationalism and unprecedented electoral volatility in England itself, reflected what can be called the "loss of gravitational power"—of cohesion or accepted ordering—which is associated with general political crisis. It is enough for the purposes of this discussion to note that the upshot had been an effort by the Heath government to force the creation of power-sharing between the dominant Protestants and the oppressed Catholic minority. Along the way, the Stormont regime, which the Protestants had set up in 1921, was destroyed, an effort to construct a power-sharing agreement (the Sunningdale agreement) foundered at the polls in the assembly election of 1973, and subsequently, direct rule from London continued (Rose, 1976).

This had fundamental consequences, as it turned out, for the outcome of the February 1974 election. The final results gave the Conservatives 297 seats (including the Speaker), Labour 301 and others (including Liberals) 37. But of these "others" 11 were Ulster Unionists, always hitherto a part of the Conservative parliamentary party but now cast adrift. Had they remained in their traditional anchoring, the Conservatives—with 308 seats—might well have succeeded in remaining in power at least for the time being. As it was, after a futile effort to set up a minority coalition with the Liberals, Heath resigned and Labour took over.

Thus, Heath's effort to win a referendum on the "constitutional issue" failed. Decisive minorities of voters responded to the call for class confrontation as though they wished to change the subject. Labour, for its part, had advanced as a solution to the power problem a return to voluntarism, i.e., a "social contract" between the government and organized sectoral-group leaders in which the latter could be made to see the necessity for restraint in claims on the national income. Its manifesto had, however, advocated a good deal more than that. Reflecting the ideological pressures from party militants, this document proposed far-reaching moves toward industrial democracy (shared decision-making in the plant between management and labor) as well as toward greater governmental command over investment flows and decisions.[10] As it subsequently turned out, very little of this set of proposed changes was moved along under either Harold Wilson or James Callaghan. This also was to be expected, as was the subsequent bitter factional infighting within the Labour party not only over future direction of economic policy but over the question of Europe as well.

Harold Wilson went to the country in October 1974 to win a majority for the "social contract," and a bare parliamentary majority was obtained. Shortly afterwards, to the surprise of most observers, Edward Heath was challenged and defeated for the leadership; out of the balloting, Margaret Thatcher became the first woman to win the leadership of any major Western political party. Of course, she won not because she was a woman, but because she was the first serious contender to enter the lists in opposition to Heath and the technocratic interventionism which he had come to represent.

By 1975, then, the general crisis which had arrived in Britain had reflected itself very broadly in four major responses by political elites to the challenge which the failing political economy presented. Two of these were associated with debates within the Labour party and two within the Conservative opposition. But it would be reasonable to suppose—as the results of the 1975 referendum on EEC membership strongly suggest—that the most profound of these cleavages lies between the left and the right-center of the Labour party. These four basic policy responses may be schematically summarized in Table 2.

(1) Socialists—i.e., those who seek a collectivist solution to the problems of political economy through the abolition of the capitalist mode of production—constitute an influential minority within the Labour party, but a minority which has never come to power within it, least of all when the party is the party of government. Their critique of the existing order in Britain stresses the irrationality of capital investment decisions, the autocratic relationships which exist in the factory, and the dead-hand stultification which the rigid British class system—reproduced through the educational system and otherwise—has brought to the country. Additionally, the Labour Left is hostile to economic incorporation in Europe, since this imposes an additional—quite possibly insuperable—barrier to the possibility of creating a socialist state in Britain. Essential, in this view, to overcoming the country's problems of economic performance and social justice is the positive and very extensive use of state power to assume command over economic decisions and to redistribute wealth-holding so that social-welfare expenditures can be maintained or even expanded. At some point, realization of these objectives would require further nationalization as well as serious conflict with the United States and other capitalist powers.

The Left of the Labour party is obviously not without influence. It was because of its passionate objections to EEC, and the certainty that Wilson could keep neither party nor government united on this issue, that he took the constitutionally unprecedented step of ordering a referendum on the issue. With equal novelty, Wilson suspended the once essential norm of collective cabinet responsibility during the referendum campaign. Yet the Left was effectively

Table 2. APPROACHES TO THE PROBLEM OF POLITICAL ECONOMY IN BRITAIN

	Formal Intervention	Voluntarism (relative Non-Intervention)
LEFT	Socialist "command" or "siege" economy BENN, "Tribune" Group	"social contract" WILSON, CALLAGHAN
RIGHT	Statutory pay policies, legal interventions to curb union power HEATH	Neo-laissez-faire: reliance on Treasury (monetary policy, cutbacks on public-sector expenditures, etc.) KEITH JOSEPH (M. THATCHER?)

isolated—along with a small minority of Tory nationalists centered around Enoch Powell—by the result.

Ultimately, the problem of the Left is that it seeks the use of government radically to modify or even to supplant the dominant mode of production. Yet it may well be argued that governments cannot really legislate away the dominant mode of production, since the latter is the basis on which the state itself rests (see Gamble, 1974:1-15). Presumably, the crisis of the British political economy would have to reach far greater heights than those of the mid-1970s for the Left to gain control of the Labour party in the first place, and then win an election subsequently. At the same time, there have been several spectacular episodes involving the displacement of right-wing Labour MPs by their constituency parties after these had been "taken over" by left-wing militants. The worries which the "social democratic" wing of the party has expressed about this are not chimerical (see Haseler, 1976: 106-162). It is possible that continued deterioration in the general economic picture could lead to such a takeover on a partywide scale. It is perhaps even more possible that the growing conflicts within the Labour party over the legitimacy of the existing politico-economic regime might at some stage rupture the Labour coalition itself.

(2) The abortive effort to establish a statutory pay-policy pattern of state intervention—in 1968-1969 under Wilson and in 1972-1974 under Heath—may also be read, in a way, as involving a "command" economy, complete with civil and criminal penalties for violators of the commands. But such an effort is as inevitably confrontationist as are the proposals from the Left for a socialist "siege" economy. The locus of the confrontation is of course different. Instead of pitting a semirevolutionary government against all the "establishments" (domestic and international) of the existing order, it pits the government and the vast majority of these "establishments" against the trade unions. The latter (as well as the broader Left) naturally regard this as command in the capitalist class interest or, more crudely, "union-bashing" which—if successful—could lead to a sharp reduction in the factor costs of labor while increasing profits and maintaining the structure of privilege and inequality intact. The first attempt to move against the intractable problems of the British political economy foundered within the Wilson government when it became clear that pursuit of the policy would place an unbearable strain on the unity of the Labour party. In other words, it would create an unbridgeable gap between the party's electoral ideologies and the government's perceived state interests. The second effort led to the spectacular smashup of 1973-1974 and repeal of the offending legislation. Edward Heath took the gamble of a general-election campaign to legitimate his policy in the electoral marketplace, and lost both the gamble and eventually the Conservative party leadership as well.

To say the least, this record is not very promising. It may well be simultaneously the case that trade-union power over the factor costs of labor in the British economy must be more or less severely curbed by formal state action involving the courts, and *also* that the mass support for doing this does not exist within the existing democratic regime. That certainly appears to be a conclusion which could plausibly be drawn from recent history. But it would be expected that leadership would attempt to find other ways out of the impasse before accepting that politics in Britain has ineluctably become the collision of irresistible forces with immovable objects.

(3) The hallmark of economic policy under the Labour government which took office in 1974 has been the "social contract." This, in sharp contrast to statutory intervention, attempts to deal with

the economic crisis through a voluntaristic compact between the government and the trade-union leadership. The former, essentially, pledges itself to minimize the damage to the lower classes which retrenchment in social expenditure and stagnation in living standards will require. The latter, essentially, pledges the trade unions to accept limits on upward wage settlements which are significantly less than the loss of purchasing power through inflation (£6 per week in 1975, £10 in 1977).

The Labour government has relied on two sanctions for obtaining compliance. In the first place, the Labour party is of course in a uniquely good position to trade on its capital of goodwill with the unions. Except among intellectuals and activists of the far Left, the party's bona fides vis-à-vis working-class Britain are as widely accepted among its representatives as those of the Conservative party are rejected. This is, therefore, the sort of policy which will "work" well, if at all, *only when it is managed by Labour in office.* Second, if fear by trade-union leadership of a Conservative government is not enough of a prod, welfare-expenditure and fiscal policy will be manipulated downwards by the Chancellor of the Exchequer to the extent necessary to compensate for excessive pay raises won by the unions against employers. The result may then be higher pay for those who continue to work, but also lower social expenditure and much higher unemployment.

For nearly three years this policy worked to hold down labor-cost increases and to preserve some degree of industrial peace to an extent that few had thought possible in 1974. Obviously, the interest which the trade unions had in preserving a Labour government— especially after the confrontationist trauma culminating in the February 1974 election—was a key ingredient in this success. But it was also true that the policy was fully engaged only after a spectacular pay explosion in 1974-1975, an equally dramatic increase in public-sector expenditures,[11] and the achievement of a 27.7% inflation rate in 1974-1975. By 1974, real hourly earnings had risen to 132.5 (1967 = 100), compared with 143.1 in Germany and 105.5 in the U.S. The problem was that 1975 output per hour in Britain was 125.2 (again, 1967 = 100), compared with 149.8 in Germany and 182.8 in Japan. In the U.S., it was 112.4, reflecting the significant fact that the overall performance of the American economy has recently been much closer to British than to continental (not to mention Japanese) levels.[12]

By the time the "social contract" was fully implemented, the British economy had reached the point where the need for deflationary fiscal policy had become acute if the well-being of the political economy was to be preserved. This was later reinforced by the "letter of intent" which the chancellor and the government had to write to obtain loans from the International Monetary Fund so that the nation's financial reserves could be preserved. Over 1976 and 1977, the decline in workers' real income became increasingly felt, as did the ceilings imposed by the government on public-sector expenditures. Accordingly, the TUC Congress, in the summer of 1977, declined further trade-union cooperation in maintaining the £10 per week ceiling on pay increases insisted on by the government. This renunciation, it is important to note, was the fruit of a rank-and-file revolt which the top leadership of the movement's peak organization could no longer contain without danger to themselves.

The government for its part—led since mid-1976 by James Callaghan—was thus in a cleft stick. Its bare parliamentary majority had long disappeared through by-election defeats, and it could survive repeated Conservative efforts to oust it only through a pact with the 13-member Liberal delegation. The pact suited the Liberals, since they had excellent reasons for wanting to avoid another general election in the near future. But its price was government adherence to a deflationary pay policy and to retrenchment in public-sector spending. Yet continued hewing to the "hold-the-line" policy necessarily involves the government in escalating confrontation with its hard-core supporters as real living standards continue to fall.

The "social contract" has had its great merits, chief among them its avoidance of confrontation, its avoidance of the use of the legal machinery of state and its success—which a non-Labour government would have a hard time duplicating—in obtaining voluntary restraint on the part of the unions. But there was a trade-off which eventually exceeded these consensual limits. Under the circumstances of the now-deepened economic crisis, the government's strategy became increasingly hard to distinguish from neo-laissez-faire policy: retrenchment in public expenditure, manipulation of the fiscal machinery, the rise of unemployment to the highest level since 1939, the decline in the worker's real standard of living for the second year in a row, and—perhaps above all—the widespread sense among the rank and file that there was little or no relief in sight. As we shall see, this sense may be quite mistaken. It may well be that the influx of North Sea oil will produce its expansionary effects just in time to reduce the acute tension between the government and rank-and-file workers. The point remains, however, that there are significant limits on the government's ability to win voluntary compliance under such conditions for any very long period of time. As of late 1977, there were signs that these limits have nearly been reached.

(4) A new "mainstream" of Conservative thinking and policy has emerged in response to the growing pressures on capitalist economies and on the institutions of state which we have discussed. This involves the rediscovery of the virtues of free enterprise and the autonomies of the economic market. While economists such as Friedrich von Hayek, Wilhelm Röpke, and Milton Friedman had never ceased defending the foundations of capitalist political economy from the collectivist postwar drift, their influence on Conservative policy in Britain during the age of the collectivist consensus had been limited. Margaret Thatcher's rise to leadership of the Conservative party in 1975 appears to reflect a major breakthrough in reception of neo-laissez-faire ideas within the party, and in the influence of its chief party theorist, Sir Keith Joseph. This, far more than the pressures from and arguments of the Labour Left, may turn out to constitute a significant—and not necessarily incremental—break in the course of contemporary British political history.

In a recent appearance on the television show *Panorama*, Mrs. Thatcher appears to have left no doubt as to her commitment to this ideology. As reconstructed by David Watt's review in *The Financial Times*, her argument advanced four ideas (Watt, 1977:21). First, the Labour party was on the high road to Communism, i.e., Mrs. Thatcher professed to believe that the Labour Left was rapidly moving toward a takeover of the party. Second, the key to economic expansion lies in the lowering of taxation. This, of course, would require sharp declines—far more than Chancellor Healey has initiated or contemplated—in public sector expenditures. The purpose of these reductions, of course, is to promote the profitability of investment in the private sector, and to stimulate individual incentives for excellence or performance. Third, Mrs. Thatcher stressed that trade unions do not confront the government but rather confront each other. This hypothesis is closely linked with monetarist economic ideology. The government sets and adheres to a monetary target. Within that "automatic" framework everyone struggles to get his or her share of wages and employment. Clearly, it is hoped that the splendid automaticity of the old gold standard could be approximated: excessive pay increases will result either in waves of bankruptcies among employers foolish enough to grant them, or to high unemployment levels or, probably, to both until the lesson was learned. Finally, Mrs. Thatcher argued in a very Hayekian vein that "freedom is indivisible." This appears to unite three elements of Conservative thought: traditional Conservative anti-socialism, the newly received neo-laissez-faire economics paradigm, and a concern—now very lively in many British circles—about the decline of respect for the "rule of law."

After this review, Watt (1977:21) remarks, "There is nothing particularly fresh about this stew of ideas. . . . What is perhaps new is the intensity with which Mrs. Thatcher now puts them forward." He then goes on to offer advice to the Tory leader from the perspective of conventional electoral politics: "The internal contradictions of Conservatism are most manageable if conservatism remains pragmatic. As soon as doctrine rears its head, the difficulties become very great—and normal voters take fright." No doubt. But Watt might have dwelt on what is really new about all this—which is the fact that this ideology (a string of commonplaces in the United States, after all, but quite exotic in the Britain of Macmillan and Butler) is espoused by the leader of a major party, a leader moreover who may very well be the next Prime Minister. As to the intensity of Mrs. Thatcher's convictions, it only needs to be remarked that such intensity is common in political situations where the need for ideological reformation is acute.

One may think what one will of neo-laissez-faire as doctrine, but it provides an emotive and envaluated commitment to the defense of existing social and economic foundations. It does so in a way which cannot even be approximated by the Fabian pragmatism of the "social contract," or the Eurocentric technocratism of Mrs. Thatcher's predecessor. It obviously represents a serious bid to reconstruct a coherent electoral ideology for the Conservative party, and even to form the foundation of a new political settlement. After all, to the extent that this ideology were accepted, a process of disentitlement—of lowering public expectations of and demand on government—would unfold. The state would gradually become depoliticized—an achievement devoutly wished by American neo-conservatives and probably actually underway in that country.[13] With the stakes so very high, it is no wonder that Mrs. Thatcher's presentation of her case is "hot" rather than "cool," ideology-ridden rather than pragmatic. And yet one wonders whether such an archaistic flight could form the basis for a new political settlement so long as the mass electoral market continues to function more or less imperfectly, but more or less freely. Can the genie be put back in the bottle? Once an electorate learns the lesson that economic policy does not just "happen" but is made, how does it unlearn the experience? If the Tribune Group's vision of a pure socialist commonwealth in Britain strikes one as utopian, Mrs. Thatcher's patent nostalgia for the Victorian synthesis seems even more so.

It seems true in any event that Mrs. Thatcher's ideological passion stands in the sharpest possible contrast to the political styles adopted by any successful Tory leadership in the past—from Disraeli to Salisbury to Baldwin to Macmillan—when the Conservative party presided, as the "natural party of government," over earlier political settlements. Indeed, nothing could more convincingly demonstrate the collapse of the collectivist consensus than this escalation of ideological warfare around the banner of free enterprise. It remains to be seen whether Mrs. Thatcher will accept Mr. Watt's pragmatic advice in the event. But when a consensus founded upon an agreed political settlement has disintegrated, and much of value to conservatives seems at risk, it is more than usually difficult to maintain a pragmatic political style. [14]

This survey draws us to the conclusion that there is now no agreed consensus among British political elites and the major social interests they represent in favor of any governmental policy which might seek to address the underlying contradictions in the country's political economy. The basic interim choice would appear to be between "muddling through" and playing for time under a Labour government following a variant of voluntaristic accommodation and a new Conservative leadership which promises ideological adventure. But at the present writing, it is extremely difficult to see from what quarter, or on what basis, a political settlement can be constructed out of the present impasse.

IV

What effects has this collapse of the postwar political settlement had on the electoral market? Assuming that a political settlement exercises strong centripetal pressure on voting behavior, we would anticipate a priori that its disintegration would involve a dramatic relaxation of this "gravitational" force. In other words, one would expect to find phenomena similar to those of "dealignment" or "decay phases" in the history of the American electoral cycle, though such effects could be expected in the British context to be on the whole much more constrained by traditional partisan attachments than has recently been the case in the United States.

Evidence for this process has been abundant in recent British electoral behavior, and has already been widely commented upon. [15] One measure is based on the monthly Gallup poll data since 1947, in response to the question, "If a general election were held today, for which party would you vote?"[16] Increases in annual variance in this measure reveal, of course, greater short-term volatility of support. When the composite variances for the three major parties, weighted by their share of the total preferences, are plotted, a clear and strong upward movement can be detected, beginning in 1965-1966. (See Figure 1.)

The "new" or post-1965 shape of volatility in electoral support is anything but stable, ranging as it does between a minimum of 2.8 (1972) and a maximum of 10.0 (1967). But, with the sole exception of 1972, each of the years 1965-1975 shows a higher monthly variance in poll support for the three major parties than occurred at any time between 1947 and 1964. Overall, if these two sets of years are grouped together, the variance in the most recent set is slightly more than 2½ times as great as in the earlier set.

Two other measurements of growing volatility, based on the analysis of by-election results from 1945 to 1977, produce comparable results. The first of these measures trends in the two-party

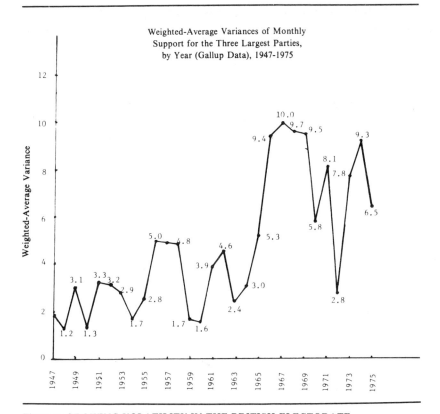

Figure 1: **GROWING VOLATILITY IN THE BRITISH ELECTORATE**

swing for or against the incumbent (government) party on an average year-by-year basis.[17] Figure 2 tells a dramatic story. Down until the early 1960s—arguably, until 1965—the swing against the government in by-elections was modest. In fact, in one unique three-year period (1953-1955), the swing was actually positive, i.e., toward the incumbent Conservative party. From 1945 through 1956, it is now striking to recall, the government party defended 73 seats in by-elections and lost not a single one to the opposition.[18] But the negative swings against the government party began to gain amplitude in the mid-1950s and, by the end of the Tories' 13 years in power, by-election losses for the incumbent party had become rather common. The full depths were not plumbed, however, until the Wilson government's rout at the polls

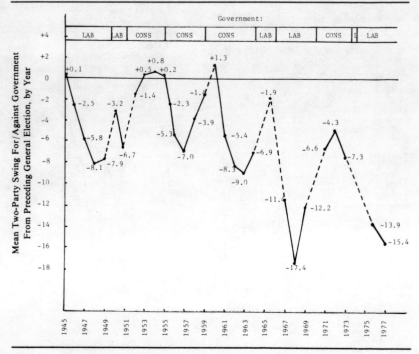

Figure 2: DECLINING SUPPORT FOR INCUMBENT GOVERNMENTS IN BRITISH BY-ELECTIONS, 1945-77

in 1968-1969. Since then, by-election losses and negative swings of 15 percentage points and more have become commonplace: under Labour, mostly to the benefit of the Conservatives, while under the Heath government—especially in the Liberals' annus mirabilis, 1973—to the benefit of the Liberals. Table 3 reviews the by-election record since the end of World War II. One further point about this by-election pattern should be noted. In the recent volatile period, it is quite clear that Labour has had much more difficulty in defending its seats—and has had overall a much larger negative swing against it—than have its Conservative opponents. This suggests a point which has been argued from survey evidence in recent literature to be discussed below: that the Labour mass base is potentially much more subject to disaffection from the party's policies under stress than is the Conservative mass base, and also that mass response to stress takes very different forms

Table 3. CONTESTS, WINS AND LOSSES FOR THE GOVERNING PARTY: BY-ELECTION OUTCOMES, 1945-1977

Years	Govt.	N Contested by Govt. Pty.	N Defended by Govt. Pty.	Won by Govt. Pty.	Lost by Govt. Pty.	Other Outcomes	% Lost by Govt. Pty.
1945–50	Lab.	46	34	34	0	0	0
1950–51	Lab.	14	8	8	0	0	0
1951–55	Cons.	44	26	26	0	(+1 Lab to C)	0
1955–59	Cons.	48	30	26	4	(1 L to Lab)	13.3
1959–64	Cons.	60	34	28	6	(+1 Lab to C)	17.6
1964–66	Lab.	13	5	4	1	(1 C to L)	20.0
1966–70	Lab.	35	24	10	14	0	58.3
1970–74I	Cons	30	13	8	5	(+1 Lab to L; + 1 Lab to Dem Lab; + 1 Lab to SNP)	38.5
1974I–II	Lab.	1	1	1	0	0	0
1974II–77	Lab.	16	12	7	5	0	41.7
1945–55		104	68	68	0		0
1955–66		121	69	58	11		15.9
1966–77		82	50	26	24		48.0

depending upon which of the two parties happens to be in power at the time of the by-election.

This latter point becomes quite clear from another aggregate analysis of by-election outcomes in the postwar period: the incidence of third-party voting in these contests, and most especially the incidence of Liberal voting. Figure 3 reveals a broad pattern of a sort we have come to expect. In the first dozen years or so after the 1945 election, voting for Liberals and other third-party candidates was heavily suppressed, in the period 1949-1955 not reaching *together* as much as 5% of the vote cast. Since then, a very clear composite pattern has emerged: heavy surges of Liberal support toward the end of periods of Conservative rule, followed by much lower levels of Liberal support during Labour governments. This corresponds to a general-election phenomenon which is by now a well-marked cyclic aspect of electoral behavior: liberal fortunes wax as grievances accumulate against Tory "ins," and wane when Labour has a record to defend. To this only one further point needs to be made: the vote for "all other" candidates does not share the same cyclic pattern. Breaking through for the first time in 1967, the "all-other" category also showed comparable levels in the 1972-1974 period, under administrations of both parties. This "all other"

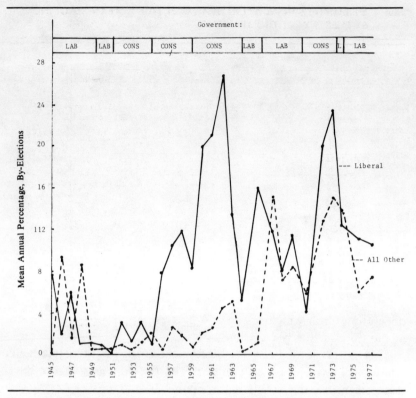

Figure 3: LONG-TERM CHANGE IN THIRD—PARTY VOTING, BRITISH BY-ELECTIONS, 1945-1977

summary category includes, predominantly, votes cast for Nationalist candidates in Wales and Scotland on one hand, and (since 1974) for candidates of the ultra-right National Front on the other. Its emergence to a new high level is a phenomenon of the past decade. To a marked extent it corresponds to the loss of "gravitational attraction" not merely of the two major parties but of the traditional British state itself.[19]

These premonitions of electoral upheaval finally became general-election realities in the February 1974 election. This election has already been very widely analyzed in the literature. The task of this discussion is accordingly limited to a review of certain aspects of that literature and the analysis of a few larger issues which the election appears to present (See Butler and Kavanaugh, 1974;

Table 4. FEBRUARY 1974 AS A "CRITICAL ELECTION"? MEAN ABSOLUTE
SWINGS, 3 PARTIES, 1880-1974 (OCT.)*

Election Pair		Mean Absolute Swing	Comment
1.	1929-1931	12.4	"National" landslide against Labour, final interwar decline of Liberals
2.	1910II-1918	10.8	Shattering of Liberals, emergence of Labour as major-party opposition
3.	1935-1945	8.9	"Realignment leading to "collectivist" cleavage structure
4.	1970-1974I	8.5	Grave economic crisis; eruption of Liberals and Nationalists
5.	1900-1906	8.4	Emergence of "New liberalism" and Labour
6.	1923-1924	8.1	Final eclipse of Liberals as majority-bent party
7.	1885-1886	7.1	Rupture of Liberals over Ireland; Liberal Unionists join Conservatives
8.	1924-1929	6.3	Liberals' "last stand" under Lloyd George
9.	1931-1935	5.8	Counter-deviating ("reinstating"?) election after anomalies of 1931 stampede
10.	1950-1951	4.7	Postwar reduction of Liberals to (mostly Celtic) hard core
11.	1906-1910I	4.4	"Reinstating" election after 1906 landslide
12.	1892-1895	4.3	
13.	1959-1964	3.8	
14.	1966-1970	3.6	
15.	1886-1892	3.4	
16.	1964-1966	2.8	
17.	1918-1922	2.4	
18.	1880-1885	2.3	
19.	1955-1959	2.2	
20.	1945-1950	2.0	
21.	1895-1900	1.9	
22.	1974I-1974II	1.8	
23.	1951-1955	1.3	
24.	1922-1923	1.0	
25.	1910I-1910II	0.6	

*Excluding Ireland, 1880-1918, and Northern Ireland, 1922-1974. Two-party measurement, 1880-1900; Mean absolute swing among three parties, 1900/06-1974I/II. Median swing among 25 pairs, 4.1; Mean swing, 4.75 (standard deviation, 3.19).

Penniman, 1975). Its most dramatic features were a sudden explosion in Liberal candidacies and electoral support, and the "take-off" of the Scottish Nationalist party toward an apparently institutionalized position as a major force in electoral politics north of the Tweed.

A disgruntled Conservative party worker was supposed to have said about the February 1974 election that it was "just a damned by-election." This remark reflected the election's violation of conventional wisdom: in all previous general elections since the war, the electorate had strongly tended to return to its traditional major-party voting, with a consequent "squeeze" against Liberals and Nationalist candidates. The "squeeze" did not materialize in February 1974. Moreover, while the Liberals were indeed "squeezed" somewhat in October (as one might expect with Labour in office), the English results far more closely resembled those of February than of any other election since 1929, while the Scottish Nationalists continued their precipitate upward surge.

Let us attempt to evaluate the relative magnitude of the February 1974 electoral upheaval in the context of British electoral history. Table 4 measures the magnitude of the mean absolute swings from general election to general election among the major parties in Great Britain (excluding Ireland and Northern Ireland) over approximately the past century. The results are striking.[20] Of the 25 pairs of elections spanning nearly a century of British electoral politics, the 1970-1974 (February) sequence shows the fourth largest amplitude of mean absolute swing. It is significant that only two postwar election pairs are to be found in the top half of this array, that of 1970-1974 and that of 1950-1951, the latter being produced by the collapse of the Liberal effort growing out of the consolidation of the postwar collectivist cleavage structure. Similarly, of the 13 elections falling below the median of this distribution of mean absolute swing, seven fall in the postwar period.

All of the eight pairs of elections with greatest swing have been clearly associated with major upheavals in British electoral politics, upheavals which—in one way or another—proved to have durable consequences. The long drawn-out process of replacing the Liberals with Labour as the major opposition to the Conservatives, not completed in some respects until the "National" landslide of 1931, accounts in large measure for three of the top eight values. Similarly, we find in this group events which include the decisive break of the Liberal Unionists from Gladstone's coalition over the Irish issue in 1886, the inauguration of a 20th century "new" Liberalism in the 1906 election, the record-breaking landslide of 1931 (which more than reinstated the "normal" pattern of major-party competition established in 1924 and lasting until World War II), and, of course, the "critical election" of 1945 which inaugurated the postwar pattern of policy and electoral cleavage in Britain. The aggregate difference between February 1974 and any of its predecessors since 1945 is patently clear; at the gross level, the outcome resembles nothing quite so much as that of the 1929 election, including the subsequent absence of a "real" parliamentary majority for any single party.

It is natural, therefore, to consider the possibility that the February 1974 election was in some sense a "critical" election. What is now known about the Liberal party's appeal suggests that this speculation may not be misplaced. The Liberals are clearly the most "American" of the three parties in policy, in outlook, and in clientele (Cyr, 1977:Chaps. 4 and 8). Their leaders eschew and deplore the freezing of alignments and policies along the dominant class-confrontation axis. They are opposed to "privilege," to what they view as the excesses of trade-union market power in the political economy, and to the electoral strategies of confrontation developed by the Heath government. For its part, the mass electorate clearly regards the Liberal party as falling midway on the conventional class/policy continuum of British electoral politics (Butler and Stokes, 1969:79-80). Its demographic profile thus cuts athwart the basic axis of cleavage in British politics and, as a result, it lacks a stable national territorial base and is heavily punished by the electoral system in consequence. Thus, in February 1974, it required 432,823 votes to elect one Liberal, as compared with 38,741 to elect one Labourite and 40,291 to elect one Conservative.

It has been patently clear for some time that the Liberal party represents a vehicle by which individuals who have supported one of the dominant parties can cast a protest vote without having to undergo the psychic strain of moving all the way over to the opposing major party. This has been amply demonstrated by Peter H. Lemieux's (1977) recent major study of the determinants of Liberal voting in Britain since 1964. Such voters at the margins, defecting to the Liberals, thus tend to act as though—following V.O. Key's (1966:1-8) argument—they were voting "retrospectively."

Developing a mathematical model of Liberal effects, stratified by continued-intervention and new-intervention constituencies, Lemieux was able to demonstrate that the model's assumptions were in conformity with the results of the 1964, 1966, and 1970 elections. In particular, Lemieux's coefficients indicated a negative Liberal effect upon the party in power at the time of the election. In February 1974, however, something very different happened. The assumptions of the model were badly violated, and the coefficients were positive instead of negative. Without attempting here to retrace in deail the argument Lemieux develops to evaluate this phenomenon, it is enough to note that he concludes—quite plausibly—that the underlying explanation may well be found in the *general* crisis of politics and the political economy then going on. In other words, the voters may not have been casting a retrospective negative judgment against one party only, *but against both*, since both had been recently in office, and since the economic-management records of both were negatively evaluated (Lemieux, 1977:Chaps. 6 and 7).

The major parties' dramatic "loss of gravitational attraction" in February 1974 stands out clearly from individual-level data as well. In a most important 1977 article, Crewe, Sarlvik and Alt (1977; see also, 1976) report the findings of their research on recent change in the British electorate. Not accidentally, the major theme is that of partisan *dealignment*, and the authors also raise very explicitly the possibility that February 1974 was a "critical election." The authors observe that while the hold of the two parties on actual British behavior had been declining since the late 1950s— as we have seen—the strength of party identification remained substantially unimpaired until February 1974. Quite suddenly, this measure of attachment to the existing institutions of the electoral market showed a sharp decline in February 1964, a decline which continued in October 1974.[21]

In attempting to account for the determinants of this change, the authors raise three hypotheses: (1) that the decline in the strength of partisan identification was the effect of the extraordinary crisis atmosphere preceding the February 1974 election;

(2) that it was the effect of generational "desocialization" paralleling the well-known American phenomenon described by Nie, Verba, and Petrocik (1976), Abramson (1975) and others; (3) that it was the effect of a long-term erosion of the once-close links between class and party adumbrated by Butler and Stokes in their classic study, *Political Change in Britain*. The conclusions they reached are striking. The first hypothesis is very strongly supported for Conservative partisanship, with clear signs of short-term rejection of Heath's leadership; but for Labour partisanship, a longer term and much more ominous process appears to have been at work, involving a growing rejection of the party's basic tenets among minorities of its supporters and increasing hostility to the economic-market power displayed by the trade unions. The second hypothesis is essentially disconfirmed. Unlike the strong generationally related decay of partisanship in the United States, the shift here was both sudden and across the board of age cohorts in the British electorate.[22] The third hypothesis—that of continuation of a long-term erosive trend away from the class-party link—receives less clear but generally favorable support in this study. The weakening of this link across the decade, as the authors observe, has not been a monotonic longitudinal process. Still, such evidence, as is adduced here, is heavily reinforced by an obvious counterfactual statement which the nature of the February 1974 campaign evokes. This campaign was explicitly structured by the government as a class-confrontation referendum. Had these class-party links not weakened across time as significantly as Bulter and Stokes have found, the mass stampede of voters from both parties to that most American and classless of British parties, the Liberals, could hardly have occurred. Moreover, the fact that by October 1974 barely half the electorate even *identified* with their "natural" class party seems mute testimony to the force of this weakening, granted the general crisis atmosphere of 1974 and the recency of the February "showdown." If so, however, we are badly in need of explanations for the causes of this continuing erosion: for surely in this context the "end of ideology" school, predicated upon the workability of political settlements and the onward march of mass affluence in high-consumption political economies, does not seem relevant to the context which we have been discussing.

The explosion of the Liberal vote in England during 1973-1974, and the subsequent rise of the neo-facist National Front to annoying but not as yet alarming levels, are probably less dramatic symptoms of political destabilization than the growth of the Scottish Nationalist party north of the Tweed. This party had been founded as long ago as 1929 and had duly contested elections in the intervening 40 years. It had a few spectacular by-election triumphs in the early period, most notably with the election of the first Nationalist to the House of Commons from the Motherwell constituency in April 1945. The party's first general-election success was registered as late as 1970, and then only in the Western Isles, not a very typical constituency. The rise of this party in recent years is concisely summarized in Table 5.

The rise of the Scottish Nationalists through the October 1974 general election was, as it turned out, more at the expense of the Conservatives than of Labour, though numerous commentaries have pointed out that further major gains by the SNP will affect Labour relatively much more adversely than the party's gains have done up to now. As Table 6 demonstrates, analysis of the cumulative swing between 1970 and October 1974 graphically reveals that Conservative strength has dropped in 1970 Conservative seats more than Labour strength has dropped in the seats Labour won in 1970. Still, the basic reality is a very large across-the-board swing to the Nationalists, irrespective of these considerations. What we are speaking about here is an aggregate two-party swing to SNP of 14.6% in Conservative seats, 13.1% in Labour seats and, in Scotland as a whole, 13.5%. The magnitude of this swing is quite without a general parallel in the rest of Britain.

Many reasons have been posited for this remarkable electoral transformation: the preexistence of many attributes of statehood in Scotland; the pervasive existence of a distinctive culture; long-term economic stagnation, which has given Glasgow some of the most noisome slums to be found in Europe; the disappearance of the Empire, and with it opportunities for young Scots to advance themselves; and, of course, oil. Very probably all of these factors have played a significant part in the rise of the SNP. But the rise of separatist movements is very much a pan-Western development of recent years. The efflorescence of autonomist movements in the West no doubt has much to do with the disappearance since 1945

Table 5: THE RISE OF SCOTTISH NATIONALISM AS AN ELECTORAL FORCE, 1959-1974

Year	% SNP of Scottish Total	N of Candidates	N of Lost De- posits	MP's Elected
1959	0.8	5	3	..
1964	2.4	15	12	..
1966	5.0	23	10	..
1970	11.4	65	43	1
1974I	21.9	70	8	7
1974II	30.4	71	..	11

Table 6. CUMULATIVE SWING FROM 1970 TO OCTOBER 1974 IN SCOTLAND: SCOTTISH NATIONALIST GAINS IN SEATS WON BY PARTY IN THE 1970 ELECTION*

1970 Seats	N	Mean Swing to/from		Standard Deviation
Conservative	25	To SNP	+17.8	3.6
		From Cons.	-11.4	5.5
Labour	42	To SNP	+18.3	7.0
		From Lab.	-7.8	3.8
Liberal	3	To SNP	+17.6	3.8
		To Lib.	+1.5	6.2
Scottish Nationalist	1	To SNP	+18.3	...
		From Lab.**	-13.7	...
SCOTLAND	71	To SNP	+18.1	5.9
		From Others	-8.8	5.4

*1970 data based on estimates of 1970 vote in 1974 boundaries kindly provided by Professor Richard Rose, University of Strathclyde, and an actual vote on constituencies with no or minor boundary changes.
**Labour last held this seat (Western Isles, 1966).

of a chief historic justification for the unitary nation-state: the maintenance of an independent national-defense establishment in a cosmos of European "great powers." This spread of demand for regional cultural and political self-determination seems also part of a larger, extremely diffuse but potent mass unrest through the West which is directed against far-off but omnipresent and un-accountable structures of concentrated power. This unrest forms an essential part of the current much-discussed "governability

crisis." There can be little doubt that, even if the Scottish Nationalist appeal has leveled off at around 36% of the vote in Scotland
(Pulzer, 1977:16), it has become an institutionalized force with
significant destabilizing potential for the existing state order in the
United Kingdom.

The processes of dissolution in the British electoral market, at
their worst, do not bear comparison with the magnitude which
disintegration of party has reached in American electoral politics.
But the evidence is clear that such dissolution of once-important
institutional channels between the voters and the candidates who
appeal for their votes is underway and, in particular, that the
electoral alignment which was functionally suited to the age of
collectivist consensus is undergoing severe erosive pressure. Since
this process seems to be most advanced among the youngest age
cohorts in the British electorate surveyed in the two 1974 elections,
there seems reason to think that it will continue to unfold in the
years immediately ahead. Granted the context which has been the
major subject of this essay, this tendency toward corrosion of
traditional partisan channels for electoral expression was perhaps
only to have been expected. Its direction—away from traditional
party voting, then from traditional party identification, and toward
support for nationalist and Americanized centrist parties—could
of course only disappoint leftist hopes. If and to the extent that
a movement out of the trenches of institutionalized class warfare
continues, and a more "American" electoral fluidity is approximated, one could anticipate two broad consequences. On one hand,
the steering capacity of the state—to the extent that it continues
to operate through traditional institutions—will be impaired by the
textbook standards of 1945: as the electorate becomes more diffuse,
so oppositions proliferate, becoming more unpredictable and more
uncontrollable. On the other hand, this growing fluidity should
in the very long term immensely simplify the primary task of governments—the defense and enhancement of the well-being of the
existing socioeconomic order. Simultaneously, and as the history
of American electoral politics in the 20th century abundantly
demonstrates, the redefinition of the mass electoral market in such
terms conduces to the preservation of its nominal structure while
modifying profoundly its substantive content.

V

Predictions of the future are often not worth the paper they are written on. Gallons of ink have already been spilled on the "problem of Britain," and much of the discussion has had a near-apocalyptic ring (see Haseler, 1976). But it may well be that this time, as has so often been the case with Britain in the past, we will find it necessary to adjourn the apocalypse to a date in the uncertain future. In the first place, it is clear that the British electorate has thus far behaved with resolute moderation—as, in the 1974-1977 period, have the trade unions and their leadership. Second, there are excellent reasons to suppose that the economic situation in Britain is about to improve rapidly, with the influx of North Sea oil as prime mover. As of the fall of 1977, Britain is obtaining about 800,000 barrels of oil a day, about equivalent to 10% of Saudi Arabia's production and equal to about half of the country's energy needs. It is anticipated that by the early 1980s the rate of extraction will be around two million barrels a day and the country will be self-sufficient in energy resources, one of the very few industrial countries so fortunately situated (see Janssen, 1977). The British balance of payments is expected to shift fully into surplus by 1978, if not before, and prospects appear excellent that with this major resource, British governments will at last find the means to break out of the "stop-go" cycles of the postwar era of economic decline.

Britain's rapidly accumulating good fortune, of course, provides opportunity, not certainty. Old problems remain: the competitive underperformance race between management and labor in the factory, the gravity of the unemployment problem and especially the heavy concentration of unemployment among the young, the issue of redefining relations between Scotland and England. New issue present themselves: assuming that the international oil price is not allowed to fall significantly (and Britain is rapidly acquiring a vested interest in the success of OPEC's price administration), the question of who controls the bonanza—what mixture is to exist between private investment and publicly directed investment—seem certain to be a basic political issue in and between future general elections.

It is thus peculiarly difficult at this obvious turning point in Britain's fortunes to assess how the recent past which we have described here will be filtered through the opportunities, issues, and conflicts of the near future. Governability in any society, we like to suppose, is enhanced whenever the stock of available resources for allocation undergoes a major increase. This, after all, was the chief hypothesis underlying the actions of the men in Britain, the United States, and elsewhere who created the postwar political order. It may accordingly turn out that the Conservatives under Mrs. Thatcher have seized upon ideology at precisely the wrong moment in history, and that the pluralist pragmatism of the present government will reassert itself as a hegemonic political style.

But man does not live by bread alone, and political conflict does not disappear as affluence spreads—this was the great error of the once-fashionable "end of ideology" school. Perhaps the collectivist-pluralist political settlement of yesteryear can be refitted by political craftsmen out of the current fragments as pressure relaxes. But one is very inclined to doubt that things will really turn out this way in the very near future. If the recent history of Western politics has any projective meaning at all for the future, it would seem to lie in the inchoate but very substantial demands by ordinary people for greater control over their own lives, and for liberation from the autocratic, immense, and impersonal structures of power which loom large over us all. This impulse toward greater self-realization—toward the revolutionary promise which democracy has always held out, and which has always been so imperfectly realized by democracies in practice—has taken an extraordinary variety of forms in the past decade of Western political history; some of these forms have been manifestly pathological. But in whatever form it manifests itself, this impulse represents the negation of certain principles which are essential to the maintenance and the management of the mixed collectivist-pluralist-capitalist state. It therefore appears, and is, a threat to technocrats and Eurocrats, and to the leaders of all the peak power groups which flourished in the heyday of the postwar political settlement.

But the resistant power of these structures is so immense, their inertial hold over the existing order of things is so strong, that it is hard to imagine a force powerful enough to displace them. Analysts should thus not be surprised to find, with Gramsci, that "in this interregnum a great variety of morbid symptoms appears." One can see certain domains of this crisis, and some of the symptoms—

morbid and otherwise—much more clearly in Britain than in the United States. The differences between the two societies are vast, but they share many of the problematics of late-capitalist society in common. The personal sympathies of scholars apart, Britain remains an important resource of comparative study by Americans—not perhaps in the older Wilsonian vein so much as in response to Karl Marx's warning: "*De te fabula narratur!*"

NOTES

1. For a conventional account, see Joseph M. Jones (1955). Leftists, of course, tend to emphasize different aspects of this basic change in American foreign policy and its background in World War II. See, e.g., Gabriel Kolko (1968).

2. One analysis of legitimation strains on the American pluralist variant is Theodore Lowi's *The End of Liberalism* (1969). A much more penetrating view of the issues involved is Jürgen Habermas, *Legitimation Crisis* (1973).

3. The classic modern exposition of the issues involved is Joseph A. Schumpeter, *Capitalism, Socialism and Democracy* (1950). The most current variation on this theme is presented by Daniel Bell, *The Cultural Contradictions of Capitalism* (1976:33-84). These books, it should be noted, were written by capitalism's friends, not its enemies.

4. Barnet (1972:112-120) also observes that the immense gains in rationalization of production achieved during the war were allowed to wither away when "business as usual" was restored after 1819.

5. Needless to say, conservatives like Enoch Powell are hypersensitive to this. See, for example, Powell, 1969:126-144.

6. Hence the literature on the "capital gap," which temporarily flourished in the American business press during the 1974-1975 slump. See, e.g., *Business Week*, "Special Issue: Capital Crisis," September 22, 1975, especially the discussion at pp. 42-53.

7. Very analogous processes have been at work in American cities—most notably, of course, in New York City. See Martin Shefter (1977). A comparative analysis of these two cases, in my opinion, virtually cries out to be done.

8. This view is argued forcefully and in detail by a leading member of the Labour Left, Eric Heffer (1973); this study contains a useful comparative discussion of labor-relations legislation in Britain and in the U.S.

9. Later, just after the February 1974 election, it was revealed that the miners were entitled to their claim even under the guidelines which the Pay Board had set up under the 1972 Industrial Relations Act, and therefore—as Enoch Powell charged at the time—that this particular confrontation was wholly unnecessary. For a discussion of this, see David Bulter and Dennis Kavanagh (1974:66-72).

10. The Labour manifesto is conveniently published in F.W.S. Craig (1975:398-405).

11. Increases in public revenues and expenditures, 1970/76, have been as follows.

Years (end 31 March)	Revenues	Expenditures (Ŀ million, current prices)	Surplus or Deficit
1970/71	Ŀ15,842.8	Ŀ14,086.3	+Ŀ1,756.5
1971/72	16,931.8	15,548.8	+1,383.0
1972/73	17,178.1	17,689.1	-511.0
1973/74	18,226.4	19,965.3	-1,738.9
1974/75	23,570.1	26,802.5	-3,232.4
1975/76	29,417.1	36,047.0	-6,629.9

SOURCE: United Kingdom Central Statistical Office, Annual Abstract of Statistics, 1976 (London: HMSO, 1976), p. 366.

12. This may also reflect a political underdevelopment which has left the United States with the most docile labor force in the Western world.

13. This is a basic, if not always fully disclosed, item on the agenda of the special 10th anniversary issue of *The Public Interest*, reprinted in Nathan Glazer and Irving Kristol (1976). The articles by Samuel P. Huntington and Aaron Wildavsky make especially instructive reading in this particular context.

14. Indeed, progmatists can and not infrequently do turn into ideologues when pressed hard by opposition on fundamentals, as the entire history of the crises of 1968 and 1972 within the Democratic party in the United States abundantly demonstrates. See, e.g., Denis G. Sullivan, Jeffrey L. Pressman, Benjamin I. Page, and John J. Lyons (1974:116-134).

15. This concern is noticeable, e.g., in the Nuffield study of the February 1974 election, where for the first time in the series the need to discuss the *meaning* of elections in the political process finds expression. See Bulter and Kavanagh (1974:1-9).

16. The basic data are found in George H. Gallup (1976). Variants of this measure have been employed by Samuel H. Beer (1974:209) and Arthur Cyr (1977:290). For some reason, both refer to "standard deviations," when in reality variances (their squares) are involved.

17. The basic data, 1945-1975, are contained in F.W.S. Craig (1976:52-64); and for 1976-1977, from return of by-elections as reported in *The Times*. Elections in Northern Ireland have been excluded. For a useful review of by-elections as barometers of public opinion, see Chris Cook and John Ramsden (1973).

18. In fact, the incumbent Conservatives actually *gained* a seat from the Labour opposition in a 1953, by-election.

19. In the remarkable year of 1973, an all-time high of 38.8% of the vote in by-elections was cast for other than Conservative and Labour candidates. It should also be noted, of course, that one essential feature of by-elections is that they reflect the "luck of the draw." As the 1973 "other" vote was inflated by the SNP success in Glasgow, Govan, the fall of the "other" vote in 1976-1977 from those highs owes a great deal to the accident that no seats in Scotland or Wales fell vacant during this period.

20. This is obviously, and admittedly, a crude measure. It includes Liberal and Conservative percentages throughout, and Labour beginning with the 1900-1906 election pair.

21. As October 1974 resembled nothing so much as February 1974 on the aggregate-data level, so it is clear from these findings that this was also true at the level of individual party identification.

22. This is an extremely carefully crafted study, a model of its kind. But there appear to be a few more signs of generationally related weakness in party identification, viewed cross-sectionally rather than longitudinally, than Butler and Stokes suggest. Thus, their Table 14 (p. 162), reworded specifically to include voters aged 30 and over in 1974, gives the following pattern:

Strength of Party ID	February 1974			October 1974		
	18-24	25-29	30 & over	18-24	25-29	30 & over
	%	%	%	%	%	%
Very strong	18	19	32	14	13	30
Fairly strong	44	41	43	49	48	45
Not very strong	28	31	19	29	28	17
No party ID	10	9	6	7	11	8
N	250	254	1958	277	271	1816

The dominant theme in this article is, rightly, that of across-the-board defection from strong identification. But the implications of this markedly weaker hold of party over younger voters for the future of the institutionalized electoral market should be noted.

REFERENCES

ABRAMS, M. (1960). Must Labour Lose? London: Penguin.

ABRAMSON, P. (1975). Generational change in American politics. Lexington, Mass.: Lexington Books.

BARNETT, C. (1972). The collapse of British power. London: Eyre Methuen.

BEER, S. (1965). British politics in the collectivists age. New York: Knopf.

——— (1974). The British political system. New York: Random House.

BELL, D. (1976) The cultural contradictions of capitalism. New York: Basic Books.

BELLINI, J., et al. (1974). The United Kingdom in 1980 (The Hudson Report). New York: John Wiley.

BUCHANAN, J., and WAGNER, R. (1977). Democracy in deficit: The political legacy of Lord Keynes. New York: Academic Press.

BUTLER, D., and KAVANAGH, D. (1974). The British general election of February 1974. London: Macmillan.

BUTLER, D., and ROSE, R. (1960). The British general election of 1959. London: Cass.

BUTLER, D. and STOKES, D. (1969). Political change in Britain. London: Macmillan.

COOK, C., and RAMSDEN, J. (eds., 1973). By-elections in British politics. New York: St. Martin's.

CRAIG, F.W.S. (1975). British general election manifestos, 1900-1974. London: Macmillan.

——— (1976). British electoral facts, 1885-1975. London: Macmillan.

CREWE, I., SARLVIK, B., and ALT, J. (1976). "Partisanship and policy choice: Issue preferences in the British electorate, February 1974." British Journal of Political Science, 6.

——— (1977). "Partisan dealignment in Britain, 1964-1974." British Journal of Political Science, 7.

CYR, A. (1977). Liberal party politics in Britain. New Brunswick, N.J.: Transaction.

EPSTEIN, L. (1967). Political parties in western democracies. New York: Praeger.

GALLUP, G. (1976). The Gallup International Public Opinion Polls: Great Britain, 1937-1975. New York: Random House.

GAMBLE, A. (1974). The Conservative Nation. London: Routledge and Kegan Paul.

GLAZER, N., and Kristol, I. (1976). The American Commonwealth 1976. New York: Basic Books.

HABERMAS, J. (1973). Legitimation crisis. Boston: Beacon Press.

HASELER, S. (1976). The death of British democracy. London: Elek.

HEFFER, E. (1973). The class struggle in Parliament. London: Gallancy.

HUNTINGTON, S. (1976). "The democratic distemper." Pp. 9-38 in N. Glazer and I. Kristol (eds.), The American Commonwealth. New York: Basic Books.

JANSSEN, R. (1977). "North Sea bonanza: Britain sees oil wealth as opportunity to end long national decline." Wall Street Journal.

JENKINS, P. (1970). The battle of Downing Street. London: Knight.

JONES, J. (1955). The fifteen weeks. New York: Viking.

KEY, V. O., Jr. (1966). The responsible electorate. Cambridge: Harvard University Press.

KOLKO, G. (1968). The politics of war. New York: Random House.

LEMIEUX, P. (1977). The Liberal party and British political change, 1955-1974. Ph.D. dissertation, Department of Political Science, Massachusetts Institute of Technology.

LOWI, T. (1969). The end of liberalism. New York: W. W. Norton.

MARX, K. (1962). "Preface to the first German edition of the first volume of Capital." In K. Marx and F. Engels, Selected works. Moscow: Foreign Languages Publishing House.

NEWFIELD, J., and Dubrul, P. (1977). The abuse of power. The permanent government and the fall of New York. New York: Viking.

NIE, N., VERBA, S., and PETROCIK, J. (1976). The changing American voter. Cambridge: Harvard University Press.

O'CONNOR, J. (1973). The fiscal crisis of the state. New York: St. Martin's.

PENNIMAN, H. (1975). Britain at the polls: The parliamentary elections of 1974. Washington, D.C.: American Enterprises Institute.

POWELL, J.E. (1969). "To socialism through inflation." In J.E. Powell, Freedom and reality. New Rochelle, N.Y.: Arlington House.

PULZER, P. (1977). "Half shores is the most the SNP can expect in Scotland." The Times.

ROSE, R. (1976). Northern Ireland: Time of choice. Washington, D.C.: American Enterprise Institute.

SCHUMPETER, J. (1950). Capitalism, socialism, and democracy. New York: Harper.

SHEFTER, M. (1977). "New York City's fical crisis: The politics of inflation and retrenchment." The Public Interest.

SULLIVAN, D., et al. (1974). The politics of representation: The Democratic Convention 1972. New York: St. Martin's Press.

WATT, D. (1977). "Mrs. Thatcher risks showing her colours." Financial Times. London.

WILDAVSKY, A. (1975). "Special issue: Capital crisis." Business Week.

——— (1976). "The past and future presidency." Pp. 56-76 in N. Glazer and I. Kristol (eds.), The American Commonwealth. New York: Basic Books.

Chapter 9

POLITICAL PARTIES AND SOCIAL CHANGE:
THE JAPANESE EXPERIENCE

T. J. P E M P E L

I. INTRODUCTION

One of the most fundamental modern political relationships is that between political parties and social change. In their role as a central link between the state and society, political parties have the potential to serve as a mechanism for autonomously generated social changes to gain reflection in governmental structure and actions. Alternatively, they serve as a device whereby the government can mobilize and channel social change. The relative strength of these linkages, the direction in which influence through them is channelled, and the uses to which such influence is put all have a profound effect on the political possibilities and political activities within any country.

In some instances, a relatively united political elite, committed to a particular vision of social change, will use parties to mobilize and channel society in desired directions. The various communist parties of Eastern Europe, the mass mobilization parties of Africa, or the reactionary parties which until recently dominated the Iberian Peninsula suggest the wide span of such possibilities. In other cases, such as the rise of parties of the left in Europe during the late 19th century and their increased electoral success, particularly following World War I, fundamental changes in society

AUTHOR'S NOTE: I would like to thank Michael Donnelly and Peter Katzenstein for reading and commenting on an earlier draft of this paper. I have also benefitted greatly from discussions of its themes with Gerald Curtis, Benjamin Ginsberg, and Sidney Tarrow.

were successfully and rather rapidly funnelled up to the state apparatus through drastic alterations in party systems. Similarly, political protection for vested social interests was achieved through the formation of various agrarian parties in Scandinavia, through religious-based parties in Italy, France, Belgium, Holland, and Germany, and upper-class aristocratic parties in England, Germany, Denmark, and the like.

One of the most well-known explanations for the relationship between party system and social change is the theory of "critical realignments" within the U.S., a theory which combines notions of responsiveness to and structuring of social change. This theory suggests that, following periods of relative political stability, broad-based social discontent with the existing political regime emerges. This crystalizes in the formation of a new major party or the capture by insurgents of an existing major party. Ensuing elections are marked by highly ideological debate and massive voter realignments. Eventually, a stable two-party system reemerges on the national level to continue until the next phase of realignment (Burnham, 1967, 1970; Key, 1955). Less developed theoretically, but resting on comparable understandings, are suggestions concerning the relationship in Britain (Butler and Stokes, 1976).

Whether linking primarily "up" to the state or "down" toward society, whether attempting to induce alterations in society or inhibit them, political parties, on the basis of this diverse evidence, are clearly a major channel for the politicization of social change. Yet the linkage function is not automatic. A one-to-one correspondence between social change and governmental action rarely, if ever, occurs. Two very important, but frequently overlooked, elements of a political system determine the potentials and actual nature of the ties between social change and political parties. First, to what extent do political parties play some significant role in the policy-making mechanisms of the country? Second, and possibly more important, to what constituencies are the existing political parties responsible? How closely intertwined are the parties with the state apparatus? What, if any, incentives exist for the party leadership to search out new bases of support or does the nature of the commitment to existing constituencies inhibit such a search?

It is highly debatable just how much most political parties exercise control over the central organs of policymaking in any society. Even students of U.S. parties who are most disposed to see parties as instruments of public control over policy formation tend to agree that the parties' role in the process is rather limited (Burnham, 1967:279). Certain private sectors outside of party control will almost always retain dominance over important elements of policy, while within the public sector certain organs will remain subject to, at best, minimal influence by parties. Even with such constraints in mind, however, different states allow for widely varying degrees of influence by parties over public policymaking, and Britain, the U.S., and most one-party modernizers demonstrate comparatively high party influence.

Where such influence is high, parties have a clear advantage in controlling emerging social trends. By using their influence, they can attempt to meet or alter new demands and thereby channel them into desired directions. Correspondingly, new groups with new demands, recognizing the influence of parties on policy, will have an incentive to work through the party system to achieve their ends. Conversely, when party influence is low or nonexistent, both of these conditions are absent and new groups will have obvious incentives to move outside the existing party apparatus in hopes of achieving their ends.

Understanding the degree of party responsibility is also critical to understanding how parties cope with social change. A high degree of responsibility toward existing constituencies may be desirable in a period of social quiescence. Under conditions of minimal social change, parties such as the Norwegian or Swedish Social Democratic parties managed to do rather well precisely by being highly responsible to their well-defined though limited social bases. But under conditions of rapid and significant social change, only parties willing to sell out past constituencies in the interest of attracting newer and more powerful support can expect to do well.

The case of Japan provides a powerful example to support these contentions, as this paper will attempt to demonstrate. During the late 1920s and throughout the 1930s, the major political parties in Japan, which had just begun to develop some element of control over organs of political power, remained adamantly wedded to their rural agricultural and urban commercial bases even though there was a surge in the number of new social groups as a result of past economic and foreign policies, and even though mass suffrage had greatly expanded the franchise. The failure of the existing parties to attract the support of at least some of these new groups led to the development of small but politically threatening proletarian parties on the left, and to attempts to implement what Hugh Byas (1942) has called "government by assassination" on the right. The social changes that occurred in Japan during the mid to late 1930s and through World War II can and have been explained by most historians with little or no reference to political parties. By the time these events were occurring, the political parties had become largely irrelevant, either as the vehicles or the reflections of social changes. Rather, the military, the Imperial household, the bureaucracy and nonparty cabinets came to occupy the central roles in adjusting to and attempting to channel these changes.

When one turns to parties in contemporary Japan, it is striking that a parallel phenomenon appears to be occurring. The two major parties have remained locked-in to past constituencies, even though major shifts in levels of urbanization, education, economic well-being, and age distribution among the populace have made it questionable whether a political majority can ever again be created from the constituencies of the past. Moreover, there is evidence that policymaking powers are slipping away from those organs controlled by the existing parties, most notably from the national Diet and the Cabinet and toward local governments, the courts, and the national bureaucracy, making it questionable whether new social groups will see such merit in working through the party system.

I will argue in this paper that, while the prewar and postwar periods are by no means identical, they are comparable insofar as the major political parties were largely incapable of dealing with social change. I will contend further that this incapacity was the result of two things: first, their collective inability to gain predominance over the central organs of policymaking within the country, and second, their continued responsibility to particular socioeconomic sectors—a responsibility that caused them to depend exclusively on support from certain social sectors to the exclusion of appeals to new and potentially more significant sectors.

II. PREWAR JAPAN: WEAK BUT "RESPONSIBLE" PARTIES IN A STRONG STATE

Political parties in Japan, as in other late and rapid industrializers, have comparatively short histories and weak claims to a share in power and legitimacy. Protoparties did not emerge in Japan until the 1870s and it took them over 20 years to gain even a modicum of political influence. Not until the 1920s did electoral success by one party or another become established as the primary basis on which cabinets were formed; and in less than 10 years even these limited forms of influence were again eliminated. If one considers that all Japanese governmental institutions were severely constrained under the U.S. Occupation, it is possible to contend that in Japan a system of meaningful party control over cabinets dates only from 1952.

By the time parties had emerged in Japan, a modernizing political elite had toppled the 250 year old feudal structure and established a comparatively strong state structure dedicated to the rapid industrialization and military protection of the country. The threat to national integrity posed by the Western imperial power plus the promises of modernization held out by the new government put the state bureaucracy in a comparatively strong position relative to the fledgling political parties. The latter were easily cast as the purveyors of an untimely and immoral urge for a self-serving fractionalization of power that could only benefit the nation's enemies (Berger, 1977; Scalapino, 1962). A strong state and an able bureaucracy, it was argued, served as a far more viable guarantor of eventual national success than the alien and threatening ideas put forward by political parties. Japan, like Germany and France, thus developed a powerful bureaucracy which served as a social control mechanism before social groups had learned how to use the weapon of political organization to secure influence (Bendix, 1964; Daalder, 1966; Tilly, 1975).

Despite the monolithic image often conveyed, under the Meiji Constitution political power was actually quite dispersed structurally. The Privy Council, the appointive House of Peers, the Imperial Household, the military and the civilian bureaucracies, the *genro,* and the cabinet all had distinct and important roles to play. In contrast to many late modernizers, Japan thus resembled far more a

Madisonian-Montesquieuian state than a Leninist or Rousseauian monolith. Multiple centers of power, each with a diverse base, were capable of utilizing their particularistic resources in competition with one another over most policy matters.

This structural diversity was, however, based on a firm under-pinning of ideological conformity and upper-class harmony and overlaid with the unifying framework of Imperial loyalty. Political participation was limited to the few. There was but one ultimate source of sovereignty, the emperor, and, though hardly articulated in the Constitution, only one driving policy goal—industrial de-velopment and catching up with the West. To these fundamental principles, all political actors seeking to exert influence were required to demonstrate full commitment.

Within these major confines, "real politics" among the competing elites with their various centers of power was highly volatile, but once a political arrangement was arrived at and had been presented for Imperial ratification, no challenge, no matter on what grounds, could claim legitimacy. Certainly any challenge based on notions of popular sovereignty, the will of the people, or a contrary electoral mandate, had anyone dared to pose it, would have been deemed irrelevant at best; more plausibly, it would have been seen as a form of lese majesté. As a result of the overarching agreement among the elites of the system, there was a great deal of cohesion despite the structural diversity in the distribution of power.

In this combination of unity in principle and diversity in the structures of power, Japan under Meiji resembled the closed political systems of much of contemporary Latin America (Ander-son, 1967; Payne, 1965). In its elite cooperation and oligarchic commitment to "the system," it is similar to the consociational model of politics suggested for many of the smaller European demo-cracies (Lijphart, 1968, 1969; McRae, 1974).

In their early statements, the major parties posed a variety of abstract and real challenges to the emerging system of power and authority. They were composed of a diversity of declassé samurai opposed to the loss of their feudal privileges and a wide array of rural interests hostile to a tax system which placed the burden of capital formation for industrialization on the rural sector. The parties' most fundamental demand was for a constitution and a representative legislature. The internal pressures they generated came at a time when the government was recognizing just how difficult it would be to eliminate the unequal treaties imposed by the Western powers and thus acquire the potential for autonomous commercial development. What seemed most to impress the Western countries was the creation of precisely those "civilized" political structures demanded by the parties. In 1881, a constitution and a parliament were thus promised; in 1890, they were delivered, but as a "gift" from the emperor, thereby undermining any popular and electoral claims that might have been advanced as the basis of their legitimacy. Had the parties' demands for a representative assembly been granted immediately, there is little doubt but that certain fundamental tenets of the Meiji Restoration would have been called into question. Through a series of politically astute moves, however, the government managed to assuage the discontent of most of the samurai, and in 1877, it militarily defeated the remaining contingent who attempted to manifest their discontents more directly. Simultaneously and also before the parliament was created, the Jiyūtō, the major party at the time, split, leaving only its more conservative wing to contest the elections that were eventually called in 1890. Although in the first few Diets there was a good deal of trench warfare between the government and the political parties over military expenses and the burdens being placed on agricultural areas, the parties were shortly co-opted into the existing system of power.

The leadership of the parties at this time was predominantly composed of ex-government leaders such as Itagaki Taisuke and Ōkuma Shigenobu who, dissatisfied with the early distribution of political offices, were comparatively easy to satisfy. Well-to-do landowners, who represented the bulk of the parties' membership meanwhile, were partly placated by land tax reductions and the introduction of income, business, inheritance, and sugar excise taxes which thereby reduced some of their tax burden. The land tax, which had produced between 85% and 93% of the government's revenue from 1871-1875, had by 1896 fallen to below 50% of government income (Halliday, 1975:46-49). Meanwhile increased agricultural productivity, a concentration of land ownership, and the increased commercialization of agriculture served to reduce further the hostility of the rural upper class to the government and to integrate it fully into the political system.

It was largely through the parties and the electoral system that this integration took place. Throughout most of the period until the introduction of universal male suffrage in 1925, elections and the Diet were the provinces of the rural areas. Scalapino calculates, for example, that before the electoral revision of 1900 all except 17 of the 300 electoral districts were rural, and as late as 1908 the breakdown was 302 rural districts to 76 urban (Scalapino, 1962:255; see also Dore, 1959:86).

Voting support, rooted in the ability of a landed upper class to deliver the votes, did not preclude the parties from acquiring financial support from the urban business sector, however. In order to insure the success of the nation's drive toward industrialization, the largest and most successful of the commercial and industrial interests—Mitsui, Mitsubishi, Sumitomo, Yasuda, Kawasaki, and the like—all came to exert major influence over one or more of the parties. In most instances, this influence took the form of direct cash contributions to the parties in exchange for both general and specific actions in parliament.

Before too long after their entry into the system, the political parties were not longer the bearers of an anti-government ideology, nor even parties of principle, to use Kirchheimer's (1966) term. Thomas (1975:14), for example, has found that Japanese parties provided far less diversity in their policy positions on socioeconomic issues and government structure during the 1910s than in any of the other eight industrial societies he examined; even during the tempestuous 1930s, the positions of the established parties were among the most homogeneous. Patronage, reelection, and pork barrel benefits for their electoral districts were the major concerns of most party politicans. As such, the parties came to represent a fusion between agricultural and rural interests and those of the emerging commerical and business elite. The latter provided the political operating expenses while the former provided the votes to allow party politicans to claim some role in the political system.

Under the political system that emerged success in elections was but one of many possible ways by which a political force could demonstrate its political resources and gain a share in the distribution of power. By no means was it the most significant. In and of itself electoral success provided little basis for exercising political authority. As has been well noted, when suffrage was introduced in

1889 it was limited to males over 25 who paid Y15 or more in taxes. The result was an electorate of about 1% of the population; candidates could be elected to the Diet with about 1,000 votes (Ike, 1964:404). A reduction in the required tax base doubled the electorate in 1900 and tripled it in 1919, but, even at this comparatively late date in Japan's political development, only slightly more than 5% of the population was eligible to vote. Universal suffrage for males over 25 was not introduced until 1925 and even then the vote was denied to the impoverished, bankrupts, recipients of public welfare, and those "without a definite domicile." Moreover, the vote's introduction was coupled, as have been most expansions in the size of the electorate, with an increase in restrictions on political liberties, in this case in the form of the Peace Preservation Law.

The comparatively late introduction of universal male suffrage can be seen when one realizes that roughly comparable expansions took place during the Jacksonian period in the U.S., 1848 in France, 1867 with the Reform Act in Britain, in each of the major Scandinavian countries at about the turn of the century, and, though only in relation to the election of a weak parliament, in Germany in 1867 (Rokkan, 1966). The timing of the introduction of the suffrage may be less significant per se than the fact that by the time Japan's suffrage was expanded significantly, industrialization was well under way. A number of other major structures of power were therefore already entrenched and closely identified with the success of industrialization. Furthermore, as will be examined subsequently, by the time mass suffrage was introduced in Japan, the political parties were so much the captives of these other forces that there was little incentive or possibility that they would be able to "reach out" to the newly enfranchised masses and bring them into the system without major social upheaval.

Japan experienced a series of different electoral systems under the Meiji Constitution, all of which made it difficult for any single party to gain an absolute majority within the Lower House of the Diet. In only four of 22 elections between 1890 and 1946 did a single party garner a majority. This made it difficult for the parties to lay even a weak claim to a popular mandate or, more importantly, to gain sole dominance over the Lower House of the Diet for a period long enough to parlay into a major policy role.

Because of the relative weakness of the Diet, even gaining total control of that body, which rarely occurred, could insure a political party of very little real political power. The Diet could not legislate; it never gained control of the national budget, and it was never the embodiment of sovereignty that parliaments were in several European countries at the time. In his *Commentaries on the Constitution,* Itō Hirobumi, like James Madison in the *Federalist Papers,* makes clear the explicit limitations on the legislature: "The Imperial Diet," wrote Itō, "takes part in legislation, but has no share in the sovereign power; it has power to deliberate upon laws, but none to determine them. The right of consent of the Imperial Diet has to be exercised within the limits allowed by the provisions of the Constitution, and is by no means an unlimited one" (Itō, 1889:62). And although the powers it was granted eventually permitted some expansion of party influence between 1890 and the 1920s (Akita, 1967; Pittau, 1967), it took 30 years before any of the major parties posed even the vaguest of challenges to the principles of an impotent Diet and Imperial sovereignty. When the Minseitō advocated "parliament-centered government" on the eve of the first general election held under male suffrage in 1925, Home Minister Suzuki delivered a stinging rebuke:

> It is inexcusable that our country be compared to others where Cabinets are directly formed by the majority party. From its inception, the Seiyūkai has been obedient to the principle of government centered on the emperor. . . . By contrast, the present platform of the Minseitō . . . is most disquieting . . . and violates the great spirit of our nation's sacred Constitution. . . . Concepts like parliament-centered politics are Anglo-American notions flowing from the current of democracy, and are inconsistent with our nation's [national polity]. They obscure the great principle that sovereignty lies entirely with the emperor. [quoted in Berger, 1977:47-49]

Even in 1934, the liberal legal scholar Minobe Tatsukichi (1934) was forced to recognize the severe limitations that existed in the Diet's power. Commenting in *Chūō Kōron,* he noted that the Diet was incapable of doing anything to initiate legislation and served only to ratify the proposals of functional specialists within the bureaucracy.

Although the Diet lacked many of the powers characteristic of moderately strong legislatures, its most striking weakness was the inability to utilize elections and control of the Diet as the basis for establishing cabinets. Of the 44 cabinets formed between 1890 and the end of World War II, at most 17 could be said to have been headed by party leaders, and these figures include the eight cabinets headed by Itō, Ōkuma, and Saionji, all of whom had left their official positions in the state bureaucracy and the court to assume party leadership, as well as that of Tanaka Giichi, a retired general who did the same. It is therefore more reasonable to speak of eight of the 44, or less than one in five. During the 1920s, the so-called "established parties" *(kisei seitō)* finally came to gain something of a veto power over cabinet formation, but even then this power was shared with other groups and hence was itself of limited import (cf. Duus, 1968).

It is even more revealing to note that during the entire prewar period not a single election resulted in the defeat of an incumbent political party (Scalapino, 1968). Governments changed, of course, as did majorities in the Diet, but the dominant pattern was for the first to take place *before* the second, rather than in reverse as is presumed to be basic to electoral control and parliamentary government. The power of the state was frequently used to insure the election of its candidates. This involved overt violence in the earliest years and later somewhat more subtle devices such as requiring the consent of all police stations in an area for a meeting by opposition parties (Quigley, 1932:267). Such actions, which reverse the direction in the presumed linkages among elections and the formation of governments, are not unheard of in other political contexts, but what is significant here is that what was the exception elsewhere was the rule in Japan. Elections served more to legitimate the state than to insure control over its activities.

The parties, like all the other actors in the system, sought to expand their relative shares of influence. Given the initial limits on suffrage, they attempted primarily to expand theirs into other organs of government. Here, they were largely stymied. The military was explicitly banned from having anything to do with parties and politicians. The Imperial Household, the *genrō,* the House of Peers, and the Privy Council were mostly hereditary and subject to only the barest and most indirect of party influence. Meanwhile, in contrast to societies such as early 19th century America or contemporary Italy (Epstein, 1967:104-111; Shefter, 1977), but parallel to the

German Second Republic, Japan early developed a series of government ordinances which made the civil bureaucracy highly meritocratic and virtually immune to penetration through patronage. Not that the parties did not try to establish such controls. In exchange for Seiyūkai support for the Yamamoto Cabinet (1913-14), for example, four bureaucratic officials who took cabinet posts enrolled in the party (Scalapino, 1962:201). But such leverage came comparatively late and was comparatively rare.

More noteworthy than party penetration of the bureaucracy was the reverse, penetration of the parties by the bureaucracy. The most notable example came when Itō Hirobumi, former prime minister, and one of the seven original *genrō* willingly took over the leadership of the Jiyūtō and reorganized it as the Seiyūkai in 1900 to insure the government of some permanent party support within the Diet. One can point also to Saionji's subsequent leadership of the party, the close cooperation between Yamagata Aritomo and Hara Takeshi, Katsura Tarō's formation of the Dōshikai and the like (Scalapino, 1962; Najita, 1967; Duus, 1968). In this regard, the Japanese pattern of party development resembles that of oligarchic cooptation by Scandinavian and British conservatives. Consequently, at least until the 1920s, the parties were far more dependent on the upper class and the state bureaucracy for leadership and favors than the reverse. The early Japanese parties thus were not forced to develop truly mass support as the basis for toppling an extent elite; rather they gained entry to the system through a politics of willing co-optation by that elite.

The major conservative parties were thus highly integrated into the political system which was bringing about major industrial successes at home, as well as developing a growing empire abroad. As a result, they were at a tactical loss when the very successes of these policies began to generate increasing discontent within Japan among those who were the policies' major victims—the urban worker and the rural tenant farmer. In reaction to the large segments of the population left behind as the dregs of the government's industrialization policies, and in response to the competing intellectual currents represented by the success of the Russian Revolution, the collapse of the German and Austrian Empires, the establishment of Fascism in Italy, the outbreak of revolution in Spain, the wave of military coups throughout Latin America, and the world depression, a new array of forces began to emerge in Japan during the late 1910s and through the 1930s. At the heart of the problem was the growing disjuncture between the purity of the national rhetoric and ideology and the sordid realities of many of its policies. In the absence of serious efforts by most elements of the existing power structures to co-opt and defuse the emerging social forces, new political organizations sprung up for their articulation. These, in turn, saw the financial and commercial establishment, the landlords, and the political parties which supported them as primary targets of opposition.

On the left and in urban areas and industrial sectors, various socialist, communist, and labor union groups developed; on the right, various forms of national socialism gained influence in the rural areas and among junior officers within the military. By the mid-1920s these forces offered fundamental policy alternatives to those maintained by the existing regime and the parties that were part of it.

The left, attempting to challenge the status quo through union and tenant organization and the electoral machinery, did gain 10% of the total vote in the 1937 election. This figure was small compared to counterpart parties in Europe at the time, but even this limited support suggested a public appeal and a threat to the existing political system which made it the target of vitriolic attacks from both the radical right and by the state apparatus itself. The left proved to be a comparatively easy target for the machinery of state suppression, particularly as the state was aided in its task by the radical right.

A series of cliques within the army as well as a more populist civilian national socialist movement abjured popular elections and dominated the political headlines by their attempts to rule by assassination, coup, and brute force. During the 1920s and early 1930s, they had elements of support within the established centers of power, particularly as they helped in the suppression of the left and in advancing Japan's interests in China. Following the most serious of the attempts by army members to topple the government in 1936, the state moved effectively to reassert its supremacy. With the outbreak of full-scale war in China in 1937 and the increased imposition of state controls, most forces outside the establishment withered or capitulated.

The role of the established political parties during this period demands attention. At no time did they demonstrate much incentive to appeal to these new forces as an additional base of support. To do so would have required a drastic alteration in the entire programmatic orientation and organization they had developed. Expansion of both the domestic economy and Japan's international sphere of influence, not redistribution of social and economic benefits at home, were the overarching goals of the parties' key supporters. The two sets of goals seemed irreconcilable within the existing system and the Japanese political leadership at the time, unlike the German leadership under Bismarck or the British under Disraeli, saw no compulsion, for example, to expand its base of legitimacy through the creation of a state system of social benefits. Such actions were simply not deemed politically necessary to insure the support of the lower and lower middle classes for the ruling conservative regimes.

Nor did the established parties find much of an appeal in the left's demand for a more pacific foreign policy. Of far more ideological congeniality was the right's insistence on greater militance abroad; however, neither the parties not the state apparatus were able to articulate policies as quickly as the right was able to carry out actions which forced both into a largely reactive stance. By the time that the threat from the radical right was at its apex, only the army could provide sufficient muscle to insure some measure of civic peace. Consequently, the party system and the established parties became increasingly tangential to the policies of the country. By 1932 they had lost their short-lived ability to form cabinets on the basis of electoral success; between 1932 and 1940 they saw their own and the Diet's influence plummet; in 1940, faced with their own impotence in the face of rising military power at home and the Pacific War abroad, they eagerly dissolved and were incorporated with other establishmentarian bodies into the Imperial Rule Assistance Association.

III. POSTWAR JAPAN: STRONGER BUT STILL "RESPONSIBLE" PARTIES

Most analyses of Japanese politics implicitly or explicitly presume a sharp distinction between the political structures of the prewar and postwar periods. The U.S. Occupation was, after all, democratically oriented and introduced a radically different constitution which, among other things, shifted sovereignty from the emperor to the people and made the Diet the "highest organ of state power," giving it effective control over the formation of cabinets. Furthermore an effort was made to resuscitate the political parties. The earliest acts of the Occupation were to remove prior restrictions on party organization and activities and to release imprisoned politicians, most of whom were from the left side of the ideological spectrum. The electorate was expanded to include women, and the voting age was lowered to 20. Repression of political thought was terminated, and the party system that emerged after the Occupation was far more ideologically diverse than that which had prevailed through the 1920s. An extensive land reform undercut the economic base of the prewar landlords, and the power of the military to influence politics was sharply curtailed, despite subsequent reverses in the original policy of eliminating the military forces completely.

In this regard, some of the fundamental obstacles to party influence in policymaking that had existed under the prewar system were removed. There can be little doubt about the fact that the political system of contemporary Japan provides more potential for popular control over state action through elections and the party system than was the case under the Meiji Constitution. Yet there is the danger of overestimating the extensiveness of the transformation that took place and of underestimating the continuities that remain.

Although the land reform sharply curtailed the economic power and local dominance of the rural landlords, at the end of the war roughly 50% of Japan's work force remained in agriculture, forestry, and fishing. The landlord was replaced by the agricultural cooperative, but few powerful individuals in rural Japan lost all influence. For the most part, the traditions of the past concerning deference to the collectivity and hierarchy of the village and its leaders remained dominant. Most of the bastions of rural conservatism remained intact and loyal to their prewar politicans. And even though the occupation forces took some early steps to break up the financial and business combines of the prewar period, these were quickly reversed in the search for economic stability and a cold war ally.

Although the Diet gained in political power relative to its prewar status, little was done to reduce the power of the state bureaucracy which had been far more dominant since the creation of modern government in Japan (Tsuji, 1958). There was very little structural overhaul, except in a few ministries; few senior officials were actually removed; most of the effort expended on "reforming" the prewar bureaucracy went into relatively trivial actions aimed at improving managerial and administrative efficiency. Furthermore, for seven years the bureaucratic agencies were the direct administrative arm of a military occupying force. This heightened further the autonomy of their power vis-à-vis other organs of government.

Practically speaking, it has been virtually impossible to become a cabinet member in the postwar period without being a party member (Fujiwara, 1974:206-207). In principle, of course, the cabinet, which in turn is responsible to the Diet, controls the bureaucracy, as the lines of the standard organization charts of Japanese government make very explicit. Detailed research on relations between cabinet ministers and the agencies below them is not available to examine how well reality comports with principle in the Japanese case; however, diaries of politicians and senior bureaucrats suggest that relations between them are more personal and political than hierarchical (e.g., Imai, 1953; Kōno, 1965; Ōno, 1964; Ojimi, 1975). In such a relationship the technical, informational and organizational resources of the civil servant are considerable (Johnson, 1974, 1975; Pempel, 1974). Surveys of top-level Japanese bureaucrats find most in strong opposition to party "interference" with bureaucratic activities and to notions that they should be more responsive to political direction (Watanabe, 1974). This contrasts sharply with the findings of Putnam (1973) on the German and British civil service which shows themselves more strongly "apolitical."

Further evidence confirms the difficult task that faces the party politician attempting to control a cabinet agency. There are only two party officials appointed to head most agencies—a minister and a parliamentary vice-minister. Unlike the United States, the level of direct political control does not reach down very deeply into an agency. Unlike France, ministers do not have a ministerial *cabinet* to aid them in gaining political control over their agencies. Moreover, because of the need to provide an unending cornucopia of real and symbolic rewards to party members, most cabinet officials hold office for only about one year. By the time they are familiar with the agency, the minister and vice-minister are rotated out and replaced by the next novices in line.

The bureaucracy, on the other hand, has considerable resources. Its top personnel are among the most proven individuals in the country. Most stay with their agency for their entire careers or, at most, spend a short time in one or two other agencies (Kubota, 1969). This gives most agencies a cohesiveness and a claim on the loyalty of its members that is difficult for bickering party politicians to match. The bureaucracy controls most of the technical information presented on a problem through its advisory committees, does the bulk of legislative drafting, and maintains close personal and organizational links with the private sector agencies it controls (Johnson, 1974; Pempel, 1974).

Finally, it is important to note that the parties—most especially the Liberal Democratic Party and its predecessors—have been subject to a good deal of penetration by ex-bureaucrats. Most noteworthy is the entry of Prime Minister Yoshida and a number of his colleagues, such as Ikeda Hayato, Satō Eisaku, Kishi Nobusuke and others less famous, immediately after the war. As Stockwin (1975: 54) has put it, "the unexpected elevation of Yoshida to the prime ministership in 1946, like the forming of the Seiyūkai party in 1900 by Itō Hirobumi, was to facilitate that partial fusion of government bureaucracy with party that has been so characteristic of Japanese politics in the modern period." This trend toward bureaucratic penetration has tapered off somewhat; nevertheless a large number of ex-government officials remain prominent and active in the upper ranks of the LDP. As with their Meiji era predecessors, the parties became the subject of bureaucratic penetration, rather than developing an independent potential to control the bureaucracy.

The resources of the Japanese bureaucracy are of long standing and its powers are highly institutionalized, while the relative resources of the elected officials are newer and fewer. This is not to say that the bureaucracy is a Frankenstein monster uncontrollable by elected officials. It does suggest that the case has certainly *not* been made that elected party officials are in fact in a position to insure that their party's will is easily implemented by the administrators of the country. Despite the changes in the constitution, much of the policymaking power in Japan today appears to remain where it was under Meiji, namely within the bureaucracy.

Hence it is clear that while some rather significant changes took place structurally and socioeconomically under the U.S. Occupation, there were strong elements of continuity with the prewar patterns. It is not surprising therefore that the organization of political parties followed the same basic lines as had been dominant during the 1920s and 1930s. The prewar conservatives reorganized quickly as the Liberals and the Democrats (later the Progressives), thereby continuing the prewar political alliance between agriculture and urban commerce and finance. By the time the Occupation entered its more conservative phase around 1947, this coalition was bolstered further by direct political and economic support from the Americans.

On the left, the unionists, socialists, and communists, who had been subject to a wide range of repression during the prewar period, found themselves free to organize. In fact, during the first two years of the Occupation, they appeared to be the targeted beneficiaries of many U.S. policies. Still they remained heavily influenced by Marxist theory and, in the case of the communists, directly responsible to Soviet policy. Consequently, the focus of their early appeals remained with the intellectual leadership and the urban worker. The rather huge rural proletariat continued to be conceded to the conservatives. Early organizational and electoral gains by the left were, however, reversed by the middle of the Occupation as initial U.S. support for the left gave way to a concern with an economically stable Japan under a government amenable to following U.S. direction in the developing cold war.

Organizationally and ideologically, therefore, Japan was split into hostile "camps." The parties were widely divided on questions of socioeconomic policy, foreign relations, state structure, police powers, controls over education, the military system, controls over labor unions, and a host of other fundamental issues. Social sectors and interest groups were forced to choose sides. By 1948, Japan reflected a distinctly bipolar pattern—conservative parties drawing their support from business, agriculture, the state bureaucracy, and the U.S. Occupation versus the progressive parties with their base in organized labor and among the intelligentsia. There was little cross-cutting of cleavages; key interests were locked in to one camp or the other, and there was little movement by voters from one camp to the other.

In 1955, this bipolarity was further rigidified by the merger of the two major conservative parties to form the Liberal Democratic Party, and the left and right socialists to form the Japan Socialist Party. With the communists reduced to one seat in the Diet, Japan seemed to be developing what appeared to many to be a two-party system, roughly comparable to that of the U.S. or Britain. What made the two parties different from these counterparts was the fixed nature of their socioeconomic bases and the rather inflexible ties that bound them to specific institutions and organizations.

At the national level, the key support organizations for the LDP were the peak associations of business and agriculture, while for the socialists they were the peak associations of labor. The policy positions (and in the case of the LDP, the policy actions) of the two major parties reflected the unyielding nature of their respective support bases. The LDP carried out a wide range of oligopolizations in key sectors of the economy, and tied Japan's military and foreign economic policies to those of the United States, while in agriculture it maintained an extensive and expensive system of price supports aimed at insuring the continued favor of its rural electoral base. Throughout the early 1970s, however, despite Japanese economic success, the LDP made virtually no significant efforts to develop the social welfare programs and labor legislation that had become so standard in Europe and North America, and on a wide range of social indicators, Japan continued to lag dramatically behind most other industrial democracies (Pempel, 1977:754-759).

The JSP, meanwhile, remained staunchly ideological. The British Labour Party, by the end of the war and certainly by the early 1950s, had rejected most of its early principles of socialism and pacifism; the German SPD, in its Godesberg program of 1959, had dropped most of its commitment to the socialization of the means of production and by mid-1960 had dropped its efforts to develop an independent foreign policy line (Kirchheimer, 1966). The JSP, however, made no such efforts to accommodate the developing realities of Japanese success and to follow the route of the catch-all parties taken by several European socialist oppositions. Instead it clung to the notion of a close foreign policy alliance with China and/or the Soviet Union, and opposed all military or economic connections wtih the U.S. For its domestic policy positions, it relied on a Talmudic Marxism, reaching into the texts of the past for a guide to the future. As of the mid-1970s, the JSP still clung explicitly to the need to establish a "dictatorship of the proletariat," a phrase rejected even by the renascent Japan Communist Party.

As is well known, the LDP and its conservative predecessors have dominated the government since 1947, continually returning majorities in the Lower House of the Diet and having exclusive control over the formation of all cabinets. Consequently, they have been in an ideal position to implement policies of benefit to their constituents whereas the JSP could only advocate from without. Although the alliance with the U.S. did involve Japan in peripheral support for U.S. military activities in Korea and Indo-China, it did not drag Japan unwittingly into a nuclear holocaust as the JSP had threatened. In fact, the two wars provided windfalls to the Japanese economy. Farm incomes were bolstered by price supports and generous, though not always scrupulous, land sales. The general citizenry, rather than suffering under the whiplash and whimsey of top-hatted capitalist exploiters, found themselves enjoying the lowest levels of unemployment in the industrial world, plus a continually rising absolute standard of living. Such successes in the policies of the LDP-dominated government blunted much of the sharpness of the class and cold war debates in Japan, and the distribution of real income and wealth within the society became a less salient issue.

At the same time, the successes had the ironic effect of generating new social problems, forces and orientations which reduced the ability of the LDP to bask in the light of past successes. The policy of rapid economic growth, focused as it was on such secondary sector industries as chemicals, shipbuilding, steel, oil refining, and heavy machinery, generated a number of fallout problems: pollution, bankruptcies of small and medium-sized firms, a rapid population shift away from agriculture and the rural sector, land use policy, industrial siting, and the like. In 1950, only 25% of Japan's population lived in cities of over 100,000; by 1975; this figure was up to 55% (calculated from Sōrifu Tōkeikyoku, 1976:16). In addition, once the immediate problems of employment and food on the table had been eliminated, most Japanese came to consider themselves "middle class" and their collective attention shifted to problems of inadequate housing and social welfare benefits, inflation, educational costs, and the like (Matsushita, 1971). Among many, a new individualism and a search for a more personally meaningful life-style became the focus of attention (Tōkei Suri Kenkyūjo, 1970). Directly or indirectly, all of this resulted from the very success of the government's policy of economic growth. None, however, could be dealt wtih through a continuation of the same measures. With the third largest GNP in the world, the Japanese state found it increasingly difficult to claim an incapacity to meet demands for redistribution and welfare spending. An expanding economic pie and trickle-down benefits would not solve these problems; most necessitated a complete reevaluation of the priorities on which these policies had been based.

Nevertheless, neither of the major parties responded programmatically to the changes that were occurring, and both sides suffered significant electoral declines. Conservatives, in 1955, received 63% of the vote; by 1976, this had dwindled constantly to 42%. The socialists fell from 29% to 21% during the same period. Meanwhile, during the same period, four smaller parties arose. On the left, the relatively conservative Democratic Socialist Party (DSP) split from the Japanese Socialist Party in 1960, and the Japan Communist Party, which was an electoral also-ran for 20 years following its success in the 1949 election, began to regain support. Meanwhile, the Clean Government Party (CGP) arose de novo with the support of the Buddhist organization, Sōka Gakkai. The conservative LDP managed to avoid any fundamental splits during most of this period, but in the aftermath of the Lockheed scandals and internal dissent over the lack of "modernization" in the LDP, a small group split to form the New Liberal Club which managed to nearly triple its small size in the Lower House election of 1976. All four of these new parties sought to claim some portion of the ground between the JSP and the LDP, thereby further reducing some of the tension along the main fissure lines within society. Not one of these parties has yet demonstrated a consistent rise in electoral success, nor has any drawn over 11% of the vote in any election. In fact, some evidence suggests they draw much of their strength from one another.[1] Still, by 1976, their combined vote was 32%. LDP hegemony was preserved only because of various imbalances in the electoral system. In 1976, the LDP margin in the Lower House was retained only by absorbing into the party several candidates who had been elected as independents.

The question naturally arises: why have the two major parties not adjusted their policy proposals and political tactics to deal with this seemingly inevitable erosion of their respective electoral bases? Part of the answer lies in the fact that there is growing public recognition of the fact that alternative channels to political influence can be exercised in Japan. A wealth of attitudinal data exists to support the conclusion that Japanese citizens have long been dubious about the prospects for political action through the party system (e.g., Hashimoto, 1975; Richardson, 1974; Tōkei Suri Kenkyūjo, 1970; Yoshikawa, 1973), but recent political actions speak even more effectively to the point than simple attitudinal research. A new phenomenon called "the party leaver" or the "disengaged" has appeared. General public support for political parties has always been low, but in 1972 surveys showed that 45% of the voting public claimed not to support a party and over one-third identified themselves explicitly as "party leavers" (Tsurutani, 1977:191).

More significantly, there has been a major rise in organized groupings which resort to direct political action outside the party-electoral-Diet nexus to insure their policy objectives. Typically focusing on local issues, such as industrial siting, consumer prices, and pollution problems, these so-called "citizen's groups" and "resident's movements," which were almost nonexistent in the mid-1960s, numbered in the thousands by the mid-1970s (McKean, 1977). In the single year 1973-1974, membership in such groups tripled; protest actions by such groups went up 27-fold between 1962 and 1970. Similar in many respects are such groups as the non-sect radicals, prominent during the university protests of the late 1960s. Beheiren, a broad-based movement opposed to U.S. actions in the war in Indo-China, and right-wing protoarmies such as Tatenokai. All of these abjure association with political parties in contrast to most earlier pressure groups which have been intimately linked to one or another of the major political parties. The pattern also differs from those pressure groups in other countries not identified with any single party, but which shift their allegiances in accord with specific promises or policy actions. While many members of these groups vote, including many who have voted for the developing smaller parties, for the most part, voting is taken to be a peripheral act and the new Japanese groups focus attention on direct political actions aimed at insuring their policy goals without any intermediation by the party system. The institutional focus of these direct actions has been more immediate to the problem at hand: individual polluting firms, local government officials, regional bureaucratic offices, the court system, and others.

Meanwhile, local governments, both those under "progressive" and those under "conservative" control, have shown a willingness to act independently of the central government, and often in complete disregard of the policies of the national parties. While the national bureaucracy, under at least putative LDP dominance, has not had to expand to deal with new social welfare programs and has remained virtually the same size as it was in 1965, the number of local government officials has risen from 1.8 million in 1958 to nearly 3 million in 1975 (Isomura and Kuronuma, 1974). Progressive administrations in the major cities have instituted anti-pollution legislation, health care and maternity benefit systems, day care centers, sewage systems, and the like, independently of the central government and often in conflict with its wishes (Aqua, 1976; MacDougall, 1977). But a "conservative" administration in Mutsu prevented the return of Japan's nuclear powered ship and extracted major financial concessions from the central government for alleged damage to the town's harbor. Conservative administrations in Sasebo, and areas surrounding the new Narita airport have been similarly independent in action and equally successful in extracting major economic benefits for central government programs impinging on these cities and villages. The socialist mayor of Yokohama, for a brief period at least, was able to prevent the use of Yokohama streets by U.S. military vehicles through rigid enforcement of local traffic regulations. Thus, the increasing autonomy and political power of local governments cuts across past ideological lines and represents a view locus of power transcending the national party system.

Similarly, the courts, most notably through the pollution cases, but also in textbook censorship cases and consumer movement cases, have begun to provide a hearing for positions not taken up by existing political channels, and the courts have responded by a new wave of activism. In the pollution cases particularly, they have forced significant changes in the activities of big business and the ruling conservative coalition.

It is clear therefore that alternative channels for coping with the new social forces have been developing outside the control of the party system. The question still remains why the major parties have been so seemingly insensitive to the changes that have been taking place. Much of the answer lies in the fact that both major parties have been high "responsible"—responsible to their respective constituencies, at the expense of attempting to be representative of society at large. The very rigidity of the alliances formed in the immediate postwar period—agriculture, big business and finance, the state bureaucracy and the LDP versus organized labor, intellectuals and the JSP —worked against any basic alteration in the policies of either party. Any significant deviation from the policies of the past was guaranteed to cost the LDP some portion of its essential electoral or financial support. The JSP, unlike the most successful Eurocommunist parties, was dominated by a trade union federation, union members, and ideological zealots, few of whose interests lay in dealing with any of the new issues that were emerging.

Neither party's policies at the national level were subject to much mass input with the result that policy in both parties was largely a function of incumbent politicians and a limited number of party cadres, all highly attuned to the demands of the key support groups. Like most parties, Japan's are responsive more to such cadres than to their voters, and incumbent politicians, in particular, have little incentive to be "issue mongers." As Rose has suggested about them: "A good policy is not defined as one in which the benefits are greater than the costs, but rather one in which there are *no* visible costs, whatever the benefits may be" (Rose, 1976:27).

At the level of the individual election district, the reluctance to change by the major parties was bolstered by the peculiarities of the nation's electoral system. The main outline of the system for electing members of the Lower House of the Diet is straightforward. Japan is composed of medium-sized districts which generally return from three to five members. But in each district the individual voter casts only a single ballot. In the Upper House election, there is a two-tier system, with one-half of the members returned from local constituencies on a basis comparable to that for the Lower House, and the other half returned from a national constituency, again with each voter casting a single ballot. There are many consequences of such a system which cannot be dealt with at great length (Nakumura, 1968; Nishihira, 1972; Soma, 1970). The most obvious and significant for this analysis is the extent to which the system fosters intraparty competition. Any party seeking to gain a majority of seats must run more than one candidate per district and, since each voter can cast only one vote, a premium exists for the candidate to develop his own personnel support organization and to separate himself from the other candidates, including particularly those from his own party (Curtis, 1970; 1971). The candidate gains nothing if, by demonstrating the merits of his party over the others, he succeeds only in insuring the election of the other candidate(s) from his party within the district.

A second and related consequence is the geographical isolation that the system fosters. Except in a very indirect way in the national constituency election for the Upper House, most voters have little way in which to act or react to national issues. In a single member district, a vote *against* an incumbent and his party automatically becomes a vote for the challenger and his. In England or the U.S., for example, a shift of as little as 10% of the vote within a district is almost guaranteed to alter the electoral results. Since in Japan most candidates are returned with somewhere between 12% and 25% of the vote in the district, a comparable shift in *party* support typically means only a 3% to 4% shift in the support level of each individual candidate from a major party. Though in some cases this is sufficient to insure defeat for one of them, the potential for the single elector to vote effectively *against* a particular party or candidate is almost nil. There is much less chance than in a single member district system that a party will lose total control of a district in a single election. The effects of this become more tangible when one considers that ex-Prime Minister Tanaka, generally regarded as a national disgrace following his indictment in the Lockheed scandal, was returned overwhelmingly in the subsequent election, as were four out of five of the other "grey" or tainted LDP members. There is little better evidence of the validity of V.O. Key's (1966:2) warning that: "It . . . can be a mischievous error to assume, because a candidate wins, that a majority of the electorate shares his views on public questions, approves of his past actions, or has specific expectations about his future conduct."

There is an additional element of the electoral system that demands attention. Its main outlines were developed immediately after the war when Japan was largely agricultural and when the population of the rural areas was glutted by returning soldiers. It has not been redistricted since, resulting in a tremendous imbalance between the representatives of urban versus rural districts. The result is a boon to rural incumbents, of course, who are relatively isolated from population shifts and as a party it is the LDP which benefits most substantially. For the 1969 elections, there were 337,000 valid electors per seat in the metropolitan Osaka's third district, with only 77,900 valid electors in the fifth district of rural Hyōgō (Stockwin, 1975:92-94). Even after a minor redistricting in the 1976 election, a communist candidate, receiving 115,000 votes in the metropolitan third district of Osaka, was defeated, while in rural Ehime an LDP candidate, receiving only 44,000 votes, was elected (Miyakawa, 1976:225-270).

All electoral systems have their biases and it is the rare system, if any exist at all, which favors the challenger. Japan is no exception and perhaps stands more at the extreme in its bias than others. It is extremely difficult to muster sufficient electoral strength to oust incumbents; during the period 1953-1976, incumbents had a return rate of well over 75%. "New faces" in the Diet, in contrast, were 41% in 1949, but were down to 19% in 1969 and 24% in 1976 (Nishihira, 1972:264; Asahi Shimbunsha, 1976:320).

Obviously the entire bias of the electoral system has benefitted the LDP, but significant as well is the fact that it does not encourage a great deal of responsibility to the individual representative's constituency as a whole or even to some shifting majority within it, but rather to that thin slice essential to his continued return to office. Moreover, these various responsibilities at the district level are splintered, if and when they ever reach the level of national party headquarters. There major policy decisions continue to reflect a responsiveness to nationally organized interests, rather than the sum of locally organized interests. The major parties are thus "free" to remain the captives of the peak associations which have supported them in the past.

The result of the electoral system has been to reinforce the incentives for the major national parties to resist, rather than encourage, the consideration of new issues and new policy solutions within the country as a whole. By being responsible to their sectorally organized supporters at the national level, and to their particularistic support groups at the level of the individual election district, the two parties manage to remain irresponsible to the nation at large.

IV. CONCLUSION

The bulk of this analysis has suggested that Japanese political parties arose in a political milieu hostile to their gaining a major role in the public policy formation of the country. A strong state bureaucracy, plus myriad other official and unofficial centers of political power, were far more significant in the process than the parties. Even at the height of their prewar power, the parties could not insure themselves control over the formation of cabinets while the Diet they did control remained severely circumscribed in its powers. Some changes of significance took place under the U.S. Occupation, most notably in the creation of a more powerful Diet and a cabinet system dependent on political parties for its formation. Nevertheless, there is a danger in overestimating the significance of these changes, since the bureaucracy remains a more central focus of policymaking power, while the courts and local governments have gained rapidly in influence.

Similarly, the argument has been raised that the major political parties, while at times a relatively accurate reflection of the key strata and groupings within society, have in times of rapid social change been rather inept at incorporating the new social forces. This was certainly true during the 1930s; it seems even more true in the mid-1970s. A wide variety of new social forces have emerged and remain largely insulated from and independent of the national party system.

What broader conclusions is one to draw from these facts? On the most general of levels, it should be clear that not all party systems adjust to and internalize the forces of social change quite so readily as the American, British, or even one-party modernizing regimes. Control of key policymaking instruments plus a modicum of irresponsibility toward old constituencies in times of major social change are essential to any comparatively easy adjustment. In Japan, limited control by the major parties of the key instruments of policymaking combined with a high degree of responsibility to dated social constituencies has worked to limit the capacity of major parties to catch up with and control rapidly changing social realities.

More specific to Japan, the analysis strongly suggests that unless some drastic steps are taken by the LDP, the JSP and their supporters, the past trend of their mutual electoral decline will continue. A continuation in the declining significance of the JSP, plus eventual defeat of the LDP would thus seem foreordained.

Such predictions, particularly as regards the end of LDP rule, have become a favorite pastime among Japan specialists. Of course much remains in the way of choices by leaders of both parties that could reverse their present declines. Still, it is hard to ignore the fact that only by creative responses to existing political problems is either party likely to stem the tide toward decline. Yet, though the LDP can no longer anticipate automatic continuity of rule and the JSP can no longer count on automatic support from opponents of that rule, because of the underlying social coalitions supporting them both parties seem collectively incapable of any alternative posture. What the present leadership of both parties fails to realize, in the words of a character in Lampedusa's *The Leopard,* is that "If things are going to stay the same around here, there are going to have to be some changes made" (quoted in Rose, 1976:7).

Still, the LDP is most likely to lose its majority without any other party coming even close to a plurality. No majority is possible without the LDP. As with the danger of overestimating the significance of the shifts in politics generally from prewar to postwar, it may also be hazardous to predict that much would change even if the LDP does lose its majority. Its coalition possibilities are virtually infinite, and the New Liberal Club, the CGP, and more especially the DSP would seem to be highly compatible with an LDP-dominated government.

On the other hand, continued success by opposition coalitions at the local level may pose a more serious long-term threat to national level LDP hegemony. If nothing else, one is likely to see the same phenomena found in France and Italy. As left-of-center coalitions continue to govern responsibly and effectively, the lie is given to much of the conservative rhetoric about the dangers of the left (Tarrow, 1977). It is not surprising, then, that there has been an increased legitimacy in voting for the left at the national level in France and Italy and, increasingly, in Japan as well. In the long run, a completely left-of-center government might be possible in Japan, but in the shorter run it seems a rather remote prospect. Far more easy to imagine is a form of coalition government, most likely with the LDP or some version of the conservation establishment in the position of dominance.

More to the point is whether such a coalition would mean much change in the policies Japan pursues. The analysis would suggest that not much change would be expected since the actual party control over public policy is limited.

The links between the senior-level civil service and the ruling LDP are well-known, and it is possible to envision an uncooperative bureaucracy thwarting the policy efforts of a non-LDP or coalition government should one come to power. The genuineness of the Japanese civil service's neutrality has never been put to such a test. Yet surveys of attitudes of senior civil servants show consistent self-evaluations of neutrality, and a consistent belief that a change in the parties of government would not require either resignation or some fundamental alteration in their policy activities (Watanabe, 1974). Whether true or not, a major political purge of top-level civil servants is certainly not feared by most of them, and does not seem to be threatened by opposition leaders. Given the high level of public support enjoyed by the top civil service, it is doubtful that any but the most revolutionary government would attempt such an act. Consequently, then, one of the major pillars of Japanese politics and public policy formation seems unlikely to be severely shaken, regardless of which government comes to power in the near future. Furthermore, an increasing proportion of government policies involve long-standing policy commitments which cannot be reversed in a period of one or two years. A significant proportion of the activities of any government, including the Japanese, will persist over time, regardless of which party controls the executive or legislative branches. It is difficult therefore to predict major alterations in policy, such as are predicted for France and Italy, should the left take power at the national level.

In short, the structural limitations on party and electoral control over public policy are severe—possibly, but not necessarily, more so in Japan than elsewhere. Thus, although a number of changes have taken place within Japanese party system since its inception, and particularly in the last decade, it would be hyperbolic to suggest that these will of necessity lead to fundamental changes in the policies followed by the Japanese government, let alone in the distribution of power within the society as a whole. It would be far more realistic to recognize the limitations that exist and to begin coping theoretically and practically with such realities. But it is perhaps more important to realize that focusing primarily on political parties and the party system, whether in Japan or elsewhere, may cause one to ignore other political structures which may be more significant vehicles of change.

NOTE

1. For example, in the 1972 election, the JCP went from 14 to 38 seats. However, they drew an identical number of these seats from the DSP and CGP as from the LDP and JSP. In 1976, when the JCP and NLC ran candidates in the same districts, the NLC candidate won in all but one and the JCP candidate lost in all but one. The constant rise and decline of the various minor parties suggests that many voters see individual parties or candidates as combinations of protest symbols against the candidates of the main parties and as sufficiently close on certain programmatic matters to warrant support. But the attachments formed seem to last for few consecutive elections and to have limited ideological, or left-right, salience.

REFERENCES

AKITA, G. (1967). Foundations of constitutional government in modern Japan, 1868-1900. Cambridge: Harvard University Press.

ANDERSON, C. (1967). Political change in Latin America. New York: Van Nostrand.

AQUA, R. (1976). "Political choice and policy change in medium-sized Japanese cities, 1962-1974." Paper presented at SSRC conference on local oppositions in Japan.

ASAHI SHIMBUNSHA (1976). Nihonjin no Seiji Ishiki. Tokyo: Author.

——— (1977). Asahi Nenkan. Tokyo: Author.

BENDIX, R. (1964). Nation-building and citizenship. New York: Anchor.

BERGER, G. (1977). Parties out of power in Japan, 1931-1941. Princeton N.J.: Princeton University Press.

BURNHAM, W.D. (1967). "Party systems and the political process." Pp. 277-307 in W.N. Chambers and W.D. Burnham (eds.), The American party systems: Stages of political development. New York: Oxford University Press.

––––– (1970). Critical elections and the mainsprings of American politics. New York: W.W. Norton.

BUTLER, D., and STOKES, D. (1976). Political change in Britain. New York: St. Martin's.

BYAS, H. (1942). Government by assassination. New York: Knopf.

CURTIS, G. (1970). "The kōenkai and the liberal democratic party." Japan Interpreter, 6(2):206-219.

––––– (1971). Election campaigning Japanese style. New York: Columbia University Press.

DAADLER, H. (1966). "Parties, elites, and political developments in Western Europe." Pp. 43-78 in J. LaPalombara and M. Weiner (eds.), Political parties and political development. Princeton, N.J.: Princeton University Press.

DORE, R. (1959). Land reform in Japan. London: Oxford University Press.

DUUS, P. (1968). Party rivalry and political change in Taishō Japan. Cambridge: Harvard University Press.

DUVERGER, M. (1963). Political parties: Their organization and activity in the modern state (B. and R. North, trans.). New York: John Wiley.

EMMERSON, R. (1966). "Parties and national integration in Africa." Pp. 267-302 in J. LaPalombara and M. Weiner (eds.), Political parties and political development. Princeton, N.J.: Princeton University Press.

EPSTEIN, L. D. (1967). Political parties in Western democracies. New York: W.W. Norton.

FUJIWARA, H. (1974). Kanryō no kōzō. Tokyo: Kodansha.

GONZALEZ CASENOVA, P. (1970). Democracy in Mexico. New York: Oxford University Press.

HALLIDAY, J. (1975). A political history of Japanese capitalism. New York: Pantheon.

HASHIMOTO, A. (1975). Shiji seitō nashi. Tokyo: Nikei Shinsho.

HIRSHMAN, A.O. (1963). Journeys toward progress. New York: Doubleday.

HUNTINGTON, S.P. (1965). "Congressional responses to the twentiety century." Pp. 5-31 in D.B. Truman (ed.), The Congress and America's future. Englewood Cliffs, N.J.: Prentice-Hall.

IKE, N. (1964). "Political leadership and political parties: Japan." Pp. 389-410 in R. Ward and D. Rustow (eds.), Political modernization in Japan and Turkey. Princeton, N.J.: Princeton University Press.

IMAI, K. (1953). Kanryō, sono seitai to uchimaku. Tokyo: Yomiuri Shimbunsha.

ISOMURA, E., and KURONUMA, M. (1974). Gendai Nihon no gyōsei. Tokyo: Teikoku Chihō Gyōsei Gakkai.

ITO, H. (1889). Commentaries on the constitution of the empire of Japan. (M. Itō, trans.). Tokyo: Government Printing Office.

JOHNSON, C. (1974). "The reemployment of retired government bureaucrats in Japanese big business." Asian Survey, 14(November):953-965.

––––– (1975). "Japan: Who governs? An essay on official bureaucracy." Journal of Japanese Studies, 2(1):1-28.

KEY, V. O. (1955). "A theory of critical elections." Journal of Politics, 17(February):3-18.

––––– (1966). The responsible electorate. New York: Vintage.

KING, A. (1973). "Ideas, institutions and the policies of governments: A comparative analysis." British Journal of Political Science, 3(3):291-313.

KIRCHHEIMER, O. (1966). "The transformation of the Western European party." Pp. 177-200 in J. LaPalombara and M. Weiner (eds.), Political parties and political development. Princeton, N.J.: Princeton University Press.

KŌNO, I. (1965). Kōno Ichirō nikki. Tokkan Shoten.

KUBOTA, A. (1969). Higher civil servants in post-war Japan. Princeton, N.J: Princeton University Press.

LIJPHART, A. (1968). The politics of accommodation: Pluralism and democracy in the Netherlands. Berkeley: University of California Press.

—— (1969). "Consociational democracy." World Politics, 21(2):207-225.

LIPSET, S., and ROKKAN, S. (1967). Party systems and voter alignments. New York: Free Press.

MacDOUGALL (1977). Localism and political opposition in Japan. New Haven, Conn: Yale University Press.

MATSUSHITA, K. (1962). Gendai Nihon no Seijiteki Kōsei. Tokyo: Tōkyō Daigaku Shuppankai.

—— (1971). Shibiru-minimamu no shisō. Tōkyō: Tokyo Daigaku Shuppankai.

McKEAN, M. (1977). "Pollution and policymaking." Pp. 201-238 in T.J. Pempel (ed.), Policymaking in contemporary Japan. Ithaca, N.Y.: Cornell University Press.

McRAE, D. (1974). Consociational Democracy. Toronto: McClelland and Stewart.

MINOBE, T. (1934). "Waga gikai seido no zento." Chūō Kōron, 553(January):2-14.

MIYAKAWA, R. (1976). Seiji Handobukku. Tokyo: Seiji Kōhō Sentā.

NAJITA, T. (1967). Hara Kei in the politics of compromise: 1905-1915. Cambridge, Mass.: Harvard University Press.

NAKAMURA, K. (1968). Nihon no senkyō kōzō. Tokyo: Hara Shobō.

NIHON KOKUSEI ZUE (1976). Tokyo: Kokuseisha.

NISHIHIRA, S. (1972). Nihon no senkyō. Tokyo: Shiseido.

ŌJIMI, Y. (1975). "A government ministry: The case of the ministry of international trade and industry." Pp. 101-112 in E. Vogel (ed.), Modern Japanese organization and decision-making. Berkeley: University of California Press.

ŌNO, B. (1964). Ōno Bamboku kaisoroku. Tokyo: Kōbundō.

PAYNE, J. (1965). Labor and politics in Peru. New Haven, Conn: Yale University Press.

PEMPEL, T.J. (1974). "The bureaucratization of policymaking in post-war Japan." American Journal of Political Science, 18(4):647-664.

—— (1977). "Japanese foreign economic policy: The domestic bases for international behavior." International Organization, (fall).

PITTAU, J. (1967). Political thought in Meiji Japan. Cambridge, Mass. Harvard University Press.

PUTNAM, R. (1973). "The political attitudes of senior civil servants in Britain, Germany, and Italy." British Journal of Political Science, 3(July):257-290.

QUIGLEY, H. (1932). Japanese government and politics. New York: The Century Co.

RICHARDSON, B. (1974). The political culture of Japan. Berkeley: University of California Press.

ROKKAN, S. (1966). "Mass suffrage, secret voting and political participation." In L. Coser (ed.), Political sociology. New York: Harper.

ROSE, R. (1976). "Models of change." Pp. 7-34 in R. Rose (ed.), The dynamics of public policy: A comparative analysis. Berkeley: Sage.

SCALAPINO, R. (1962). Democracy and the party movement in pre-war Japan. Berkeley: University of California Press.

—— (1968). "Elections and political modernization in pre-war Japan." Pp. 249-291 in R. Ward (ed.), Political development in modern Japan. Princeton, N.J.: Princeton University press.

SCALAPINO, R., and MASUMI, J. (1962). Parties and politics in contemporary Japan. Berkeley: University of California Press.

SHEFTER, M. (1977). "Patronage and its opponents." Western Societies Program at Cornell University, Occasional Paper No. 8.

SOMA, M. (1970). Nihon no sōsenkyō. Tokyo: Mainichi Shimbunsha.

SŌRIFU TŌKEIKYOKU (1976). Nihon no tōkei. Tokyo: Author.

STOCKWIN, J.A.A. (1975). Japan: Divided politics in a growth economy. New York: W.W. Norton.

TARROW, S. (1977). Between center and periphery. New Haven: Yale University Press.

THOMAS, J. (1975). The decline of ideology in western political politics. Berkeley: Sage.

TILLY, C. (ed., 1975). The formation of national states in Western Europe. Princeton, N.J.: Princeton University Press.

TŌKEI SURI KENKYŪJO (1970). Daini Nihonjin no kokuminsei. Tokyo: Shiseidō.

TSUJI, K. (1958). "Shihai taisei no seisaku to kikō." Pp. 53-166 in Y. Ōka (ed.), Gendai Nihon no seiji katei. Tokyo: Iwanami Shoten.

——— Seiji o kangaeru shihyō. Tokyo: Iwanami Shinsho.

TSURUTANI, T. (1977). Political change in Japan. New York: McKay.

WATANABE, T. (1974). "Kōkyū komuin no ishiki." Pp. 425-464 in B. Ari et al. (eds.), Gendai gyōsei to kanryōsei. Tokyo: Tōkyō Daigaku Shuppankai.

WATANUKI, J. (1976). Nihon seiji no bunseki shikaku. Tokyo: Chūō Kōronsha.

YOSHIKAWA, Y. (1973). "Shakyō wa shiminundō wo riyō dekinai." Chūō Kōron, 88(June):209-216.

YOSHIMURA, T. (1973). Nihon seiji no shindan. Tokyo: Tōkai Daigaku Shuppankai.

ZOLBERG, A. (1964). One-party government in the Ivory Coast. Princeton, N.J.: Princeton University Press.